B O D Y

B O

Marina Abramovic
Francis Bacon
Balthus
Richard Baquié
Georg Baselitz
Max Beckmann
Hans Bellmer
Joseph Beuys
David Bomberg
Pierre Bonnard
Louise Bourgeois
Arthur Boyd
Gunter Brus
Dinos and Jake Chapman
Francesco Clemente
Gustave Courbet
John De Andrea
Edgar Degas
Willem De Kooning
Dennis Del Favero
Cathy de Monchaux
Otto Dix
Orshi Drozdik
Jean Dubuffet
Marcel Duchamp

Thomas Eakins
Lucio Fontana
Lucian Freud
Paul Gauguin
Adam Geczy
Robert Gober
Natalia Gontcharova
Antony Gormley
Richard Hamilton
Mona Hatoum
Bill Henson
Roger Hilton
Edward Hopper
Rebecca Horn
Frida Kahlo
Anish Kapoor
Ernst Ludwig Kirchner
Yves Klein
Pierre Klossowski
Oskar Kokoschka
George Lambert
Zoe Leonard
Bracha Lichtenberg-Ettinger
Edouard Manet
Man Ray

D Y

Henri Matisse

Paul McCarthy

Ana Mendieta

Joan Mirò

Paula Modersohn-Becker

Pierre Molinier

Otto Muehl

Eadweard Muybridge

Alice Neel

Helmut Newton

Hermann Nitsch

Tony Oursler

Gina Pane

Mike Parr

Vettor Pisani

Michelangelo Pistoletto

Jackson Pollock

Marc Quinn

Arnulf Rainer

Auguste Renoir

Auguste Rodin

Georges Rouault

Julie Rrap

Doris Salcedo

François Sallé

Egon Schiele

Carolee Schneemann

Rudolf Schwarzkogler

Cindy Sherman

Kazuo Shiraga

Walter Sickert

Kiki Smith

Stelarc

Laura Torrado

Ken Unsworth

Suzanne Valadon

Jacques Villon

Gert Wollheim

Zai Kuning

Contributing Writers

Jill Beaulieu

Jill Bennett

Susan Best

Anthony Bond

David Bromfield

Sarah Faunce

Philippe Grand

Alan Krell

Charles Merewether

Mary Roberts

This publication accompanies an exhibition
at The Art Gallery of New South Wales entitled

BODY

Exhibition dates:
12 September to 16 November 1997

Published by Bookman Schwartz
A division of Bookman Pty Ltd
227 Collins Street Melbourne Victoria 3000 Australia
and The Art Gallery of New South Wales
Art Gallery Road Sydney New South Wales 2000 Australia

National Library of Australia
cataloguing-in-publication entry
Bond, Anthony: 'BODY'
ISBN 0958720606

Exhibition Curator and Editor: Anthony Bond
Assistant Curator: Caroline Butler-Bowdon
Copy Editor: Suzannah Biernoff
Design: Ian Robertson
Film Separations: Hi-Tech Graphics, Melbourne
Printing: Vaughan Printing, Melbourne

Front cover: Auguste Renoir, *Young Boy With Cat*, c.1868–69
Collection: Musée d'Orsay, Paris
© photo RMN – R. G. Ojeda
Back cover: Gustave Courbet, *The Source*, 1862
Collection: The Metropolitan Museum of Art, New York

Contents

Foreword

BODY is the most comprehensive exhibition devoted to the representation of the naked body in Western Art that Australia has seen. It is the culmination of an ambitious project that has been passionately pursued, developed and curated by the Gallery's Head Curator of Western Art, Anthony Bond. The exhibition demonstrates with some persuasion the Gallery's commitment to undertaking exhibitions that consider and explore contemporary art in a broader historical context.

The exhibition includes an impresssive 160 works on loan from 60 international and national collections and ranging from the nineteenth-century Realism of Courbet and heroism of Rodin, to the more discomforting experiences offered by contemporary artists such as Hermann Nitsch and Mike Parr. BODY traces continuities between nineteenth-century Realist painters and certain key explorations in avant-garde art of the twentieth century, thereby providing a contemporary perspective on the art of the Western world of the last 150 years. Concentrating on images of the naked body provides a particularly challenging theme for such an investigation, for perhaps more than any other it seeks out our strengths, our vulnerabilities, our secrets and aspirations.

The substantial catalogue provides a fully-illustrated source for the exhibition combined with nine essays which explore, among other topics: voyeurism; gendered views of the body; total bodily perceptions contrasted with purely visual appreciation; issues of the tactile in relation to erotic imagery; the negotiable body and social identity; masculine anxiety, cleanliness and modernity; and the relationship between body and landscape.

An exhibition of this scope could not materialise without the remarkable generosity of international and national collections, both public and private, from Japan, Austria, Germany, Switzerland, Italy, the United States, Colombia, Singapore, France, England, Scotland, Spain and of course, Australia. The commitment of contemporary artists to this exhibition is also noteworthy. The Gallery is delighted that several of the artists are here and can participate in the symposium and events associated with the exhibition. It is a pleasure also to acknowledge the unreserved commitment of Anthony Bond and staff in the Curatorial Services and Exhibitions Departments at the Gallery in realising this profound and rewarding exhibition.

Edmund Capon Director

Lenders to the Exhibition

Alexander and Bonin, New York
Anna Schwartz Gallery, Melbourne
Anthony d'Offay Gallery, London
Art Gallery of South Australia, Adelaide
Art Gallery of Western Australia, Perth
Barbara Schwartz, New York
Courtauld Institute Galleries, London
Fonds National d'Art Contemporain, Paris
Galerie der Stadt Stuttgart, Stuttgart
Galerie Gmurzynska, Koln-Marienburg
Galerie Krinzinger, Vienna
Galerie Jennifer Flay, Paris
Galerie Lelong, New York
Galleria Schwarz Collection, Milan
Giovanni and Anna Rosa Cotroneo, Naples
Giuliana and Tommaso Setari, Milan
Hirshhorn Museum and Sculpture Garden, Washington DC
Ivor Braka, London
Jay Jopling, London
Kunstammlungen Böttcherstraße, Bremen
Kunsthaus Zurich, Zurich
Kunstmuseum Dusseldorf im Ehrenhof, Dusseldorf
Kunstammlung Nordrhein-Westfalen, Dusseldorf
L. F. Toninelli
Lisson Gallery, London
Ludwig Museum of Contemporary Art, Budapest
Mary Anne Martin Fine Art, New York
Metro Pictures, New York
Musée d'Art Contemporain Lyon, Lyon
Musée d'Art Moderne de la Ville de Paris, Paris
Musée d'Orsay, Paris
Musée National d'Art Moderne, Paris
Musée Rodin, Paris
Museum Ludwig, Cologne
Museum Moderner Kunst Stiftung Ludwig Wien
Museum of Contemporary Art Tokyo, Tokyo
National Gallery of Art, Washington DC
National Gallery of Australia, Canberra
National Gallery of Victoria, Melbourne
Newcastle Region Art Gallery, Newcastle
Paula Cooper Gallery, New York
Philadelphia Museum of Art, Philadelphia
Rheinisches Landesmuseum, Bonn
Richard Nagy Fine Art, London
Robert Miller, New York
Sammlung Friedrichshof, Zurndorf
Sammlung Hubert Klocker, Vienna
Sammlung Julius Hummel, Vienna
Scottish National Gallery of Modern Art, Edinburgh
Sean Kelly, New York
Stedelijk Museum, Amsterdam
Tate Gallery, London
The Metropolitan Museum of Art, New York
Ubu Gallery, New York
Victoria Miro Gallery, London
Von der Heydt Museum, Wuppertal
Wallraf-Richartz-Museum, Cologne
Whitney Museum of American Art, New York

Acknowledgements

BODY has been evolving over a three year period and during that time so many people have been involved offering formal and informal advice and other assistance that it will be impossible to adequately record every instance. However I would like to thank all the museum staff and academics around the world who have shared their ideas whether or not they led to specific outcomes for the selection. Many ideas that were not followed up were of importance because of the way in which they focused my curatorial response and helped me to hone down the themes of the exhibition.

I would like to single out a few people however who have been of particular importance to the realisation of the exhibition. Caroline Butler-Bowdon above all has been Assistant Curator and my constant support with every aspect of the project. She has coordinated the research efforts to track down items corresponding to my gradually refined specifications and has kept me supplied with relevant reading matter and followed through on much of the administration of the exhibition and coordination of this book. Anna Hayes has been the Registrar for the exhibition arranging the enormously complex loan and freight details. Victoria Lynn has contributed to the selection of the performance work and has devised the related film programme with the assistance of Rilka Oakley. Morry and Anna Schwartz have also been strong supporters and the quality of this book is a result of the very favourable conditions Morry has provided for publishing it. Ian Robertson's sensitive and intelligent design has ensured that my conception of the exhibition is realised visually in this book. Anne Graham, my wife, not only gave me moral support but is my first reader and final proof reader.

The research for the exhibition and the book has involved many volunteers and contract staff. I would like in particluer to mention Jane Richards who came to us as an intern and stayed on as a contract researcher. It was Jane who first completely understood the exhibition I was trying to create. Her suggestions guided some of my early research trips and a number of the works selected resulted from this research. Dr David Bromfield who is my doctoral supervisor has done much to sharpen my thinking on realism and is a continuing source of intellectual and moral support. Dr Susan Best has undertaken a rigorous critical reading which prompted several significant improvements to the text of this book. Suzannah Biernoff has been a very creative and acute copy editor whose comments have also assisted in clarifying the many interweaving themes that I have been trying to construct. Brendan Winter has been employed here during the final stages of the publication process and has made a valuable contribution.

The Research Library staff at the Gallery have been very helpful chasing up bibliographic references and assisting our many volunteers: I would particularly like to thank Kay Truelove and Robyn Louey. Simone Korn, Margaret Long, Susan Long, Susan Manford, Kathryn Parker, Sky Reidy and Shannon Wood have been willing volunteers working in support of Caroline Butler-Bowdon.

I would like to acknowledge the efforts of our Public Programmes and Marketing teams who have made a great effort to interpret this complicated project for a wider audience. I appreciate their patience. The generosity of lending institutions has been extraordinary as the catalogue demonstrates and I must express my deep gratitude for their support. Finally I want to thank Edmund Capon, the Director, and the Board of Trustees for their support of such a demanding exhibition. I am conscious of being given a great deal of freedom to develop the exhibition concept and I hope that their confidence has been justified.

Anthony Bond Curator

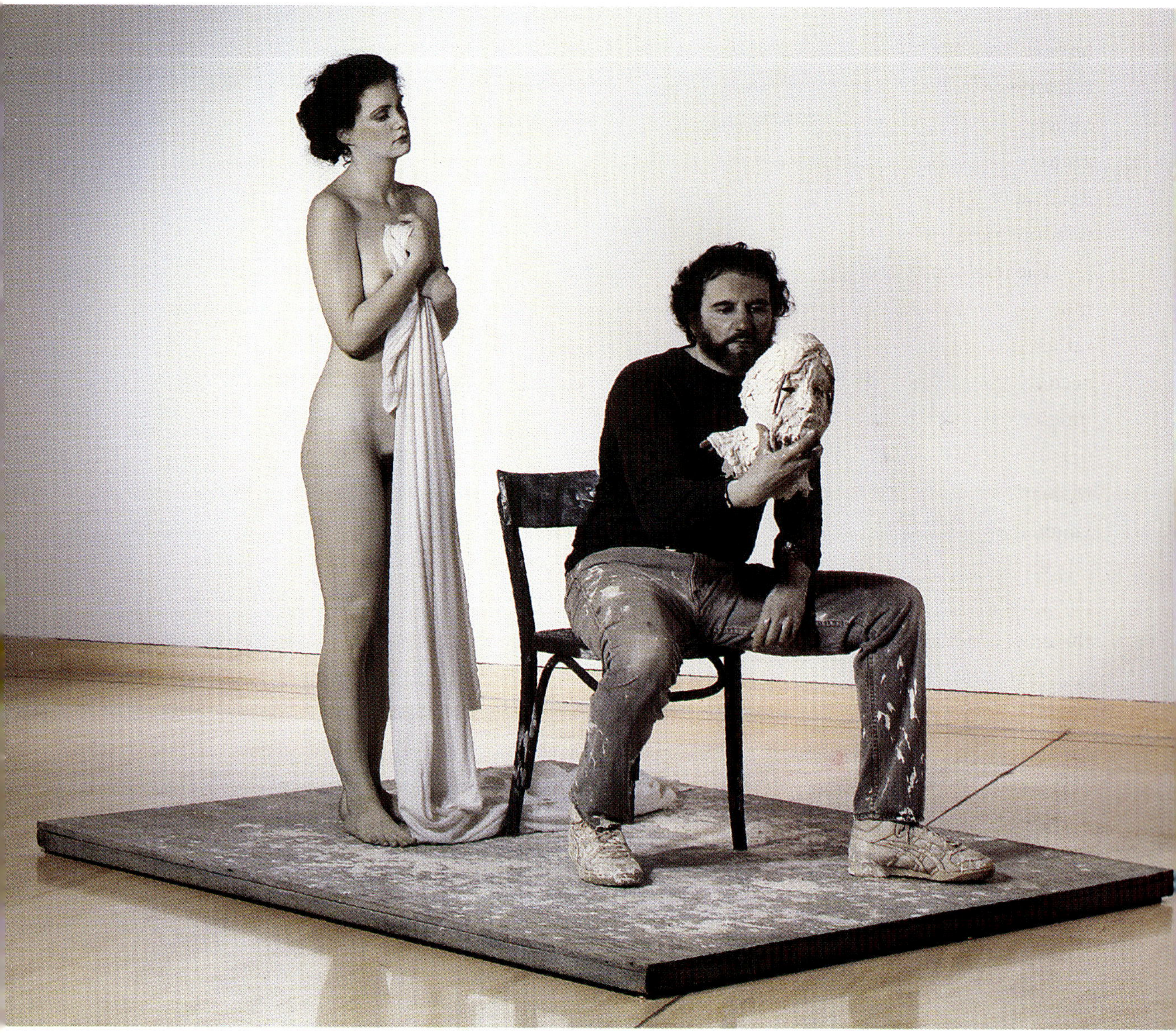

Fig. 1. John De Andrea *Allegory: After Courbet* (1988) Cat. 35

Anthony Bond

Embodying the Real

The original concept for the exhibition BODY was simply to present a realist view of the naked human body. In 1997 the Gallery will also present an exhibition of Orientalism, the high point of romantic, academic painting in the mid nineteenth-century. By way of contrast BODY represents a radical alternative starting with Gustave Courbet and following a realist thread through modern art to the present day. The process of selection brought other critical ideas into play such as: Realism versus Salon painting, empathy rather than voyeurism, gesture as a trace of the artist, the relationship between art and life, and self-reflection.

The most apparent distinction between Courbet's Realism and Orientalism, or other forms of nineteenth-century Salon painting, is the choice of subject matter. Realism depicts everyday life rather than fantasies of far-away places and legendary histories. This exhibition and the accompanying book will show that Courbet's preference for modern themes not only entailed an intellectual embrace of modern political thought, but also frequently involved a significant personal identification with the model and with the natural environment. One of the major thematic strands in BODY is the distinction between empathy and voyeurism, where empathy is engendered through this emotional identification.

Empathy is usually precluded by certain cultural and artistic conventions that sanction voyeurism. Such conventions have provided an acceptable context for looking at bodies, even in the most prudish societies (at least within the West). One of the ways in which this has been done is through strategies which distance the viewer from the model. Orientalist and academic paintings, for example, which commonly appeared in the official French Salon exhibitions of the ninteenth-century, portray the nude as exotic, mythological or historically distant. Equally, the classical nude described by Sir Kenneth Clark is intellectually appreciated as an embodiment of classic ideals and proportion, rather than as a body amongst others.[1] This distance secures an indemnity for the voyeur from the threat of a gaze returned: the odalisque will not challenge the viewer's consuming eye. The voyeur may wish to possess the object of the gaze imaginatively, but not at the expense of forgoing the protection of anonymity. On the other hand, the intimacy of an empathic gaze may be confronting because it engages an erotic and bodily response, without the distancing filter of these conventions. It may also lead a viewer to identify with the body of the model, producing an imaginative merger of beholder and image.[2]

The selection process began with extensive viewing of major public collections. The initial framework was based on the principles outlined above, but there was also an intuitive component. Some works seemed to support the concept of an empathetic gaze perfectly while others did not. In several cases these readings of individual works went against the grain of orthodox art historical classifications of the artist's work. These intuitions therefore needed to be supported by careful visual analysis. One of the factors which emerged from my subsequent reflection on the work was the relation of eye and hand in the realist paintings that I had selected. The nineteenth-century collection of the Musée d'Orsay in Paris is arranged with the Realists along one side of the main aisle and Salon and Orientalist paintings opposite. If the viewer inspects each work in the

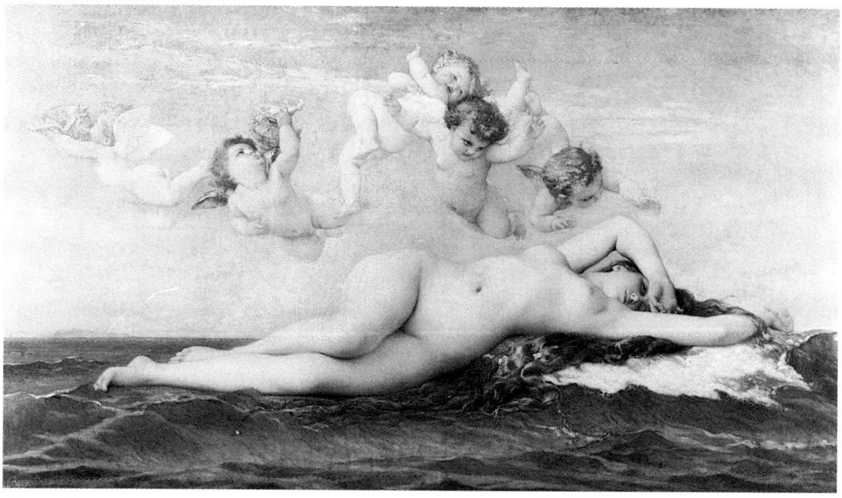

Fig. 2. Alexandre Cabanel *The Birth of Venus* (1863) Ref. 1

Realist section and compares the brushwork with those on the opposite walls they will find a surprisingly consistent distinction. Artists like Ingres and Alexandre Cabanel not only project their subjects into an exotic scenario, they also brush away any trace of their hand. It is as if they distance themselves from the voyeurism facilitated by their art (Fig. 2). Experiencing the Realist works, in contrast, entails a full sensory engagement because in tracing the form, the viewer's eye follows the gesture of the artist. This is a process which brings the viewer very close to the artist and to the subject matter. In a way it is as if the viewer recreates the moment of production with each glance.

This idea of the work of art as a trace of the artist's bodily presence provided an important link to certain twentieth-century practices, culminating in performance art in the 1960s. In many ways a precursor to performance art, Jackson Pollock's dripped paintings can readily be interpreted as the trace of a physical action, an observation confirmed by Namuth's famous film of Pollock in the studio. Later in this introduction I will outline how Yves Klein created his *Anthropometries* using his models as living paintbrushes and how the Vienna Aktionismus group moved from painting to performance, enacting rituals in which the body of the model and sometimes that of the artist no longer functioned as figures but as the field on which the paint was splattered. Such an emphasis on the artist's presence could easily lead to solipsism and self-indulgence. On the other hand it can be a means to engage the viewer more completely in the work. The body art of Gina Pane, Mike Parr or Marina Abramovic from the 1970s is confronting precisely because the viewer – and not just the artist – is included within the work.

By replacing the objectifying and distancing conventions of academic painting with an emphasis on sensory and emotional engagement, the works selected for BODY lessen the gap between art and life. Making art which addresses the boundary between representation and lived experience is an important aspect of realism. Art that makes this border visible presents visual language as a kind of screen or veil which reveals yet separates and obscures the represented.

Another artistic strategy in this exhibition contrives to position the viewer in ways that focus attention on the specific nature of their gaze. The most dramatic example of this is Richard Baquié's faithful reconstruction of Marcel Duchamp's *Etant Donnés: 1° La chute d'eau 2° Le gaz d'éclairage* (1991) henceforward referred to as *Etant Donnés* (Figs. 18, 84 and 113).[3] In this installation, originally completed by Duchamp in 1968, the viewer is compelled to stoop and peer through a peephole to see the bizarre tableau created within.[4]

The gap between art and life is further eroded by the substitution of objects and materials in place of images of the body. Doris Salcedo, for example, presents the shoes of those who have disappeared in the political violence in Colombia as attributes of the departed, in such a way that their presence is invoked more forcibly than any portrait could hope to do.[5]

Many of the exhibitions and publications that have addressed the body in the last five years have considered it from an inter-disciplinary perspective. They have charted social and scientific visions of the body and traced the evolution of different perceptions throughout history. These exhibitions have been very informative and have brought together fine art with comparative cultural material, from scientific, medical and social history. Outstanding amongst these were the exhibitions *l'Âme et Corps*, curated by Jean Clair and shown at the Grand Palais in Paris in 1994, and *Identity and Alterity: Figures of The Body 1895/1995* at the Venice Biennale in 1995. Also notable is *fémininmasculin*, curated by Marie-Laure Bernadac at the Centre Georges Pompidou in 1995. BODY shares some concerns with the latter project, which examined many aspects of sexuality in art. It differs, however, in its emphasis on the act of looking as a bodily function: to this end I have focused on artistic strategies by which the viewer is made aware of the particular quality of their own gaze.

The many intertwining themes of this exhibition reveal unexpected relations between the work of certain contemporary artists and their nineteenth-century precursors. In particular, many works selected emphasise an intimacy born of shared bodily sensations. The display of objects throughout the gallery spaces follows this thematic closely, beginning with an acknowledgment of the essentially voyeuristic business of peeking into private places.

1 Private spaces, voyeurism or intimacy

Many of the works in this first section conform to our expectation of an exhibition focusing on the nude. Luminous paintings by Edgar Degas, Pierre Bonnard, Suzanne Valadon, Edward Hopper and Balthazar Balthus accord with our desire for an aesthetic vision of the human body. Two contemporary artists, Bill Henson and Tony Oursler, make images which raise critical questions about privacy. This group of works jumps ahead of the chronology for the exhibition which actually begins with Courbet in 1862. I have presented them first, partly because they meet a certain expectation but also because they raise the issue of voyeurism. Each image shows a figure engaged in personal activities, for example in the bathroom or the bedroom: private spaces in which we prepare our bodies for eventual exposure in the outside world. The artists take us into this private domain, thus parting the veil of discretion which allows for a reasonable distinction between private and public space. In most cases the artist seems to be an unseen watcher and the viewer is, by association, a 'fellow-voyeur'.

Not all of the images in this room leave the viewer unseen. Helmut Newton's photograph *Self-portrait with June and Models* (Fig. 3) is a study of gazes returned and deflected. The viewer's eye is most likely to be captured by the gaze of the artist's wife, who is actually looking at the artist as he lines up the shot. We stand in place of the artist although unlike him, we are not reflected in the mirror. This work clearly harks back to Velasquez's great composition *Las Meninas* where viewers find themselves standing on the spot where the king and queen – the probable models for the picture – must have stood. The royal couple only appear as a shadowy presence in the mirror on the rear wall of the artist's studio.[6]

At the entrance to the exhibition John De Andrea's sculpture, *Allegory: After Courbet* (Fig. 1), also shows the artist and the model, but as with Courbet's great allegorical painting the model is shown watching the artist and not the other way round.[7] In the Courbet the artist depicts himself sitting so close to the canvas, upon which he is painting a landscape with waterfall, that he appears to be merging with the painting.[8] The artist in *Allegory: After Courbet* is staring into a plaster mould of his own face. The mould acts as a sculptural equivalent to Courbet's compression of the figure against the pictorial surface in the self-portraits and *The Painter's Studio* (Fig. 119); it also introduces the concept of a trace or imprint of the body. For Marcel Duchamp and other artists in the exhibition, such as Yves Klein, Julie Rrap and Arnulf Rainer, the mould becomes a marker of presence and absence and an indication of physical contact.

Degas is represented by a drawing and a sculpture, the former (Fig. 144) depicting a naked woman drying herself after the bath. He is one of the many nineteenth-century artists apparently obsessed with washing. This could be thought of as simply a convention for revealing nudity, as in traditional themes such as *Susanna Surprised by the Elders*. There are however more particular associations between modernity, washing and prostitution in the French nineteenth-century imagination which Alan Krell has touched upon in his essay.[9]

Fig. 3. Helmut Newton *Self-portrait with June and Models* (1981) Cat. 112

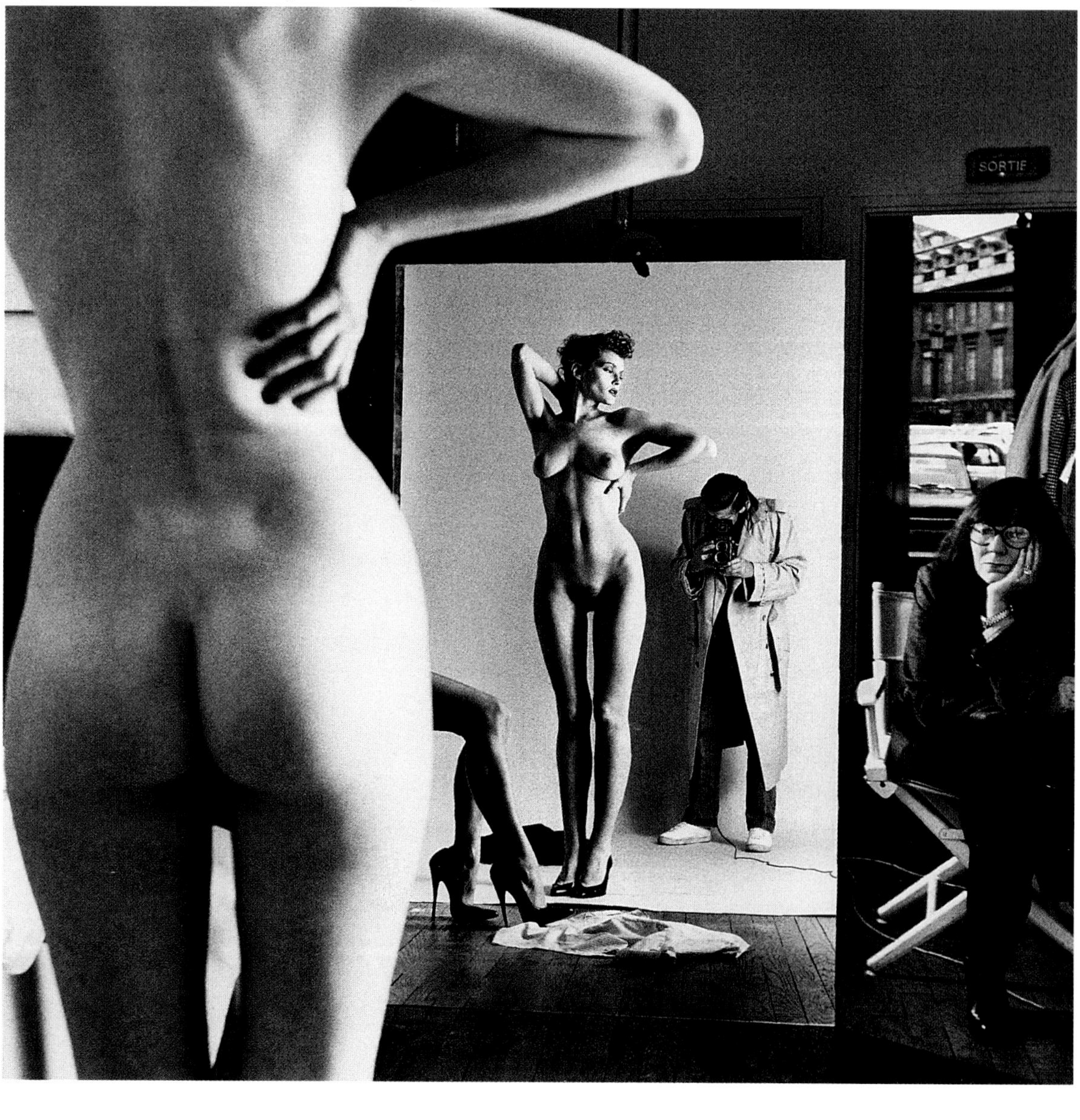

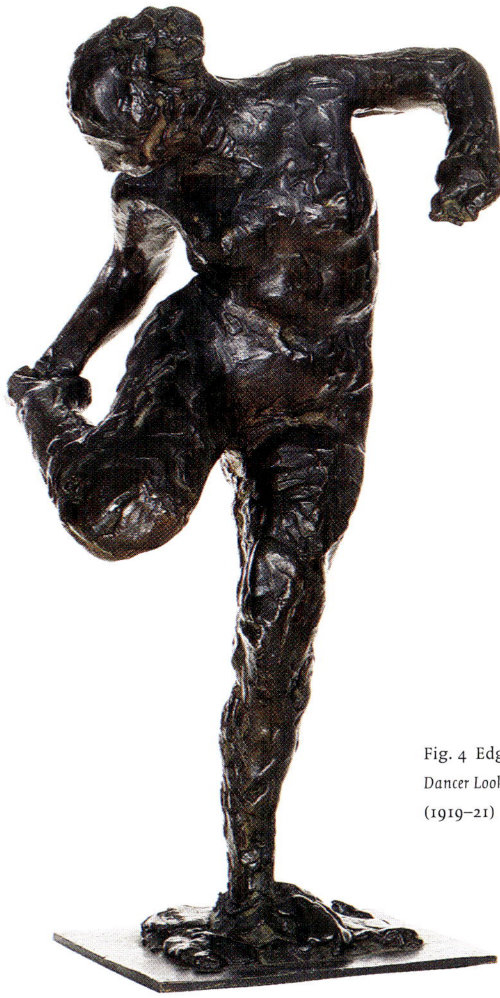

Fig. 4 Edgar Degas
Dancer Looking at the Sole of her Right Foot
(1919–21) Cat. 36

Bonnard always seems to be disclosing a private world. The earlier paintings in this room, *Siesta – The Artist's Studio* and *L'homme et la Femme* (both 1900) (Figs. 5 and 141), are at first glance charming domestic scenes with a strong hint of post-coital regret.[10] In the latter, the man gathers up his clothes while the woman turns her attention to the kittens on the bed. Both paintings make much of the tumbled bedclothes which provide a luxurious opportunity for the painter's brush and heighten the level of sensuality in the image. Courbet was a master of this use of fabric. In *The Sleepers*, for instance, he allows the hand of the brunette sleeper to dangle at the edge of the bed where the silky white slip parts to reveal a fleshy pink fold in the bed covers (Fig. 132).[11] Fabric easily translates into flesh in the hands of the artist and in the imagination of the viewer.

Nu de Dos à la Toilette and *The Bath* (Figs. 6 and 8) by Bonnard return to the theme of the toilette. Marthe de Méligny, his partner for over 50 years, seems to have been a compulsive bather and the artist took every opportunity to paint her during her long periods of immersion. The shimmering colours of the tiled bathroom provide a luxurious bourgeois background to the figure, yet there is something sinister about this obsession with bathing which is conveyed by the lifeless pallor of Marthe's flesh and morbid stillness of her body in *The Bath*.

Suzanne Valadon's *Nu à la Couverture Rayée* (Fig. 9) by contrast, seems very straight-forward. She also makes much of the fabric, but here the pleasure seems to be in the visual delight with no sexual overtones. Unlike the sickly flesh tones of Marthe's body, Valadon's figures are flushed with vitality. I have included the dressed odalisque in *La Chambre Bleue* (Fig. 10) because it was made as a response to Edouard Manet's *Olympia*. Unfortunately the Manet can only appear as an

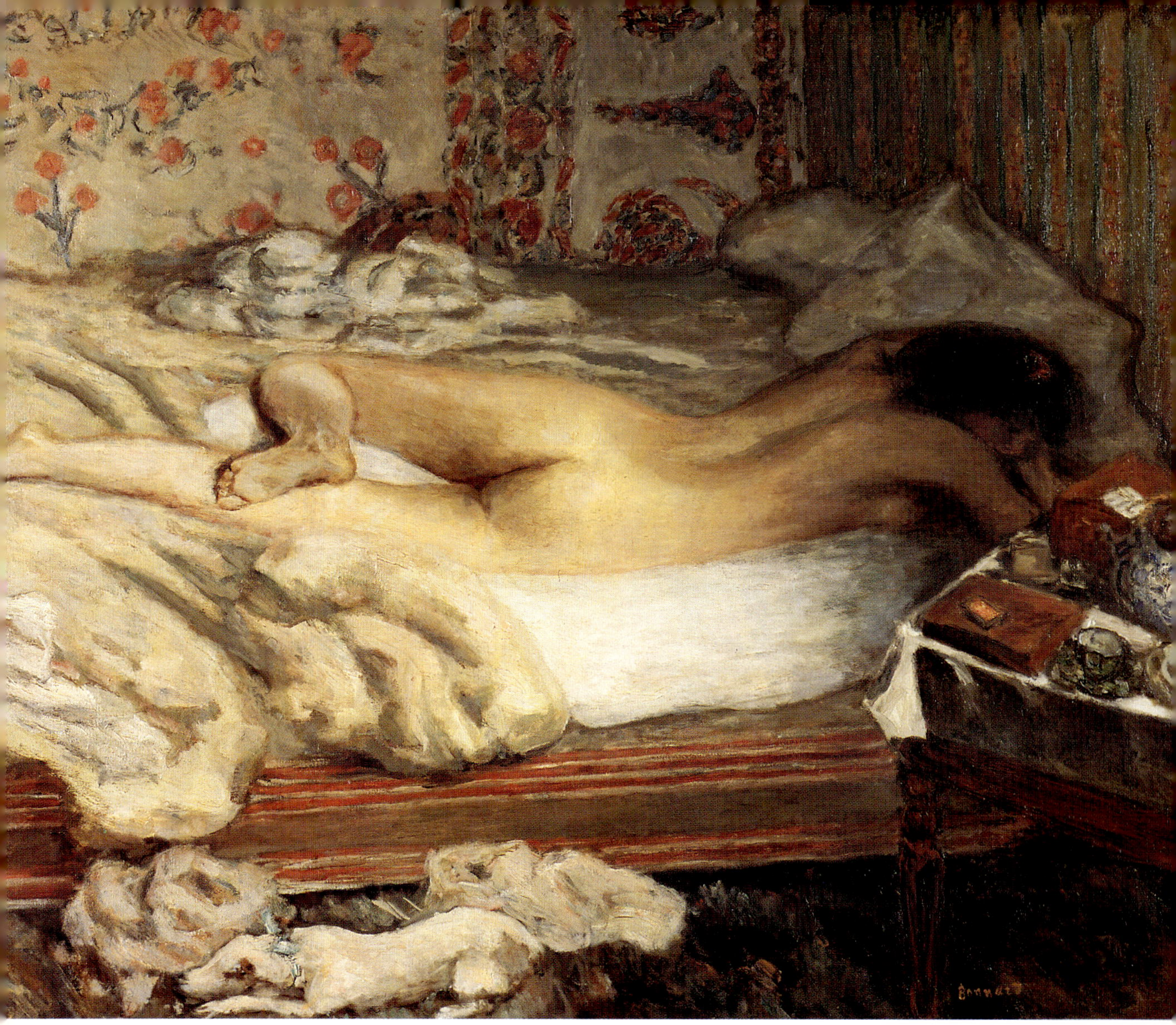

Fig. 5. Pierre Bonnard *Siesta – The Artist's Studio* (1900) Cat. 25

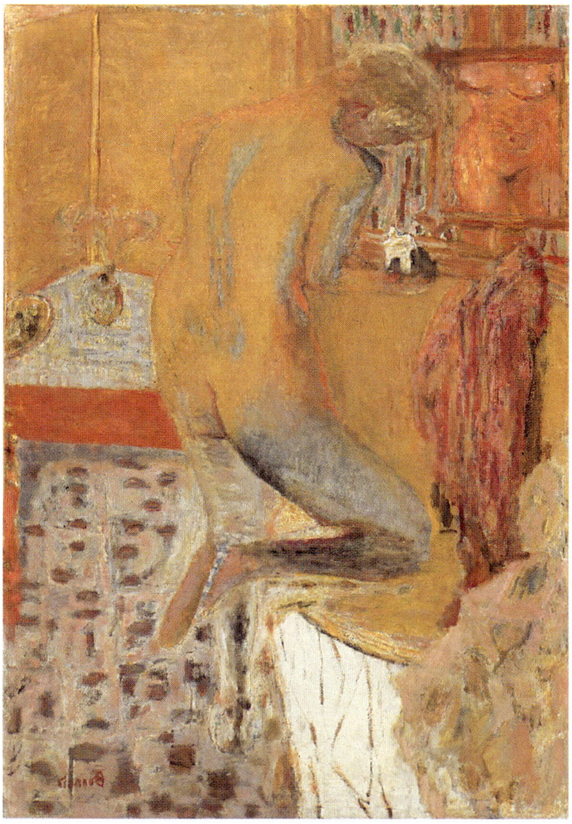

Fig. 6. Pierre Bonnard
Nu de Dos à la Toilette (Nude at Toilette, back view) (1934) Cat. 23

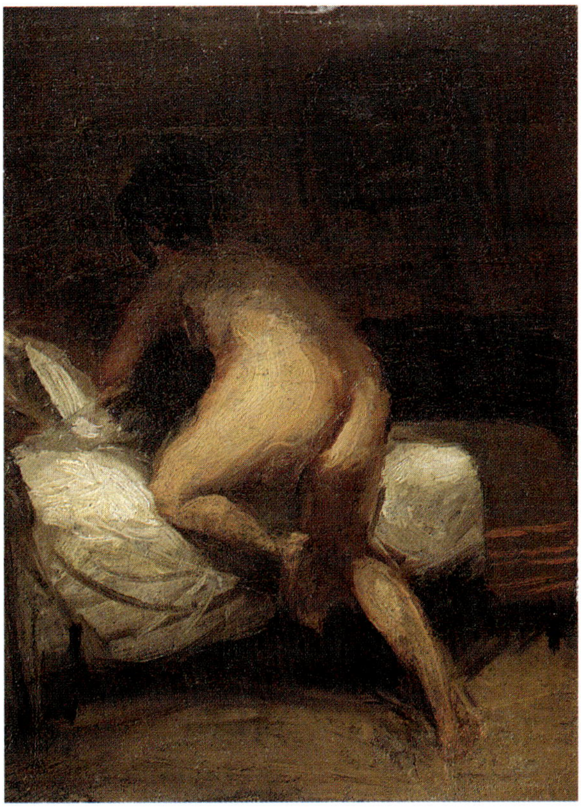

Fig. 7. Edward Hopper *Nude Crawling into Bed* (c.1903–05) Cat. 66

Fig. 8. Pierre Bonnard *The Bath* (1925) Cat. 22

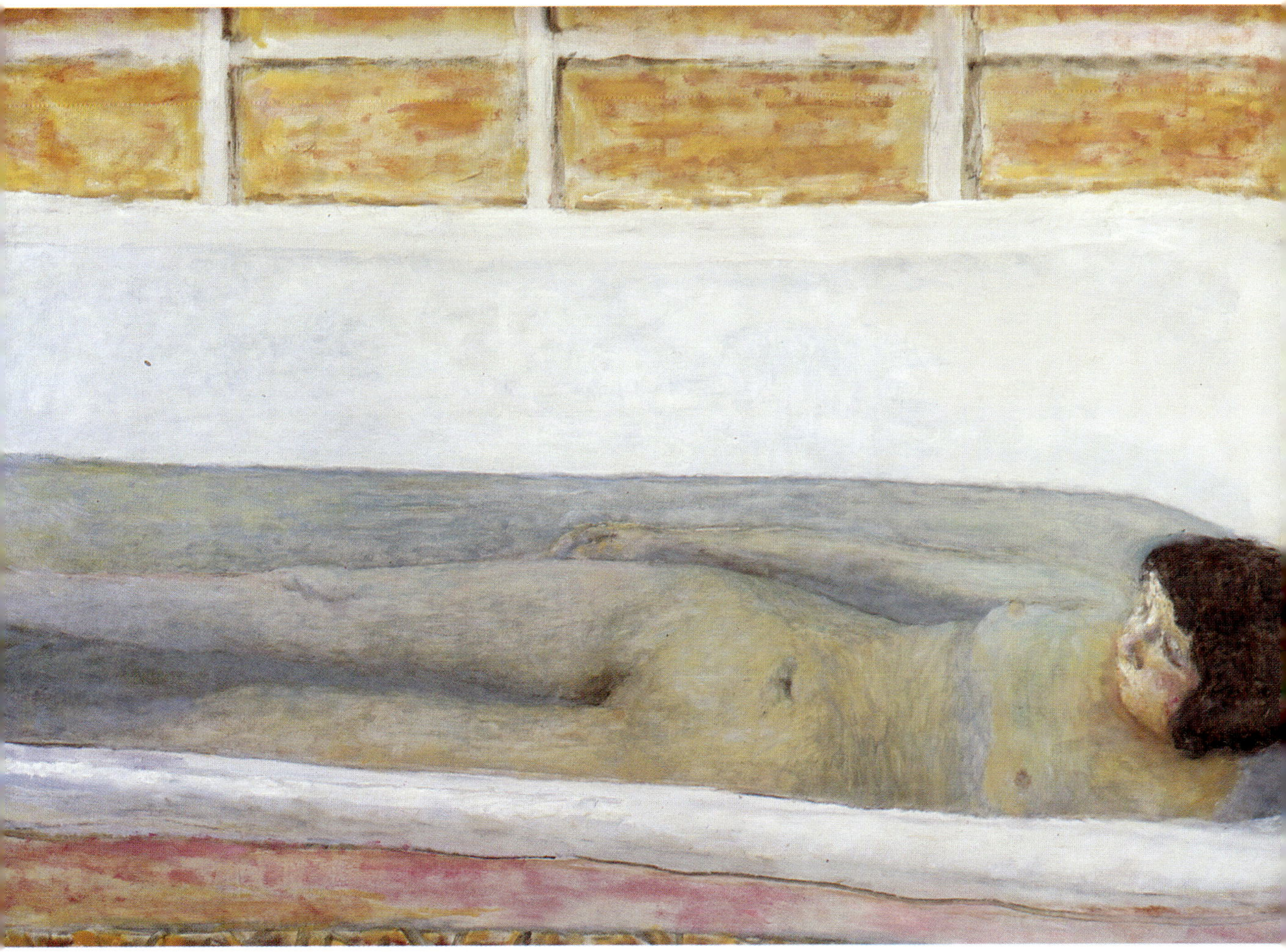

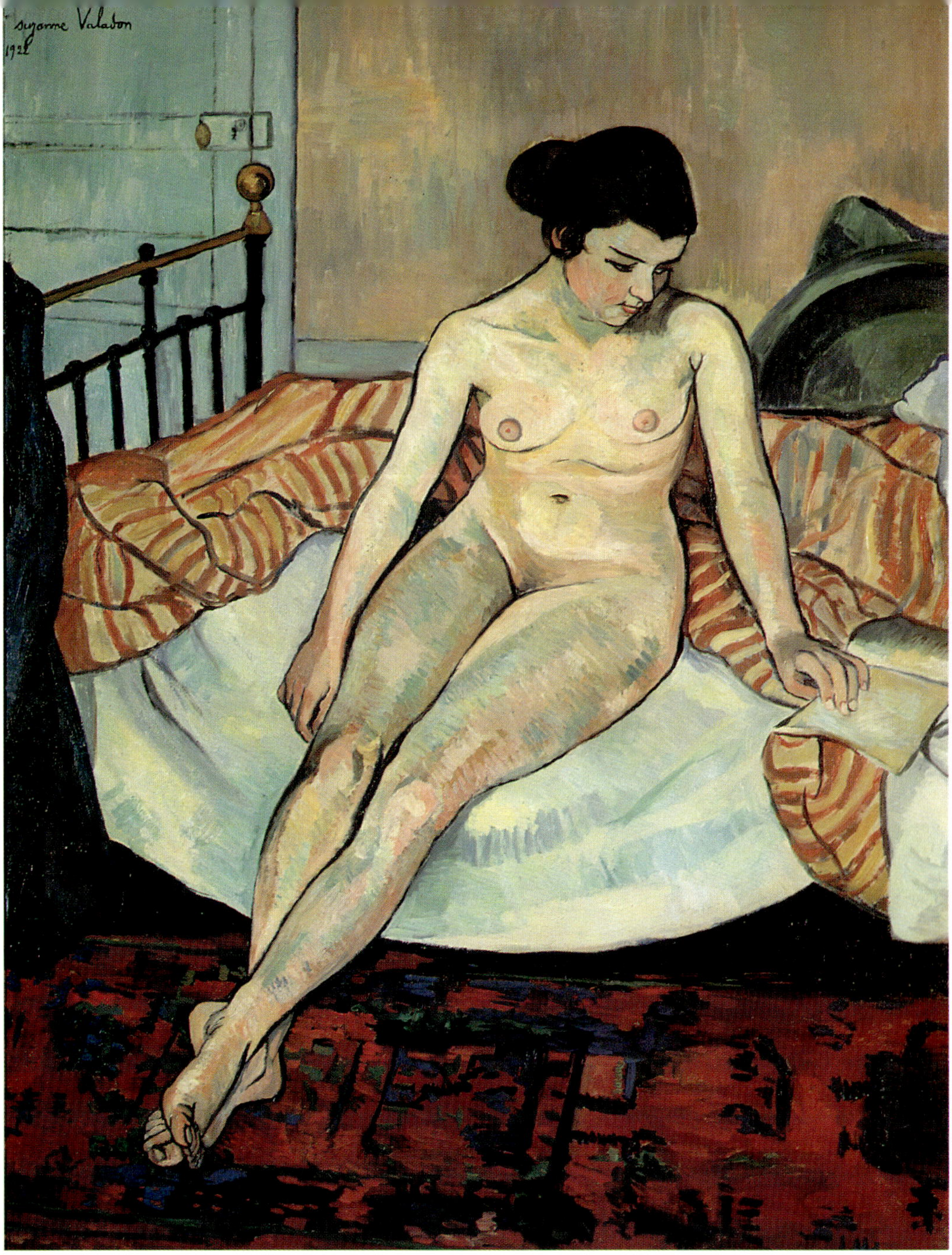

Fig. 9. Suzanne Valadon Nu à la *Couverture Rayée* (*Nude on Striped Blanket*) (1922) Cat. 153

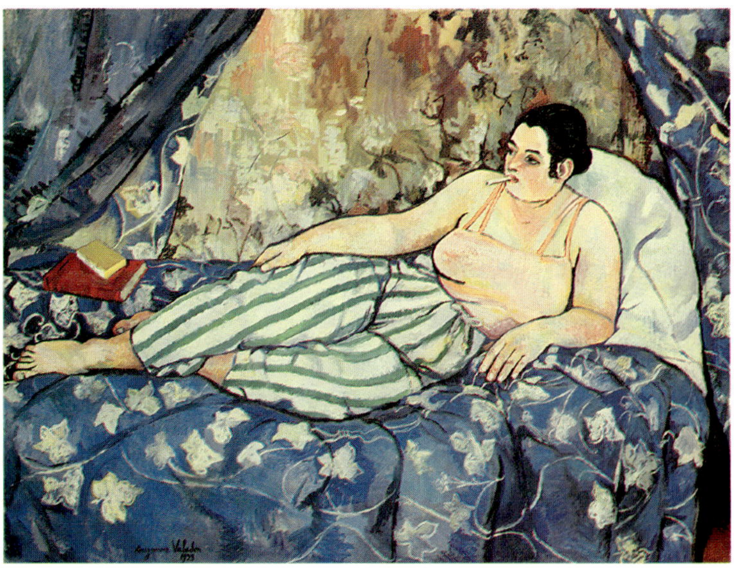

Fig. 10. Suzanne Valadon
La Chambre Bleue (*The Blue Room*) (1923) Cat. 152

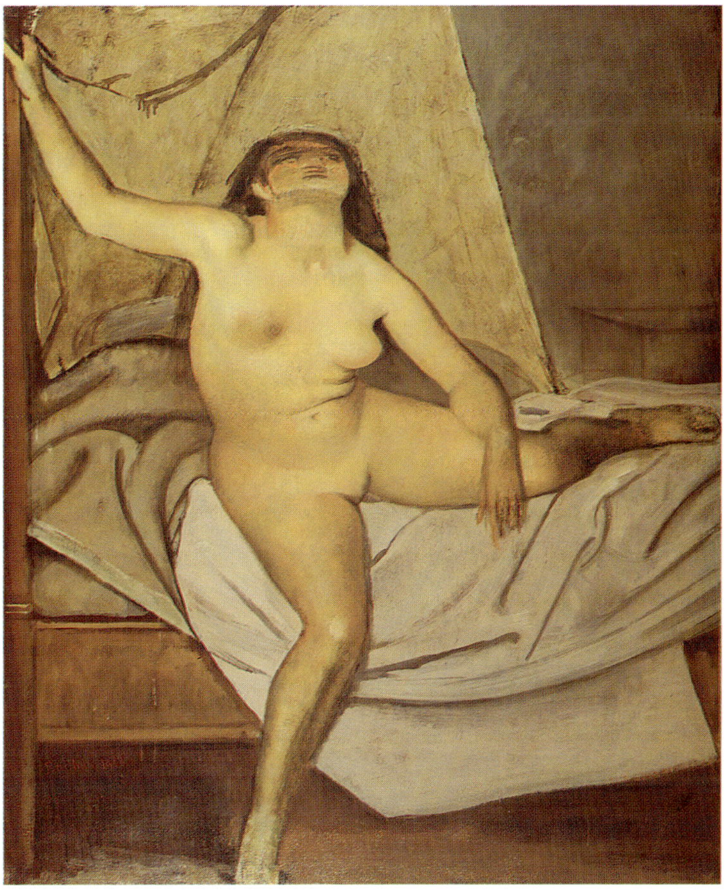

Fig. 11. Balthus *Le Lever (Getting Up)* (1955) Cat. 6

Fig. 12. Balthus *Nude with Cat* (1949) Cat. 8

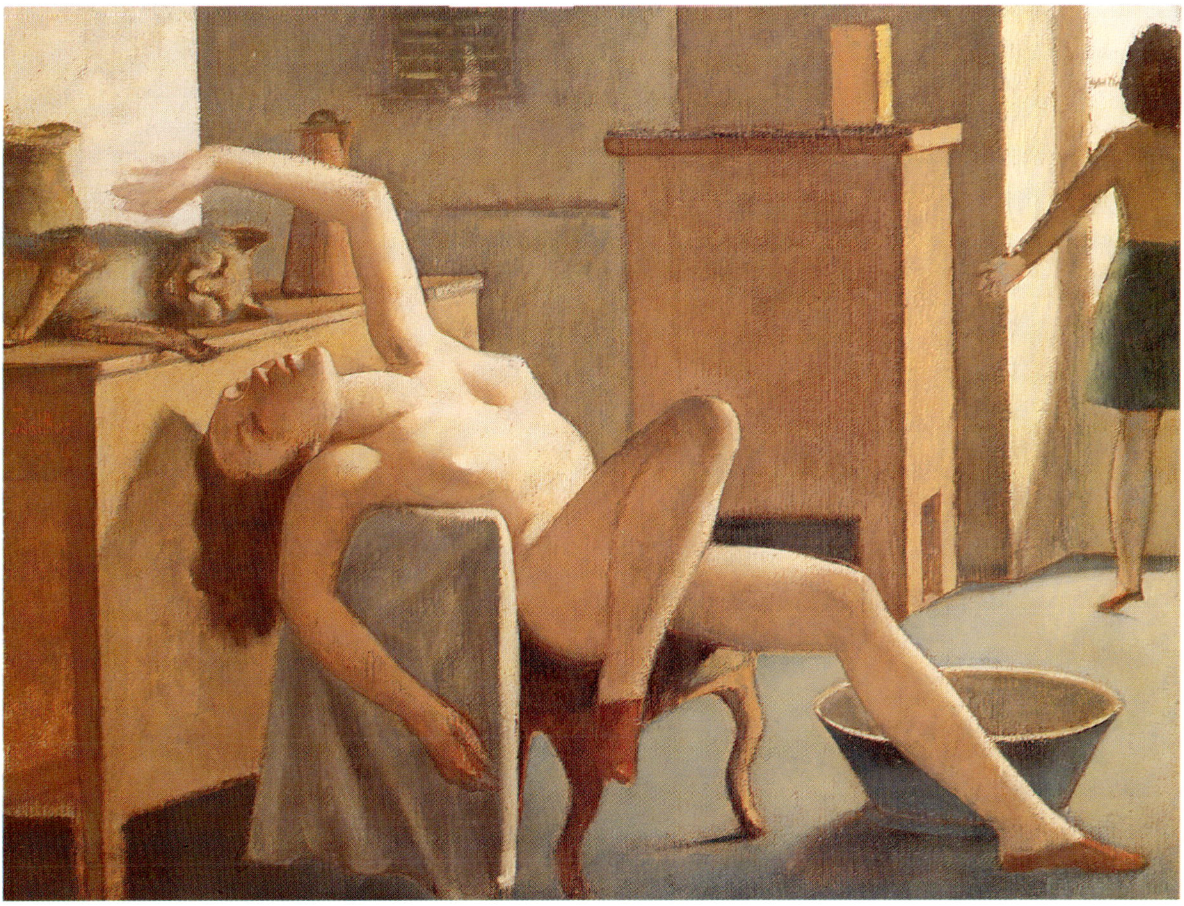

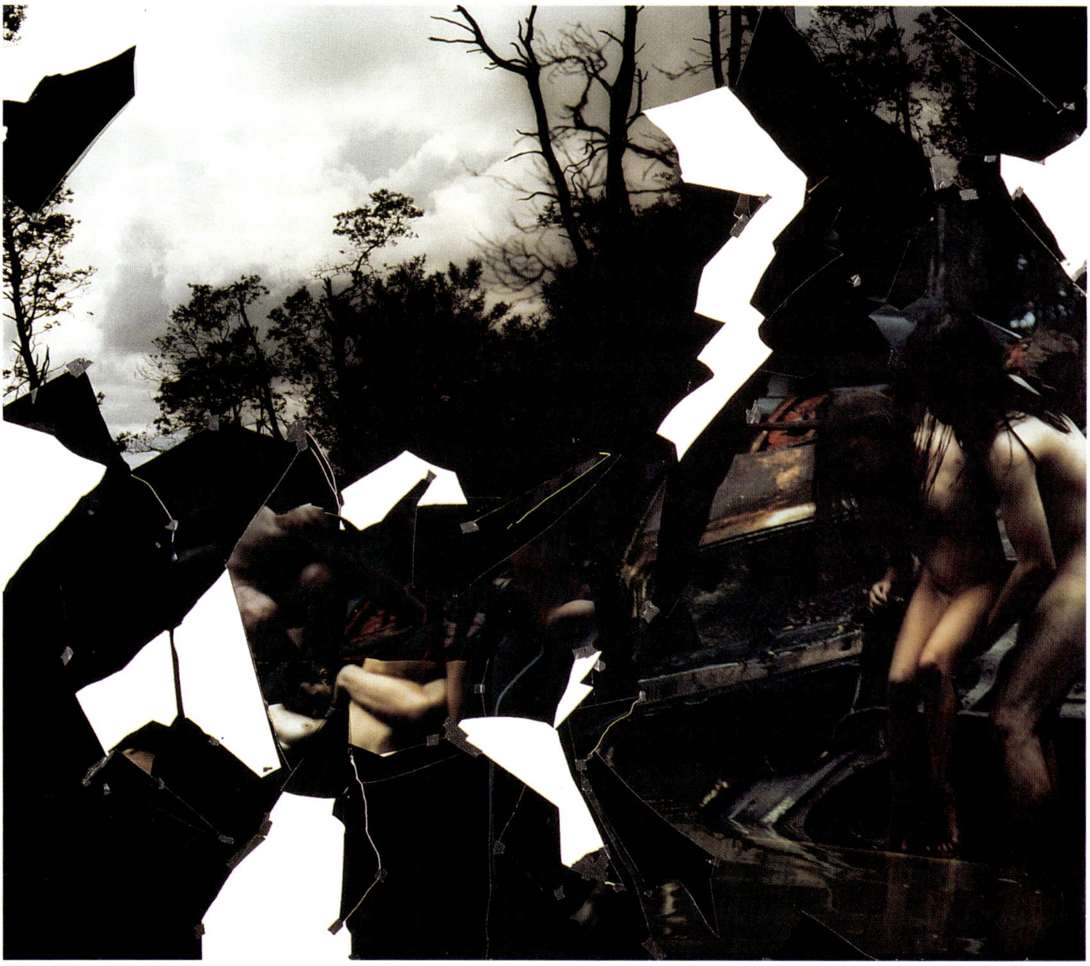

Fig. 13. Bill Henson *Untitled 1994/95* (1994–95) Cat. 64

etching, but its echo in *La Chambre Bleue* reveals how time and taste move on. Manet was reviled in his time for exposing the everyday in the realm of painting which convention reserved for higher fancies. Valadon, in her turn, rejects Manet for simply modernising the objectifying gaze of nineteenth century male artists. Her heroine is self-absorbed, clothed and smokes a cigarette. Manet's *Olympia* may have flaunted the conventional notion of beauty in the 1860s, but she was nevertheless desirable and available because implicitly a prostitute.[12]

Edward Hopper is best known for his observations of everyday life in the public domain. The little study *Nude Crawling into Bed* (Fig. 7) is an exception. As in the self-portraits by Courbet, Hopper has brought the figure very close to the picture plane. The room is divided by the play of light and shade, creating a plane of illumination through which the figure passes into the dark recesses of the bedroom. This implied movement from the viewer's space into the veiled interior evokes a movement from consciousness into reverie or sleep.

In *Le Lever* and *Nude with Cat* (Figs. 11 and 12) Balthus depicts pubescent girls in erotic and mysteriously theatrical poses. The light falls from the side, as if from an open window, yet this only serves to heighten the intimacy of the acts which have occurred or are about to occur within the privacy of the room.

Balthus' nudes are often accompanied by a clothed admirer or witness. He also makes use of fabric and other tactile materials to amplify our awareness of touch. Fabric hangs alongside skin, the hand brushes the breast or reaches out to touch a cat. These are moments in which Balthus suggests arousal through the medium of obsessively worked paint. This is handled in the manner of Degas, by layering pigments and rubbing them back until a skinlike surface is developed. This technique translates again into a tactile, sensual response and yet the models are children and unthinkable as objects of desire.

Bill Henson's photographs purport to capture erotic rituals being played out by adolescents on an urban tip (Fig. 13). The site is presumed to be away from the public gaze but the photographer, who has either commissioned the event or has been tolerated by the participants, allows the viewer to intrude. The images are collaged to re-situate the action in grand romantic landscape settings. The figure groupings in this scenery are suggestive of dramatic history paintings in the Baroque manner, and yet the source of the imagery is of abject and dysfunctional adolescent behaviour. The surface of thc imagery is ruptured violently by jagged areas collaged from the white reverse of the photographic paper. This rending of the surface of representation exaggerates the contextual disruption of the collage, making it hard to focus on the pictures as a straight narrative. They acquire an abstract dynamic which reads across separate panels, transforming the whole wall into a dance. The viewer is compelled to move back and forth between a formal reading of the whole and voyeurism of its parts. Henson deliberately places compositional difficulties in the way of an uncritical gaze, thereby requiring the viewer to work hard at looking.

Towards the end of the exhibition we are invited to participate in an intensely private moment in the video installation, *Stuck*, by Tony Oursler (Fig. 14). A roughly formed rag doll of human scale lies in a corner, its face is a projected video image. The actress who has performed the portrait of the doll vividly simulates a sexual experience. Because we can not see the partner who is producing these gasps and grimaces we are left to imagine the particular nature of the act. By requiring us to visualise the invisible source of the doll's experience Oursler involves us as active participants: the viewer's response in effect completes the work.

Fig. 14. Tony Oursler *Stuck* (1996) Cat. 114

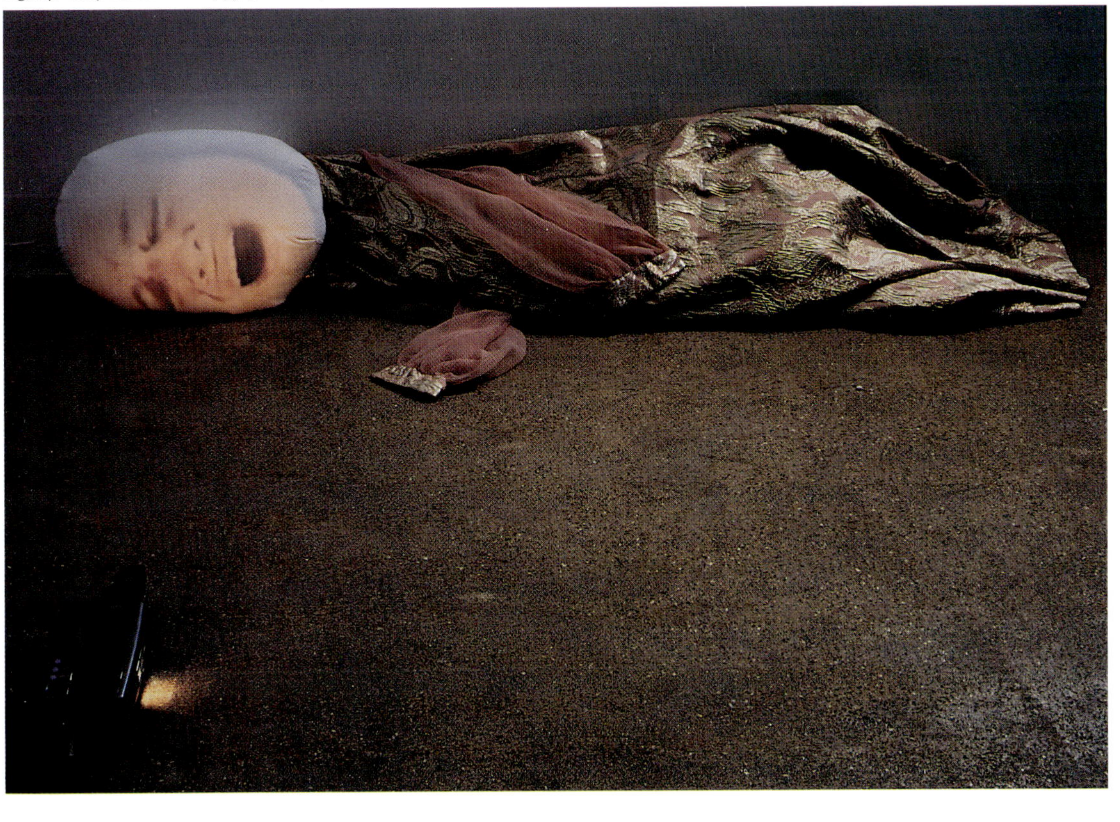

2 Landscape, waterfall and hole: sexual allegories

The next group of works links nineteenth and twentieth-century images of the landscape as an allegory of the female body to reclamations of the land as a productive site by later feminist artists. Courbet was particularly committed to the association between female creativity and the earth. His best known paintings of the nude are intimately associated with nature: *The Painter's Studio* (Fig. 119) and the two versions of *The Source* (the version from The Metropolitan Museum is represented in this exhibition, Fig. 16) are key examples which Michael Fried has analysed most provocatively. One feature of his interpretation is the intense identification Courbet is supposed to have demonstrated with his female models.[13] Another is the artist's identification of women with nature and the use of landscape features as metaphors for aspects of the feminine. The waterfall, the source, and the cave are obvious enough associations which can be reduced to banal sexual innuendo. Linda Nochlin supports this view, regarding Courbet's merger with the female body as yet another instance of a male artist presenting 'woman' as available for imaginative penetration.[14] Arguably, however, there is an intense investment in this female presence in nature throughout the art of Courbet which seems deeply personal and empathic.[15] These opposing interpretations are most dramatically exposed in Courbet's specifically erotic compositions.

L'Origine du Monde (Fig. 15) painted by Courbet in 1866 was commissioned by Khalil Bey, a wealthy businessman and Turkish diplomat. It was undoubtedly intended as erotic if not pornographic, but Courbet's title would seem to be more than a nineteenth-century euphemism. The image depicts a woman lying with her legs spread. It is framed to focus on the pubic area, with the lower legs and the torso above the breast falling beyond the edge of the composition. Courbet transfers this anatomical meaning of 'origin in a woman's body' to the earth as the 'source of all life' and, in doing so, he sexualises the landscape itself. Courbet's landscape paintings often depict the rocky gorges of the river Loue which flowed through his home town of Ornans. *The Source of the Loue* in this exhibition – which has often been discussed in relation to *L'Origine du Monde* – shows the river gushing out of a cave towards the viewer (Fig. 17).[16]

The association of water welling up from the ground with human procreation is a common theme and the representation of the spring or source as female is a conventional allegory in ninteenth-century painting. In the case of Courbet, however, his profound identification with the land seems to arise more from his historical and political circumstances and his daily experience

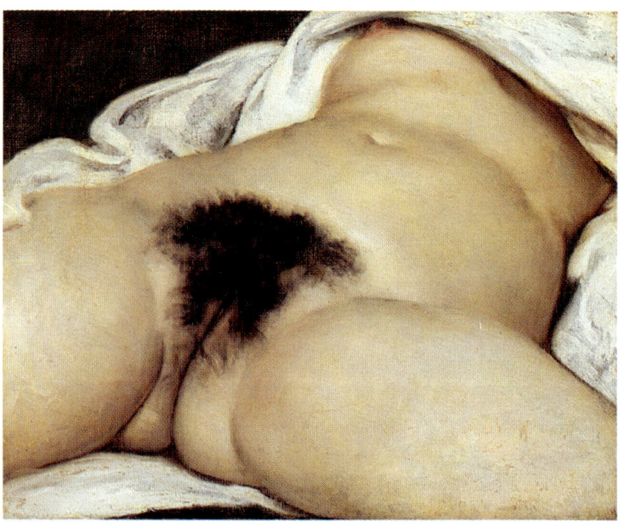

Fig. 15. Gustave Courbet *L'Origine du Monde* (*The Origin of the World*) (1866) Ref. 12

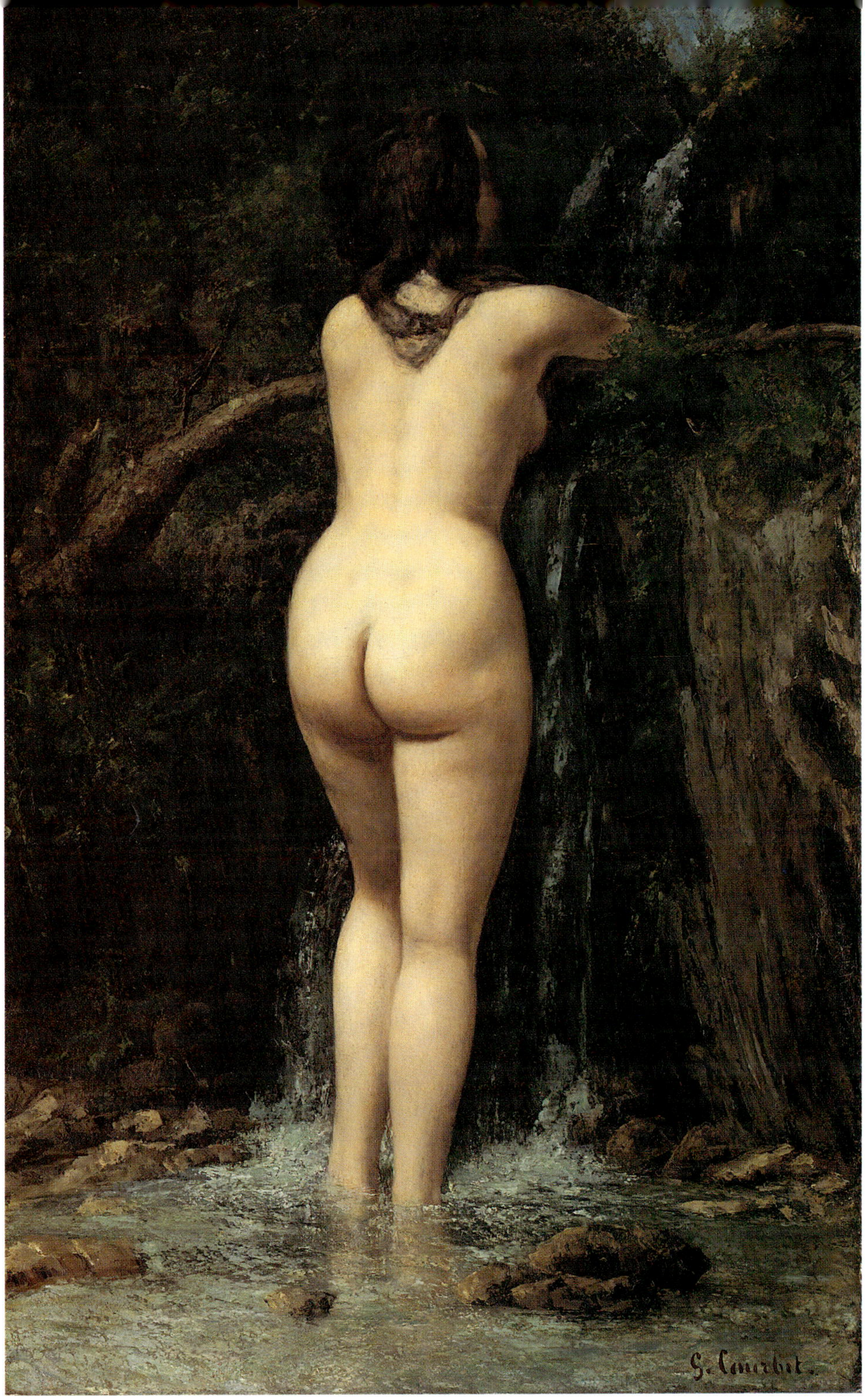

Fig. 16. Gustave Courbet *The Source* (1862) Cat. 33

of the countryside. Courbet came from a rural community that had benefited under the Republic's re-distribution of land between 1848 and 1851. For these middle-class land owners the land was a major political issue. For the first time in modern history those who worked the land also owned it, and participated in government. Later in his life Courbet served as a minister in the short-lived Commune of 1871 and was subsequently thrown into prison for his political activities. Much of his work is allegorical, not so much as an aesthetic device but because of the very real fear of political censorship felt by his class. *The Painter's Studio* for example was intended as a satirical criticism of Napoleon III.[17] It was submitted to the Salon in 1855 at the time of the Great Exhibition in Paris which had been initiated by Napoleon. Although Courbet's criticism was encoded as allegory it was still not acceptable to the officials. He responded to rejection by creating his own pavilion near the official exhibition. While the allegorical nature of his criticism gave him some protection from the law his position with regard to the authorities was permanently compromised.

Courbet was an active naturalist and a member of the *Societé d'emulation du Doubs*, a society formed to promote scientific studies to improve the land in his native region. He was also called upon by geologists to render rock formations for scientific publications. In other words, he was actively involved in the daily management of the environment and not just an objective observer. His painterly treatment of rocks and water is as obsessively rendered as his handling of skin and hair. He evolved techniques for handling paint that approached the concept of equivalence which was later articulated by English painters such as Francis Bacon and Frank Auerbach. When painting rock, for instance, he preferred to use a palette knife to simulate the hardness and angularity of the crystalline nature of stone.

In *L'Origine du Monde* the intimate detail of flesh and pubic hair is meticulously recreated so that the viewer's experience is almost as tactile as it is visual. A consistent feature in Courbet's compositions is a framing that brings the viewer very close to the subject. This adds to the sensation of merger and encourages the viewer's imaginative projection into the picture. While contrived for figure painting, and most particularly *L'Origine du Monde*, this effect is equally evident in Courbet's landscapes and his later studies of animals. The combination of this compositional strategy with the sensual paint quality produces a striking material presence for the viewer.

Michael Fried argues that Courbet attempts a quasi-corporeal merger with the subjects of his painting.[18] By implication the viewer follows the artist as beholder, experiencing something of this sense of passage through the pictorial surface. In paintings such as *The Source of the Loue* the flow of water out of the composition towards the viewer and the deep, inviting recesses of the cave initiate an imaginative movement in and out of the composition, binding the viewer in a sexual allegory. Passage through the screen of a pictorial surface may be thought of as a passage from the world of representations and language to the material world. This passage is made more explicit in some contemporary art such as Yves Klein's *Leap into the Void*, Lucio Fontana slashing the 'veil' of representation in his *Concetto Spaziale* paintings, and the work of performance artists of the

Fig. 17. Gustave Courbet *The Source of the Loue* (c.1865) Cat. 34

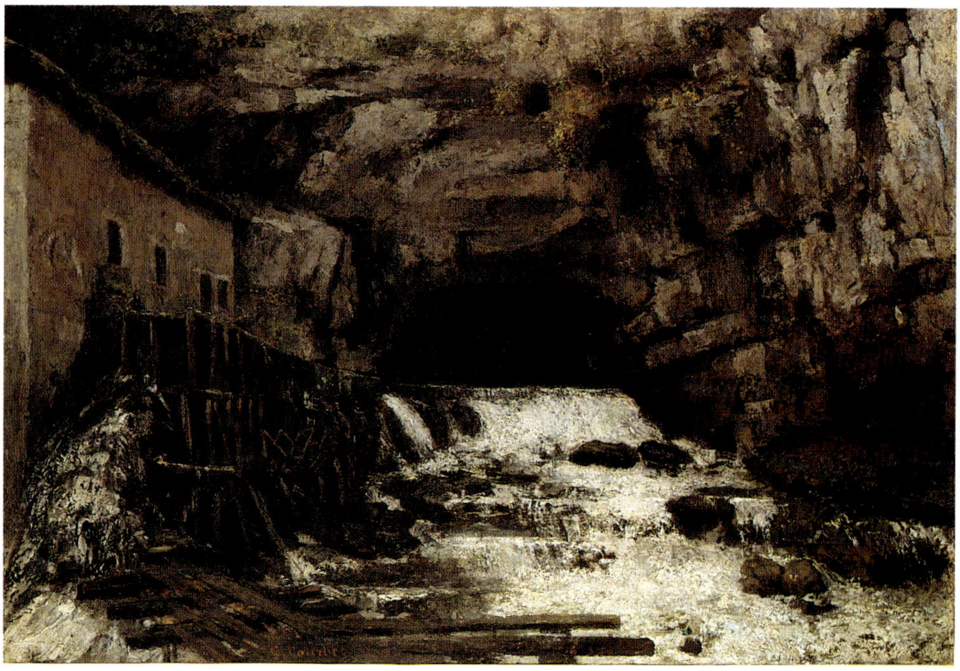

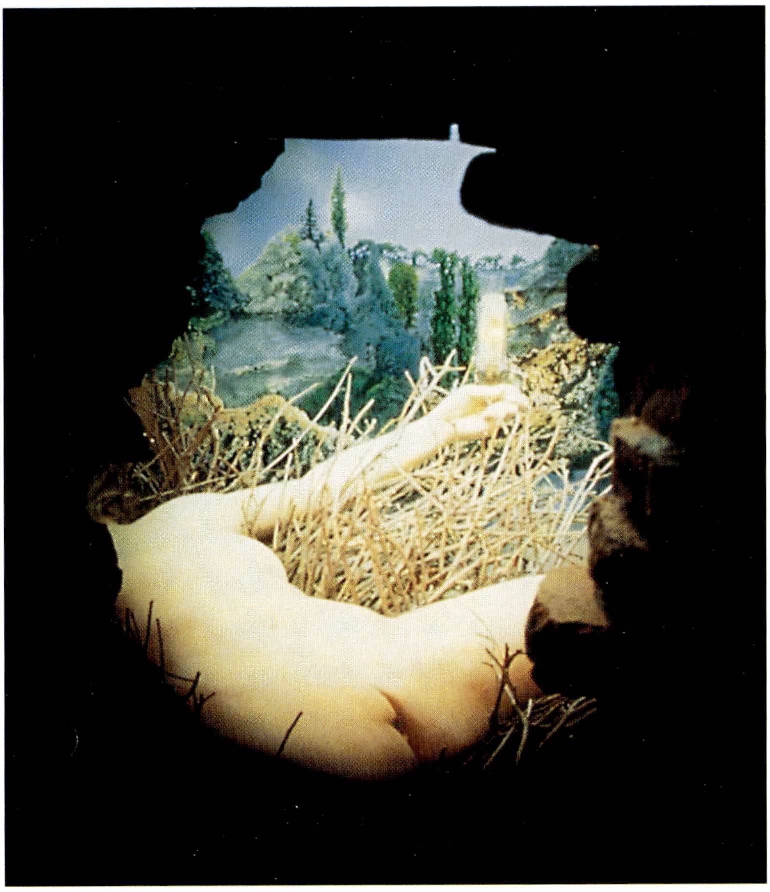

Fig. 18. Richard Baquié *Sans Titre. Etant Donnés: 1°La chute d'eau 2°Le gaz d'éclairage (Untitled. Given: 1. The Waterfall 2. The Illuminating Gas)* photograph by J. B. Rodde (1991) Cat. 9

1960s and '70s who are discussed later in this introduction.

Landscape as sexual allegory is taken up in the exhibition by the proximity of Courbet and Baquié, who has faithfully replicated Duchamp's last great work, *Etant Donnés* (Fig. 18). In this work the viewer must look through a small hole in a wooden door to see the secret image. By stooping to peer the viewer becomes a conspirator with the artist and perpetrates an act of visual penetration. The view which meets the eye through the keyhole is an extraordinary tableau. Through a ragged hole in a brick wall there is a landscape which includes a waterfall animated by a crude lighting device. In the foreground a naked woman is seen lying on a bed of twigs. The framing of the figure is similar to that of *L'Origine du Monde*. She is holding up a glowing gas lamp which draws our gaze towards the waterfall in the distance. Auguste Rodin's sculpture *Iris, Messenger of the Gods* continues the theme of water, Iris being a water nymph in classical mythology. Another bronze by Rodin, *Figure Volante* (Fig. 20), is a closely related work whose pose could well have inspired Duchamp's original study for *Etant Donnés* in 1947.[19]

Flanking the doors with their infamous peepholes is a body of small works by Duchamp to one side and Anish Kapoor on the other. Duchamp's nine etchings entitled *The Lovers* selectively quote from erotic paintings including *Woman in White Stockings* by Courbet, and Ingres' *Turkish Bath* (Figs. 19 and 21). The small collage *A la Manière de Delvaux* (Fig. 22) shows a cameo or detail from a painting by the Surrealist artist Delvaux of a woman's breast reflected in an oval mirror. Duchamp has framed the oval within a further circle cut from a sheet of tin foil. The net result is a keyhole vision of a woman in the privacy of her bedroom. The keyhole effect relates to *Etant Donnés* while the invasion of privacy reverts to the theme of the first room.

Kapoor's five drawings are all highly material works depicting sexualised voids which are inevitably linked to the image of *L'Origine du Monde* by Courbet and its connection with the grotto. This gallery wall with its actual peepholes and its many represented apertures paradoxically conceals more than it reveals for behind it there lies a cabinet of erotic curiosities. Further into the exhibition the viewer encounters the verso of Baquié's reconstruction of *Etant Donnés*. This room of sexualised fragments and Surrealist fantasies of the body lies unseen behind the gallery wall in Room 2, just as the fetishisation of the female body lies behind the body as landscape.

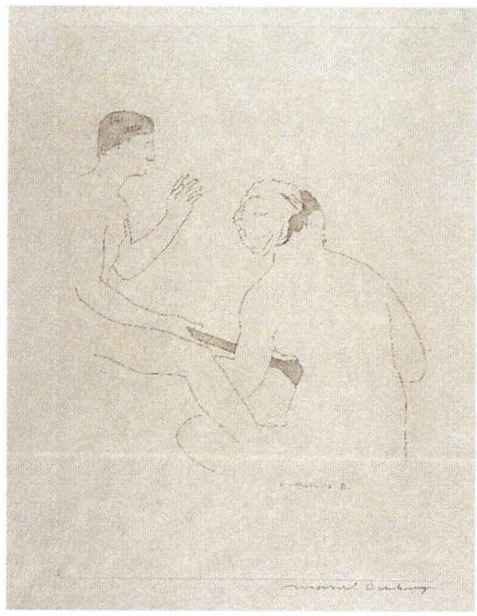

Fig. 19. Marcel Duchamp *Morceaux Choisis d'après Ingres, 1 (Selected Details after Ingres, I)* (1968) Cat. 50 (ii)

The waterfall and the grotto are combined in the works of Courbet and Duchamp, but there are many other manifestations of the hole. While an orthodox psychoanalytic reading would ascribe negative connotations to the hole, it can in fact become the exact opposite of a lack. Anish Kapoor's drawings of sexualised voids bring the vagina and infinity together in a powerful allegory of becoming at the threshold of being and not being (Fig. 23). Kapoor has been influenced by Klein's attempt to manifest the void; his *Void Field*, for example, creates a void within a stone which is visible as a 'black hole' in the top of the stone. Noting Kapoor's Indian background, Thomas McEvilley has identified the hole with the Hindu Goddess Kali whose womb gives life and subsequently devours it in a cycle of renewal.[20] Lucio Fontana punctured the pictorial surface in his slashed canvases, bringing painting and action together in a decisive gesture, but he also returns us to the desire for merger and passage through the veil which was discussed in relation to Courbet.[21] In one form or another this investment in the productive space of the void will be encountered throughout the exhibition.

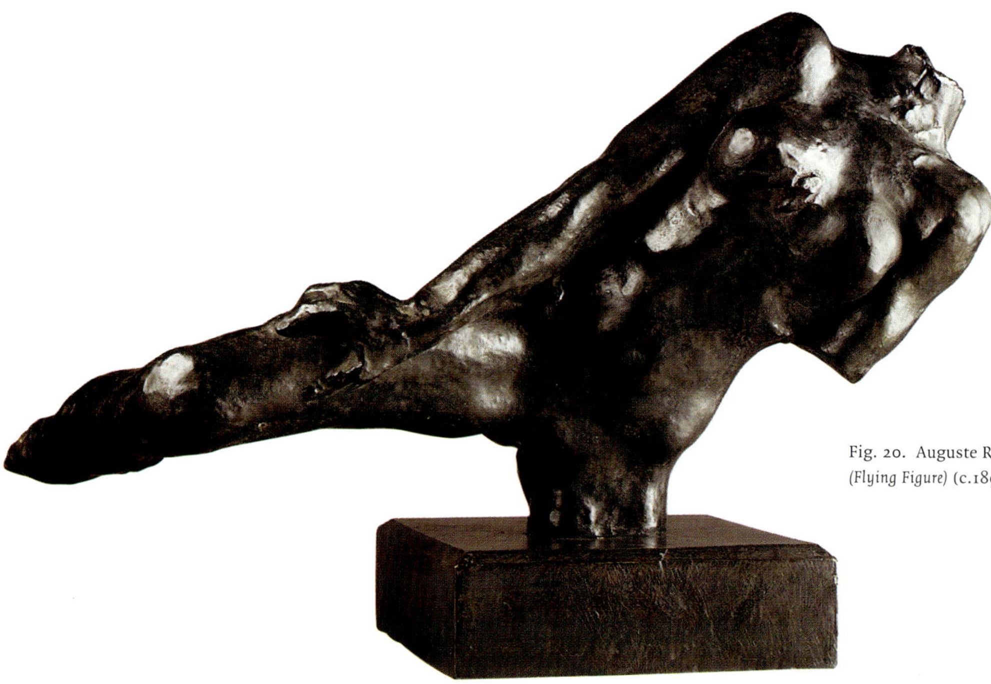

Fig. 20. Auguste Rodin *Figure Volante (Flying Figure)* (c.1890–91) Cat. 131

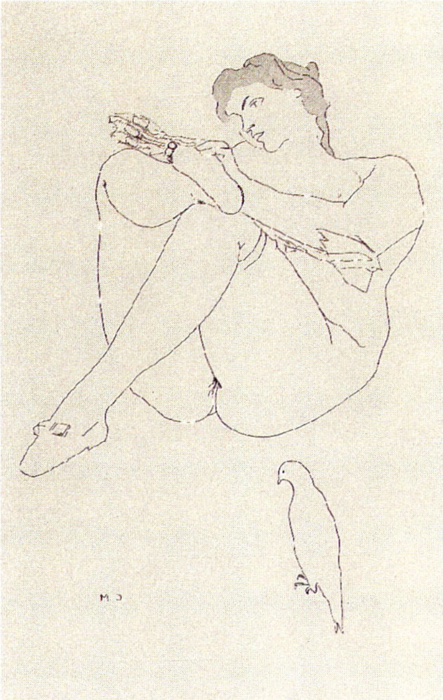

Fig. 21. Marcel Duchamp *Morceaux Choisis d'après Courbet (Selected Details after Courbet)* (1968) Cat. 50 (v)

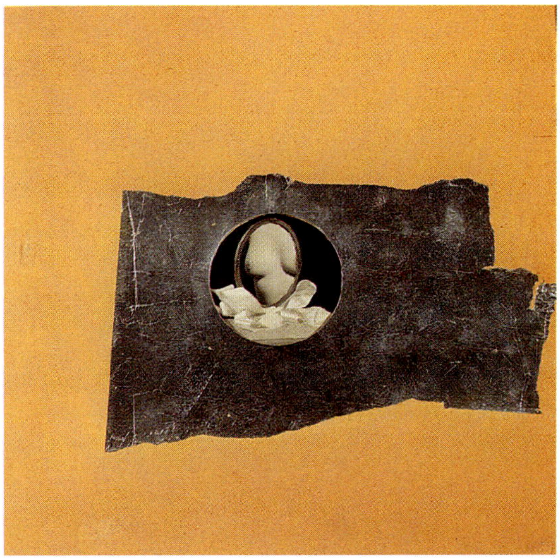

Fig. 22. Marcel Duchamp *A la Manière de Delvaux (In the Manner of Delvaux)* (1942) Cat. 46

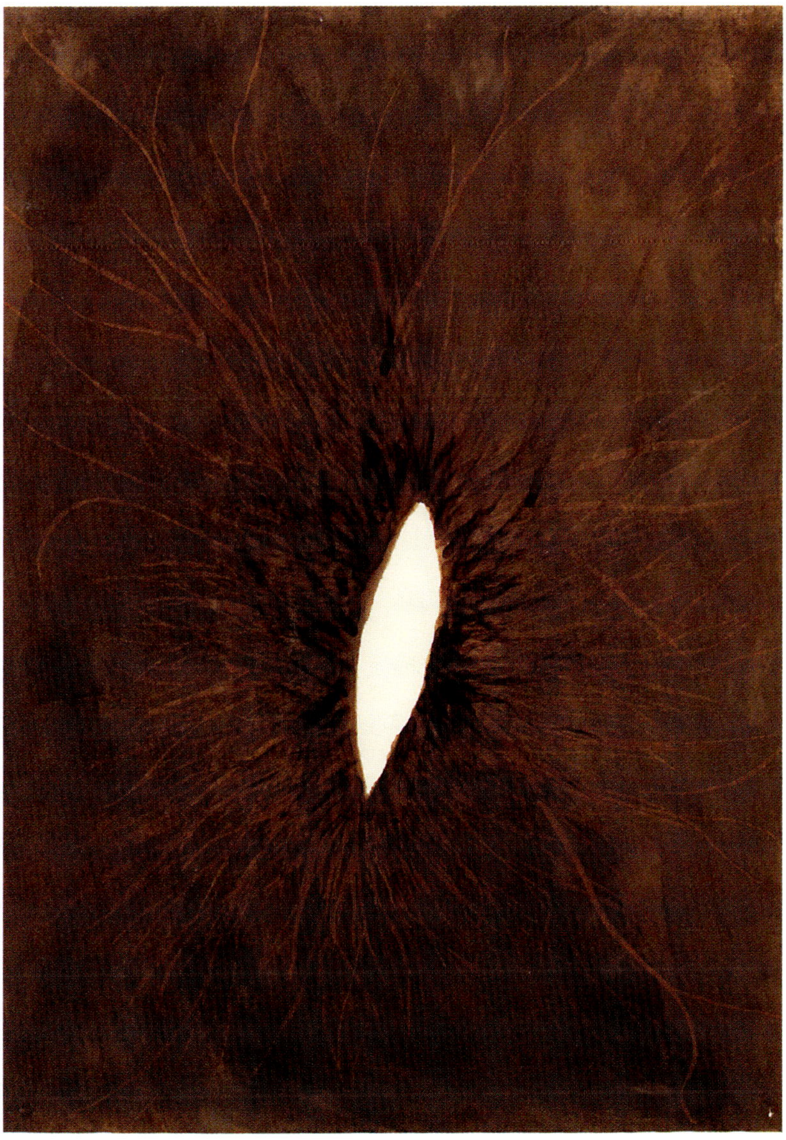

Fig. 23. Anish Kapoor *Untitled* (1988) Cat. 71

3 Feminising the landscape allegory

Elsewhere in the exhibition, women artists respond to the male identification of the feminine with nature by claiming it as a site of power rather than a mechanism which silences or de-humanises. They may, for instance, place the figure intimately in the earth, reclaiming the association of femininity and the creative power of nature. In an unusual painting entitled *The Earth Itself* or *Two Nudes in the Jungle* (Fig. 25), Frida Kahlo reveals two nude figures lying together in a pose which implies their intimacy. This composition parodies popular ninteenth-century erotic depictions of lesbians, in which the light and dark skins of the women implied the racial and class distinction of maid and mistress. The two figures could also be interpreted as representing culture and nature, where the exotic other is identified as primitive and close to nature while culture is the prerogative of the white coloniser.[22] Kahlo may be representing herself as a post-colonial hybrid of Europe and the new world by acknowledging both aspects of her own identity in a double self-portrait. The figures are at the edge of a bank which also functions as a transparent screen, revealing roots below the surface. The effect is to make the women appear to be a part of the tropical luxuriance. Above their heads the vegetation writhes in convoluted knots suggestive of a sexual embrace. In the trees there is a black monkey staring intently at the resting women as if it were an alter ego, the watcher and the psyche of the protagonists.

Ana Mendieta is represented by the *Silueta Works in Iowa* (Fig. 24) consisting of video and photo-documentation of a series of actions performed by Mendieta in the Iowa landscape.[23] In these performances she left traces of her body in the soil and vegetation. In the video we barely detect the human form as it slowly moves under the weeds in a swamp or the sand of a riverbank. The photos reveal her presence more emphatically, while paradoxically consisting of her absence. They were made by drawing her own silhouette in the ground or leaving an impression of her figure in the mud. Sometimes the trace of her presence is retained in selectively weeded fungus or flowers or by the effect of fire. In an earlier series of performances made in Mexico her presence is

Fig. 24. Ana Mendieta *Silueta Works in Iowa*
carved earth at riverbank, Old Man's Creek, Iowa (1976–78) Cat. 95

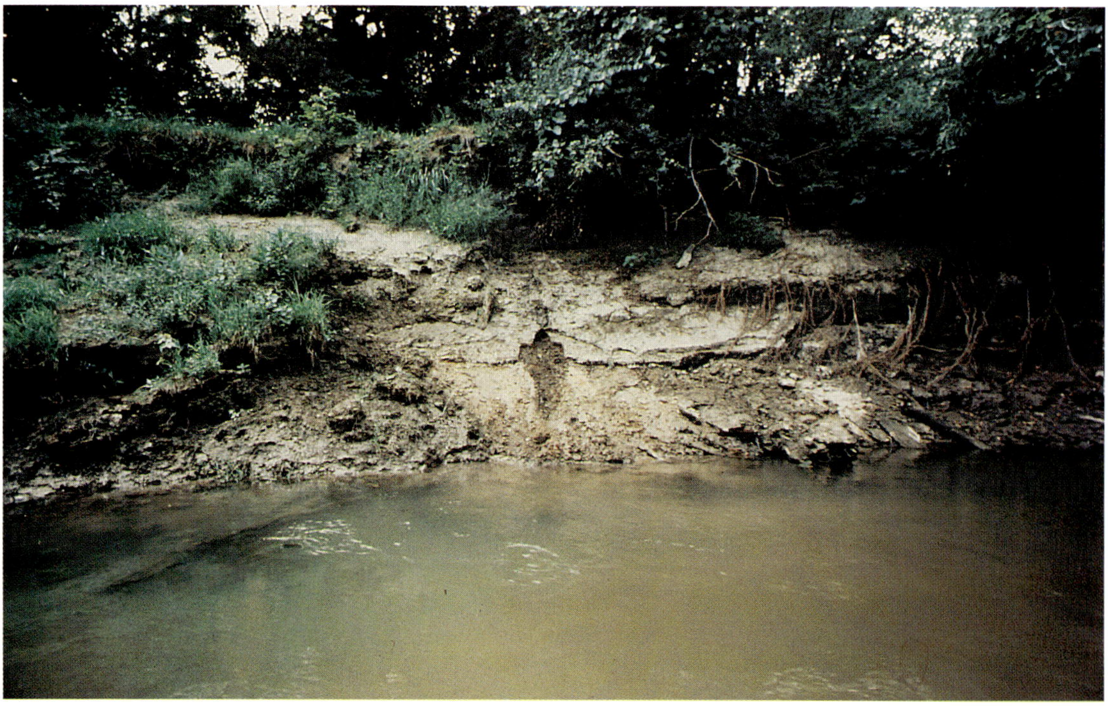

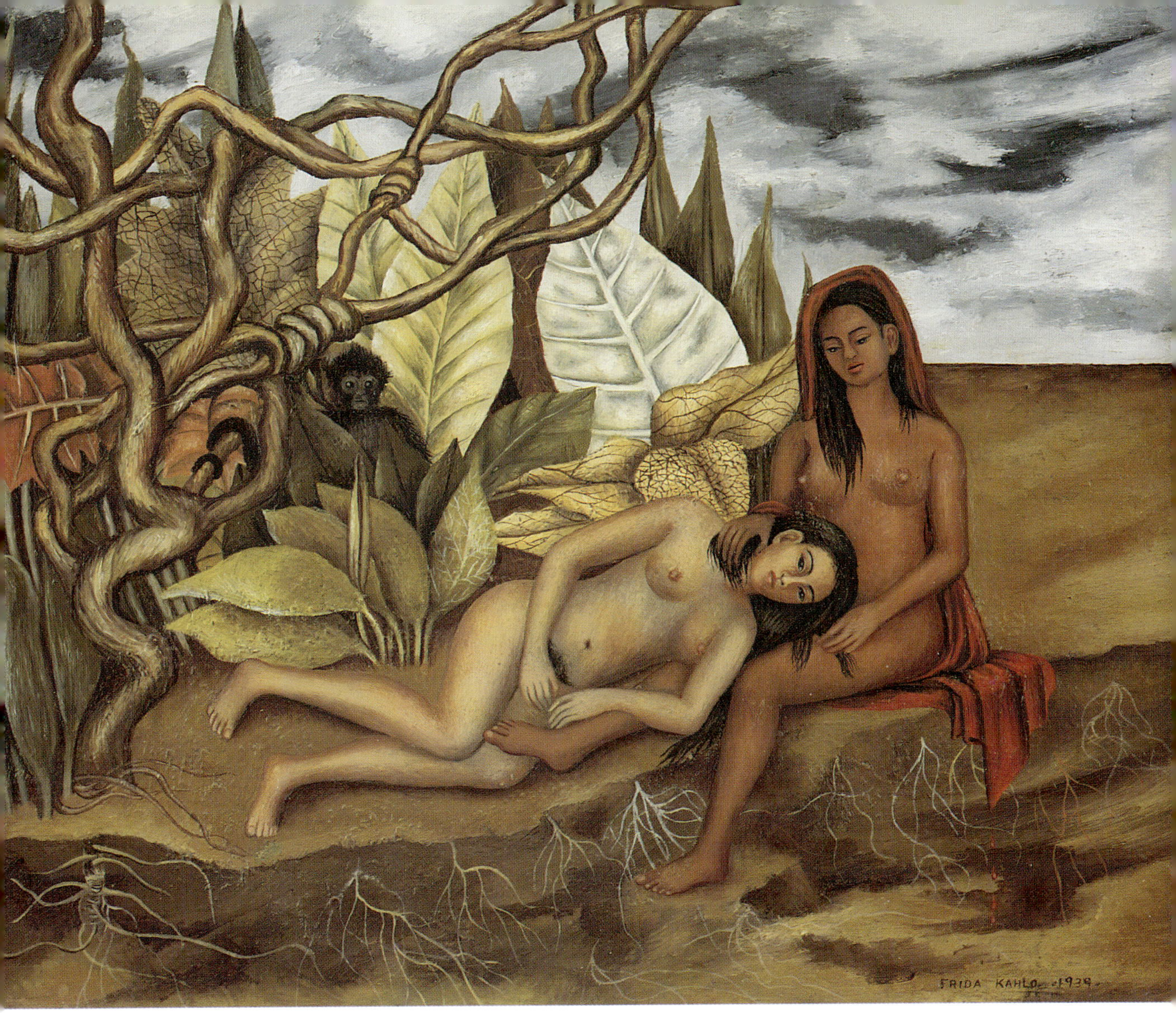

Fig. 25. Frida Kahlo *Two Nudes in the Jungle* (1939)

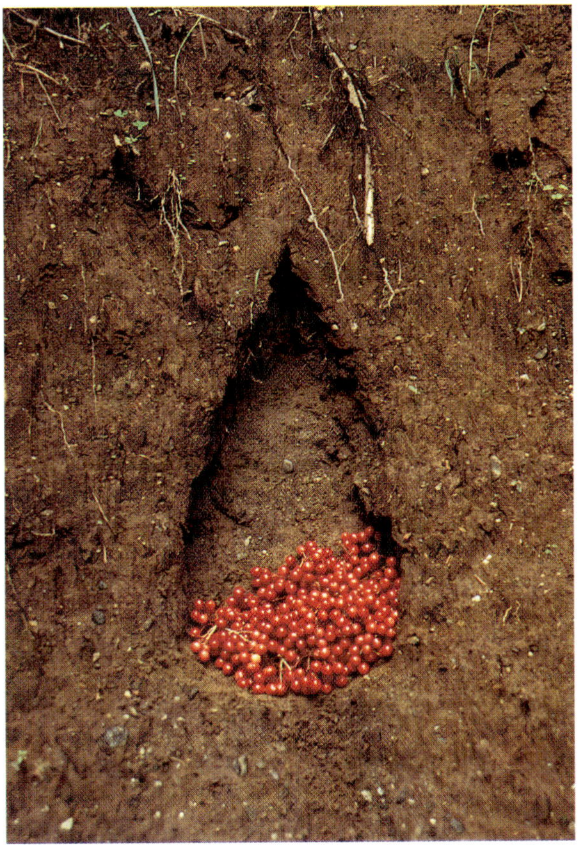

Fig. 26. Laura Torrado Red Inside I (1993) Cat. 149

marked by rituals of Catholicism. Mendieta ended her life on a New York pavement after falling to her death from her apartment window. This hindsight lends these imprints of her form a particular resonance.

In the two series of photos by Laura Torrado represented in *BODY*, *Red Inside* and *Island*, installations in the landscape take the form of female genitalia (Fig. 26). They lay claim not only to the productive power of nature, but also the creativity of culture associated with the transformation of the earth into pottery and bricks.[24] The chief distinction between the male view of a feminised landscape and a woman's claim to the earth is one of agency. It is very easy for the former to neutralise the role of woman by naming her as natural and therefore pre-cultural. For a woman to identify with the productive power of nature may, however, be empowering.

4 Anxious males

"Fearful Desires: 'Embodiments' in Late Nineteenth-Century French Painting," is the title of the essay by Alan Krell in this book which looks at the anxiety engendered by male bodies in artistic representations of the nineteenth-century. This section of the exhibition follows landscape metaphors of femininity and inevitably leads into the section dealing with tactility.[25] Of particular interest is François Sallé's, *The Anatomy Class at the École des Beaux-Arts* (1888) from the collection of The Art Gallery of New South Wales (Fig. 143). The male model is half naked and is being examined as if he were just a piece of flesh. In spite of his cocky stance, his sturdy muscled torso

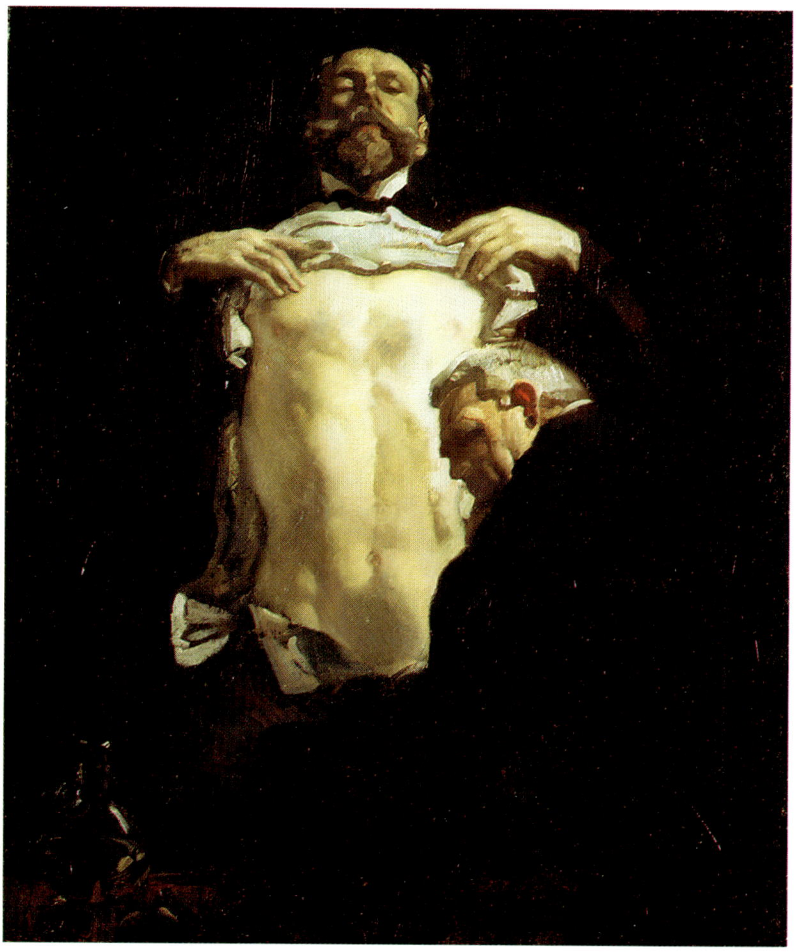

Fig. 27. George Lambert *Chesham Street* (1910) Cat. 79

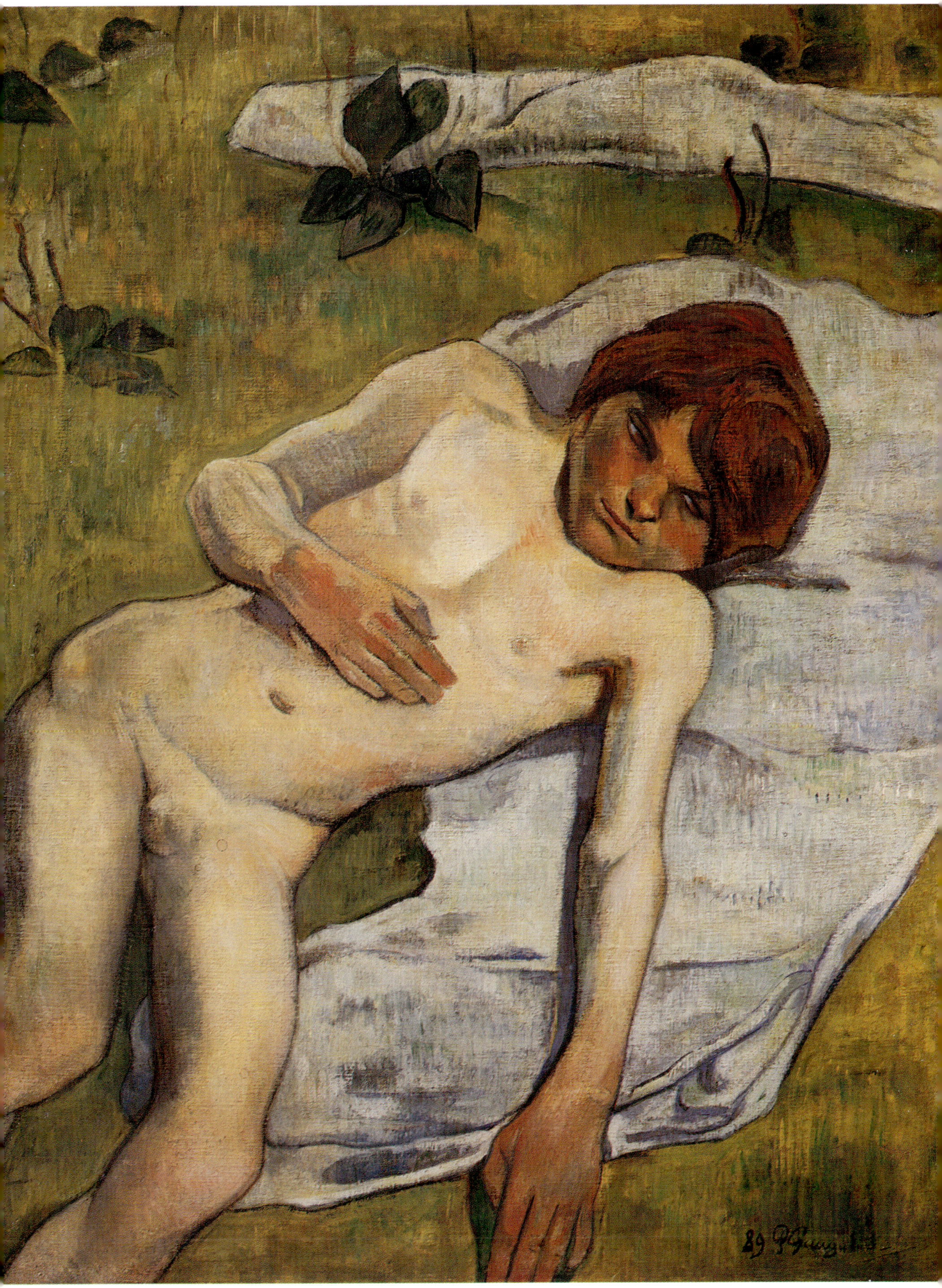

Fig. 28. Paul Gauguin *Breton Youth* (1889) Cat. 56

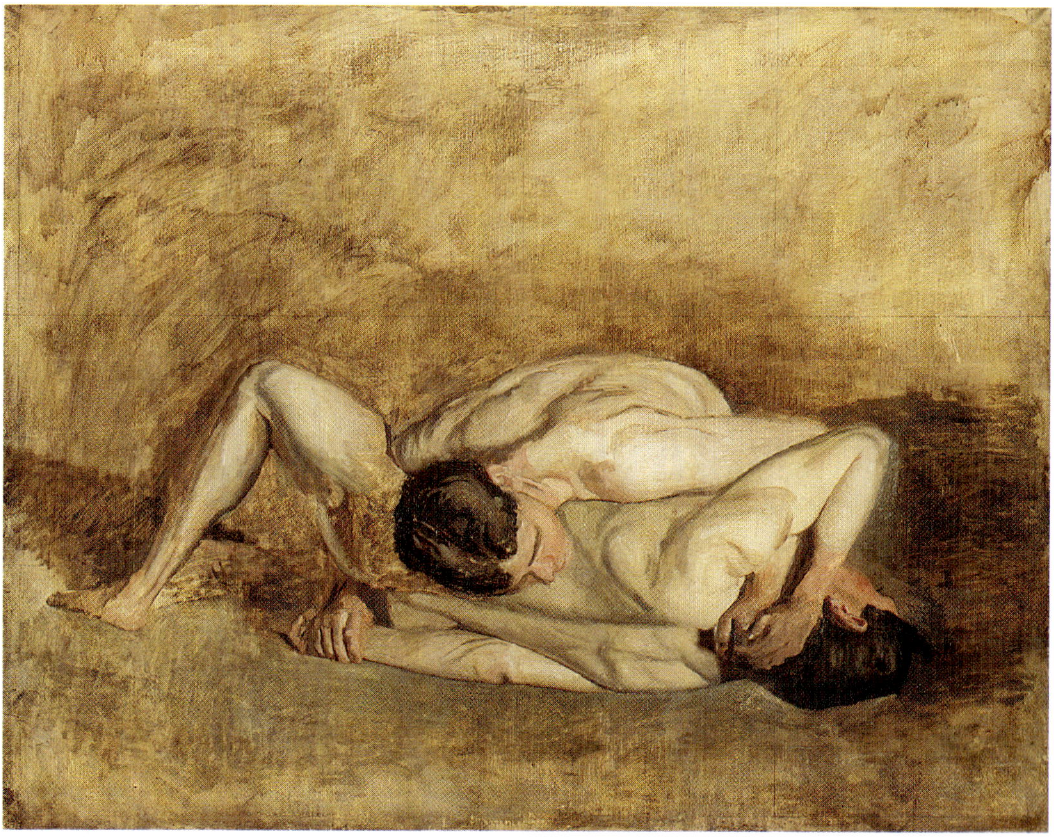

Fig. 29. Thomas Eakins *Wrestlers* (1899) Cat. 51

and rough trousers attest to his lower class status thus rendering him available for objectification by the gentlemen at the academy. The model's standing as a specimen is enhanced by his juxtaposition with a flayed figure, bones and anatomical charts.

The bare torso of the gentleman being examined by a doctor in *Chesham Street* by George Lambert is somehow an incongruous exposure only permitted by the notional discretion of the doctor's surgery (Fig. 27). Thomas Eakins uses the context of athletics to permit male body contact in *Wrestlers* (Fig. 29). This image is accompanied by Eadweard Muybridge's study, *Wrestling* (Fig. 155), which later formed the basis for Francis Bacon's lovers in paintings such as the central canvas of *Triptych* (1974), also included in this exhibition (Figs. 153 and 154).

Auguste Renoir's *Jeune Garçon au Chat* (Fig. 30) and Paul Gauguin's *Breton Youth* (Fig. 28) are sexually ambiguous images of young boys. The two works are very different from each other, Renoir's being a finely finished and elegant painting while the Gauguin is awkward with strangely blurred features. Both figures are disconcertingly androgynous. *Jeune Garçon au Chat* shows the youth from the back in a pose similar to one of the three graces in classical painting. His face is nuzzling a cat's head while the cat returns the affection, yet the boy's gaze is partly turned towards the artist or the beholder. The cat seems to function as a vehicle for sympathetic contact between the viewer and the model, just as it does for Bonnard and Balthus. Gauguin's youth is self absorbed and on the edge of consciousness, his eyes half closed and cast to one side. The boy's face and the hand resting upon his solar plexus are vividly coloured, combining reverie and touch.[26]

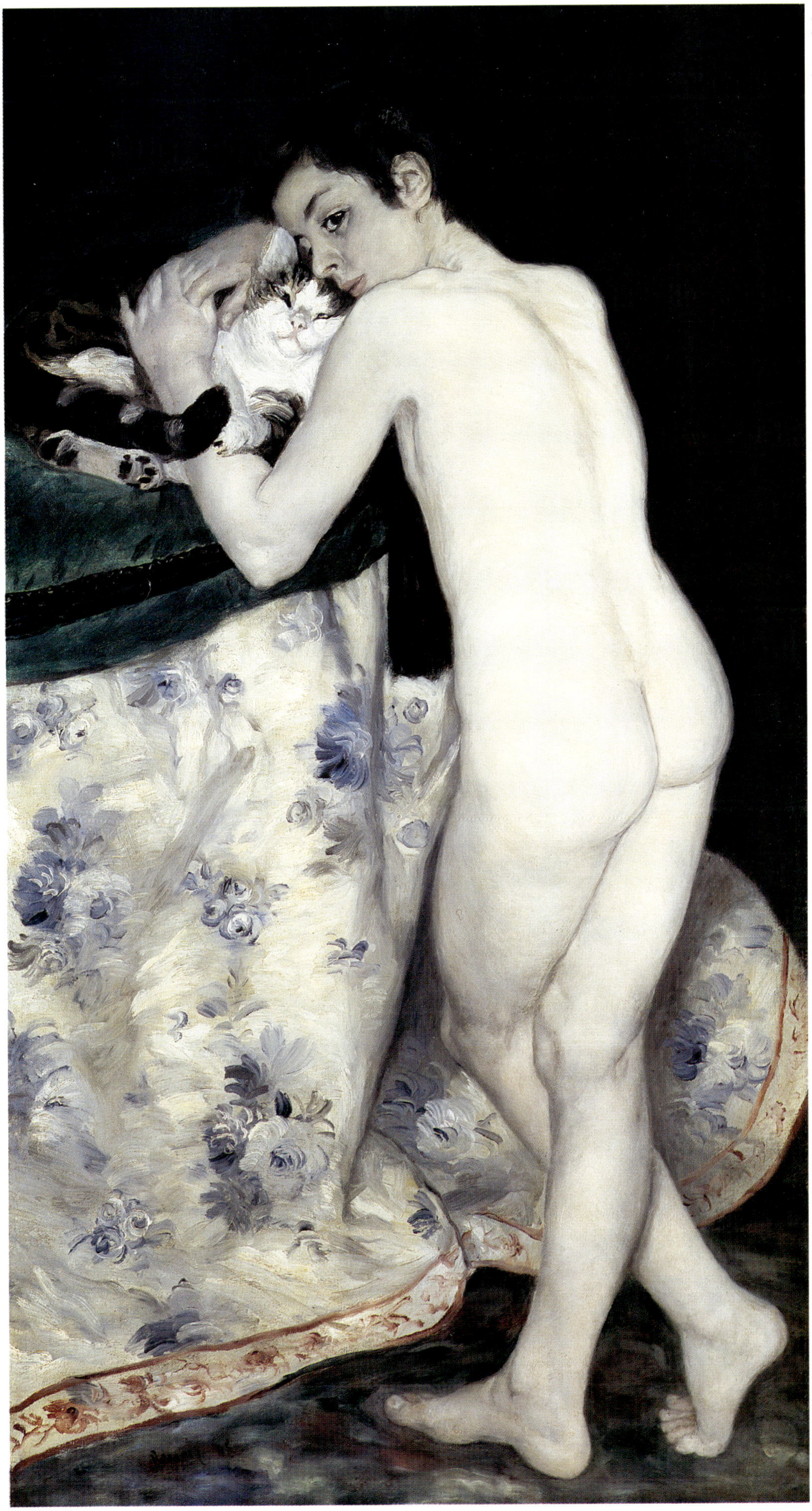

Fig. 30. Auguste Renoir *Jeune Garçon au Chat (Young Boy with Cat)* (1868–69) Cat. 125

5 Tactility and the trace of the artist

Jill Bennett writes in this book about tactility and vision, focusing on images that represent and engage all our senses without privileging the purely visual. In this way intimacy and even leakage between bodies is invoked.[27] The images in this section combine intimate visualisations of touch with the tactility of the painted surface. This tactile apprehension of the artist's mark continues the theme introduced in my discussion of Courbet.

Egon Schiele's preoccupation with erotic imagery finds expression in *Eros (Self-portrait Masturbating)* (Fig. 31). Apart from the obvious references to touch, there are some more subtle indicators of implied contact in the drawing. The gown is pulled back to reveal a breast which seems sexually ambiguous, and the fabrics the figure is sitting on are draped to suggest female genitalia. Schiele believed that the marks an artist made could capture the way in which the outer form reveals something of the inner world of the subject. His use of watercolour paint is surprisingly tactile and is laid on in dabs and strokes which enhance the sensitivity of the image. *Die Siegerin* (Fig 33) by Gert Wollheim is an even more eccentric sexual image. The rather lumpen ballerina in her 'Ned Kelly' mask appears to be tickling the deformed worshipper's hump with a whip. The mask carries the connotation of carnival, when the normal relations between men and women are traditionally reversed; it may also signify the diabolic possession of the wearer. Alice Neel's portrait *Joe Gould* (Fig. 34) is ambiguous and extreme in its fantastic distortion, presumably revealing an aspect of Gould's eccentric life. Neel remarks that:

> Joe wanted this painted, and I was still imaginative enough to give him a whole tier of penises. I thought that was so clever, hanging that one set from a stool. He was uncircumcised. This could be a propaganda picture against circumcision.[28]

Touching is a recurrent feature of Klossowski's work (Fig. 35). The figures are often ungainly and the poses stiff, making the points of contact, such as a finger resting on the top of a thigh or the simple holding of hands, all the more noticeable. The partially dressed figures of women in his drawings maximise the ambiguity of revealing and concealing. The series of 12 drawings

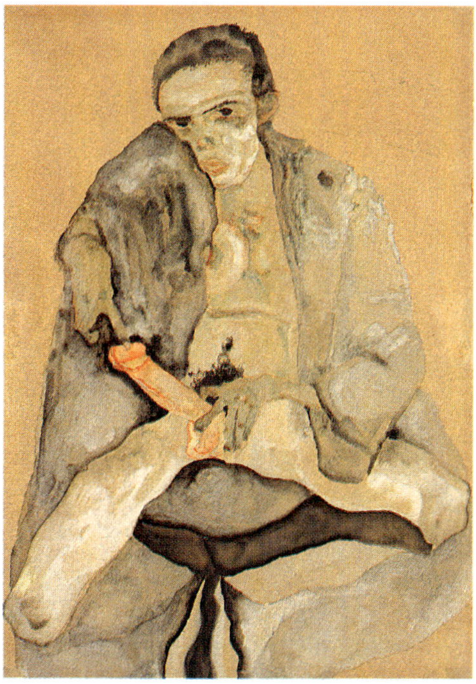

Fig. 31. Egon Schiele *Eros (Self-portrait Masturbating)* (1911) Cat. 137

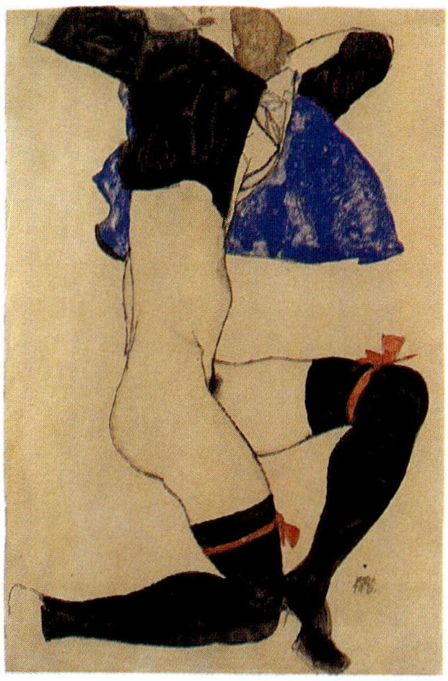

Fig. 32. Egon Schiele *Reclining Semi-nude with Black Stockings* (1913) Cat. 138

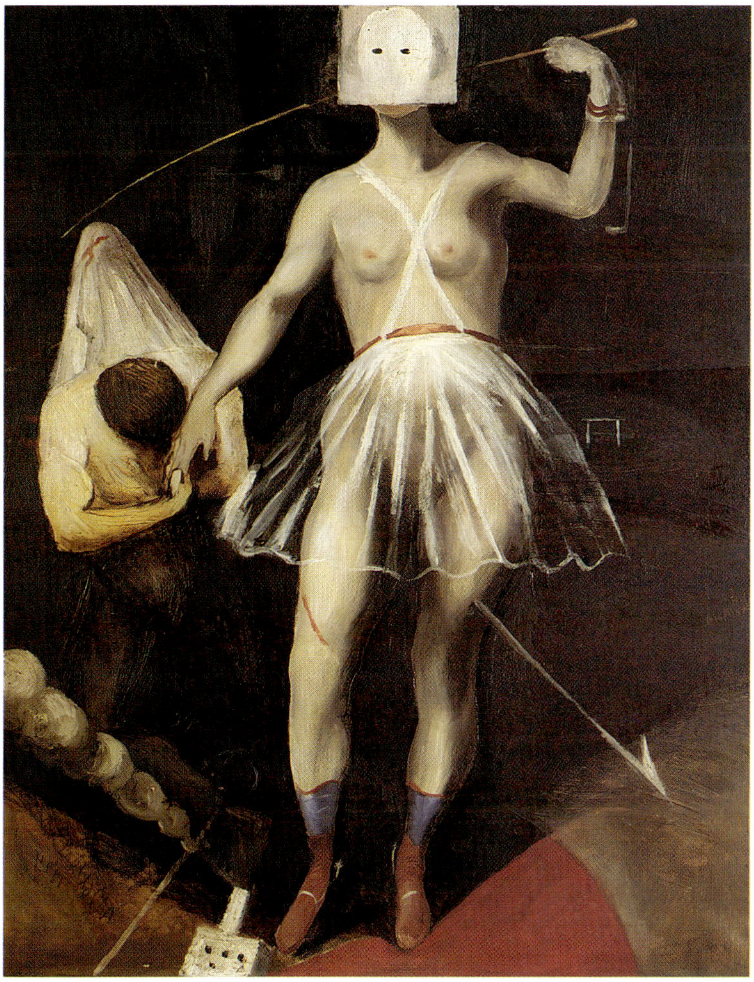

Fig. 33. Gert Wollheim *Die Siegerin (The Champion)* (1924) Cat. 155

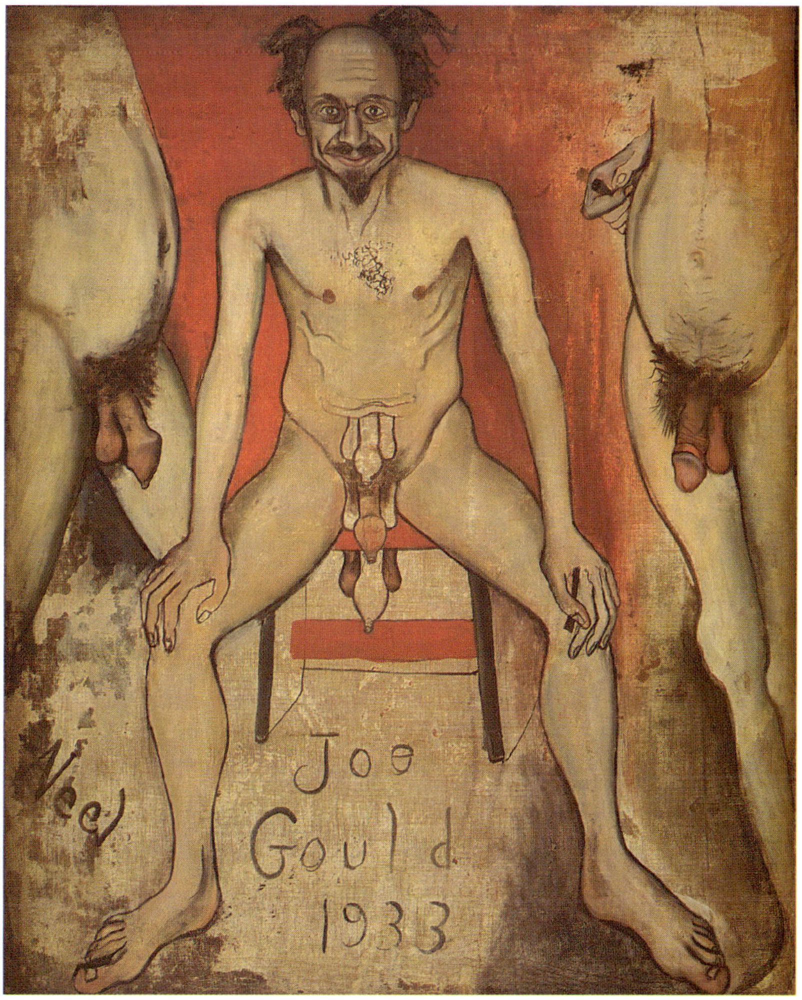

Fig. 34. Alice Neel *Joe Gould* (1933) Cat. 111

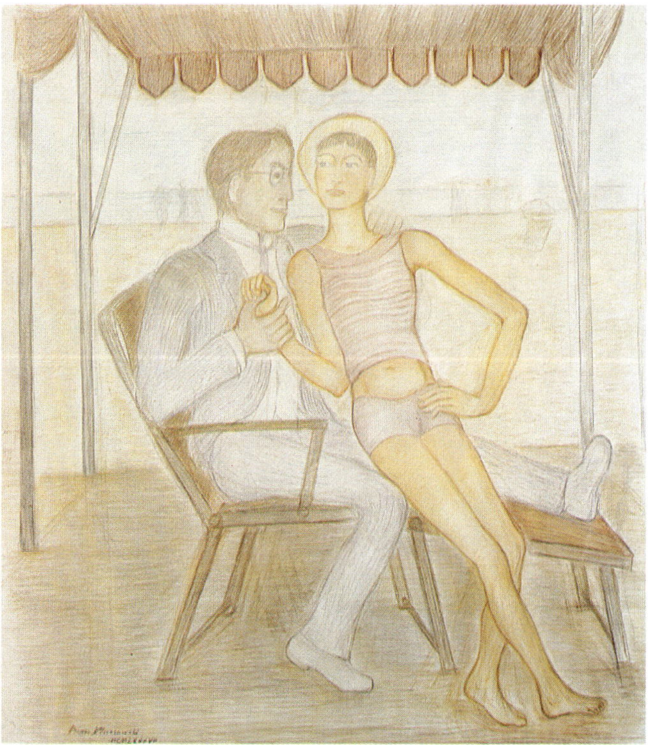

Fig. 35. Pierre Klossowski *La Réalisation Invraisemblable de l'Entente de Tadzio et Aschenbach II (The Improbable Understanding of Tadzio and Aschenbach II)* (1987) Cat. 77

entitled *The Purification of The Twelve* by Francesco Clemente are devised to express something about each of the senses, emphasising touch, taste and smell over the purely visual (Fig. 37).[29] Each image represents a part of the body and also a month of the year, for example *April: Left Eye*, but the image has no obvious connection to the bodily part as such. April consists of a woman lying on top of an ant hill, being impregnated by a giant turtle with a crucifix on its back. Above the figures, ant-like demons wheel around in the sky.

Lucian Freud's *Naked Man with Rat* (Fig. 36) makes the sense of touch, implied by his visceral brushwork, even more acute by the inclusion of a live rat whose tail is draped across the thigh of the young man. This contact is an electric pointer to the sensation of bodily contact. The expressive brushmark not only heightens our sensation of the form but can also suggest the presence of the artist. In this section the artist's incarnation in the trace becomes increasingly assertive and finally obliterates the image that is ostensibly being represented.[30] This tendency is introduced through two early paintings by Henri Matisse (Figs. 38 and 40) and concludes with a photographic self-portrait by Arnulf Rainer where the figure is completely obliterated by the gesture of the artist (Fig. 60). *Le Modèle* by Matisse is a classic modernist reduction of the body through the simplification of its planes, a process which eventually led him to the vibrant colour fields which characterise his later work. Like Matisse, Georges Rouault uses line to define forms; but whereas Matisse's line gently contains the form leaving the colour as pure as possible, for Rouault line becomes the main force and energy of his compositions (Fig 39).

There are three sculptures in this room: Rodin's small study for the nude, *Balzac "Athlete" (study F)*, Matisse's study from the same model, *The Serf* and De Kooning's *Clamdigger* (Figs. 41, 42 and 43). Each of these works uses the material in a way that parallels the gestural qualities of in the painter's brushmarks. The clay carries the marks of the artist's hand as much as it takes on the form of the model.

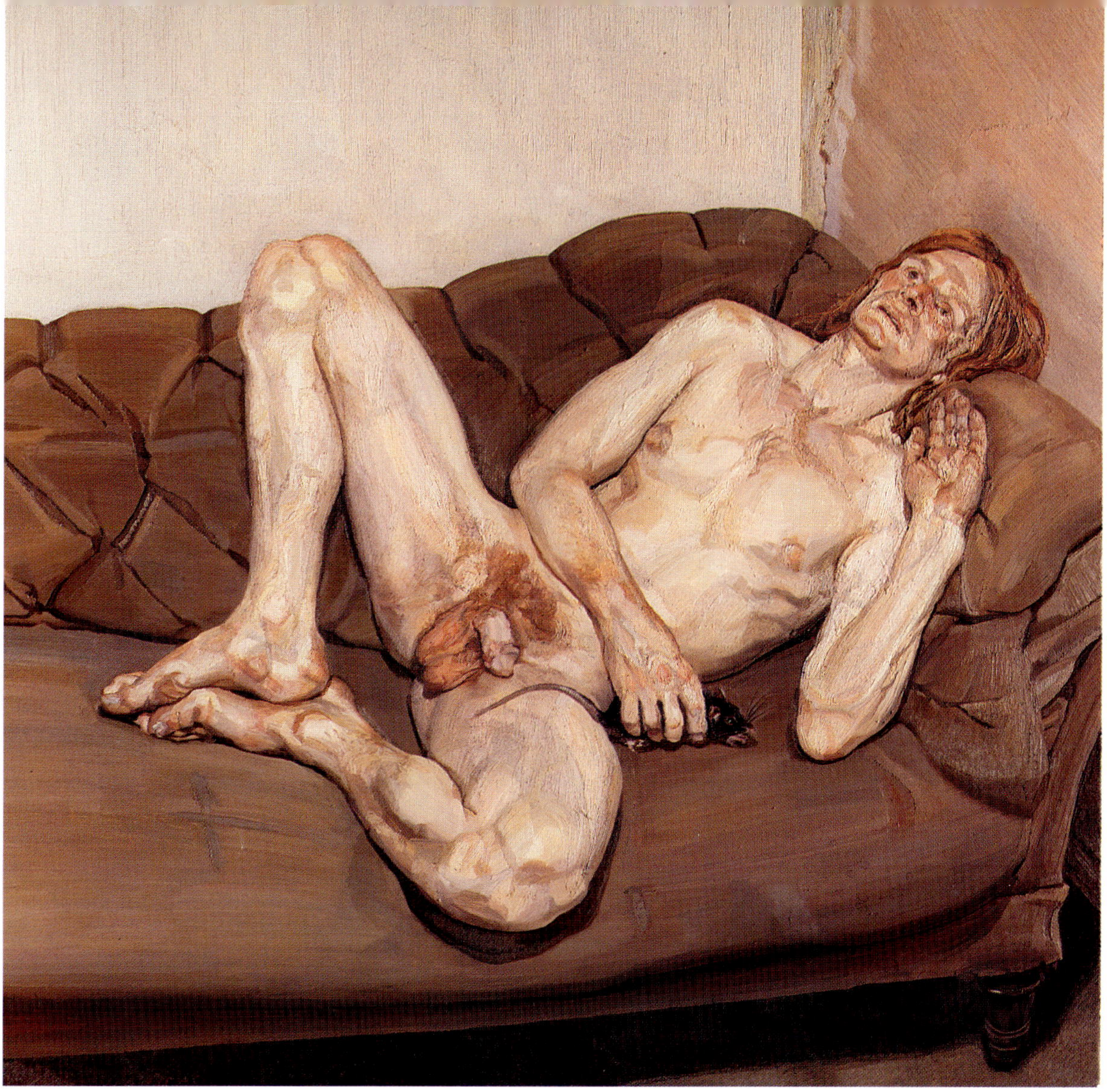

Fig. 36. Lucian Freud *Naked Man with Rat* (c.1977–78) Cat. 54

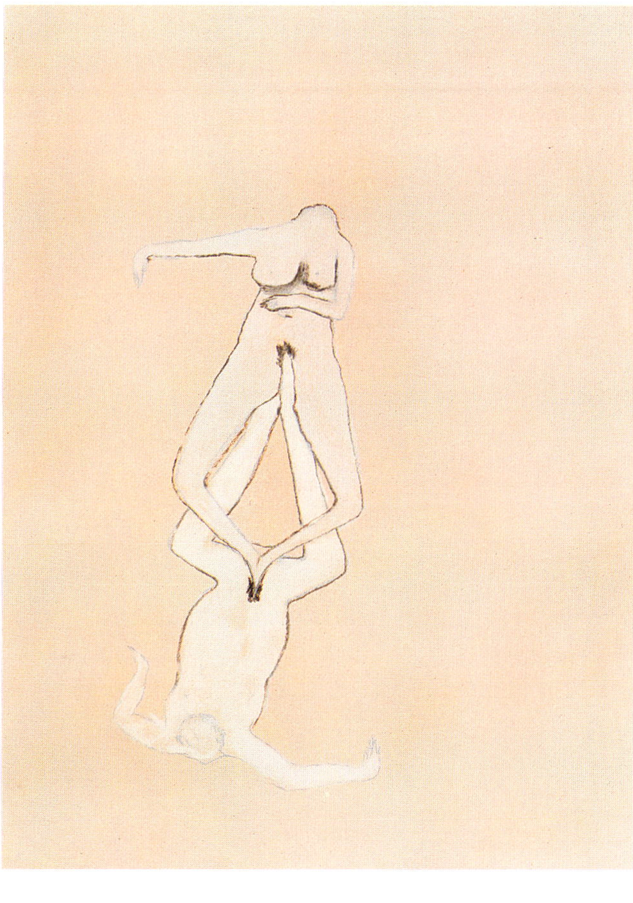

Fig. 37. Francesco Clemente *December* from *The Purification of The Twelve (A Calendar for 1988)* (1987) Cat. 32

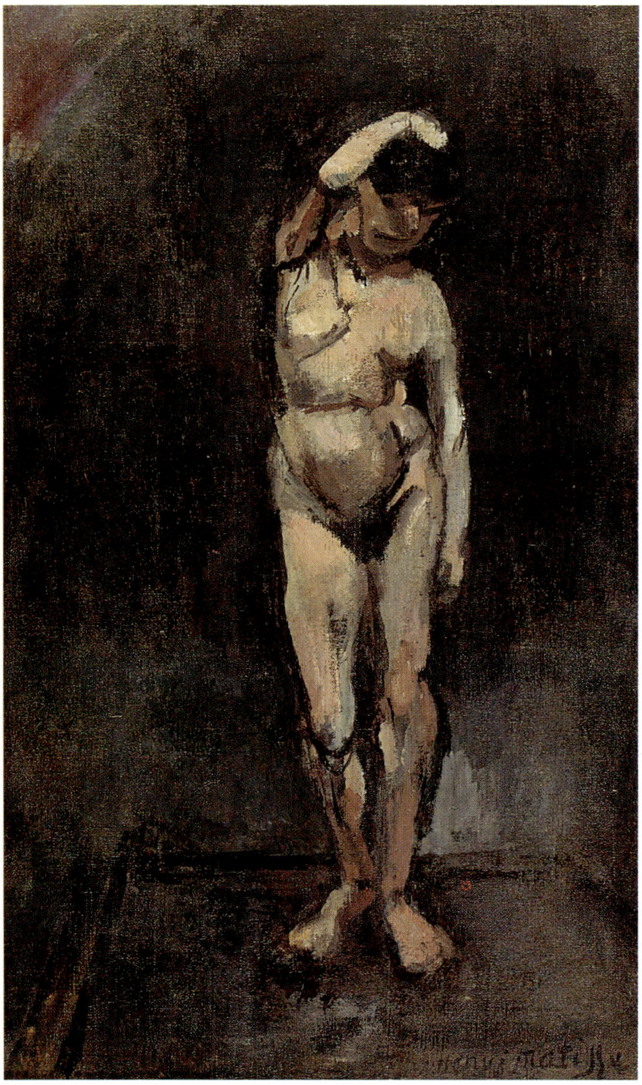

Fig. 38. Henri Matisse *Le Modèle (The Model)* (1900) Cat. 91

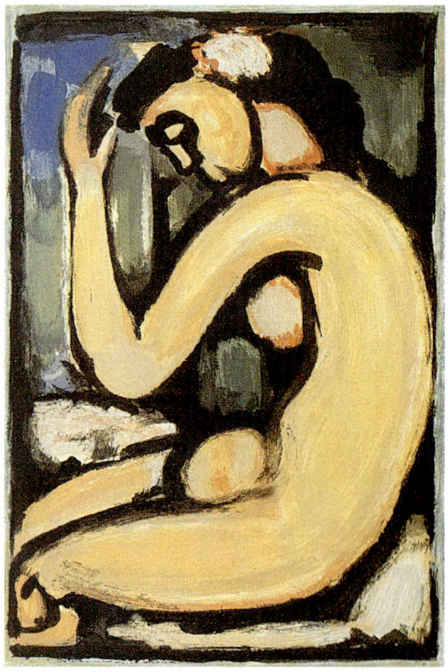

Fig. 39. Georges Rouault *No Title ("Nu de Profil") ("Profile of a Nude")* (1936) Cat. 133

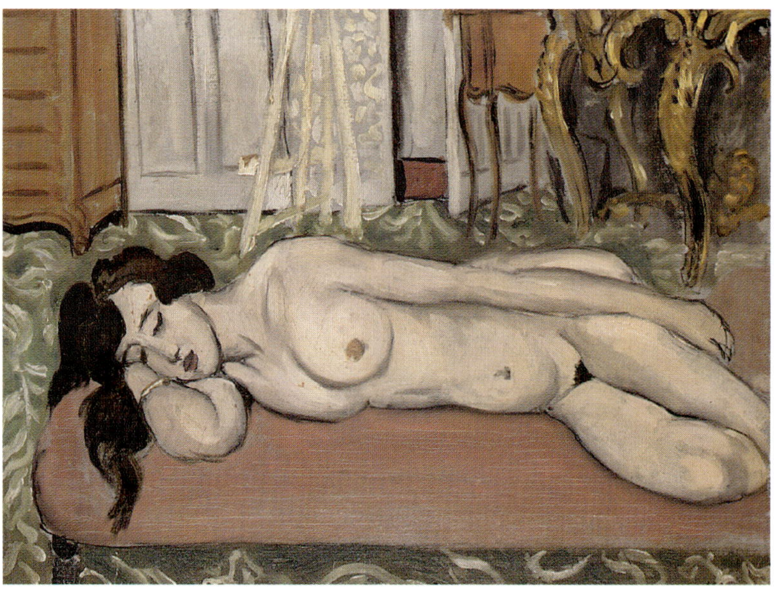

Fig. 40. Henri Matisse *Reclining Nude* (1919) Cat. 92

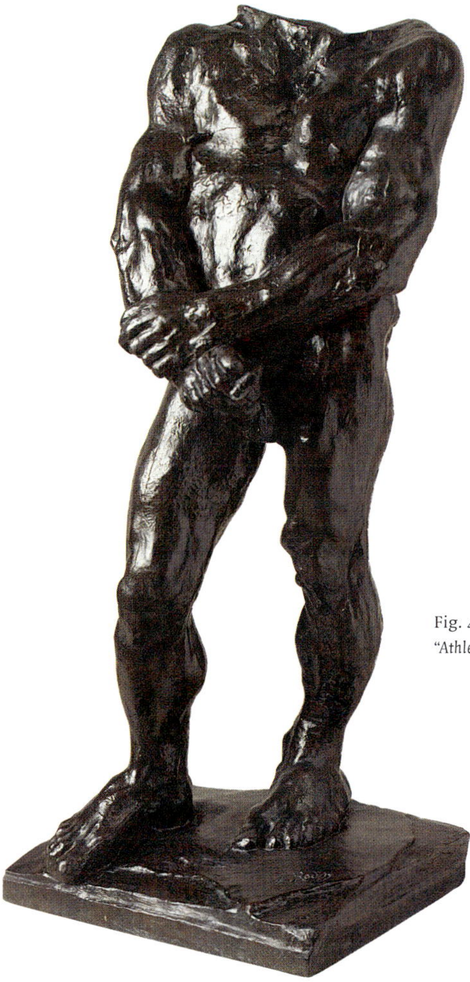

Fig. 41. Auguste Rodin *Balzac "Athlete" (study f)* (c.1896) Cat. 126

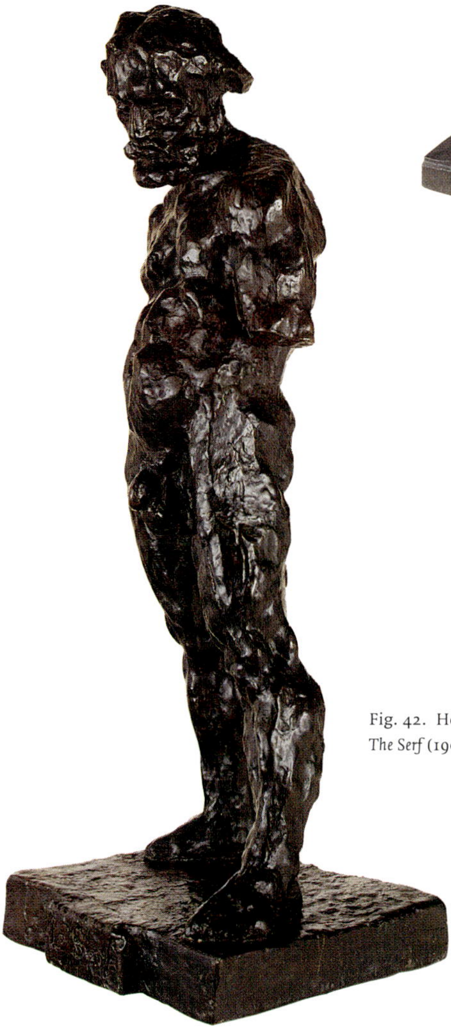

Fig. 42. Henri Matisse *The Serf* (1900–03) Cat. 93

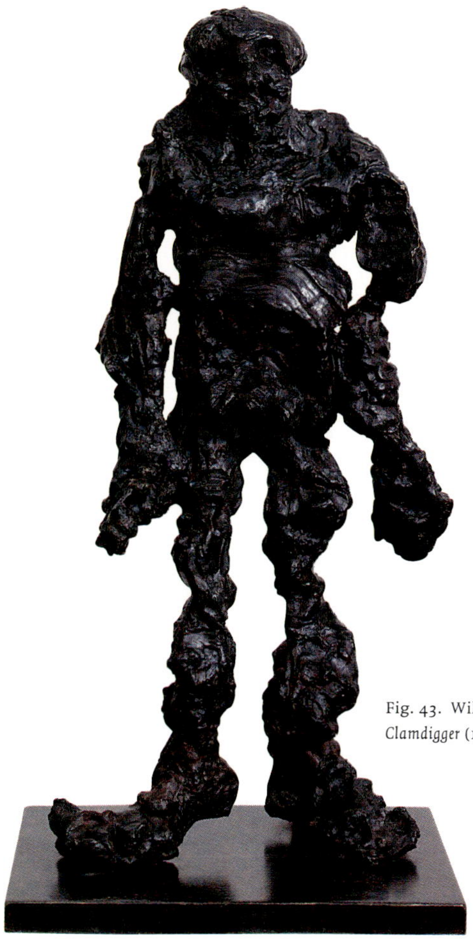

Fig. 43. Willem De Kooning *Clamdigger* (1972–79) Cat. 39

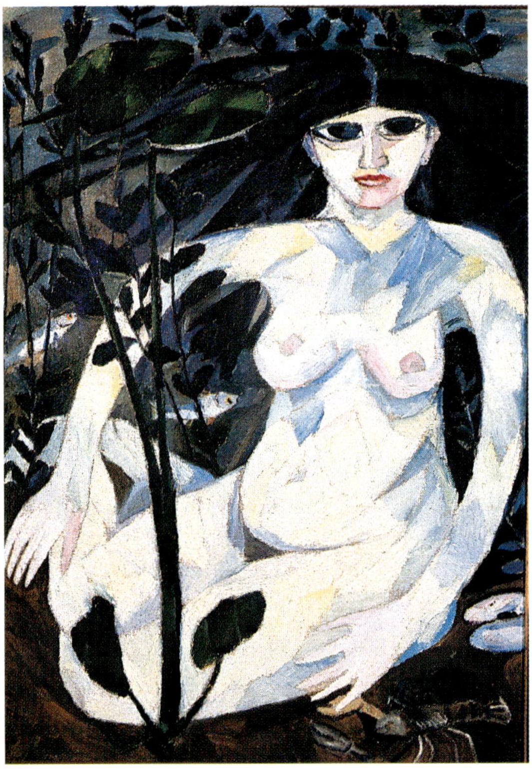

Fig. 44. Natalia Gontcharova *Mermaid* (1908) Cat. 59

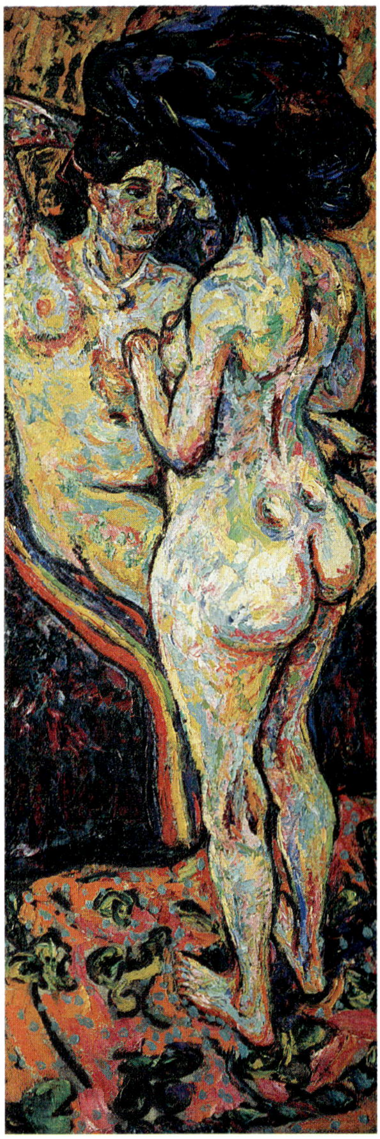

Fig. 45. Ernst Ludwig Kirchner *Two Nudes* (1907) Cat. 74

Fig. 46. Oskar Kokoschka *Zrani (High Summer)* (1938–40) Cat. 78

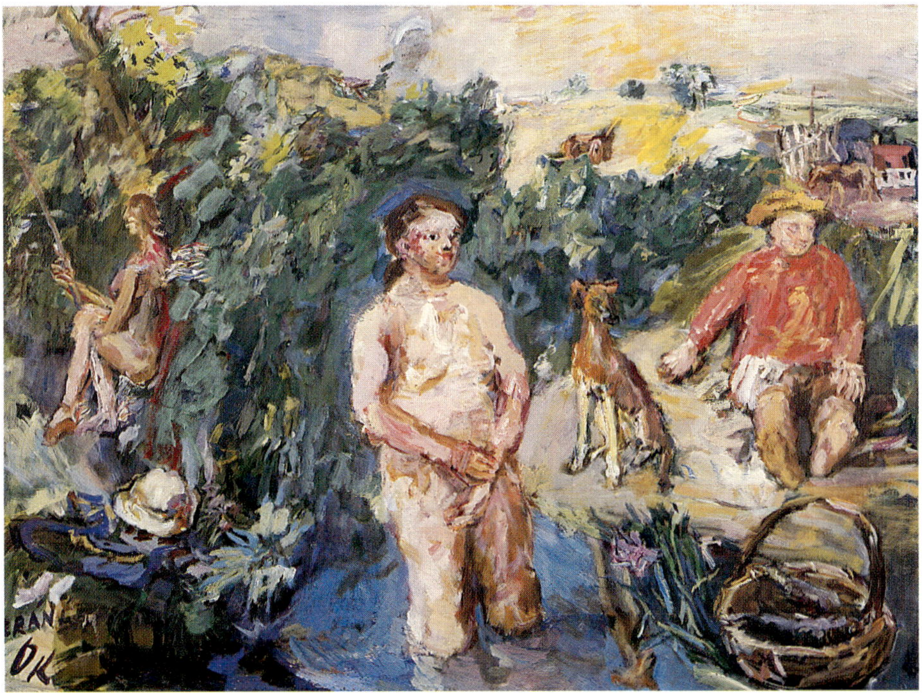

Natalia Gontcharova is represented by a painting that is characteristic of the convergence of primitivism and cubism which occurred in the Russian Avant-garde and particularly within the *Jack of Diamonds* Group. The energy of her brushmarks typifies this convergence (Fig. 44). Expressionist paintings by Max Beckmann, Ernst Ludwig Kirchner and Oskar Kokoshka are also shown here and are discussed in the essay by David Bromfield (Figs. 45, 46 and 152).[32]

The two paintings by Otto Dix in this room are vicious parodies of the human form that satirise aspects of Weimar society. His painting of *Three Women* (Fig. 48) cruelly exaggerates the shape of the models. The attention to detail is obsessive, with veins and blemishes meticulously rendered. In spite of the undeniably grotesque appearance of the three women, the intimate attention Dix pays to the minute details of their skin and hair makes the viewer acutely sensitive to their vulnerability. *The Odd Couple* (Fig. 47) is another gross satire which contrasts the shrivelled and varicose body of the old man with the plump perfection of the young woman on his knee. The contact between their respective bodies is loaded with pathos. We are caught between disgust for

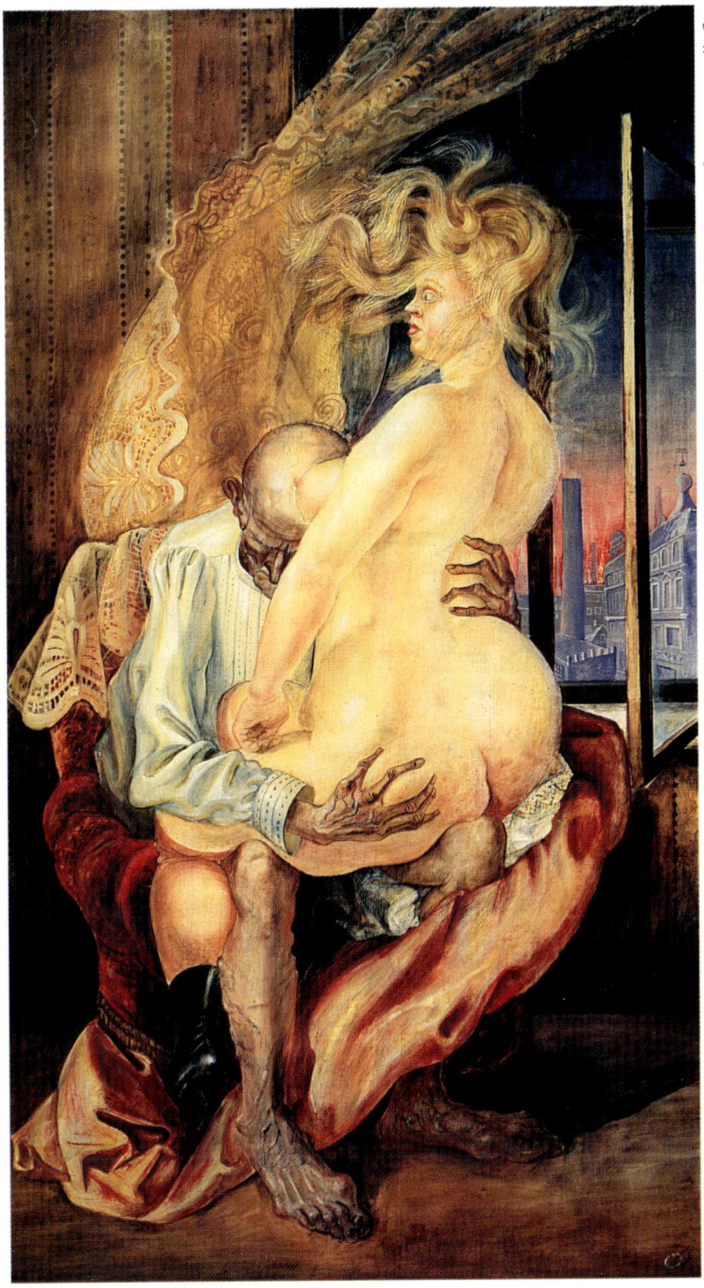

Fig. 47. Otto Dix Ungleiches Liebespaare (*The Odd Couple*) (1925) Cat. 43

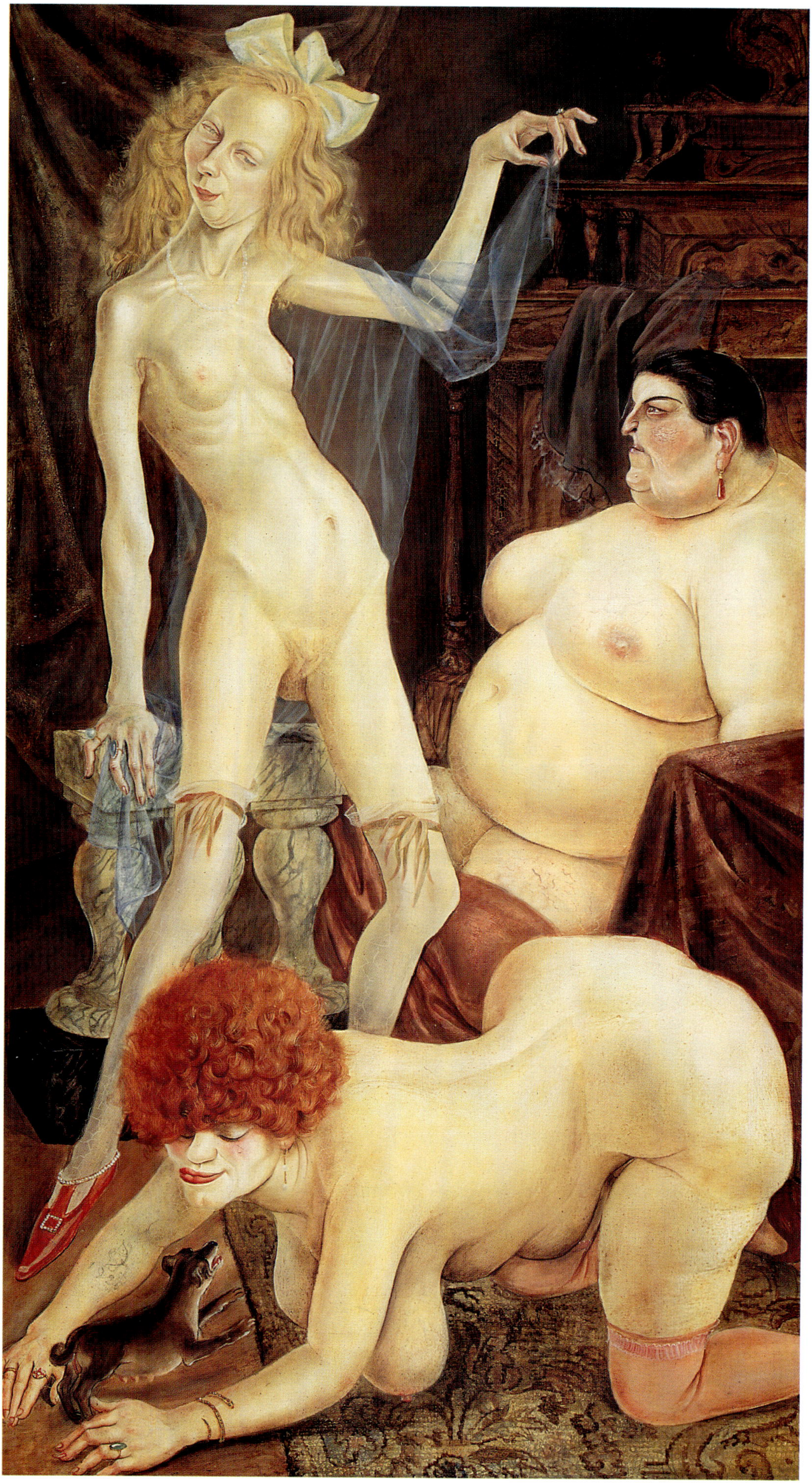

Fig. 48. Otto Dix *Drei Weiber (Three Women)* (1926) Cat. 42

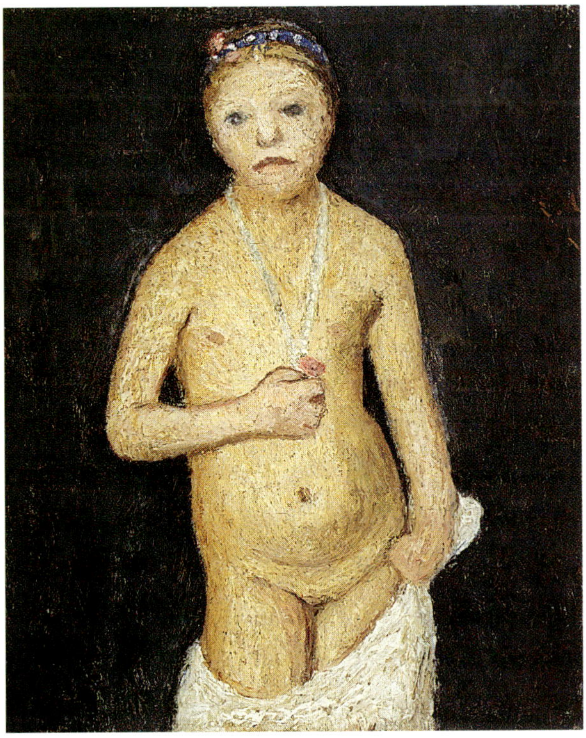

Fig. 49. Paula Modersohn-Becker *Kleiner Mädchenakt (Nude Girl)* (1906) Cat. 98

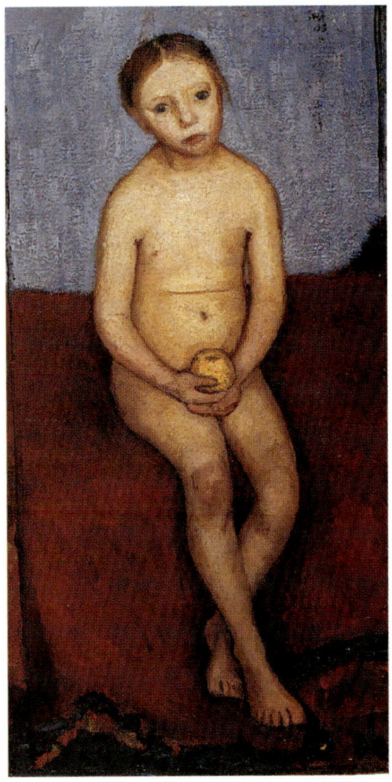

Fig. 50. Paula Modersohn-Becker *Nacktes Mädchen mit Apfel (Nude Girl with Apple)* (1906) Cat. 99

his desire and terror at her potential to consume him. The wind from the open window blows her hair and the curtain into serpentine shapes which suggest the head of Medusa or of a fearful Valkyrie. The juxtaposition of Paula Modersohn-Becker and Dix creates a dramatic contrast. Dix's grotesque figures are set against the self-absorbed and rather tragic figures painted in almost classical purity by Modersohn-Becker. The paint is built up with sculptural attention to form in the rendition of these sad little girls (Figs. 49 and 50).

Another group of paintings in this room prefigures the works of the London school and in particular the paintings of Francis Bacon. The paintwork and colour in Walter Sickert's *Mornington Crescent Nude, Contre Jour* (Fig. 51) evoke a mysterious dark luminosity and brooding atmosphere in this intimate London interior which was to become a trade mark of the London Group. David

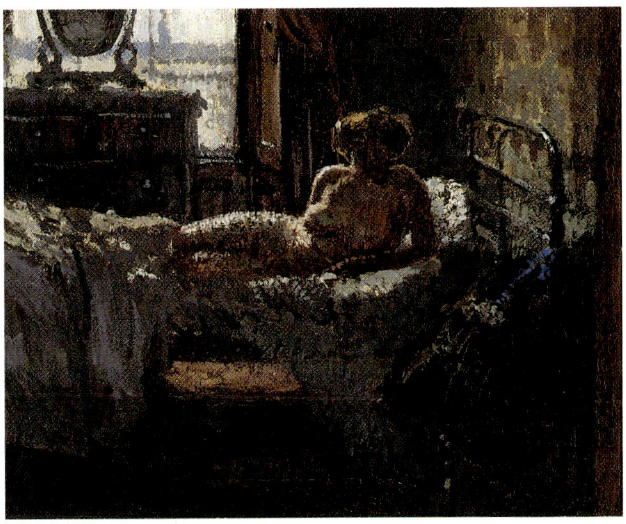

Fig. 51. Walter Sickert *Mornington Crescent Nude, Contre-Jour* (1907) Cat. 145

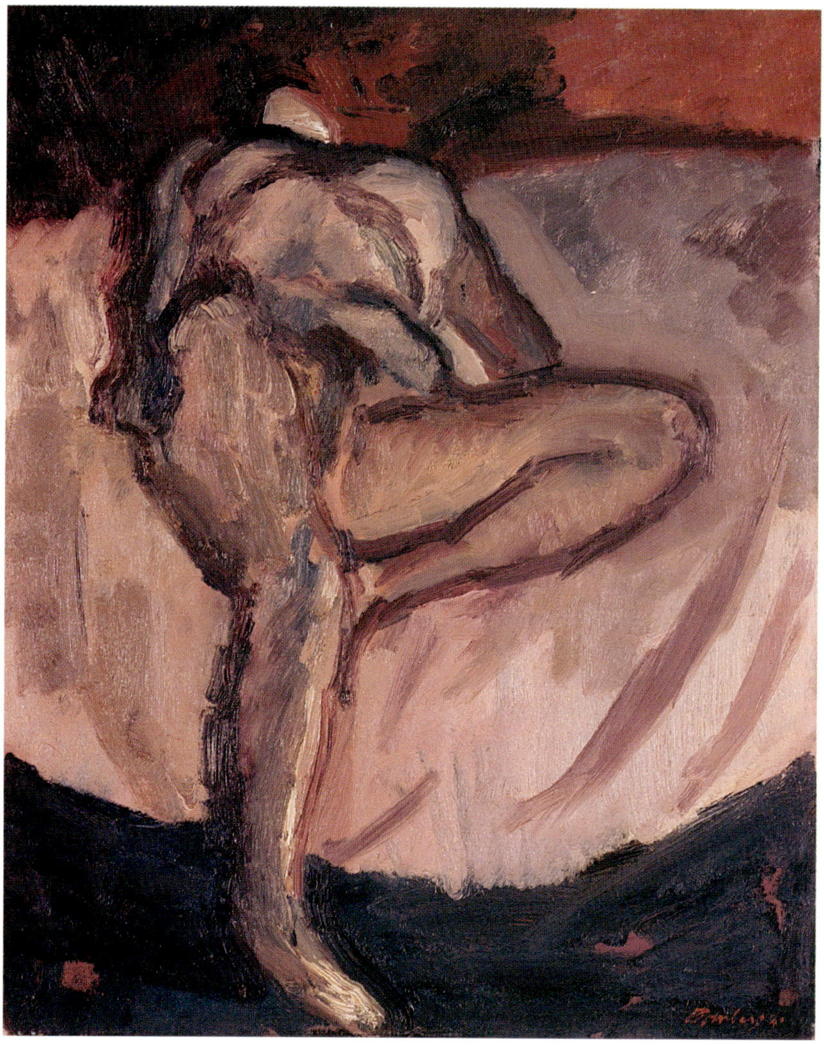

Fig. 52. David Bomberg *Nude* (1943) Cat. 21

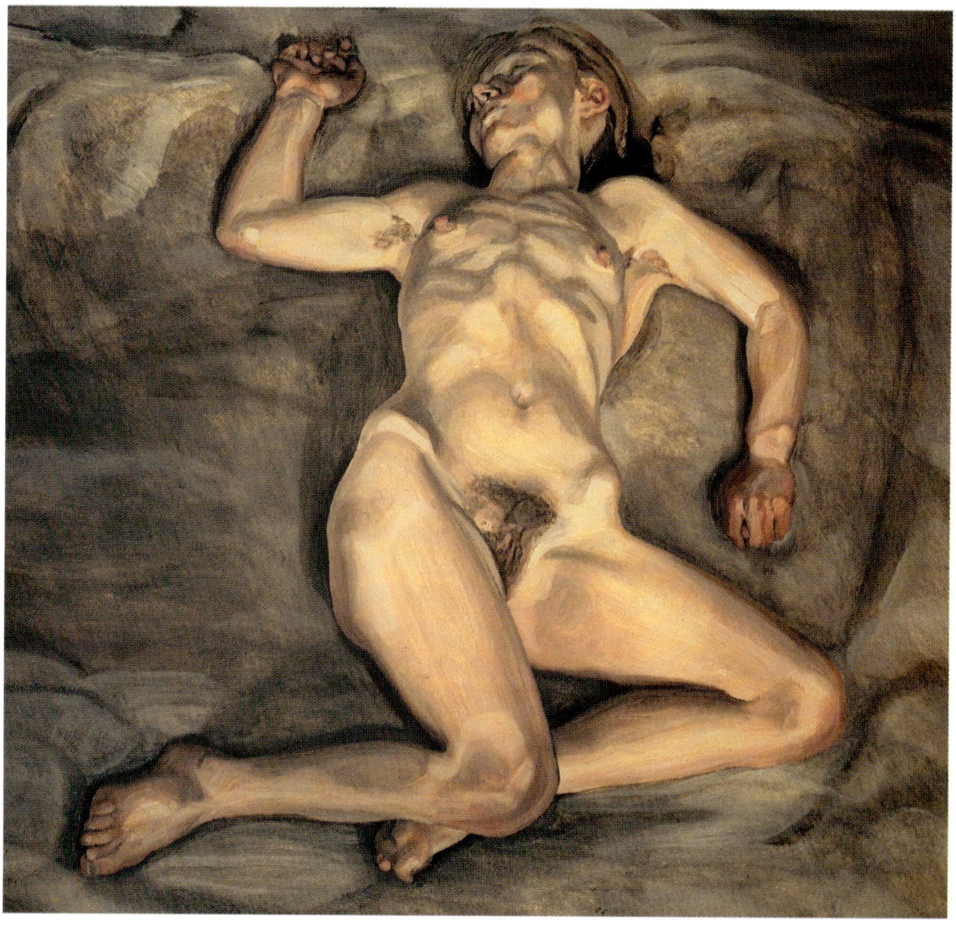

Fig. 53. Lucian Freud *Naked Girl Asleep II* (1968) Cat. 55

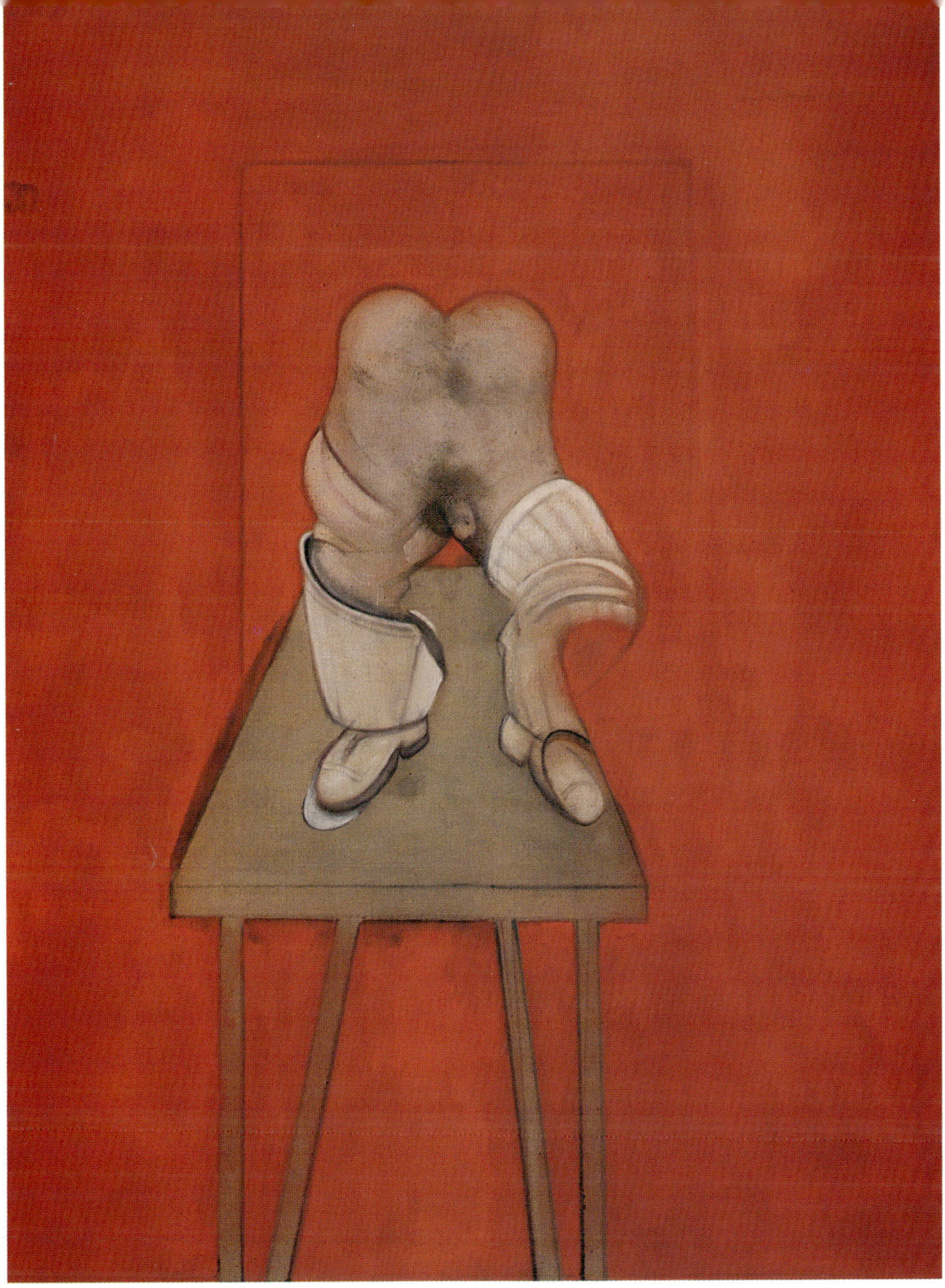

Fig. 54. Francis Bacon *Study of the Human Body* (1981–82) Cat. 4

Bomberg transmitted this influence to another generation (Fig. 52). Lucian Freud emerged from this tradition, painting highly tactile images. His brushmarks retain the freshness and intensity of the moment when they were first laid down. The viewer's eye follows each stroke as it traces the forms of the body, but the brushmarks do not always follow the form: sometimes they are in jarring tension with it and this is what makes Freud's paintings so disturbing. Because of this tactile 'interference' we are unable to gain a seamless illusion of reality. We are constantly returned to the intractable quality of the paint itself and to the hand of the artist as it 'sculpts' each fragment of the body (Fig. 53).

Francis Bacon's statements about the immediacy of the artist's gesture, which allows the paint to act upon the nervous system of the viewer, form a key to enjoying much of the art in this part of the exhibition.[32] Bacon admired the work of Jean Dubuffet, in particular his earlier figures such as *Gymnosophie* (Fig. 55), where the outline is scratched into paint like a child scratching in wet cement. Bacon felt that these images captured the urgency of feelings rapidly expressed, like the graffiti on the back of a lavatory door. Bacon articulated the principle that paint should be made to

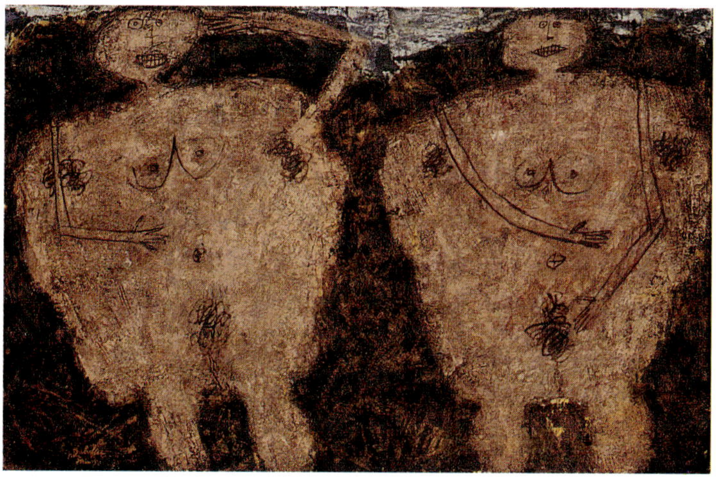

Fig. 55. Jean Dubuffet *Gymnosophie* (1950) Cat. 45

function as an equivalent to the sensations of the body rather than merely reproducing the body's appearance. In his last filmed interview, with Melvyn Bragg, at the time of his retrospective at the Tate Gallery London, Bacon said "I wanted to bring about the sensation of the thing without the boredom of its conveyance." This is in part achieved by the simple response which I am proposing between hand and eye that binds artist and viewer through the action of the body.

Figure in Landscape (Fig. 56) by Arthur Boyd makes great use of gesture and thickly slashed paint marks. The figure is shown to be partly transparent against the bush, picking up on the theme of identification or fusion of the figure and the landscape discussed in section 3. In the background a black ram watches the nude washing. This presence of a mute witness recurs throughout the exhibition: in the form of the cats in the first room, Balthus' companion figures, Frida Kahlo's monkey, the watchers on the edge of Francis Bacon's triptych, and the gaze of the wife in Helmut Newton's photograph.

Fig. 56. Arthur Boyd *Figure in Landscape (Nude Washing in a Creek III)* (1961) Cat. 27

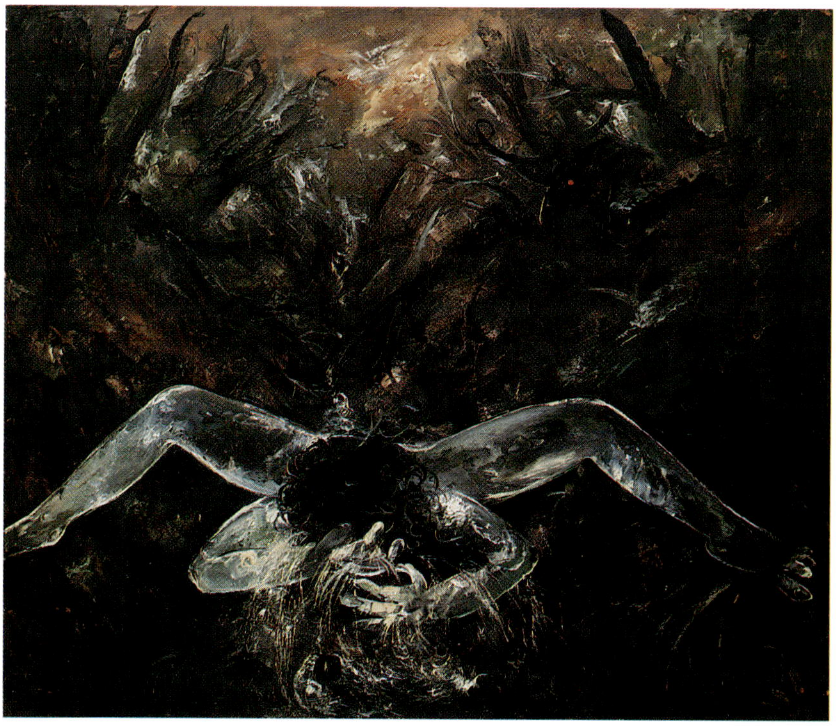

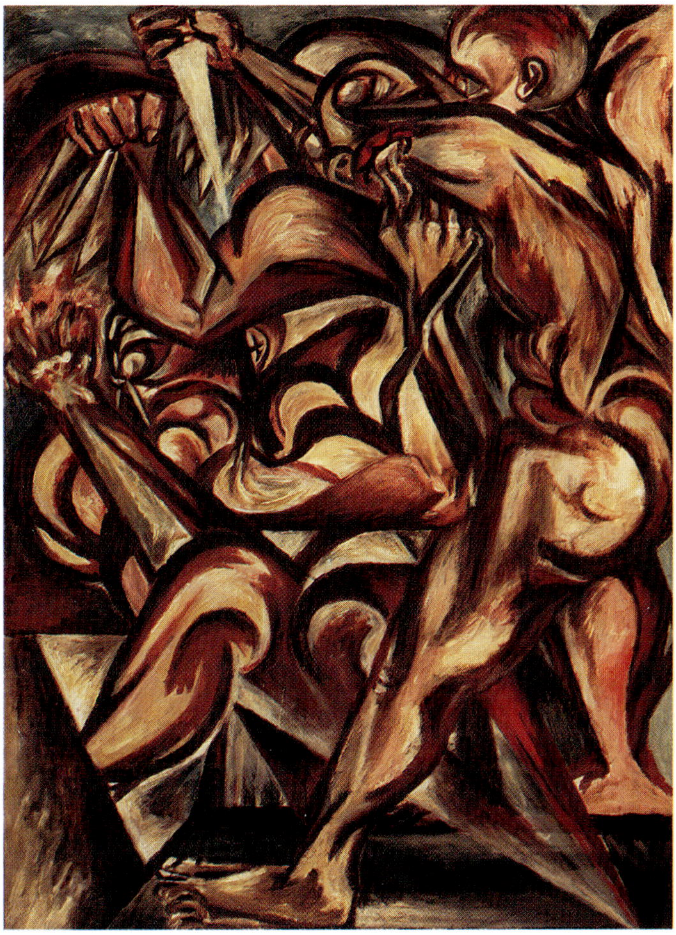

Fig. 57. Jackson Pollock *Naked Man with Knife* (c.1938–41) Cat. 122

Jackson Pollock is better known for his Abstract Expressionist drip paintings such as *Blue Poles*. It would be possible to present these paintings in this exhibition as a transition from painting to performance, and indeed the Namuth film of Pollock at work in his studio will be a part of the programme. *Naked Man with Knife*, however, predates these action paintings (Fig. 57). This is a violent image which exploits Cubo-Futurism and in particular Picasso's more political works of the 1930s. Willem De Kooning's *Two Figures in Landscape* (Fig. 58) is a particularly loose painting where the images of the two figures almost dissolve in the gesture of the paint. This kind of distortion, also explored by Georg Baselitz (Fig. 59), may be considered misogynistic in its painterly brutality, but it is also a record of the artist's body and a trace of his tantrum. This sequence comes to a head with *Overpainting-Totem* by Arnulf Rainer which is a photographic self-portrait that has been almost completely covered over with daubings of paint (Fig. 60). The trace of the artist's fingers has virtually taken over from the image.

Yves Klein was a complex and contradictory artist whose overall project seems to have been inextricably linked to aspects of transcendence (discussed in the next section), yet he was also a realist with a passionate dislike of solipsism and expressionism in art, particularly when it purports to be a revelation of genius. In the postwar years, Abstract Expressionism in America and Informel painting in France dominated the contemporary art market. A significant component of the meaning of this art was supposed to be the expressive quality of the artist's gesture. The gesture was reported to reflect the inner world of the artist which was presumably more interesting than average because of their heightened state of consciousness. Francis Bacon was

Fig. 58. Willem De Kooning *Two Figures in Landscape* (1968) Cat. 38

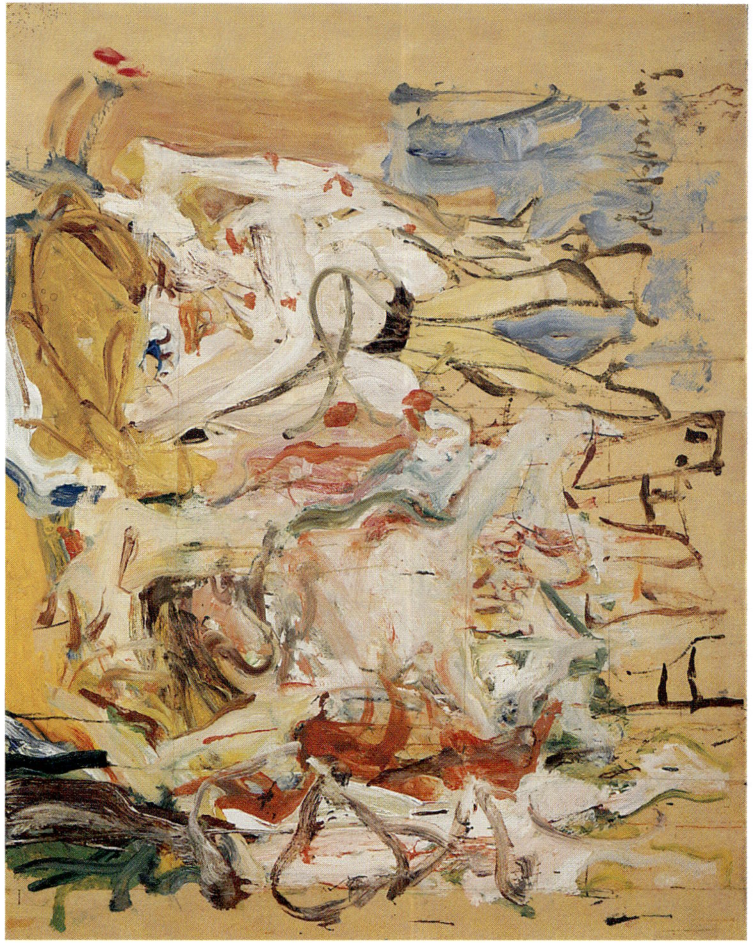

Fig. 59. Georg Baselitz *Akt Elke III (Nude Elke III)* (1976) Cat.10

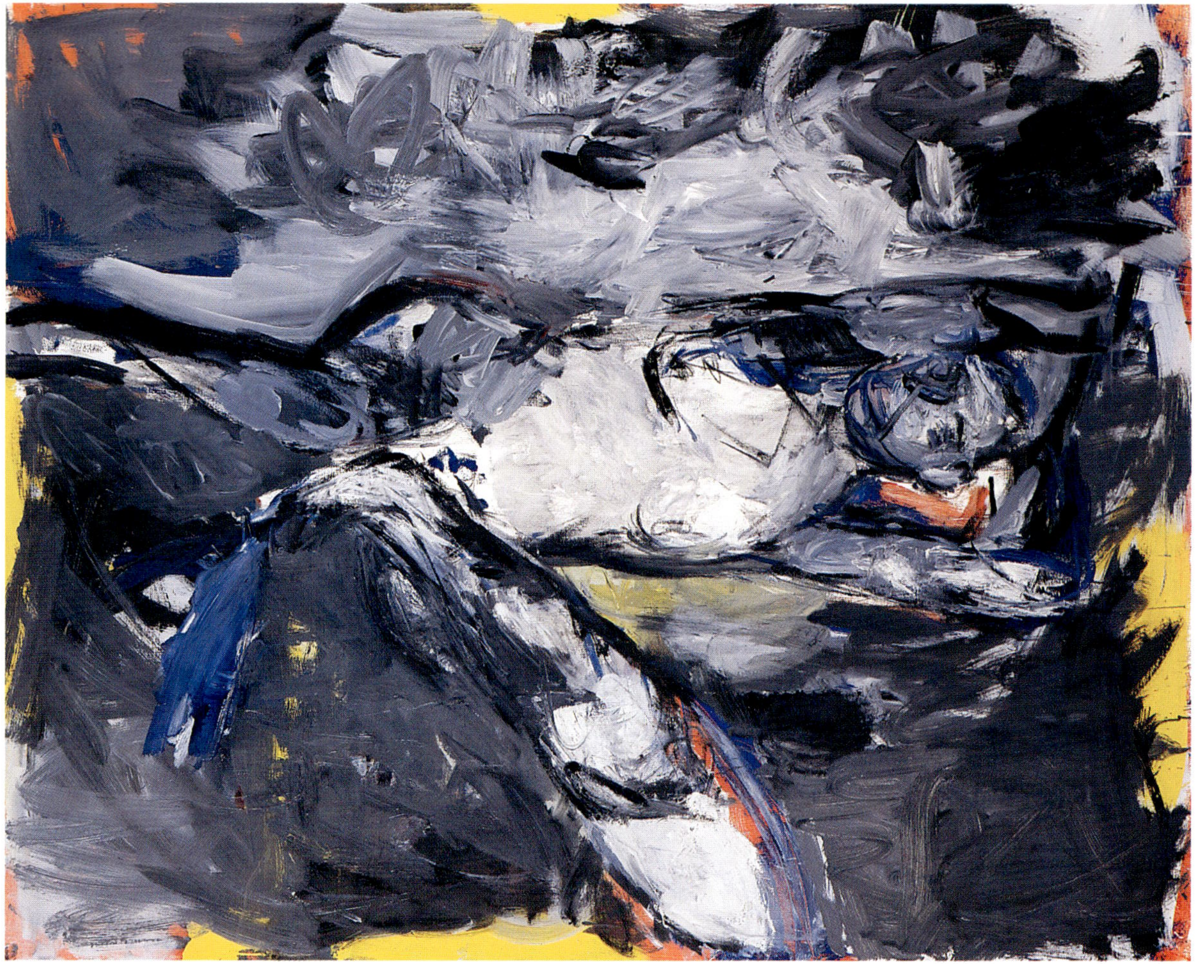

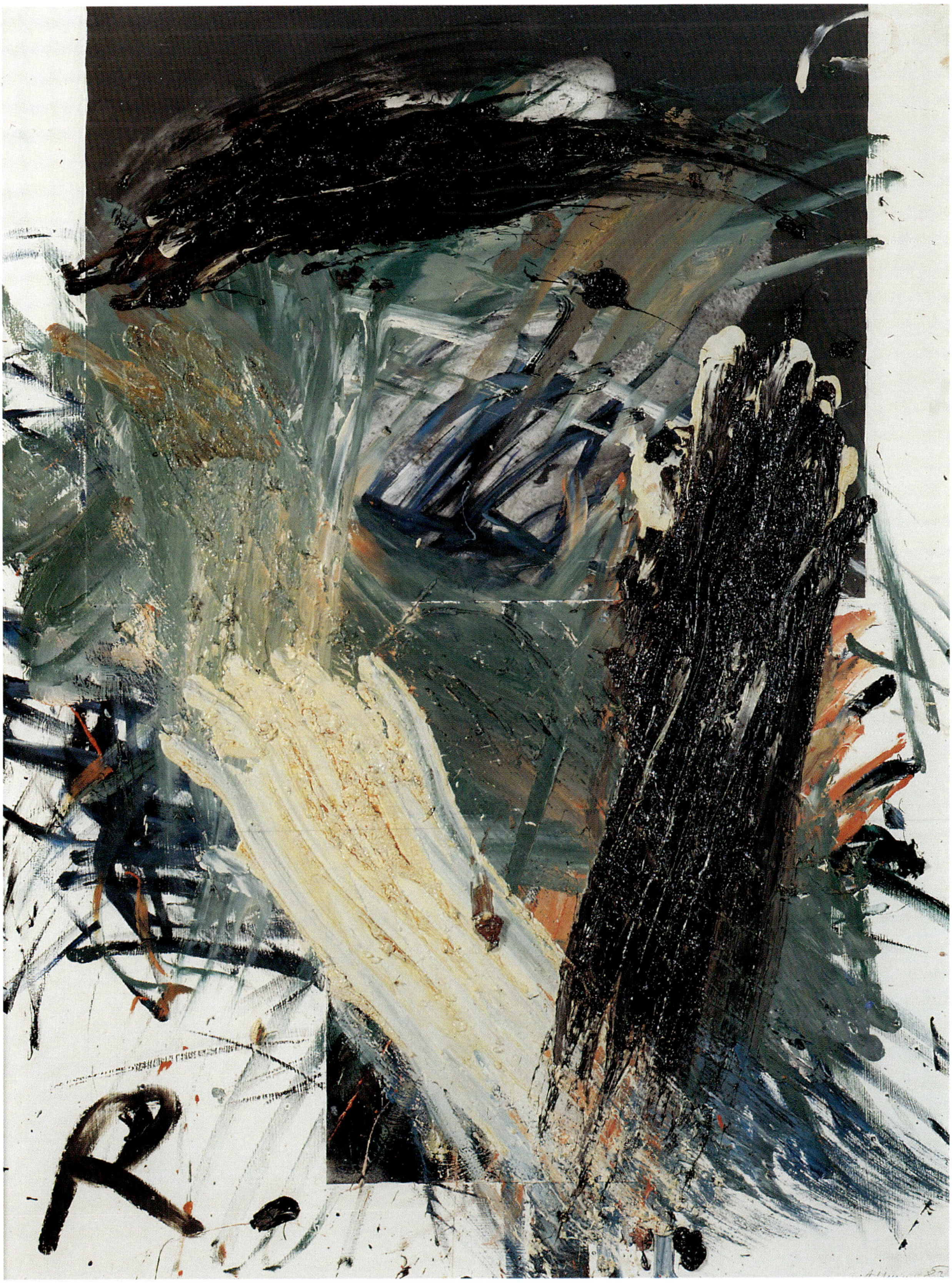

Fig. 60. Arnulf Rainer *Totem-Übermalung (Overpainting Totem)* (1983-84) Cat. 124

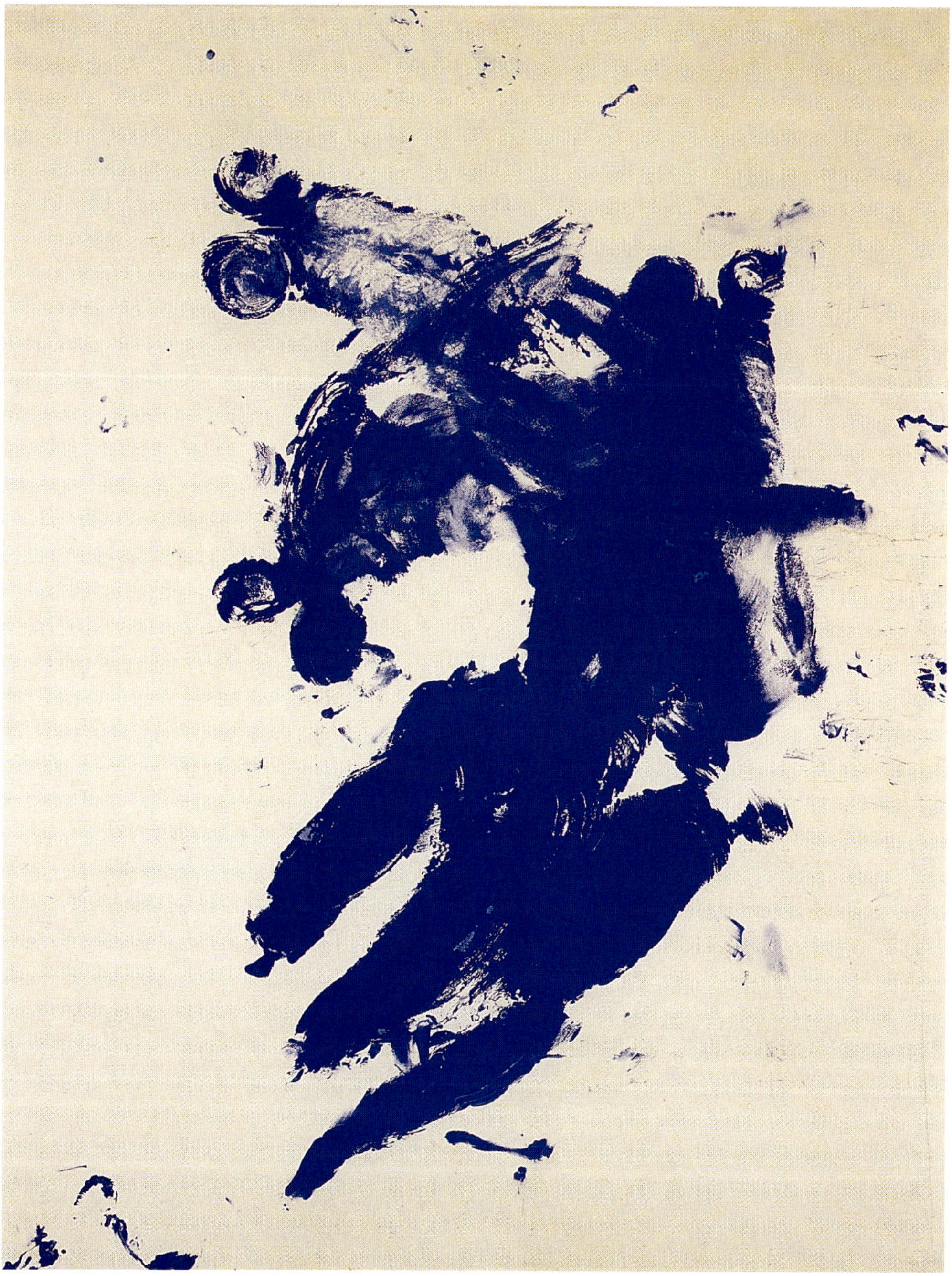

Fig. 61. Yves Klein *ANT. 118* (c.1960) Cat. 75

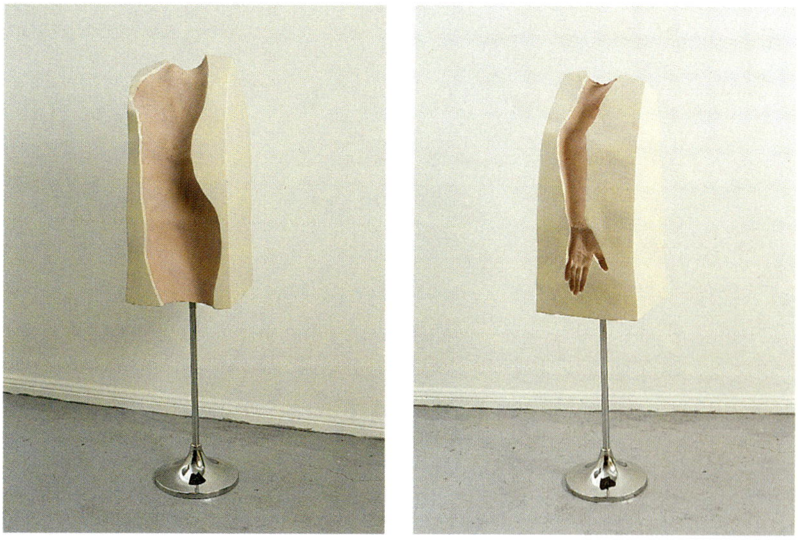

Fig. 62. Julie Rrap *Vital Statistics* (from the series, *Prosthetics*) (1997) Cat. 134

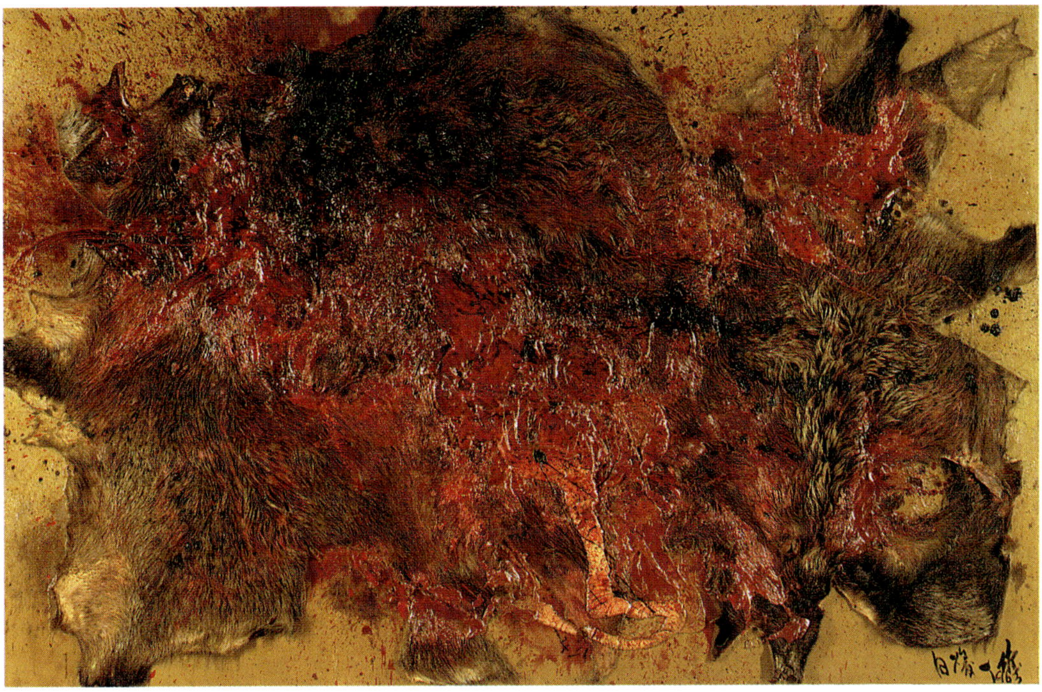

Fig. 63. Kazuo Shiraga *Wild Boar Hunting (part 1)* (1963) Cat. 144

also scathing about Abstract Expressionism and constantly affirmed his desire to make work which would resonate with sensations of reality rather than express his feelings.

Klein's view was that the internal world of the emotionally disturbed was best left where it was. He believed that an artist's efforts should be directed outwards to reveal something in the real world. In *Anthropométries* such as *ANT. 118* (Fig. 61), Klein used a model's body as a means of applying paint to the canvas. He claimed that these images capture the energy and the presence of the body. The *Anthropométries* are part of a series in which he 'collaborated' with nature to produce the paintings. As a variation on the 'living paintbrushes' of the *Anthropométries* he tried holding his prepared canvases up against grass waving in the rain and the wind to capture the vitality of the elements. Many of the *Anthropométries* were executed as performances intended for photographic documentation. The stage was designed by his photographers so that the documentation would most effectively show the performers, an orchestra playing Klein's *Monotone Symphony* and the audience dressed as for a formal theatrical event. Klein himself wore a tuxedo and white gloves. The venue he chose was the gallery where the Informel artist, Mathieu, exhibited. Mathieu had given public displays of gestural expressionism inspired by the Namuth film of Jackson Pollock in his studio. Klein's performance was a deliberate parody of Abstract Expressionism.

In the context of this exhibition a body print acts like a trace of the real model and the viewer has the sense of being able to reach out and touch the trace where the body touched the canvas. Julie Rrap also presents a trace of her own body in rubber moulds that carry the impressions of her skin and hair (Fig. 62). While Klein performed his *Anthropométries* in France in 1960, in Japan, Gutai artists were also 'performing' paintings. Shiraga made his dramatic paintings by dancing in paint over the canvas and in the case of *Wild Boar Hunting (part 1)* (Fig. 63), a performance was enacted on a boar's skin. The tactility of the boar's hairy body enhances the sensation which these works generate. These paintings are traces of the artist's dance rather than representations of the artist's psyche. They are evidence of an actual event, and as such they have as much in common with Klein's *Anthropométries* as they have with Abstract Expressionism.

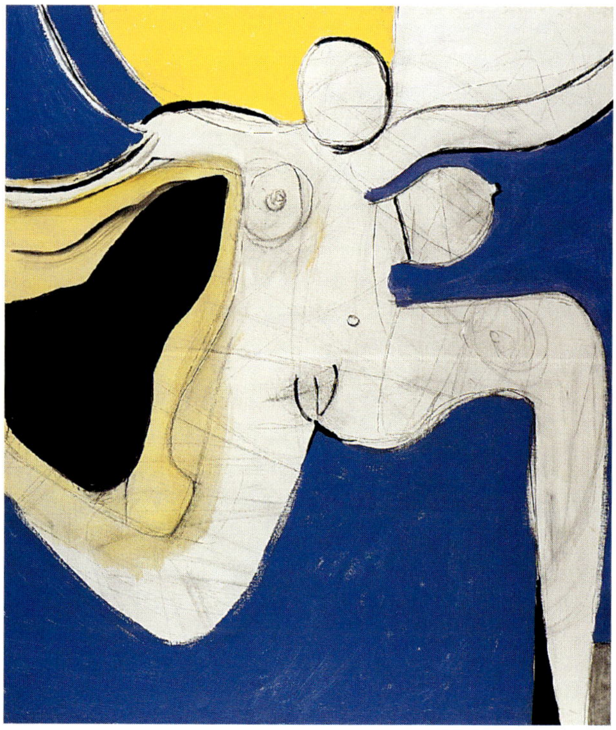

Fig. 64. Roger Hilton *Dancing Woman December* (1963) Cat. 65

6 Leaping, puncturing and levitating

The traditional representational surface acts as a kind of screen on to which images of the world are projected. But when the surface of the painting becomes evidence of the artist's actions rather than the site of an illusion we are made aware of the literal presence of the support. The visual penetration of this surface by the illusion of pictorial space may now become literal penetration. Courbet's self-portrait, *Man Mad With Fear* (Fig. 65) provides a graphic image of the desire to pass through this screen. Courbet has been discussed in several other places in this book in relation to quasi-corporeal merger.[33] In particular his self-portraits show the artist pressing up against the pictorial surface or the frame of the composition as if he was about to burst through the viewer's side of the canvas. This dramatic painting provides an extraordinary metaphor for the terror of representation because absorption entails a partial loss of self for the artist and the viewer. The surface of the painting may be thought of as a veil or screen which separates the material world from our understanding of it. The veil reveals, just as it conceals, because perceptions of the world can never be the equivalent of reality. For the painter the struggle to dissolve the border between representation and the real world may become obsessive, as seems to have been the case with Courbet. In this painting the figure of the artist leaps into the pictorial void – signified by the cliff at the lower right hand side – and into the viewer's space.[34] Michael Fried has argued that such voids at the margin of a composition are linking spaces which provide entry for the artist and the viewer.[35] In *Man Mad With Fear* the void is 'fortuitously' left unfinished: precisely at the point where the artist is about to leap through the pictorial surface the paint breaks down into an abstract scumble. Representation is seen dissolving in front of our eyes.

Bob Law painted a series of virtually blank canvases in the late 1960s entitled *Nothing to be afraid of*. They consisted of unpainted stretched canvas with a biro line that framed the space just inside the edge. In the corner were the words "Nothing to be afraid of." He said that this partly referred to the banal comfort people give to anyone mad with fear or having a nervous breakdown: "There there, there is *nothing* to fear." But for someone who is in fact afraid of fear itself, *nothing* or the void is of course the most terrible thing.[36] It is not reasonable to suggest that an artist in 1843 could have consciously depicted the breakdown of the surface of representation, an idea that comes into play through the investigations of twentieth-century modernism. For a contemporary viewer, however, the implications of this work are striking.

Juxtaposed with a reproduction of the Courbet is a photograph of Yves Klein's *The Leap* (Fig. 66). Klein tried to manifest thought materially by impregnating spaces with his psychic emanations as a part of his *Immaterial* projects. He practiced Judo, achieving a 4th Dan Black Belt from a Judoka school in Japan. He also studied Rosicrucianism under Max Heindel and practised spiritual exercises which would hasten the onset of the age of the immaterial. His leap from the second floor window of Iris Clert's studio in 1960 was in part a demonstration of his achievements

Fig. 65. Gustave Courbet *Le Fou de Peur (Man Mad with Fear)* (1843) Ref. 9

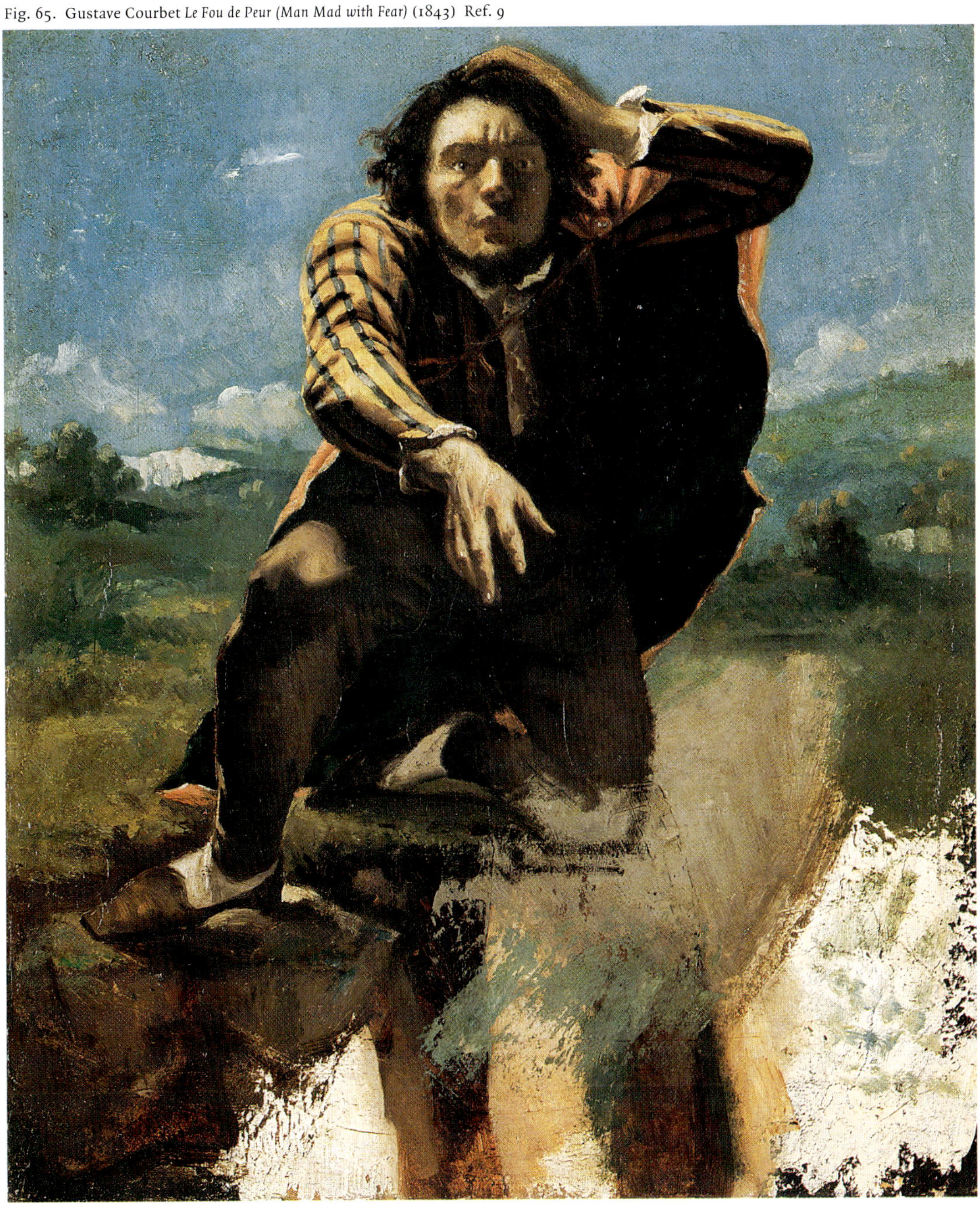

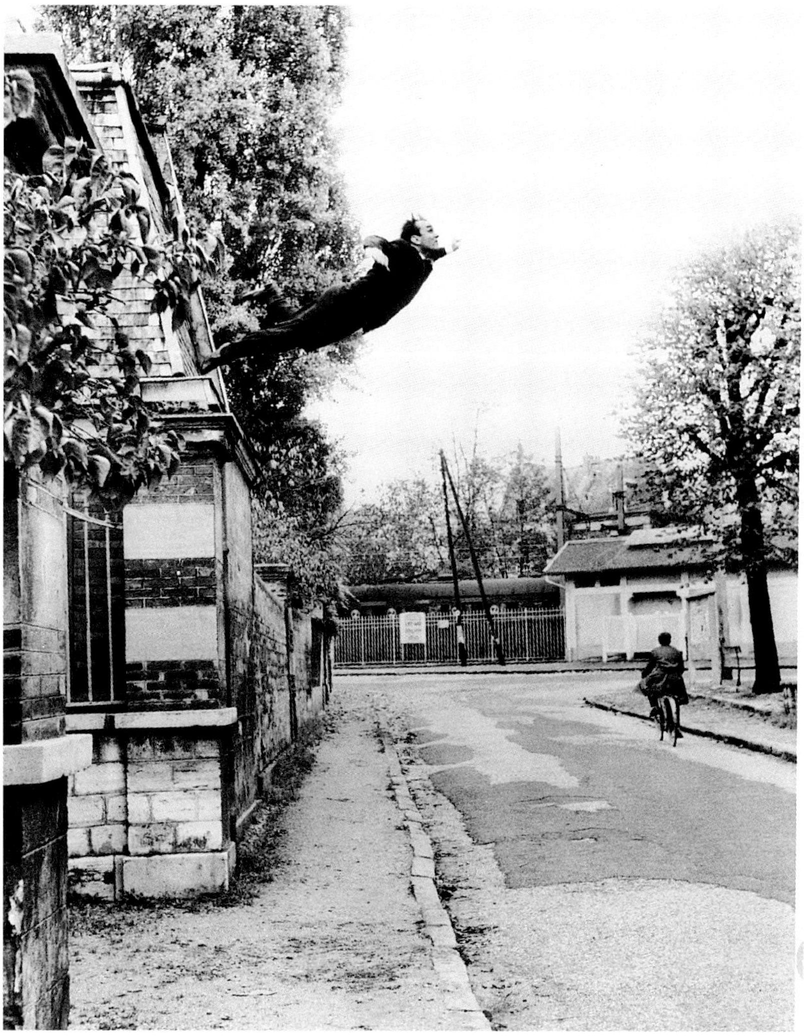

Fig. 66. Yves Klein *The Leap* photo by Harry Schunk (1960) Cat. 76

in this work, yet he deliberately set himself up to be caught faking the evidence. This photograph by Harry Schunk shows a cyclist on the road and a tram across the end of the street. This was the image Klein inserted in a simulated edition of *Dimanche* which he placed on news stands all over Paris immediately after the event. Within a short time he had the same photograph, but this time without the cyclist and tram, published as a poster for his exhibition in Krefeld. A careful study of the photograph shown in this exhibition reveals that it has been spliced, presumably to remove the image of a safety net.

The authenticity of the performance has been much debated.[37] The interesting thing, however, is the fact that the photograph as an art work is authentic irrespective of the means of production. If we want it to be literal evidence we are not accepting its role as an art object. The viewer may be curious about whether Klein actually leapt, but they will see in the photograph a convincing image of someone flying upwards into the void with a fiercely determined expression. There can be no doubt that Klein wanted to fly and this photo conveys that as expressively as Courbet renders a man fleeing from fear itself. *ANT. 118* (Fig. 61) has been included here because it echoes the feeling of levitation in *The Leap*. This work also brings the skin of the model into contact with the skin of the paper, triggering an awareness of the connection between skin and the pictorial screen.

Suspension pieces by Stelarc and Ken Unsworth from the 1970s provide an Australian response to these issues (Figs. 67 and 68). These images continue the theme of levitation introduced by Klein. In the case of Stelarc, transcending bodily limits has always been important. In more recent times he has made use of medical technology to extend the performance of the body and to disrupt its boundaries. In the suspension works, however, Stelarc draws our attention to the limits of the body in another way: by attaching the wires which hold his body aloft to meat hooks pierced through his skin. Unsworth presented his body as an element in formal sculpture in the same way that he balances and props plates of steel and rocks in his Minimalist sculpture and installation. Balance and equilibrium were the constant themes of these works, yet the body is placed in highly uncomfortable positions sometimes reminiscent of medieval martyrdom.

These works introduce performance art in which the body of the artist becomes the site of the work, thereby conflating figure and field. Some of the issues associated with performance and body art in the 1960s and '70s are discussed in an interview with Mike Parr. In this section of the exhibition more theatrical forms of performance art, for example the rituals of the Vienna Aktionismus group, are contrasted with the direct investigation of bodily limits Gina Pane, Mike Parr and Marina Abramovic (Figs. 69–80).

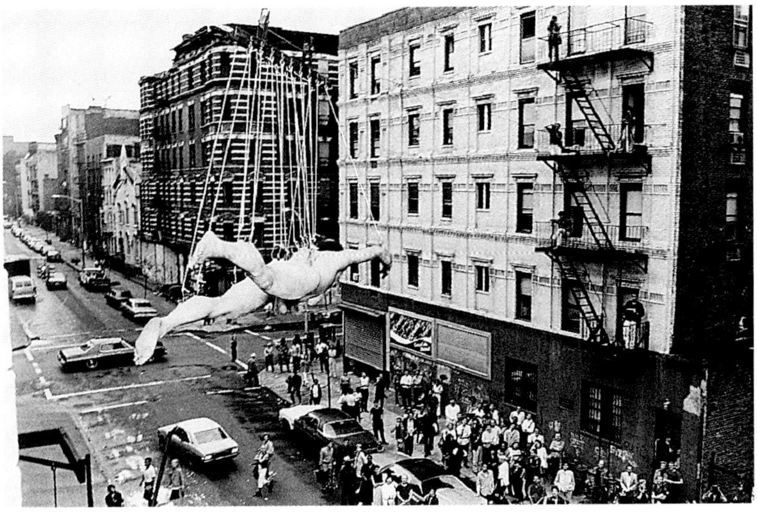

Fig. 67. Stelarc *Street Suspension* (1984) Cat. 147

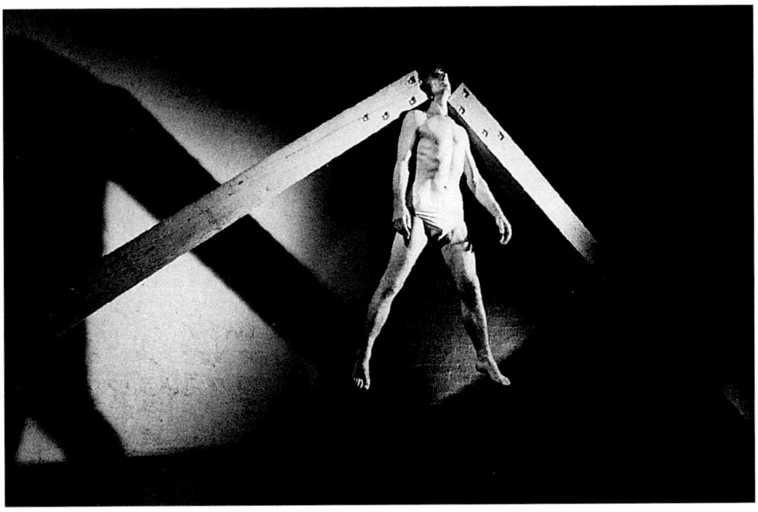

Fig. 68. Ken Unsworth *Five Secular Settings for Sculpture as Ritual and Burial Piece* (1975) Cat. 151

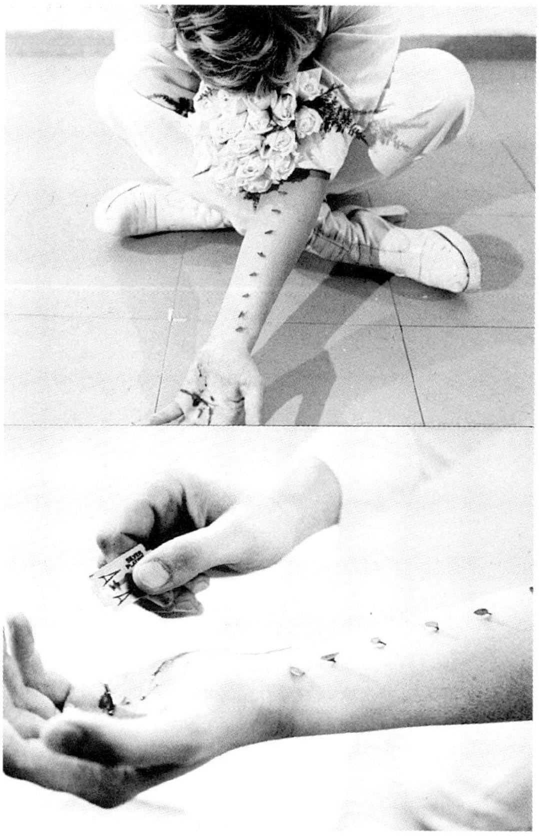

Fig. 69. Gina Pane *Aktione Sentimentale* (1973) Cat. 115

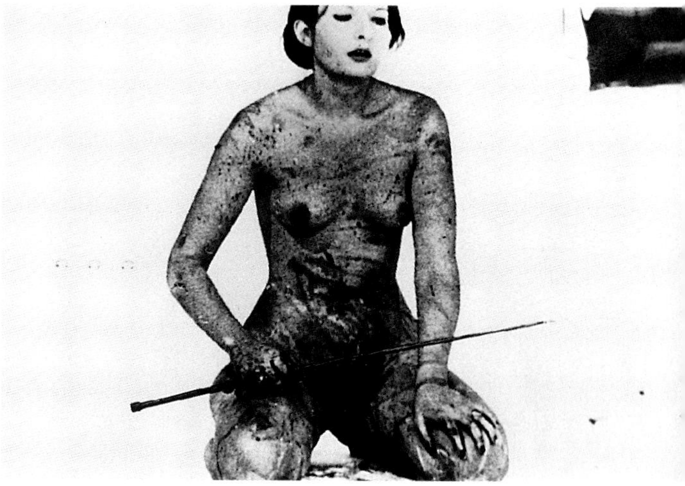

Fig. 70. Marina Abramovic *Lips of Thomas* (1975) Cat. 2

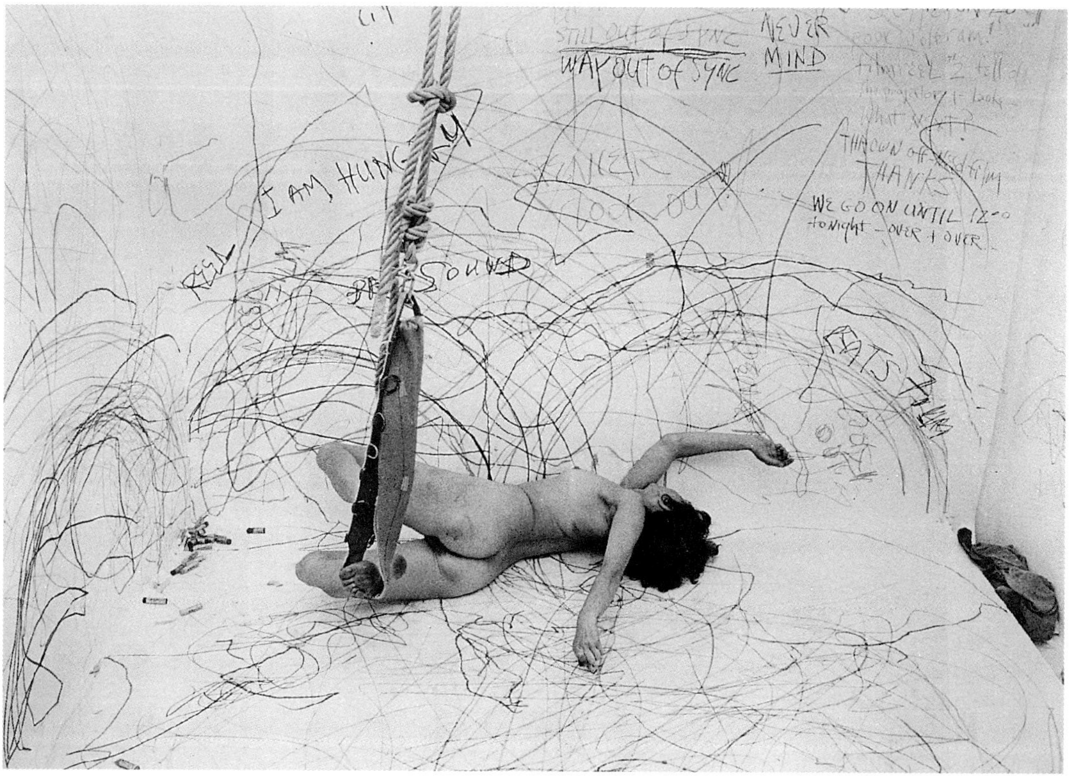

Fig. 71. Carolee Schneemann From the performance *Up To and Including Her Limits* (1975) Cat. 139

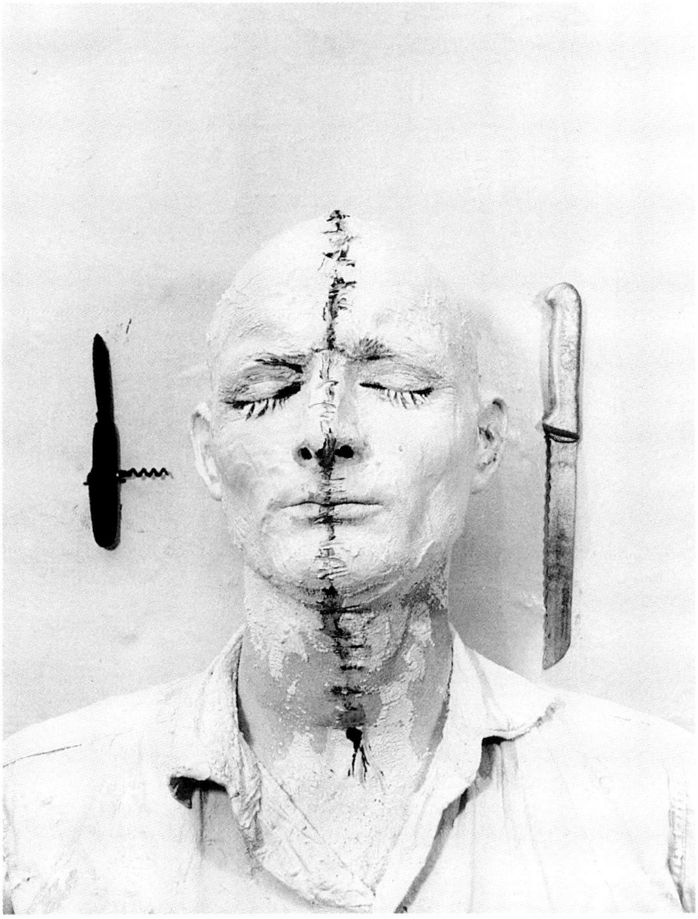

Fig. 72. Gunter Brus *Selbstbemalung (Body Painting)* (1964) Cat. 29

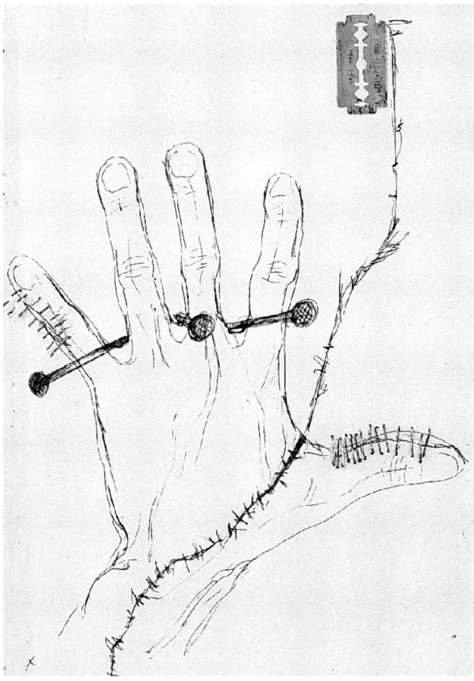

Fig. 73. Gunter Brus *Selbstbemalung III (Body Painting III)* (1964–65) Cat. 28

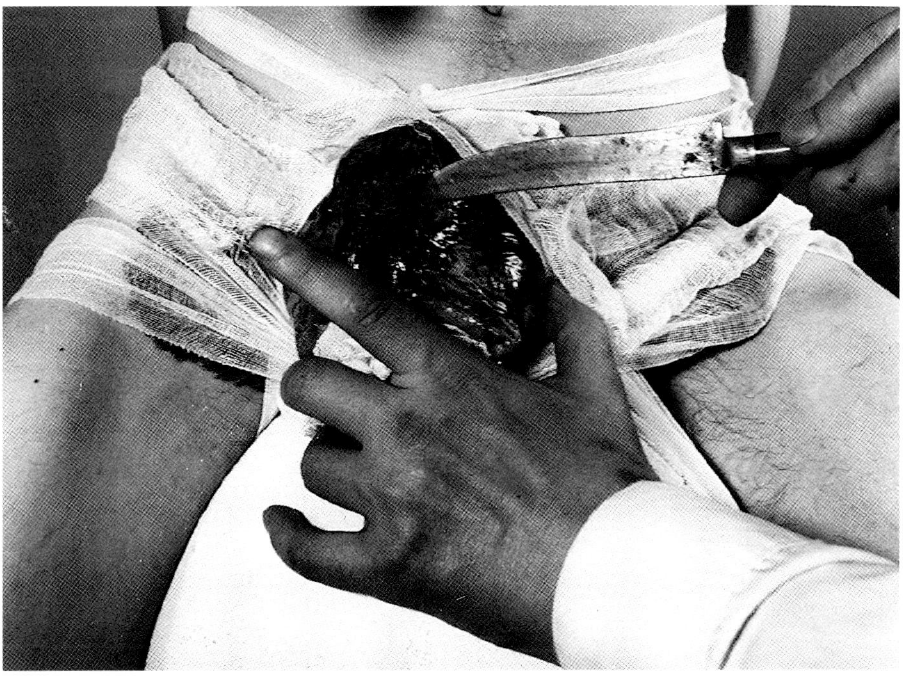

Fig. 74. Rudolf Schwarzkogler *Aktion Wien* (1965–66) Cat. 140

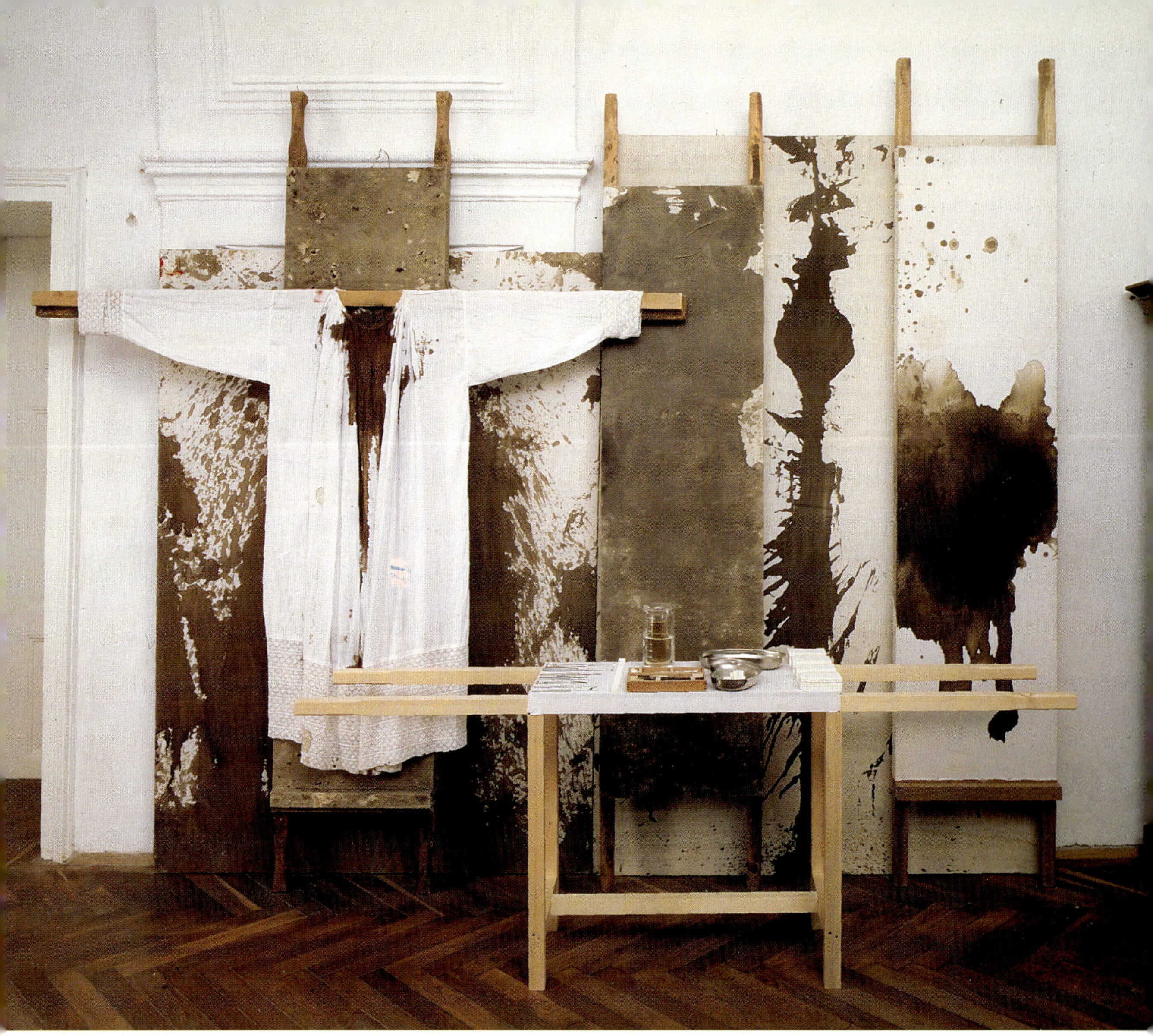

Fig. 75. Hermann Nitsch *Altar Piece* (1984–96) Cat. 113

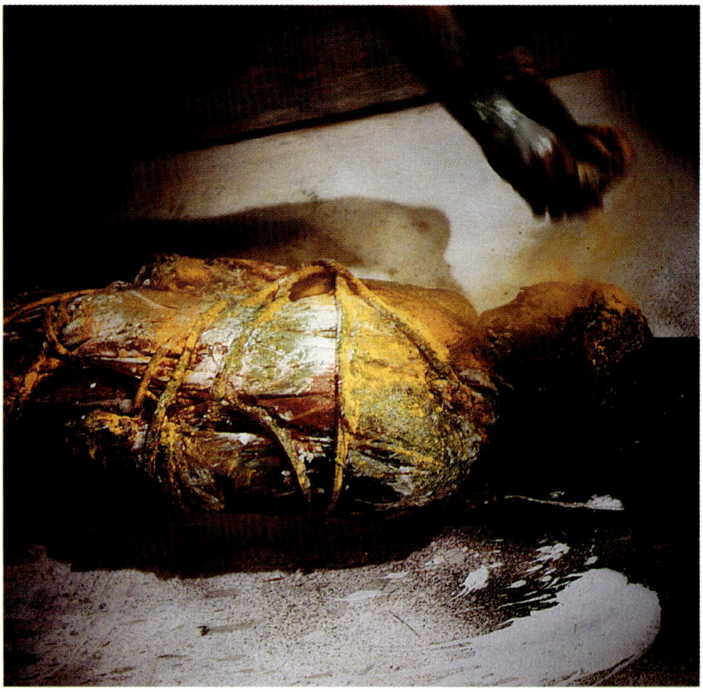

Fig. 76. Otto Muehl *Materialaktion 29* (1966, printed 1994) Cat. 108

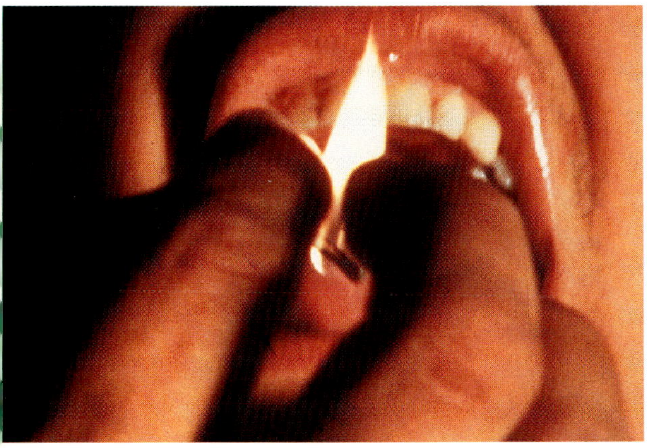

Fig. 77. Mike Parr *Hold a Match in your Mouth for as Long as Possible* (1972) Film List

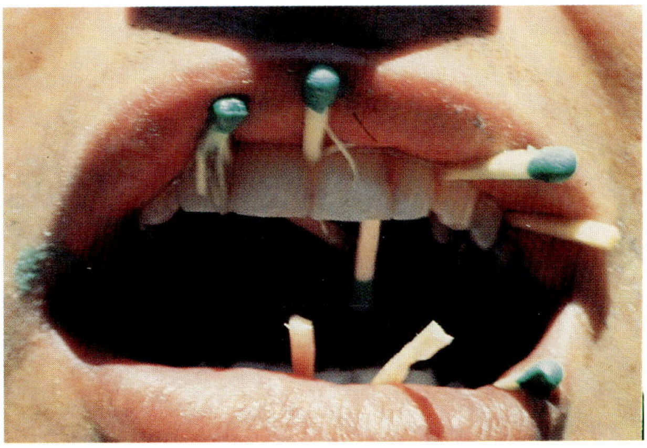

Fig. 78. Mike Parr *Push Matches into your Teeth until your Mouth is Filled with Matches* (1972) Film List

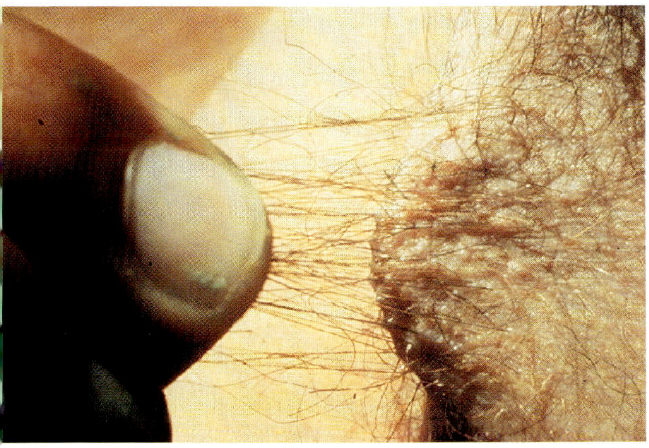

Fig. 79. Mike Parr *Untitled* (1972) Film List

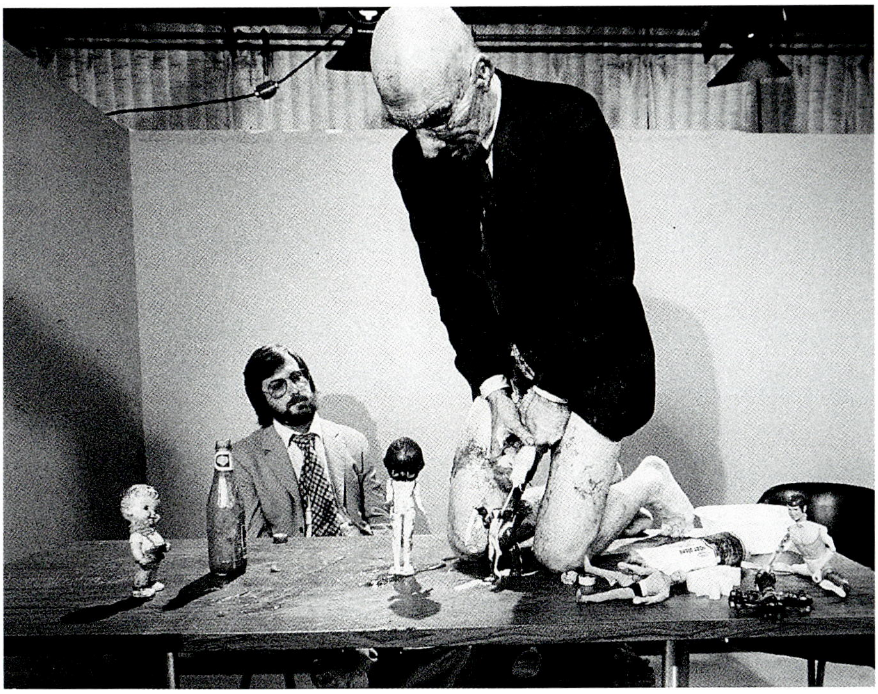

Fig. 80. Paul McCarthy *Grand Pop 1977, Los Angeles California* (1977) Cat. 94

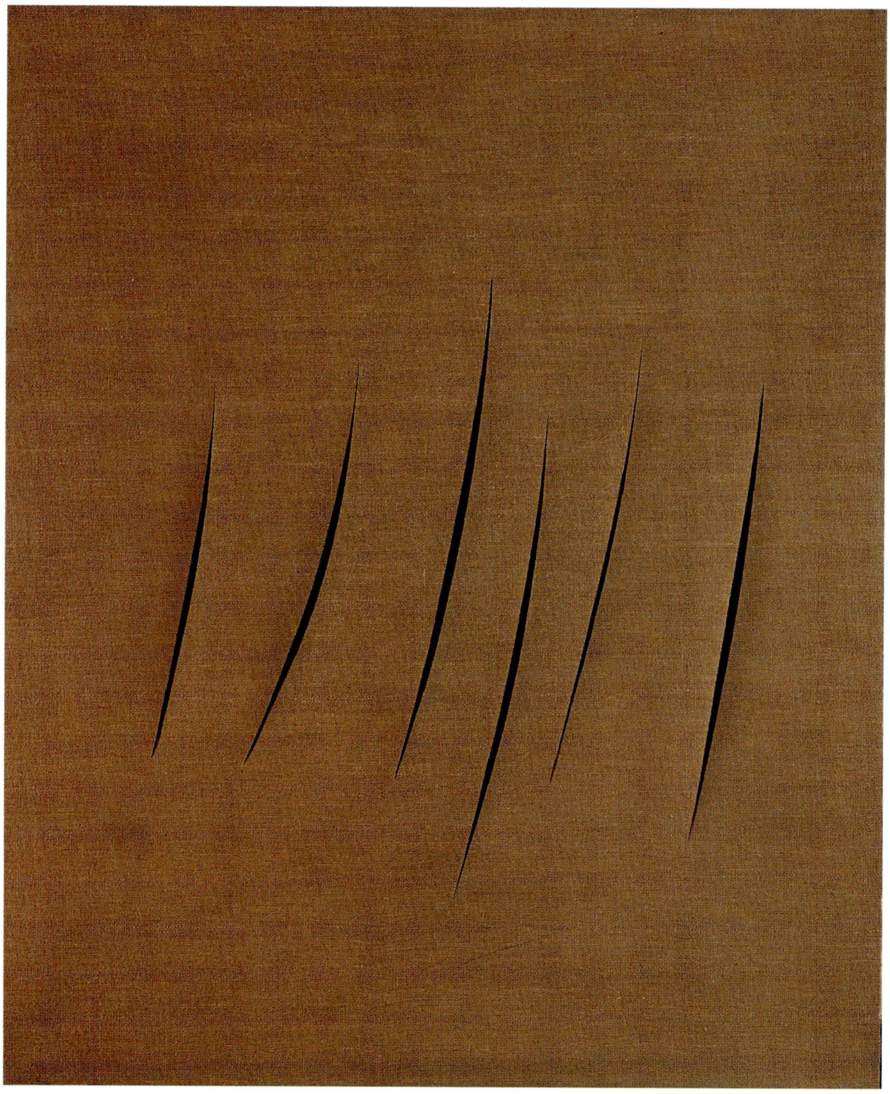

Fig. 81. Lucio Fontana *Concetto Spaziale, Attese* (1962) Cat. 53

Fig. 82. Lucio Fontana *Concetto Spaziale* (1962) Cat. 52

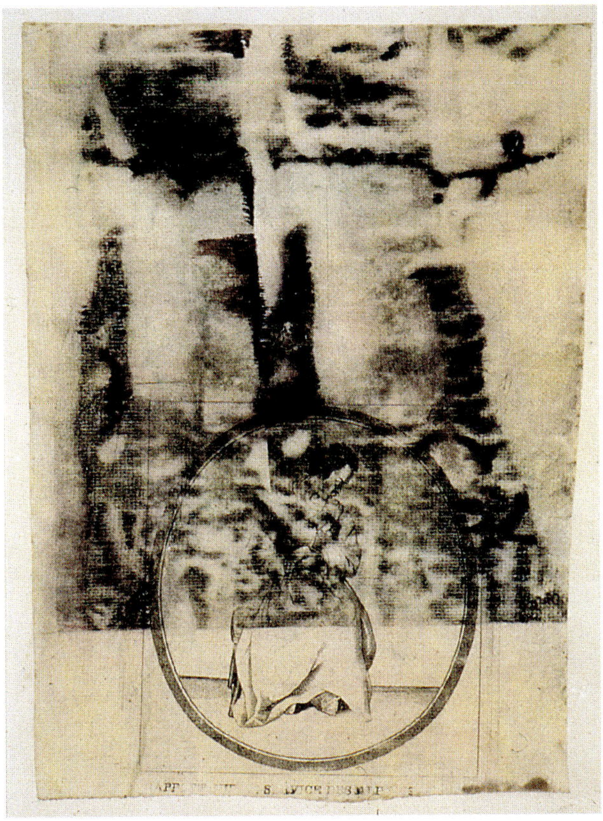

Fig. 83. Bracha Lichtenberg-Ettinger *Eurydice*, no.2 (1992–94) Cat. 81

Lucio Fontana, previously referred to in relation to sexual allegories, is included in this section of the exhibition with two paintings from the *Concetto Spaziale* series (Figs. 81 and 82). These works entail the artist puncturing or slashing the picture plane. While there may be visual associations between these cuts and sexual orifices, they also rupture the veil or screen of representation at the brink of the void. Because this veil is metaphorically related to the skin which separates the body from its surroundings, the orifices created by Fontana naturally evoke the openings of the body itself. The paintings are also relics of actions more decisive than the gestures of painters discussed in *Tactility and the trace.*

In her series entitled *Eurydice* Bracha Lichtenberg-Ettinger creates fugitive and mysterious images in which presences seem to appear between and amongst the fragments of found images (Fig. 83). These paintings are evolved from photocopies made from a particularly loaded source: photographs of naked women and children taken just prior to their execution by officers of the Third Reich. Fragments of these images are assembled and only partially fixed. Consequently they retain a fugitive appearance, having the quality of haunting and fragmentary memories. The surface of these images is finished with oil paint which is systematically stroked on, touching the surface like a divining rod capturing moments of intensity within the image. The artist is also a practicing psychoanalyst who is contributing provocative ideas within the orthodoxy of Freudian and Lacanian analysis. In essence she posits a matrixial border space resulting from early experiences of separation. These spaces are libidinally invested and act as a productive alternative to the absence proposed by castration theories.[38] The paintings seem to be veils or screens that capture images coming from beyond the subject's direct field of experience.

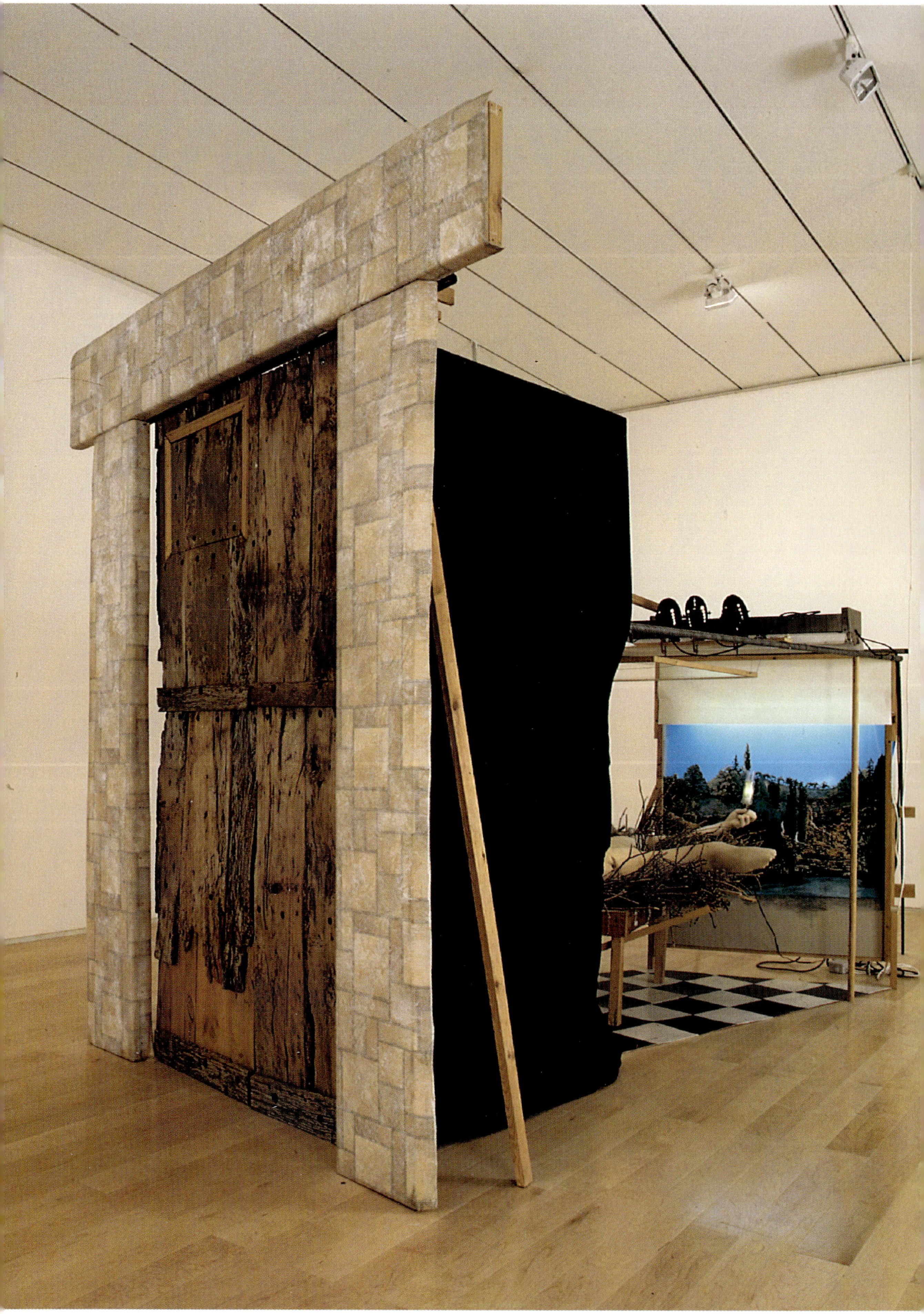

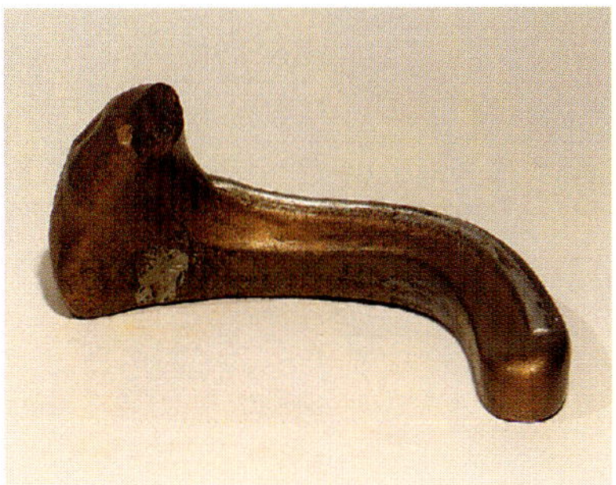

Fig. 85. Marcel Duchamp *Objet Dard* (1951–63) Cat. 47

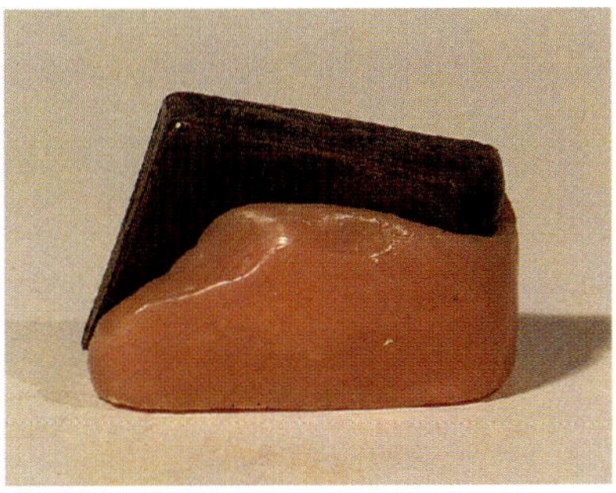

Fig. 86. Marcel Duchamp *Coin de Chasteté (Wedge of Chastity)* (1954–63) Cat. 48

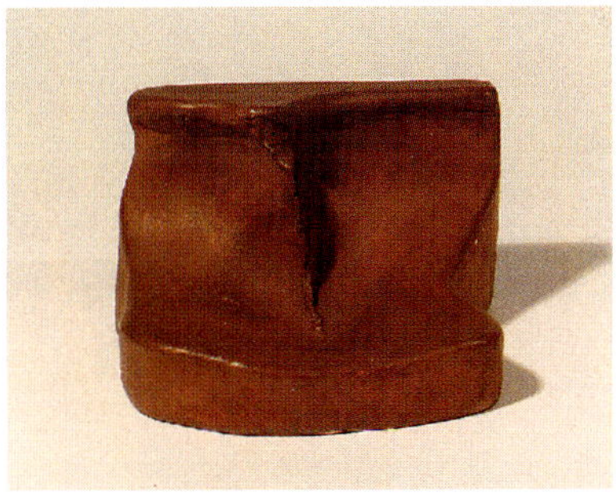

Fig. 87. Marcel Duchamp *Feuille de Vigne Femelle (Female Fig Leaf)* (1950–51) Cat. 49

7 Surreal fragments and recombinations

The most disturbing quality of *Etant Donnés* is the fragmentation and depilation of the model. What is not obvious from the original view through the keyhole is that the figure is incomplete. Baquié has faithfully reproduced Duchamp's installation which only provides as much of the body as the viewer could see through the hole in the bricks (Fig. 18).[39] Now that we are permitted behind the scenes, the image is revealed as the site of an atrocity (Fig 84). The carcass, for that is how it looks, holds up the lamp as if locked in rigor mortis. Surrounding this bizarre tableau in the central part of the exhibition is a cabinet of curiosities including fragments and recombinations of the body.

First, there are Duchamp's sculptures *Objet Dard*, *Coin du Chasteté* and *Feuille de Vigne Femelle* (Figs. 85, 86 and 87), which relate to the process of producing *Etant Donnés*. Although these appear to be casts of genital areas they remain visually obscure. Moulding and casting are the sculptural equivalents of the trace in painting. Duchamp uses the idea of the mould to suggest the border of matter and thought, where representation may be characterised as being like a veil draped over matter, concealing as much as it reveals. The mould shares this association with the Wilson/Lincoln effect where two possible readings of an image alternate perceptually (Fig. 88).[40] Duchamp uses this effect in describing the horizon in *The Large Glass*. The horizon, which is also the bride's dress, separates consciousness from its object just as it binds them together. The process of moulding is erotic since it implies the pressure of material on the body and in the case of Duchamp's *Feuille de Vigne Femelle*, on the genitals. Rodin's *Iris, Messenger of the Gods* reappears in a smaller version in this room recalling Duchamp's debt to this work in *Etant Donnés*. As the messenger, Iris could pass between the material and the immaterial domains.

Fig. 84. Richard Baquié *Sans Titre. Etant Donnés: 1°La chute d'eau 2°Le gaz d'éclairage (Untitled. Given: 1. The Waterfall 2. The Illuminating Gas)* Photograph by Blaise Adilon (1991) Cat. 9

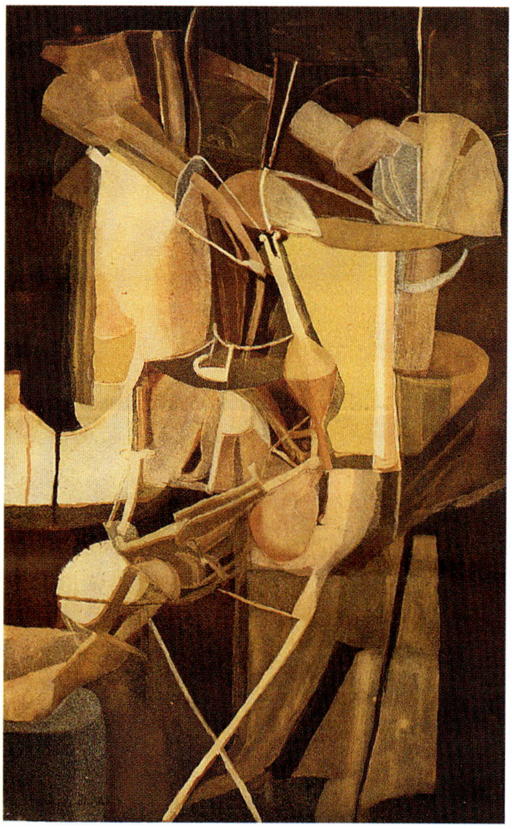

Fig. 88. Jacques Villon after M. Duchamp *Duchamp's Bride* (1912–34) Cat. 154

Fig. 89. Rebecca Horn *Pendulum with Emu Egg* (1987–94) Cat. 67

The theme of the fragmented body returns in a vitrine of works by Rodin. Rodin kept in his studio a vast collection of casts of fragments: arms, legs, heads and torsos. These casts were repeatedly recombined to produce the great array of figures in his compositions (Fig. 90). This vitrine contains a small group of assemblages from such fragments.[41] Joan Mirò's *The Tightrope Walker* (Fig. 91) is a surreal figure composed of fragments including bones, a gourd and a dolly, all assembled and cast in bronze.

Hans Bellmer also used dolls. His *La Demie-Poupée* (Fig. 92) is one of a series of near life-size articulated dolls that he had fabricated to his specifications by craftsmen.[42] He subsequently played games with the dolls where they were placed in various situations and photographed. Bellmer also produced drawings of the body in which it seems to be turned inside out. Sexual organs are enlarged in proportion to their sensory potential, creating images that represent tactile rather than purely visual experience. Distortion takes the form of mutant or morphed human bodies in the sculpture *Doggy* by Dinos and Jake Chapman (Fig. 93). Fantasies of corporeal merger and of the doppelganger take on perverse form here, seriously undermining the stability of the body's boundaries. These artists belong to a new generation who imbibed weird cartoons with their mother's milk.

Pierre Molinier is represented by photographs of multiple figures modified to produce almost flower-like patterns of human bodies in complex sexual combinations (Fig. 95). A delightful note is struck by Richard Hamilton's *Study for Leopold Bloom* (Fig. 94), made as an illustration for James Joyce's *Ulysses* in 1948.[43] Hamilton is fascinated by the circumcised penis that floats on the water's

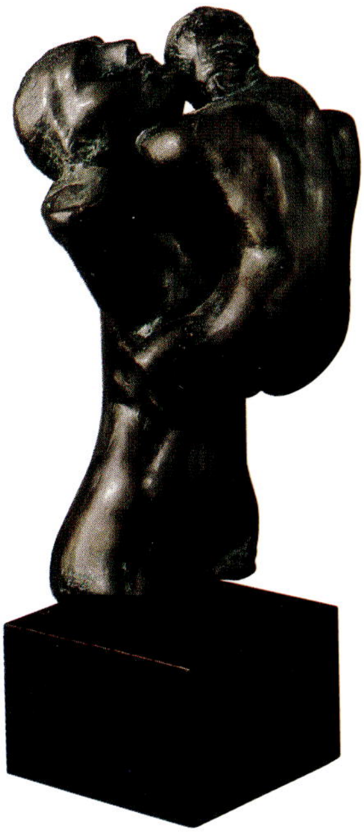

Fig. 90. Auguste Rodin
Assemblage: Torse del Centauresse et Étude pour Iris (1910)
Cat. 129

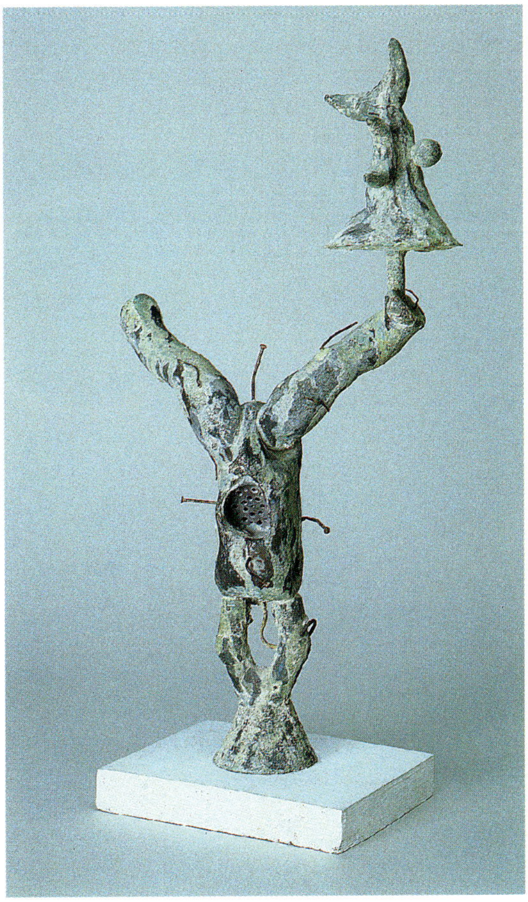

Fig. 91. Joan Mirò *The Tightrope Walker* (1970) Cat. 97

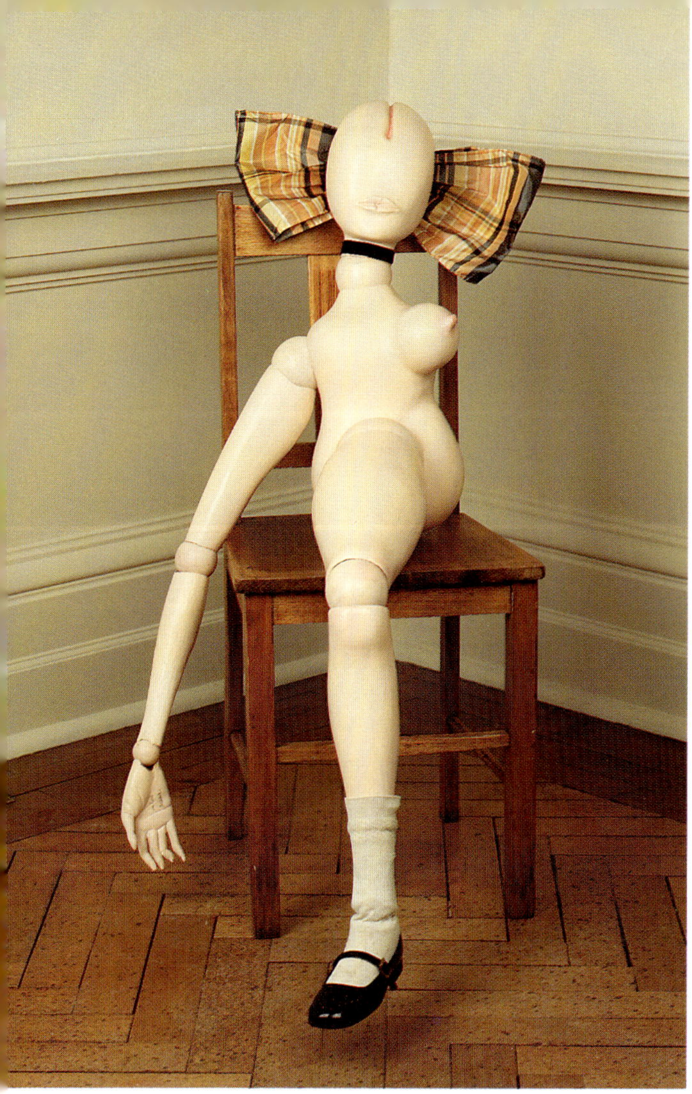

Fig. 92. Hans Bellmer *La Demie-Poupée (Half-Doll)* (1971) Cat. 12

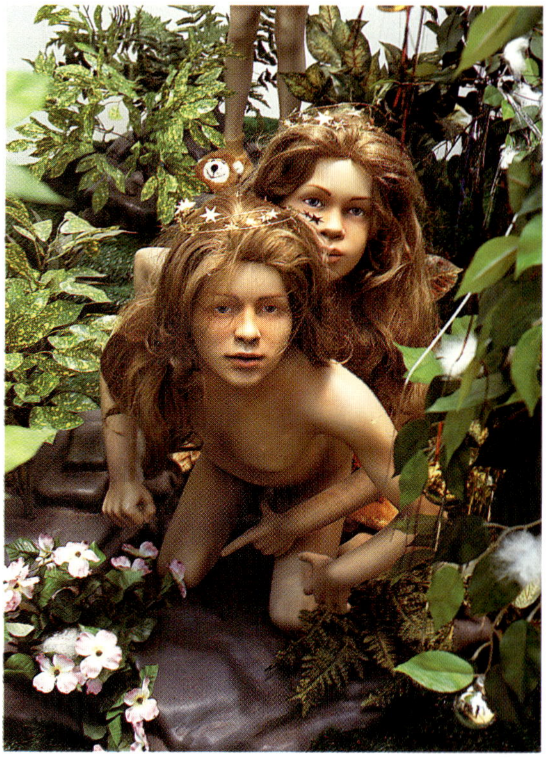

Fig. 93. Dinos and Jake Chapman *Doggy* (1997) Cat. 31

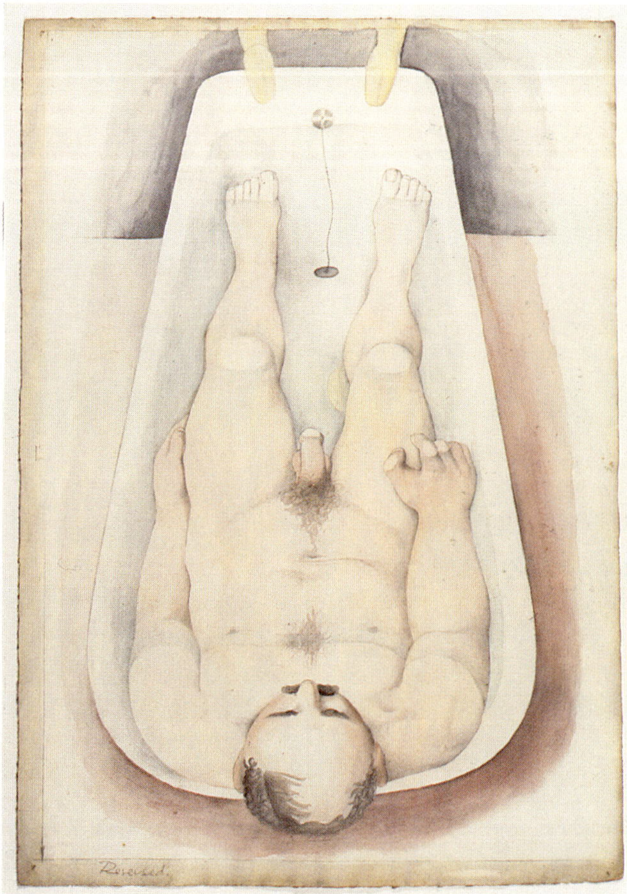

Fig. 94. Richard Hamilton *Study for Leopold Bloom ("He foresaw his pale body")* (1948) Cat. 61

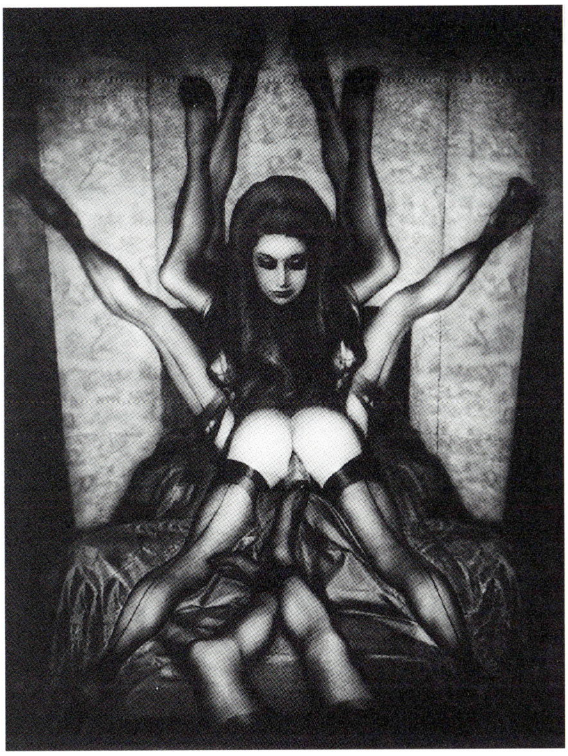

Fig. 95. Pierre Molinier *Le Festin de Manès* (no. 34) (1968–70) Cat. 101

surface, making parallel notations of flowers and fungi all around the edges of the composition in an echo of this form.

Rebecca Horn's *Pendulum with Emu Egg* and *Thermomètre d'Amour* (Figs. 89 and 96) are two erotic sculptures which play off Duchamp's idea of the mechanical bride. Precariously attached to the wall by a small rod, the pendulum hangs like a javelin or pointer with its sharp end almost touching an emu egg. Suddenly the pendulum jerks into action, swinging wildly from side to side. It threatens to smash the fragile egg with each swing yet as it slows down before returning to the rest position it begins to seem more like a caress. The machine threatens but also completes the bride's orgasm. *Thermomètre d'Amour* plays a counterpoint to this 'blossoming of the bride'.[44] The oversized glass thermometer rests in a lined case like a piece of precious jewellery or a violin. If

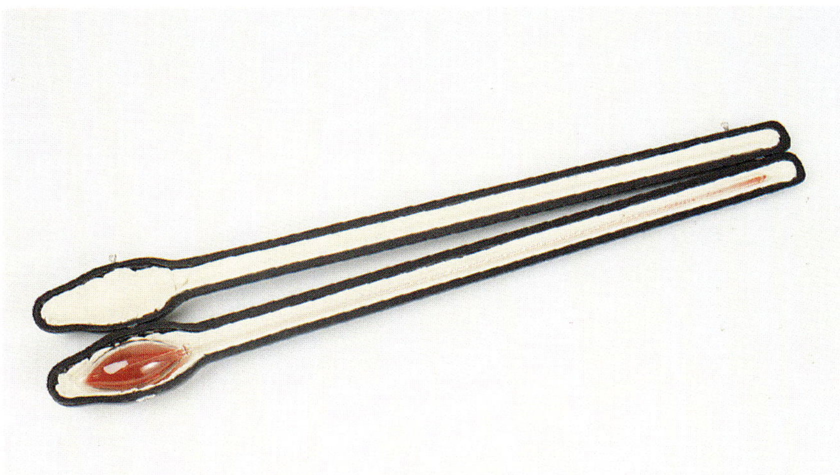

Fig. 96. Rebecca Horn *Thermomètre d'Amour (Love Thermometer)* (1988) Cat. 68

the viewer picks up the instrument by the bulb the heat of the hand causes the red fluid in the bulb to be forced up the stem in an image of engorgement.

More assertively surreal and allied to the work of Bellmer are Cindy Sherman and Robert Gober. Sherman's photographs reveal figures poorly assembled from prosthetics and rubber body parts (Fig. 97). Robert Gober's *Man Coming Out of Woman* (Fig. 98) is a wax sculpture which disturbingly simulates flesh, although the waxwork quality lends it a macabre effect that jars with the subject of an improbable birth scene.[45] This fantastic scenario seems to link the original object of fixation, the mother, with the artist's sexual investment in the male body.

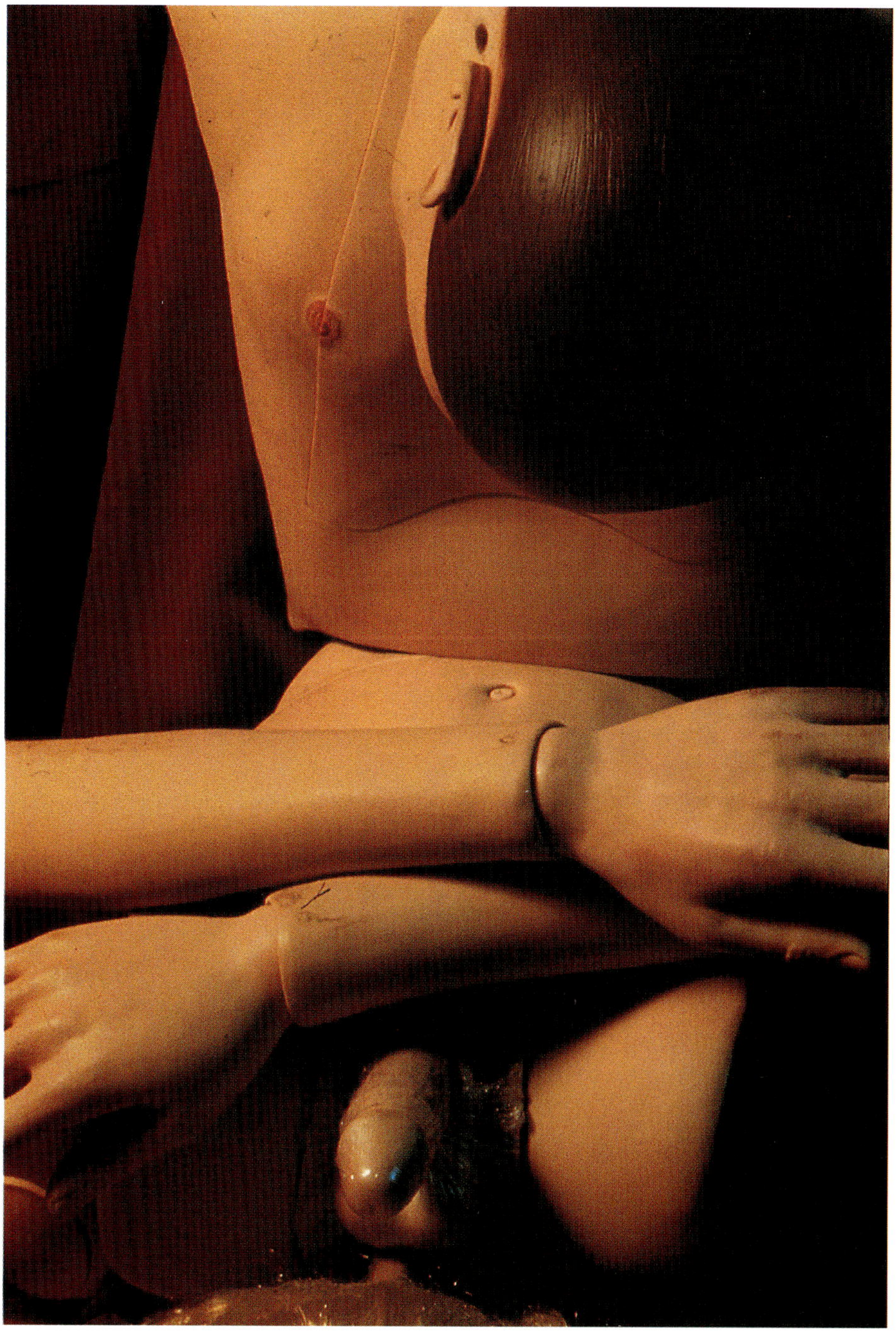

Fig. 97. Cindy Sherman *Untitled* (1992) (MP#259) Cat. 143

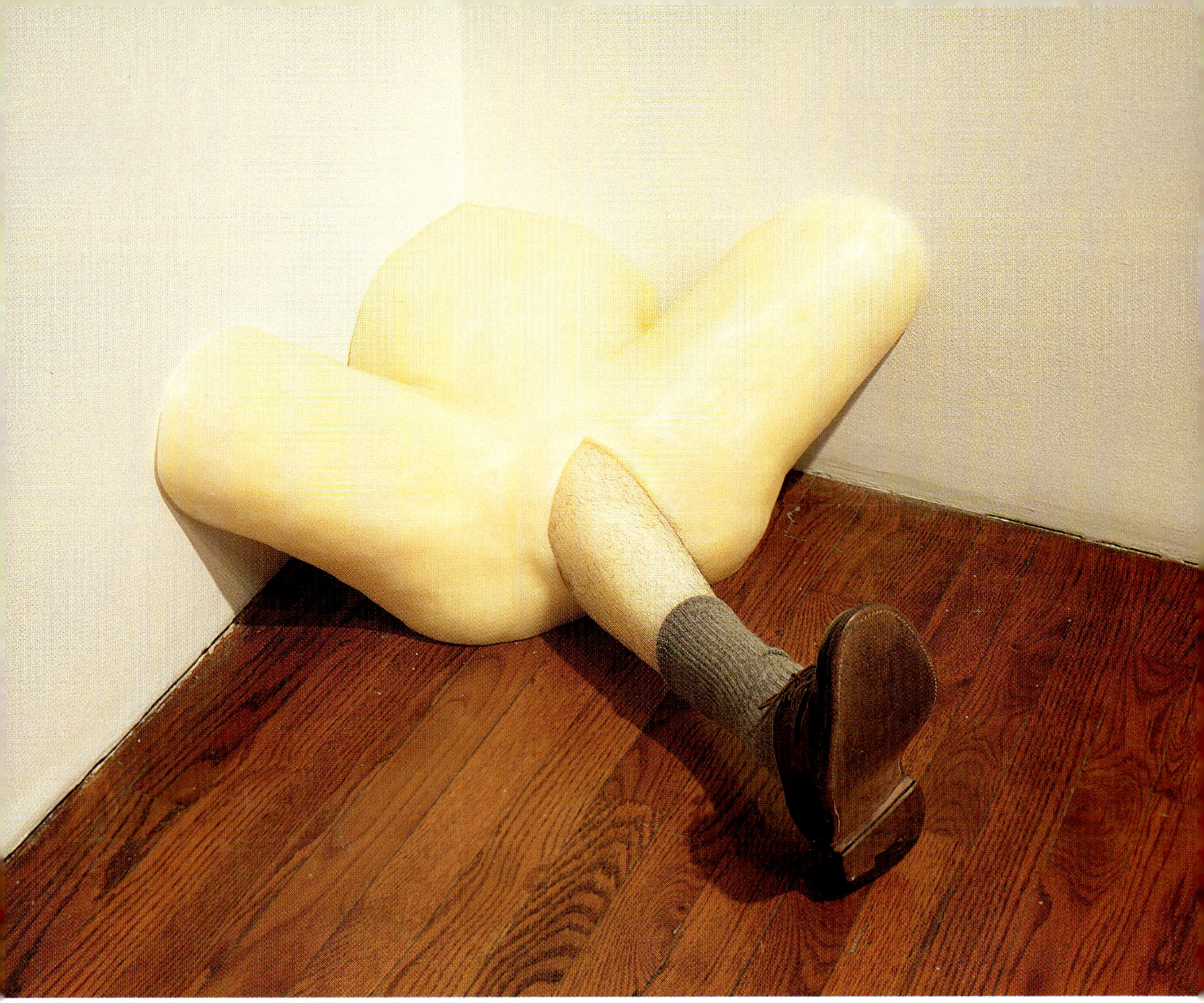

Fig. 98. Robert Gober *Man Coming Out of Woman* (1993–94) Cat. 58

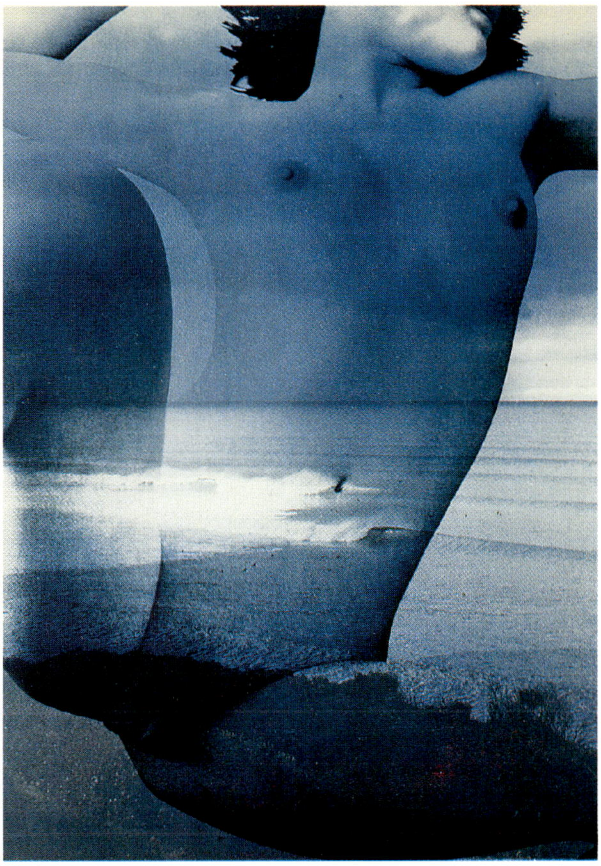

Fig. 99. Vettor Pisani *La Tempesta (The Storm)* (1990) Cat. 120

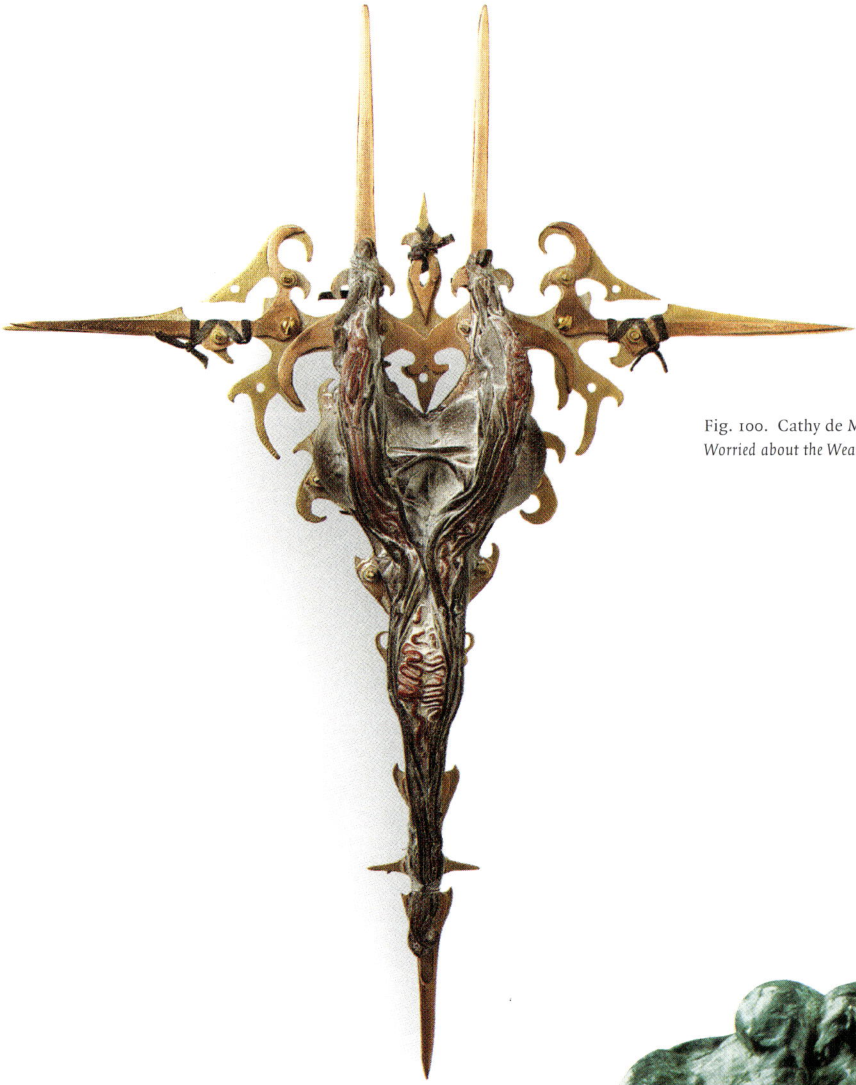

Fig. 100. Cathy de Monchaux
Worried about the Weather? (1996) Cat. 41

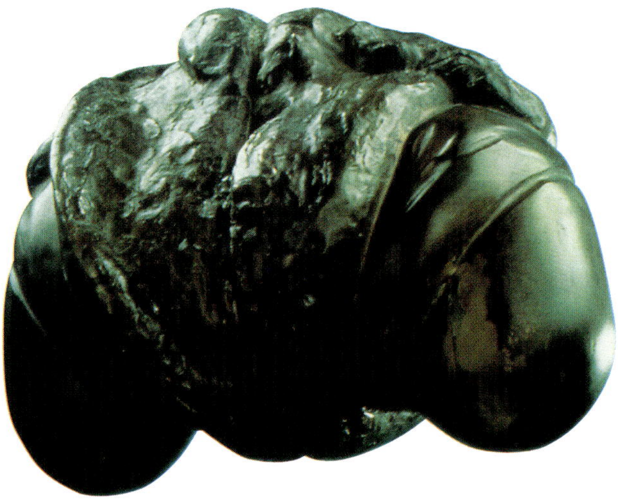

Fig. 101. Louise Bourgeois
Janus Fleuri (1968) Cat. 26

8 Imagining the inside out

Imagining the body, and in particular representing the inside on the outside or recreating the feel of a body rather than its appearance, is also a critical component of this project. Louise Bourgeois' sculpture, *Janus Fleuri* (Fig. 101), is a highly concentrated form which is based on female genitals framed by polished mounds.[46] It does not simply present the visual appearance of the body, and is not reducible to a deformed fragment such as *Objet Dard* by Duchamp (Fig. 85). It refers to the sensation of sex rather than depicting the outward appearance of organs. The wings of the form, corresponding to thighs, are smoothly finished and polished bronze. The central area which

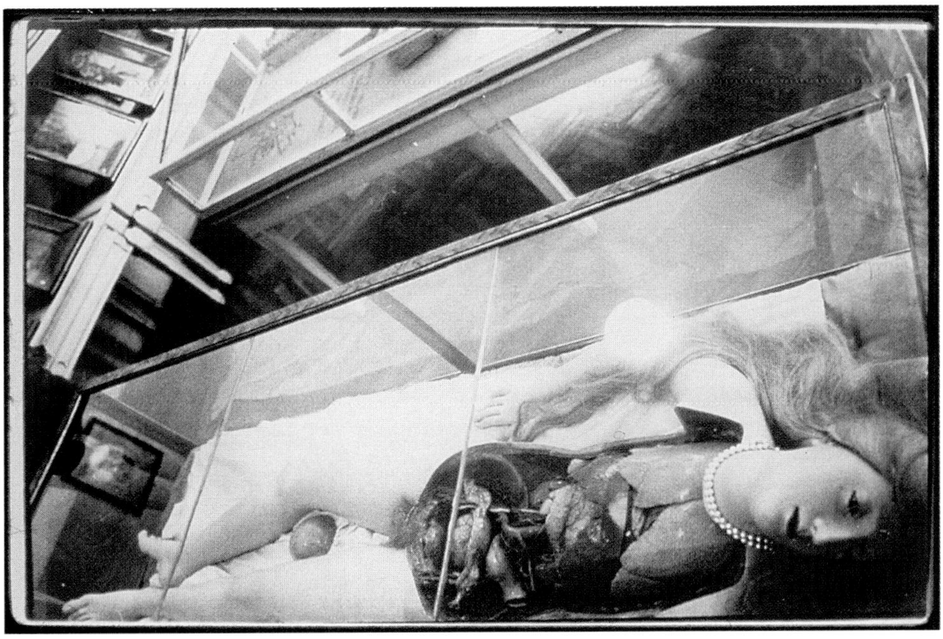

Fig. 102. Zoe Leonard *Wax Anatomical Model Shot Crooked from Above* (1990) Cat. 80

occupies the space of the genitals is, in contrast, roughly formed and ill defined. It seems more like an accumulation of fatty matter than an anatomical detail. The polished area becomes an outside or a skin while the contrasting unformed part seems to be the interior normally available only by touch.

Cathy de Monchaux also produces forms which convey sensation rather than imaging the body as such. She creates a world of fragments which partly suggest genitalia, but they are equally possible to read as independent entities, insects, fungal growths and elaborate jewels, all at the same time. The spiky fractal metal forms that clasp the soft folds of talcumed leather strongly suggest sexual pleasure as well as throbbing pain (Fig. 100).

Zoe Leonard is represented by a photograph taken of a medical Venus in a glass case (Fig. 102). This is a beautiful and terrible image. The model is an attractive naked woman with long blonde hair wearing only a string of pearls round her neck. Her abdomen has been dissected to lay bare her entrails and organs. Francis Bacon has spoken of the beauty of a diseased mouth or a road accident, but it is more compelling to hear Orshi Drozdik describe her first encounter with an anatomical dissection when she was at art school. After the initial shock of seeing a beautiful woman lying disembowelled she discovered that the lining of her stomach was a gorgeous, lustrous purple material while the texture of the organs provided a wealth of exquisite forms and colours. From horror to aesthetic pleasure there is a short loop (Fig. 103). To see the corpse as beautiful requires a suspension of our awareness of the circumstances of death and mutilation. Inevitably we find the outward appearance of the innards shocking because in everyday life we only experience this sight as catastrophe. On the other hand we are not normally repelled by the sensations of our innards unless we are ill, indeed it is in the hidden recesses of our interior that we feel warmth and comfort after a good meal, or experience sexual arousal. Confronting this paradox may simply be perverse but it is also part of coming to terms with mortality and overcoming the tyranny of appearances. Mona Hatoum takes us on a journey through her body using a medical video probe but the image appears in a dish set for dinner (Fig. 104).

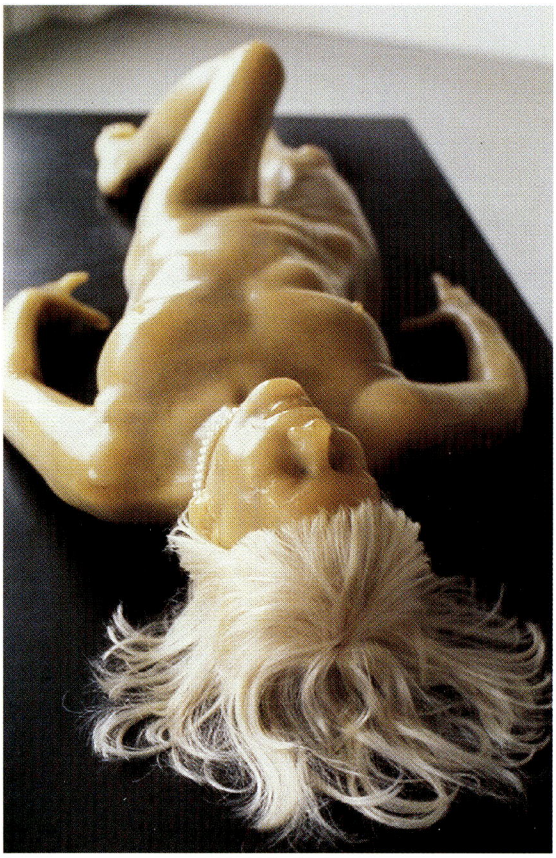

Fig. 103. Orshi Drozdik *Body Self* (1983–93) Cat. 44

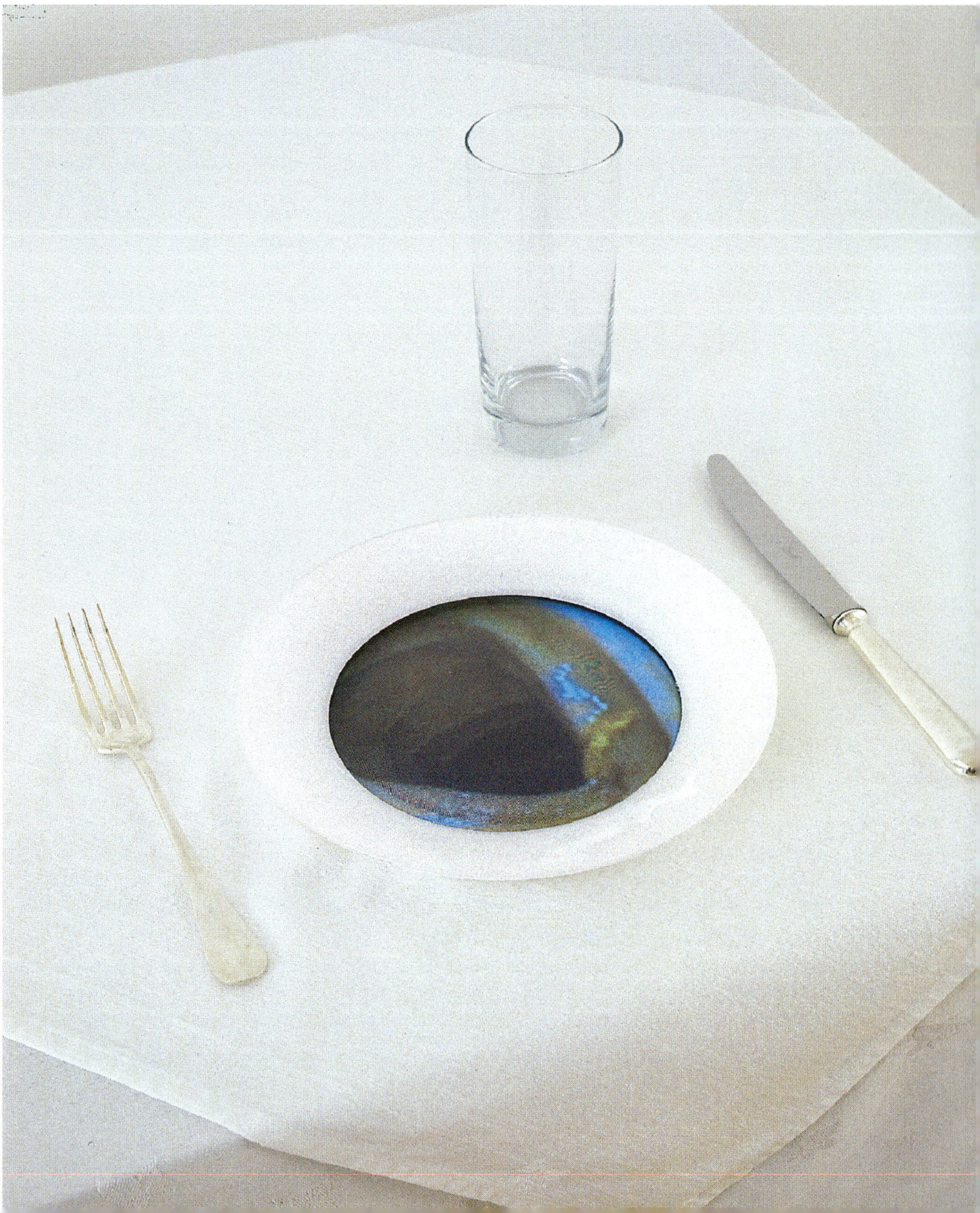

Fig. 104. Mona Hatoum *Deep Throat* (1996) (detail) Cat. 63

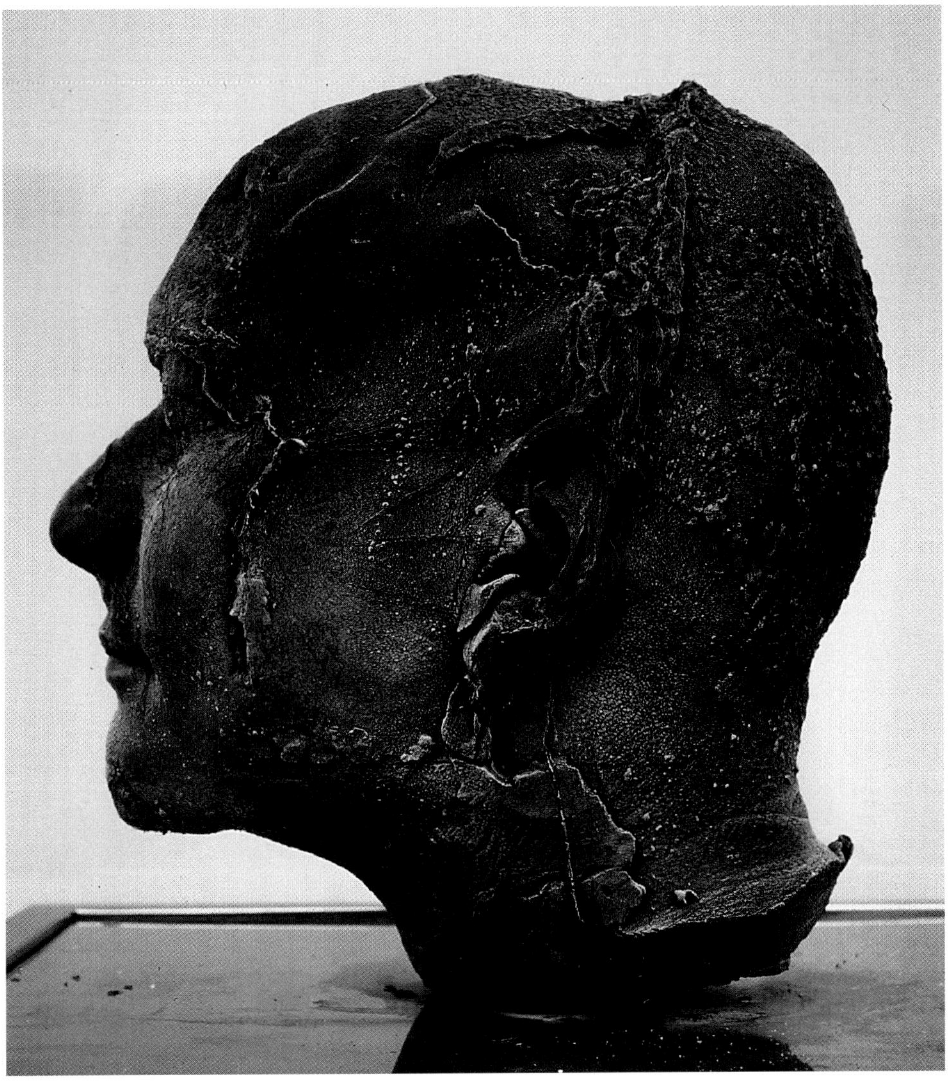

Fig. 105. Marc Quinn *Self* (1991) (detail) Cat. 123

Marc Quinn has produced a second version of his 'bloodhead' sculpture, *Self* (Fig. 105). This work consists of nine pints of the artist's own blood collected over a period of time and frozen into a mould of his head. Nine pints is the normal amount of blood in a body: for Quinn the fact that it perfectly matched the volume of his head was a compelling coincidence. The plinth for the work is a refrigeration unit which lends it a particularly medical or scientific appearance.

Zai Kuning is a young artist from Singapore who recently exhibited at the *Asia Pacific Triennial* in Brisbane. He is a performance and installation artist and these objects can therefore be thought of, in part at least, as residues of performance. Zai Kuning has created forms by layering sheets of wax or cloth around unknown objects (Fig. 106). These bundles are suggestive of body parts or of the abattoir but they remain ambiguous forms. The idea of secret parcels relates to Duchamp's ball of string within which Walter Arenberg has hidden an undisclosed object. These secrets also suggest bodily mementos, hence Zai Kuning's parcels have an affinity with Doris Salcedo's shrines to the lost citizens of Colombia (Fig. 107). [47]

Salcedo is able to take the empathic process to an exquisite level of pain. In *Atrabiliarios* she evokes absence and loss by using materials and processes that locate memory in the body. The viewer's response is, in turn, emotional – even visceral – rather than purely intellectual. Niches cut

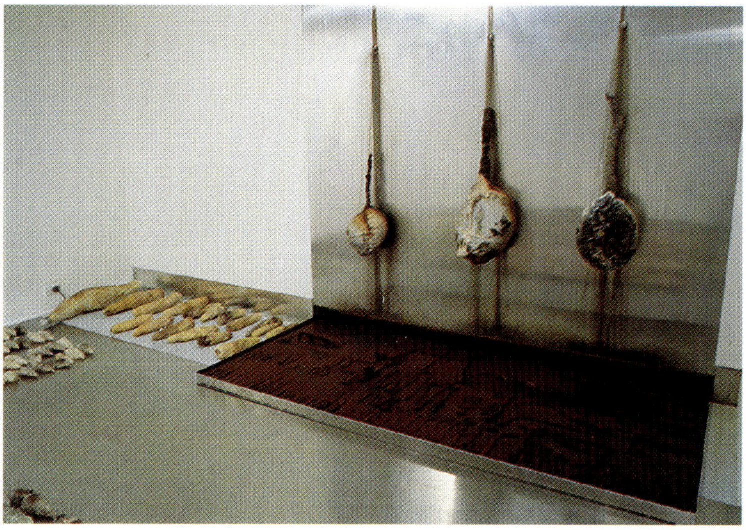

Fig. 106. Zai Kuning
HYDROGEN: The lightest element
HYPOCAUST: Hot air was sent as a form of heat
IDIOCY: Extreme mental imbecility; utter foolishness
HYSTERIA: Functional disturbance of psychoneurotic origin
INANE: Enigma of a sexless toad (1996) Cat. 156

into the plaster wall contain shoes as relics or attributes of lost people donated by the families of those who have disappeared in the political and economic violence that has racked her native Colombia. The niches are then sealed with a membrane of animal caul which is literally sutured into the plaster of the wall. Barely visible through the membrane, the shoes are a particularly haunting evocation of their absent owners. The animal skin and the shoes inevitably recall the grizzly souvenirs of Nazi death camps.

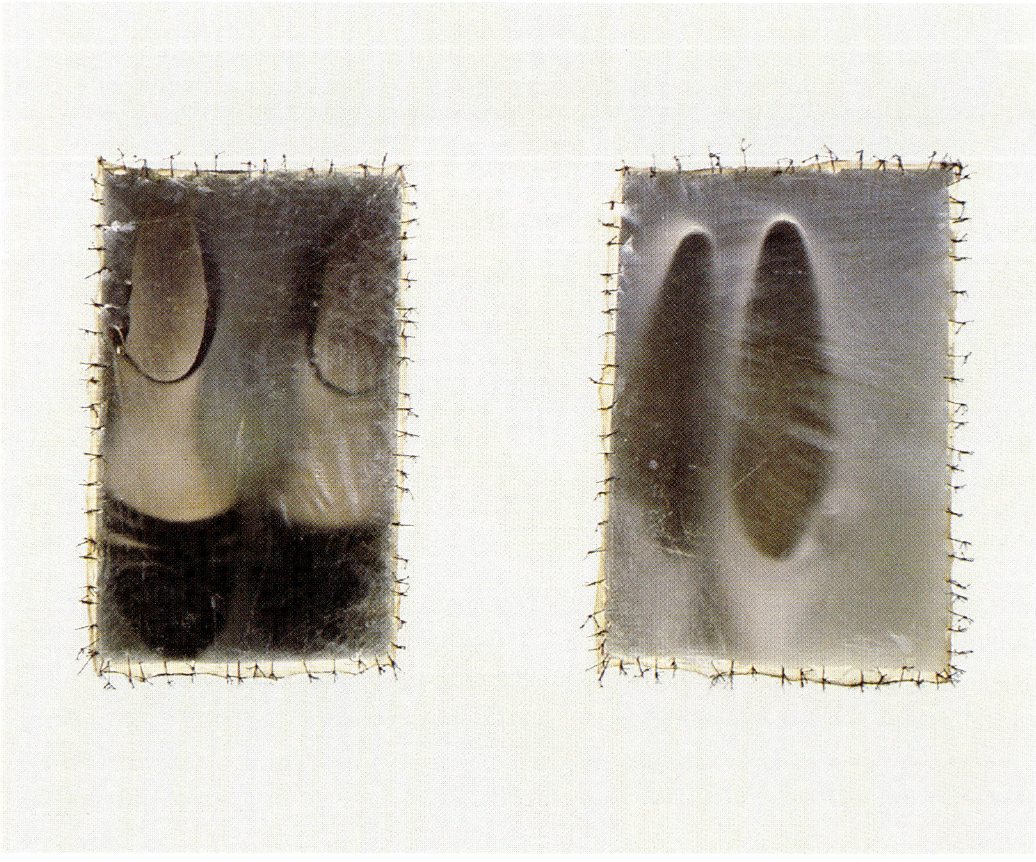

Fig. 107. Doris Salcedo *Atrabiliarios* (1992) (detail) Cat. 135

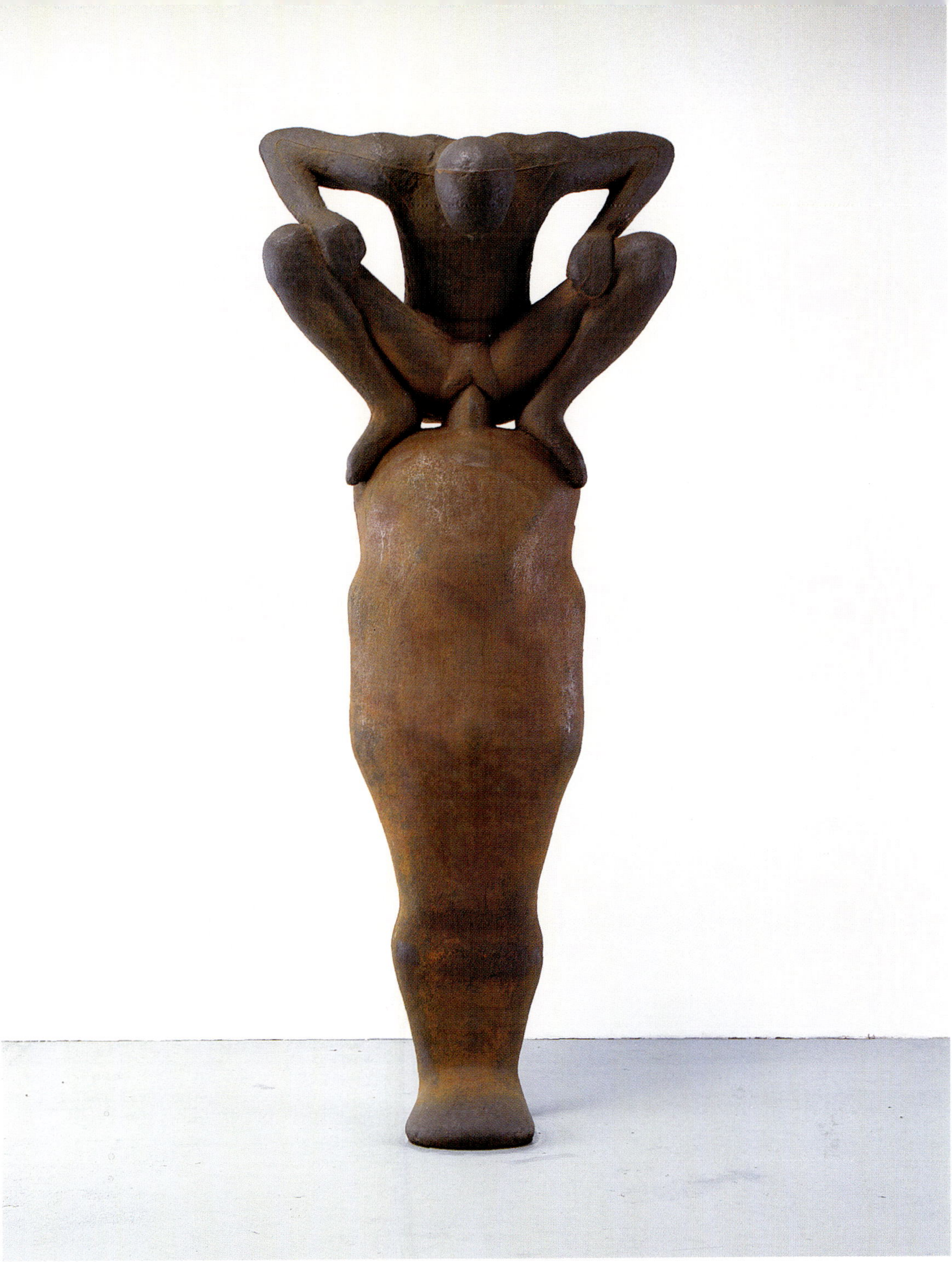

Fig. 108. Antony Gormley *Bearing* (1987–95) Cat. 60

9 Seeking reconciliation with nature

Antony Gormley represents his own body as a measure of the world. Through the image of his body he depicts humankind arising from the earth and coming to reflect upon its own mortality. In human form clay becomes aware and in this moment shares some of the understanding reserved for the angels thus bridging the material and spiritual divide. This double figure, *Bearing* (Fig. 108) replaces the head of the standing figure with another body crouched as if in childbirth. It could also be an image of the artist returning to the womb. The figure bears and is also born.

Kiki Smith's *Mary Magdalene* (Fig. 109) is reminiscent of Donatello's wooden *Penitent Magdalen*. Her body is covered in hair, half human and half animal. She drags a chain from one ankle like an escaped beast. When she was making this work Smith was thinking about French legends of the penitent Magdalen who wandered in the wilderness for seven years after Christ's death. The stay in the wilderness carries with it many of the connotations of humanity's search for reconciliation with nature, a theme which connects this work with the work of Ana Mendieta and Frida Kahlo in this exhibition. The hair is also a trace of the artists fingers clawing at the surface of the clay. Only the face, breasts, stomach and knees are polished and smooth, highlighting their erogenous nature as points of contact with the earth and with other bodies.

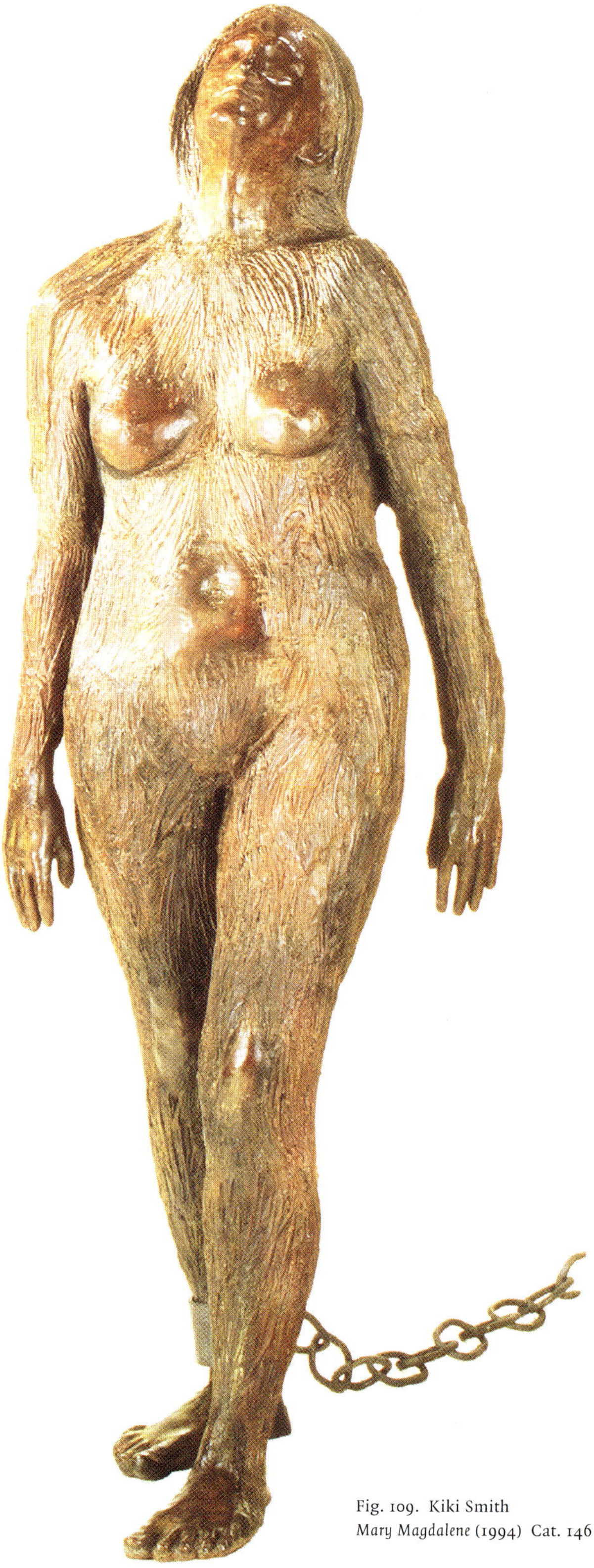

Fig. 109. Kiki Smith
Mary Magdalene (1994) Cat. 146

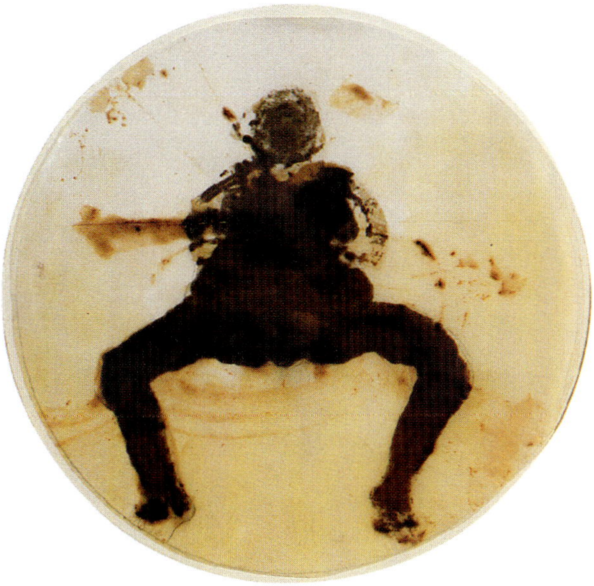

Fig. 110. Joseph Beuys
Dickes Mädchen (Fat Girl) (1955) Cat. 16

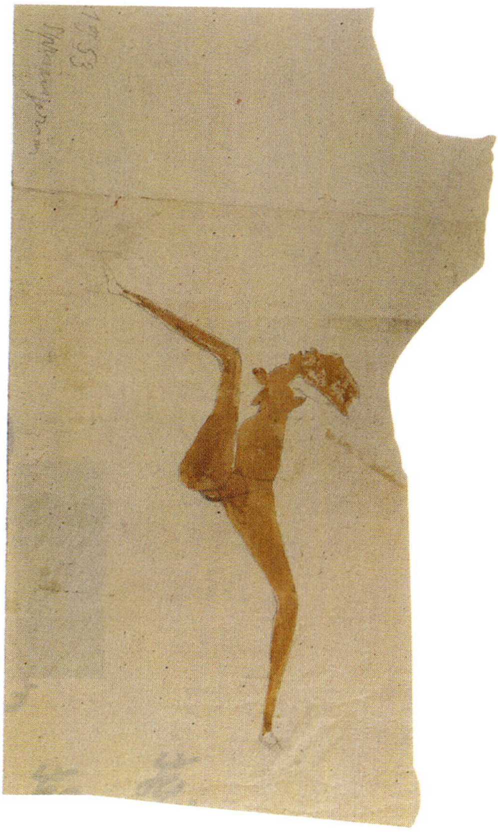

Fig. 111. Joseph Beuys
Springerin (Leaper) (1953) Cat. 19

Joseph Beuys spent some years recovering from the trauma of his time as a fighter pilot in the Luftwafe and subsequently discovering the reality of the holocaust. During this period his own return to life was equated with the need for humanity's reconciliation with nature. These early drawings of the figure (Figs. 110 and 111) deal with the pre-linguistic animal origins of humankind, prior to the separation or expulsion of humanity from nature. The Palaeolithic figure of the goddess, which Beuys has called *Beast Woman* or *Animal Woman* in his earlier sculptures, reflects his dismay at modern humanity's separation from nature: a moment of loss referred to in many of our key myths. In *Genesis* and in the Greek story of Prometheus, for instance, loss of innocence is linked with separation from the natural order. The relationship between humankind and nature is one of the fundamental problems of being, and is as central to art as it is to philosophy. A reminder of the use history has made of the body as language comes with Adam

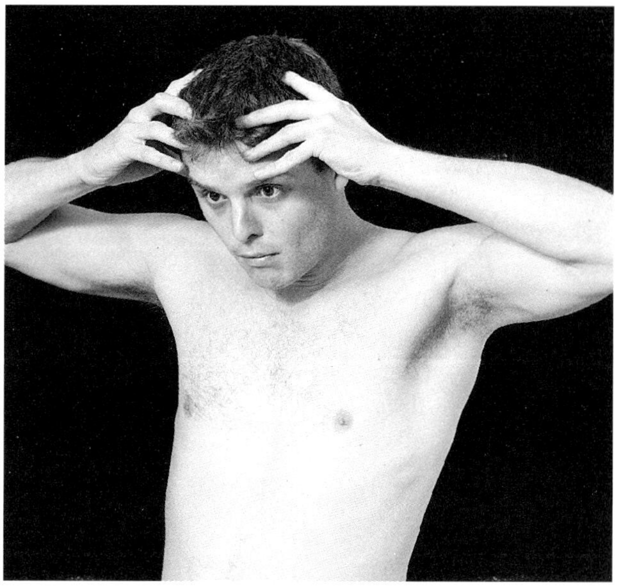

Fig. 112. Adam Geczy *Invocation and Exorcism* (1997) Cat. 57

Geczy's photomontage in which he studies the way Hitler codified bodily gestures taken from Wagnerian staging (Fig. 112). Geczy's intensity of facial expression sits oddly with the stylised rhetoric of the body language leaving meaning and affect in tension.

Empathy has been at the heart of all of these themes. Beuys's ideas about reconciliation are both practical and metaphorical. They assume a responsibility for the world we occupy and promote a sense of inhabiting the world rather than accepting a scientifically distanced and objective or instrumental view. An empathic attitude to other people involving a degree of identification is in keeping with this idea and underscores the selection of works for *BODY*.

Notes

1 Jill Bennett, "Kama and Eroticism: the Five Senses in the Work of Francesco Clemente and Pierre Klossowski," in this volume.

2 See Jill Beaulieu and Mary Roberts' analysis of Michael Fried's concept of merger in "Courbet's Corporeal Realism: The Phenomenological Body and the Anti-Theatrical Tradition," in this book.

3 Given: 1. The Waterfall 2. The Illuminating Gas.

4 *Etant Donnés* is discussed later in this essay, and in depth by Susan Best, "Just Looking? The Body, the Gaze and Syncope," and Philippe Grand, "Baquié," in this book.

5 Best, "Just Looking?"

6 Michel Foucault, "Las Meninas," *The Order of Things: An Archaeology of the Human Sciences* (London: Tavistock, 1970) 3–16. Also see Best, "Just Looking?"

[7] Courbet's painting, *The Painter's Studio*, is referred to in other parts of this book. See for example Sarah Faunce, "Courbet: Feminist in Spite of Himself."

[8] Beaulieu and Roberts, "Courbet's Corporeal Realism."

[9] Alan Krell, "Fearful Desires: 'Embodiments' in Late Nineteenth-Century French Painting," in this book.

[10] As discussed by Krell, "Fearful Desires."

[11] Sarah Faunce refers to this image in her catalogue essay, as do Jill Beaulieu and Mary Roberts.

[12] Krell, "Fearful Desires."

[13] Michael Fried, *Courbet's Realism* (Chicago: U of Chicago P, 1990). Fried proposes a theory of embodiment, which is analysed from a feminist perspective in two essays in this book: one by Jill Beaulieu and Mary Roberts, the other by Sarah Faunce, joint Curator with Linda Nochlin of the exhibition *Courbet Reconsidered* at the Brooklyn Museum New York, 1988.

[14] Linda Nochlin in her catalogue essay for *Courbet Reconsidered.*

[15] Sarah Faunce argues this case in detail in her essay.

[16] Faunce and Nochlin, *Courbet Reconsidered.*

[17] Helen Toussaint in her essay for the exhibition *Gustave Courbet (1819–1877)* (Paris: Grand Palais; London: Royal Academy 1977–1978).

[18] Beaulieu and Roberts, "Courbet's Corporeal Realism."

[19] See David Bromfield's essay, "Posing the Question: Rodin's *Iris* and the Modern Body," in this book.

[20] Thomas McEvilley, "The Darkness Inside a Stone," *Anish Kapoor* exh. cat. (Venice: XLIV Venice Biennale, 1990).

[21] See my notes on Fontana later in this essay.

[22] Courbet also made reference to this fashionable trope in his painting *The Sleepers*, which is discussed in this book in the essays by Sarah Faunce and also Jill Beaulieu and Mary Roberts.

[23] Best, "Just Looking?"

[24] See Charles Merewether's essay in this book: "The Unspeakable Condition of Figuration."

[25] Krell, "Fearful Desires."

[26] Krell discusses these works in some depth in "Fearful Desires."

[27] Bennett, "Kama and Eroticism."

[28] Interview with Alice Neel in P. Hills, *Alice Neel* (New York: Abrams, 1983).

[29] Bennett describes these works in more detail in "Kama and Eroticism."

[30] In "Posing the Question" Bromfield discusses other aspects of the work by these expressionists and links them to the advent of performance art in the 1960s.

[31] See Bromfield, "Posing the Question."

[32] See Bromfield, "Posing the Question."

[33] Beaulieu and Roberts in this book.

[34] Courbet has used the image of a hole at the edge of the painting as a connection between the viewer and the represented space before, notably in *The Burial At Ornans* where the grave, which is the centre of the action, disappears out of the pictorial frame at the base of the composition.

[35] Fried, *Courbet's Realism* 61-65.

[36] Bob Law in an interview with the author, 1966.

[37] Thomas McEvilley and Nan Rosenthal in their respective essays in *The Art of Yves Klein* exh. cat. (Houston: Institute for the Arts, Rice University, 1982).

[38] Bracha Lichtenberg-Ettinger, "Metramorphic borderlinks and matrixial borderspace," *Rethinking Borders*, ed. John Welchman, papers from the symposium for *The Boundary Rider*, 9th Biennale of Sydney (London: Macmillan, 1996).

[39] Grand describes Baquié's motives for replicating Duchamp's work in "Baquié."

[40] This is another of Duchamp's names for the gilled cooler, the bride's dress and the horizon which forever separate the bachelors from the bride in the *Large Glass*.

[41] Bromfield, "Posing the Question."

[42] Best, "Just Looking?"

[43] Sarat Maharaj in a paper presented at *The Boundary Rider*, a Symposium for the 9th Biennale of Sydney, 1992/93.

[44] Marcel Duchamp refers to the pink cloud in the bride's apparatus of *The Large Glass* as the blossoming of her orgasm.

[45] Best, "Just Looking?"

[46] Discussed by Best, "Just Looking?"

[47] Merewether and Best discuss this work in their texts in this book.

Philippe Grand

Baquié

Baquié's work belongs to a tradition in the plastic arts initiated by artist/bricoleurs such as Duchamp, Rauschenberg and Tinguely. From the early '80s he has produced some astonishing and heteroclite constructions from salvaged materials and objects, often animated by machinery producing wind, frost, etc. Words – poetic, humorous and contradictory – form an integral part of these sculptures; their letters fashioned from steel, the words are treated like the recycled objects he uses; like them they are diverted from their usual meanings.

Such diversions of materials, techniques and words proliferate in Baquié's works. In them he not only adopts practices made part of the vocabulary of twentieth-century art by his famous elders, he perpetuates their very mentality. Against harmony and equilibrium – the effects of a spontaneous seduction by a fixed, closed form (itself the transposition of a complete and positive thought) – Baquié forwards the principle of an open and irreducible sculpture, always surpassing commentary and – in terms of a sculpture presented as a fragment of reality where meaning homologically circulates without end, like a moment of forms reflecting its own morphogenesis – allowing the individual to think his relation to reality as a perpetual becoming.

Sculpture doesn't produce a centre, it's simply a mark.[1]

The notion of circulation, or movement, is essential to Baquié's art – essential in that it adds a temporal dimension to it – and it is evoked as much by the mechanisms that are always displayed in his assemblages (refrigeration plants, hydraulic pumps, electrical conductors) as by his choice of material (car bodies, fuselages, cards, empty boxes). Baquié's work is as much a 'work in time' as a work in space. In exhibitions conceived as installations the juxtaposition of the pieces allows observers to weave them together with threads of their own memory and imagination into a sort of story. But above all, the formal structure of the works – whose refusal to be pure plastic objects is clearly readable – necessarily delays their apprehension. This suggests to observers, in their progressive discovery of the works, that there is a parallel between what they are seeing and the way they are thinking about it.[2] It is as though the very object of Baquié's sculptures was, starting with the 'hypotheses' they embody, the unrealisable constitution of meaning, or meaning as adventure.

My works are propositions . . .[3]

What we might call Baquié's 'propositional' art couldn't avoid engaging the figure of Duchamp, entering into a dialogue not with inventor of the readymades, but with the altogether more secret and complex Duchamp of the assemblages, the Duchamp of the *Grand-Verre* and *Etant Donnés*.

Baquié's piece acquired by the Musée Contemporain de Lyon, which literally cites Duchamp's enigmatic posthumous masterpiece in its title (*Sans Titre. Etant Donnés: 1° La chute d'eau 2° Le gaz d'éclairage*) explains/ratifies an affiliation in his approach, while denouncing its own far too systematic reference and the misunderstanding it involves. For Baquié, 'copying' Duchamp's fascinating artistic testament is a way of reframing their relationship and a modest attempt to follow him into the complexity of a work that is slightly overshadowed by the fame of the readymade.

. . . interest in copying is above all related to the interferences between what one thought one knew but that became something else . . .[4]

This meticulous bricolage produced over three years is atypical, yet it is within the logic of Baquié's oeuvre. It is simultaneously a sort of exercise in identification across time (he 'remounts' the work in an attempt to achieve the state of mind that engendered it); an appropriation of Duchamp's work as material (he questions the symbolism of ownership in the artistic field); and the continuous exploration of this transformation, this endless becoming of forms where the same is always already the other, like the formula in terms of the 'infra-thin' difference in Duchamp himself.

Remember that *Etant Donnés*, exhibited in Philadelphia since 1969, is Duchamp's final work, to which he dedicated himself exclusively and secretly for twenty years. This "demountable approximation," in the words of its creator, of "indeterminate" status (still Duchamp), consists of an environment that one can observe through two holes drilled into a massive wooden door where a nude woman with spread legs and shaved vagina lies on a bed of twigs clutching an illuminated gas lamp in her left arm. This arrestingly realist foreground is set against a naturalistic landscape complete with waterfall. Such is the environment: this astonishing scene of desire reconstructed by Baquié from the Manual of Instructions written by Duchamp in 1966 and published by the Philadelphia Museum of Art in 1987. But where Duchamp managed to make the work untransportable and inaccessible, and forced the observer act as a voyeur, by making it viewable only through the two spy holes, Baquié circumvents the obstacles erected by Duchamp to the penetration of his work. Here is *Etant Donnés*, now not simply transportable but visible from every angle wherever it is displayed, exposing all its machinery.

To reduce Baquié's work to simple replication would be to ignore the fact that "historical circumstances penetrate the substance of art,"[5] and fail to understand that "two indiscernible objects dating from different historical periods are, or can be, totally different works of art with different structures and significations, calling for different responses."[6] Further, if the difference involves the same 'same' – implied in the Duchampian question (and summarised by Danto: "Why is one thing a work of art when another absolutely identical thing isn't?") – then it is right to accord effective differentiation to the manifest difference. In Baquié's work, the walls of *Etant Donnés* – which turned it into an inverted camera obscura where the observer projected his desire – these walls have crumbled; no longer a solitary activity, seeing becomes once again a communal experience. The exploded volume reveals the image's construction; isolates the planes; destroys the illusionary and illusionist unity granted it by one-eyed perspective, and finally decomposes representation before our eyes – and for all that without ever robbing it of its mystery. Not so much a reply to what Duchamp's work replicates, *Sans Titre. Etant Donnés* throws up the question of appearances involved in Duchamp's construction. With and through this construction, Baquié will have attempted "to see whether the image contains something other than the image."[7] It is perfectly consistent with his entire oeuvre that such a project would provoke a meeting between Baquié and *Etant Donnés*.

Notes

1 Baquié quoted in O. Kaeppelin, "R. Baquié au Carré d'Art de Nîmes," *Morphogène* exh. cat. (3 July – 9 Sep. 1990).

2 Baquié's own words in 1986: "Je veux que mon travail déplace les gens par rapport à leur façon de penser." *Art Press* (1986): 104.

3 Interview with R. Baquié and B. Blistène in *Richard Baquié, constats d'échec* exh. cat. Fondation Cartier, Jouy-en-Josas, 10 Mar. – 5 May 1991.

4 Interview with R. Baquié in *Richard Baquié* 16.

5 Arthur Danto, *l'Assujettissement philosophique de l'art* (Paris, 1993) 12.

6 Danto 35

7 Interview with R. Baquié in *Richard Baquié*.

[Translated by Julian Pefanis and Peter Raissis]

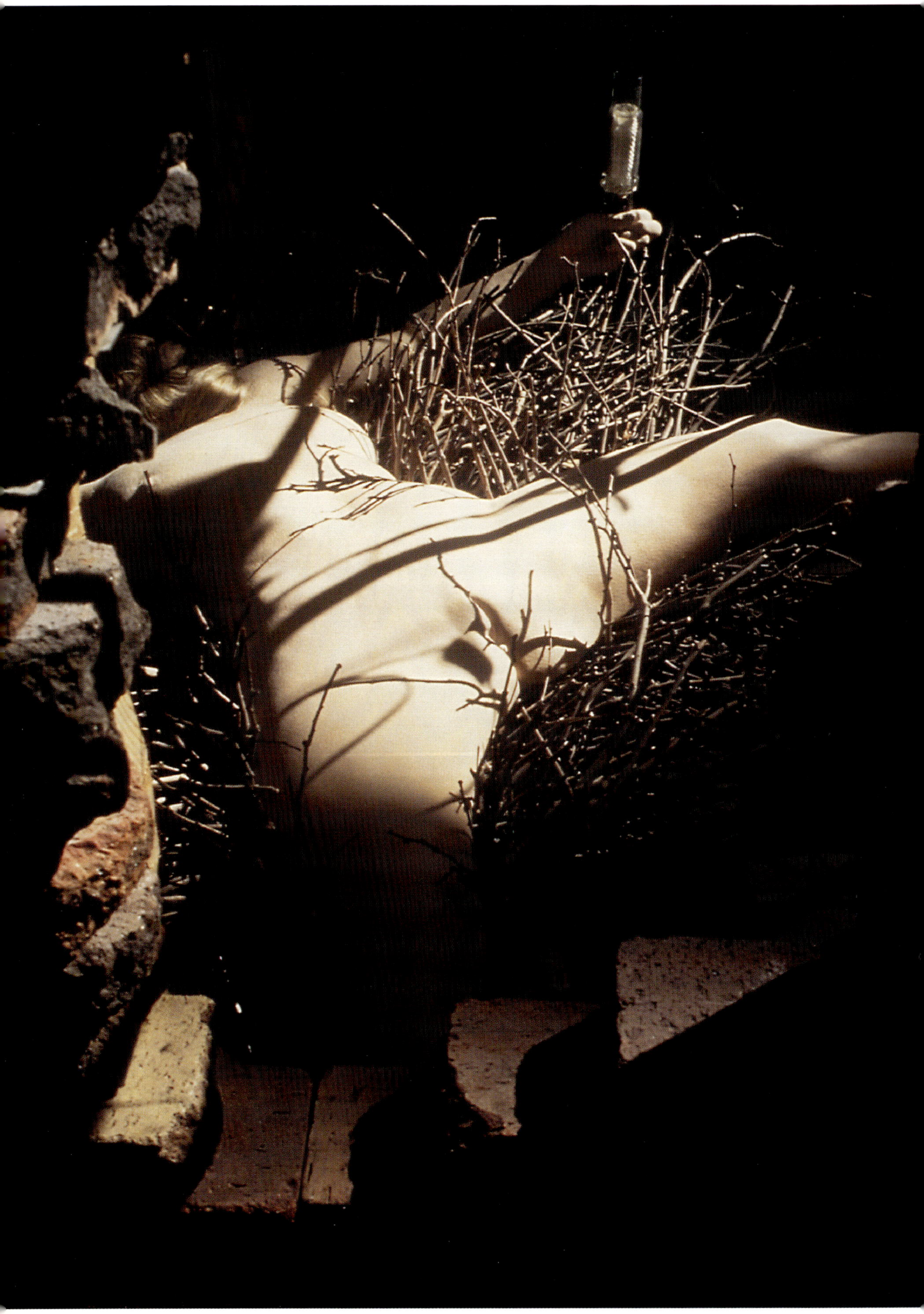

Susan Best

Just Looking? The Body, the Gaze, and Syncope

"Perception is *ex hypothesi* a form of affection and being moved, and the same goes for thinking and knowing." – Aristotle[1]

Set into the wall in the last room of this exhibition, behind veils of skin are shoes; some single, others in pairs. The skin is translucent so that the eye is arrested and tantalised by the blurred shapes that sit partly in and partly just out of focus. There is something at once tender and brutal about the entombment of these shoes. Shoes like second skins mould to the foot's contours, they take and hold the marks of life, their entombment signals both the end of that life and a desire to honour and memorialise it, no matter how humbly.

Herein lies the tenderness, yet brutality is attached like a shadow to its heel. Like the transformations of nightmares, the skin-membranes that frame and make possible the scenes of remembrance also call up their opposite – annihilation. The stitched skin suggests a body pierced and pried open: the shoes start to float below the surface like strange viscera. But there is no body below this skin, the skin has been sheered away from the body and stretched into diabolical service like some Nazi relic. The body has been reduced to mere substance. The corporeal transformations do not rest with annihilation, the nightmarish twist also uncoils: as the casing of memories, the skin again resumes human form as the fragile outer limit of our bounded existence.

These shoe-reliquaries, assembled by Doris Salcedo, are called *Atrabiliarios* (loosely translated as melancholy) (Fig. 107). Even without the title to guide us toward a suitable affective response, we are lead to feelings of loss, horror, sorrow, and anxious fearfulness at our fragile mortality. If this work is about the evocation of melancholy, how do we discuss the way it so surely moves us in that direction?

• • • • •

We are accustomed to thinking of art as a 'moving' experience, yet in recent times very little has been said about this responsive 'movement' in the viewer. As any attentive observer of Art History will know 'movement' is mainly attributed to the makers of modern art: 'movements' describes the successive waves of artistic invention, not the changes wrought in the accompanying generations of viewers. The viewer is not exactly rendered impassive by this concentration on the

Fig. 113. Richard Baquié *Sans Titre. Etant Donnés: 1°La chute d'eau 2°Le gaz d'éclairage (Untitled. Given: 1. The Waterfall 2. Illuminating Gas)* photograph by C. Ganet (1991) Cat. 9

production of art, but certainly the viewer's affective reaction is not central to our understanding of the meaning of art, nor to the experience of looking. This subtle shift away from affect is the consequence of what has been termed the anti-aesthetic impulse in modern art.

A complex cluster of ideas can be investigated under this heading 'anti-aesthetic': from the demise of beauty as the central category of art-evaluation (nineteenth-century Realism mortally wounds this guiding precept), through to the critical 'negations' performed by modern art movements bent on illuminating, attacking or unpicking the conventions and protocols of pictorial representation.[2] The result of collecting these changes and critical interventions under the heading 'anti-aesthetic' is that aesthetics, as Christine Battersby has noted, is now a much maligned body of knowledge, particularly in feminist and left-oriented approaches to art history and film theory.[3] Nowhere is this rejection of aesthetics more clearly illustrated than in Laura Mulvey's classic essay of 1975, "Visual Pleasure and Narrative Cinema."[4]

Mulvey's stated aim in this article was to destroy the visual pleasure which derives from the fascination with the human form. In the process she substantially and irrevocably changed our understanding of visual pleasure. From an innocent enough affect – the feeling of liking was the concern of Kant's aesthetics – visual pleasure became instead something intimately tied to patriarchal ideology. Mulvey identified two kinds of viewing pleasure – identification and objectification – both of which presumed, or conformed to, an asymmetrical relation between the sexes. Women it seemed were usually objectified by mainstream realist cinema; visual pleasure here derived from voyeuristically looking at the woman-as-spectacle. Men, on the other hand, were the active figures with whom one should narcissistically identify. Much has since been made of this gendered division of roles into looked-at and bearer-of-the-look in both art history and film theory, however very little has been said about the subsequent loss of affect as a key term of critical discussion.[5]

In scholarly discussions of art, the viewers' affective response has not been central to the conception of art since Kant. So it is with reference to Kant that Mulvey's intervention can be best understood. For Kant, an aesthetic judgement is not, as we now think of it, primarily about the appearance of the object judged, instead it concerns the sensation that the *subject* experiences in relation to the representation of an object.[6] The assumption being that others should share this same feeling of pleasure. Indeed, we act as if our response is universally shared, we presume others will feel as we do: share our taste in the beautiful and our standards in judging the sublime.

This is precisely where Mulvey's essay has intervened. In the wake of her essay, visual pleasure has become highly suspect, given its demonstrated complicity with voyeurism, narcissism and the perpetuation of rigid gender roles. Perhaps most importantly, the unity of viewers around shared taste is stripped of its universalism: it is revealed that the gaze of (white, heterosexual) man was masquerading as the universal. Mulvey's intervention leaves us much better informed about the sexual dynamics of looking, but also impoverished when it comes to discussing visual pleasure. Her ground-breaking account is so convincing that it seems to exclude the possibility of other modes of looking or other sources of pleasure. But are narcissistic identification and voyeuristic objectification really the only ways in which we experience pleasure in looking at the human figure?

• • • • •

Many of the realist paintings and sculptures in BODY conform to Mulvey's argument – female bodies are indeed opened out for the gaze – but there are also a number of works in this exhibition that push up against the limits of this scopic regime, and others still which seem to thwart it completely. There are three categories of works I want to discuss here: works which directly address the problematics of voyeurism and objectification, works which complicate identification, and then a further category which suspend the viewer between identification and objectification.

In the first category, works which thematise objectification and voyeurism include: Helmut Newton's *Self-portrait with June and Models* (1981) (Fig. 3), Richard Baquié's *Sans Titre. Etant Donnés: 1° La chute d'eau 2° Le gaz d'éclairage* (1991) (Fig. 113), and Michelangelo Pistoletto's *Mirror Diptych* (1962–71) (Fig. 114). All three images replay and rework images that already addressed the theme of looking. Newton's *Self-portrait* borrows its structure and concept from the quintessential metapicture Velasquez's *Las Meninas*. Pistoletto reworks Man Ray's *Erotique-voilée*, an image whose title points to a visual pun: the model's body is partly hidden by the wheel, but the wheel is itself a partly concealed source of erotic frisson, it adds a phallus to Meret Oppenheim's body. In Baquié's case, *Untitled* is a third generation 'reworking.' He appropriates Duchamp's *Etant Donnés*, a work which in turn uncannily traces the form of Courbet's *The Origin of the World* (1866) (Fig. 15). Crucially, Baquié's *Untitled*, unlike Duchamp's prototype which it in all other ways exactly copies, allows access to the 'back' of the work (Fig. 84).

The first encounter with Baquié's work coincides with the only view offered of *Etant donnés*: one is compelled to look at the work through peepholes. One's act of voyeurism is then further underscored when the view offered is that of a supine naked woman. The unnaturalness of this restricted view in a gallery space essentially given over to the act of looking, cannot fail to make the viewer self-conscious. Indeed, the view itself is so unnatural and puzzling, that a distinct edginess pervades the whole experience. A woman lies, or rather is sprawled, uncomfortably on a bed of spiky, wiry twigs redolent of the very pubic hair she so clearly lacks. One would assume she was dead but for the hand holding aloft a burning lamp. Why else would she be lying on twigs?

Her hand has a solidity, muscularity and energy singularly lacking in the rest of her body which exhibits the kind of slackness one might associate with a mildly deflated doll. Her ambiguous genitals reinforce the sense of rubbery dollness: her peculiar genital gash, a kind of jagged tear punctuated by a dark hole, is doll-like in its reduced simplicity. Alternatively, one might interpret the absence of labia and the anus-like vagina as depicting the rear, and not the front, of the body so that the lower half of the body is in some way twisted or reversed (a point amplified by another work in this exhibition by Duchamp, *Female Fig Leaf* (Fig. 87), a cast taken from the pudendum of *Etant Donnés* which resembles the indentation left by a bottom).[7] The jagged recessed shape is more like the indeterminate hole displayed in Courbet's *Nude with White Stockings* (c.1861) which is also simultaneously suggestive of both the anus and the vagina. (A copy of this image, an etching by Duchamp (Fig. 21), is also in this exhibition).

The ambiguity of the genitals is also a feature of Courbet's *The Origin of the World* which, despite claims of its pornographic status, in actual fact shows nothing at all of the genitals. A profusion of pubic hair, and a faint suggestion of the clitoris between tightly clamped labia majora, are all that can be seen. It is the prototypical image which appears to open everything to view only to withhold the very parts it is supposedly offering for us to see. In *Etant donnés* this disparity between what seems to be offered and what is actually given applies also to the act of voyeurism itself. To see without being seen is what the peephole promises and yet it is precisely when one's eye is up against the hole, straining to view the spectacle behind the door, that the viewer's body becomes most vulnerable and visible to others who can effortlessly feast their eyes on them.

The theme of reciprocal visibility is played out even more explicitly by Helmut Newton's *Self-portrait*. Here the photographer, the one who traditionally operates the controlling, objectifying gaze from outside the frame, is also in the frame; he is in the picture as he takes the picture. Indeed he presents himself as not only part of the spectacle for us, but also as watched by his wife as he constructs images of woman-as-spectacle.

The spectacle is very 'stagey': the model is in a highly clichèd pose designed to open out the body and lift the breasts for maximum visibility. To enhance the spectacle, we are given two views of her. Indeed, the contortions of the Mannerist nude, which work to maximise the surface area presented to the eye, are easily surpassed here by this simple double-sided view. Yet her exquisite body cannot hold our undivided attention: the puzzling space of representation overtakes our fascination with her form.

The image seems to pose a series of spatial questions which the viewer must resolve. The questions partly stem from the unorthodox incorporation of the photographer in the image. His position is not immediately obvious. But once we see him, we have to work out where he is. He is a diminished, hunched figure barely half the size of the statuesque nude and dressed in a flasher's overcoat, hardly a strong figure for identification. He seems to be looking back at us from the depth of the picture plane, taking our picture. The usual positioning of the viewer in the photographer's stead is thus disrupted by his stance facing us, coupled with his distance from us. Eventually we realise that the view we have is exactly what is in the photographer's viewfinder, the image is then like a closed-circuit: the photographer looking at himself with us oddly excluded, or at least, having great difficulty gaining visual anchorage in the image.

The disorientation is complicated by the full-length mirror. There is an initial failure to compute the mirror space as a mirror space, aided and abetted by the objects in the mirror which do not appear in the room: the mysterious legs without a torso, fabric on the floor. The 'disappearance' of these objects in the real space of the room is enabled by the drastic truncation of space between the model and the mirror. This truncation disrupts the scale of the image, making the distance between the model and her reflection appear unusually long. The disruptions to scale, space, and point of view keep the eye moving and uncertain, the gaze thus cannot easily alight upon the sumptuous visual feast that has so clearly been prepared for it.

Pistoletto's *Mirror Diptych* is also a disorienting image. This time we are incorporated into the picture, or more precisely, we are caught in the mirror-space of doubling. We cannot look without being seen. The two nudes are positioned on the threshold of the two worlds: we appear behind them in the virtual looking-glass world, at the same time as they appear to be pressing up against our world. The replication of the same pose partly undercuts this, reinforcing their artifice and underscoring their position as images at the surface of the mirror rather than beings in the world. The doubled pose is also strangely confronting: in its obvious theatricality it addresses us as viewers, despite the models' averted gaze. It is as though we are mocked, accused or in some way to blame for the ludicrousness of their melodramatic poses.

Despite this theatricality the images also resonate with a kind of quiet ambiguity. The image of Meret Oppenheim by Man Ray (replicated on the right) which is the prototype for the diptych, turns on a certain corporeal ambiguity: Oppenheim's heroic integration with the machine. Her inky pose at the printing press allows her to become an extension of it – her blackened hand and

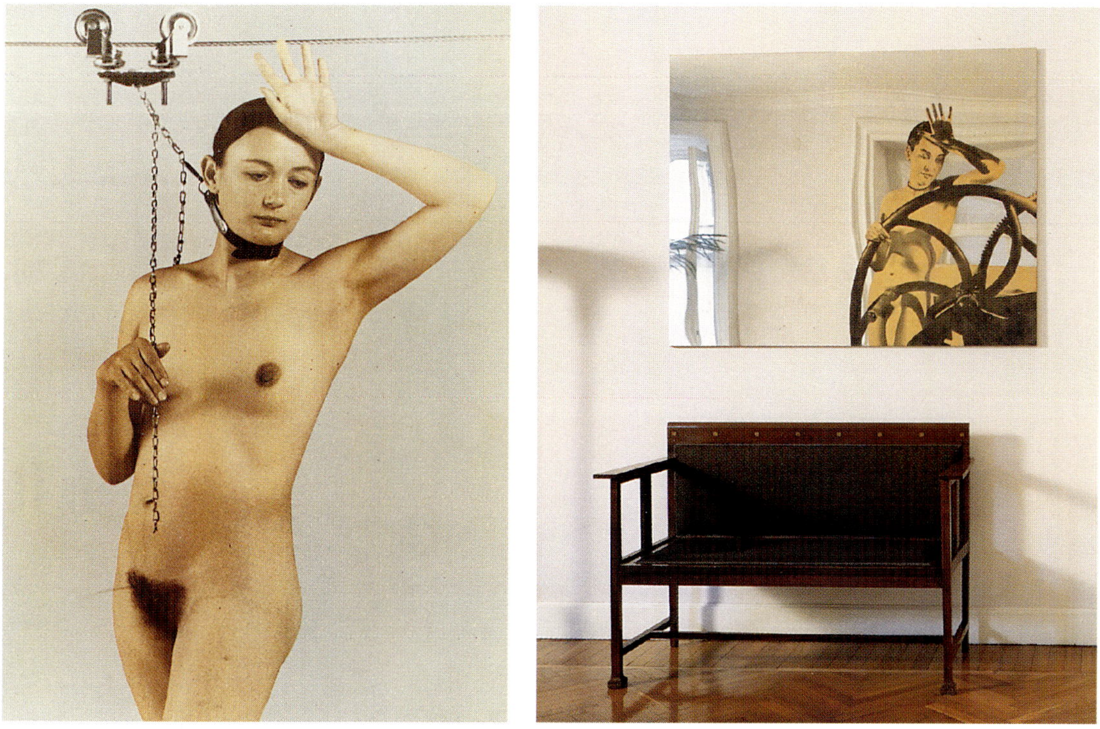

Fig. 114. Michelangelo Pistoletto *Mirror Diptych* (1962–71) Cat. 121

arm repeat the zig-zag of the spoke and wheel, her outstretched fingers echo the cogs. In turn, the press extends her, providing her with a very erect black phallus. The same pose, duplicated on the left half of the diptych, now stripped of the empowering wheel-veil, and secured by wires, pulleys and chains, becomes a stylised image of limp, feminine bondage recalling the pose of numerous other chained women of Art History such as Angelica and Andromeda. Yet in this instance there is a dead-pan humour about her captivity; indicated by the ironic repetition of Oppenheim's pose as a sort of camp gesture of lament, and underscored by the peculiar nature of the model's partial mobility.

Sitting between these works which tease, provoke, and yet frustrate voyeurism and the next category of works which court and complicate identification, are two works by Hans Bellmer: *La Demie-Poupée (Half-Doll)* (1971) (Fig. 91) and *The Doll's Games* (c.1940) (Fig. 116). At first sight these works may seem irredeemably fetishistic and our gaze at them necessarily voyeuristic: the impossible double legs of the doll, enclosed at both ends in little girl shoes and socks; the one-legged, one-armed half-doll with its one beacon-like, swollen breast. But these dolls are *so* blatantly perverse; they push objectification to the point where it collapses and dissolves into the kind of polymorphous perversity which is said to precede the capacity for objectification.

Similarly, the dolls, despite initial appearances, are highly unsuitable fetishes. A fetish should cover over the threat of castration posed by female genitals and thus foreclose upon the possibility of any continuity between male and female genitals. The dolls, on the other hand, demonstrate a slippage between phallic and vaginal forms. The half-doll's girly beribboned head is scored down the middle like a bottom or a penis-head, the torso thus functions as a shaft for the penis and a body for the womanly spherical breast. The only facial feature is a mouth that is distinctly vulval in form, a kind of play on lips worthy of Luce Irigaray. A similar gender indeterminacy is suggested by the doll. The doll's legs seem suitably phallic, as two independent entities they appear to commune on the seat of a chair, and yet they are also joined together to create a rosy vaginal form

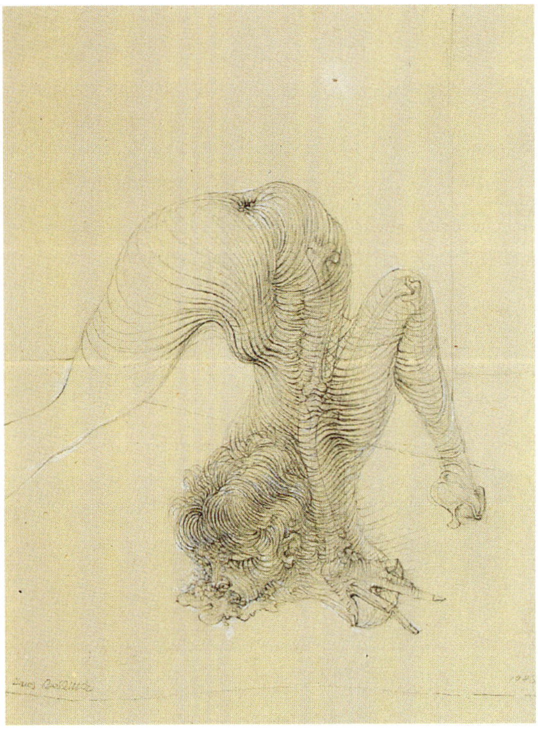

Fig. 115. Hans Bellmer *Erotic Drawing* (1948) Cat. 13

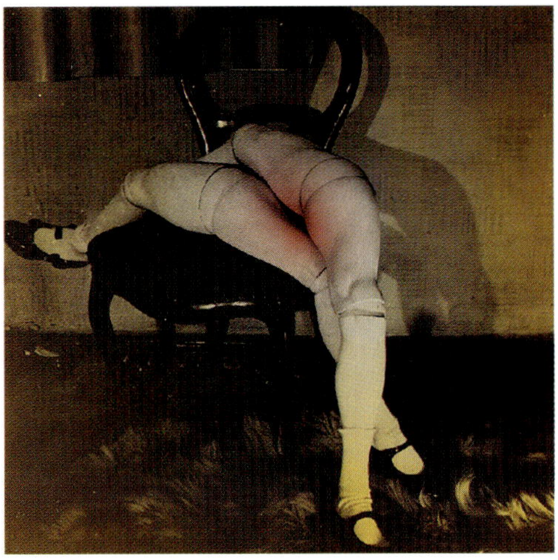

Fig. 116. Hans Bellmer *Variant from Les Jeux de la Poupée (The Doll's Games)* (c.1940) Cat. 14

accentuated by the pink tint overlaid on the photographic image. This body is even more unstable; the hair that should be between these legs is instead underfoot, as though substance and form have somehow drifted apart.

The next three works – Dennis Del Favero's *La Linea Sfumata (The Blurred Line)* (Fig. 117), Louise Bourgeois' *Janus Fleuri* (Fig. 101), and Robert Gober's *Man Coming Out of Woman* (Fig. 98) – are also sexually fluid or sexually indeterminate. They ask us to identify with them as bodies, as beings like us, despite their strange or attenuated forms. Yet they do not offer up any sense of "unity, mastery, and control" – the characteristics of the narcissistic identificatory gaze.[8] If narcissistic identification is about a kind of quasi-merger with a whole and more perfect being, then these images, like Bellmer's perverse constructions, make this kind of identification extremely difficult.

Del Favero's *La Linea Sfumata* is the most complete and identifiable form in this group. Yet the body is insubstantial, quivery and unstable like a mirage or an apparition which has emerged from the blackness and will sink back again out of sight. The outstretched figure is an uneasy amalgam of man and woman which gives the body a strange unevenness, as if the two forms are forces pulling the outer skin in opposite directions, making the body kink, shudder and refuse to settle.

The head and the Christ-like pose set the sex as in the first place masculine. The body is then feminised by the addition of breasts, an additional pubis, and attenuated arms. But the transformation is more than an addition of body parts, it utterly destabilises the original form. Not only does the surrounding blackness threaten to engulf the frail form, as it gnaws deeply at the edges of the body, there is also a subtle dissolution of the body: the face seems to be slipping away, and the arms are already returning to nothingness. Identification here is with a feminised man of sorrows – a figure in retreat, an image of passive, and possibly redemptive, suffering – but certainly not a masterful man of action.

The Gober work is also a disturbing image of gender indeterminacy. While the wax corner-piece is a very small slice of two bodies, it manages to conjure up the idea of two bodies. We imagine the emergent hairy leg complete with sock and shoe is just the visible tip of a fully-dressed man carried inside the woman's body. Her shapeless splayed legs fold back into the wall cavity where it is cleverly suggested the rest of her can be found.

His emergence or 'birth' suggests horrible pain, even death; he cannot emerge without splitting his mother-host apart. But then again surely he is stuck there, and hence he is her appendage, her captive. Woman becomes man. There is a very black sense of humour at play here which seems to mix the fact of man being 'of woman born,' the doubled subjectivity of pregnancy, and a kind of wacky mythological version of coming into being that bypasses gestation, like Minerva, Venus et al. The great power of this work is its capacity to make parts of bodies evoke whole bodies. This makes a measure of identification possible, but the situation of these bodies stuck (permanently it seems) together and in a wall cavity is hardly fortifying for the narcissistic ego.

The Louise Bourgeois sculpture is another fragment of being. It also combines both sexes, and thus demands the regard of a human form. While the work joins body-parts – it is formed by a rough vulva-like middle surmounted by two smooth penile ends – it does not evoke whole bodies in a manner which would render it as a mere part or parts. The combination of parts forms a very

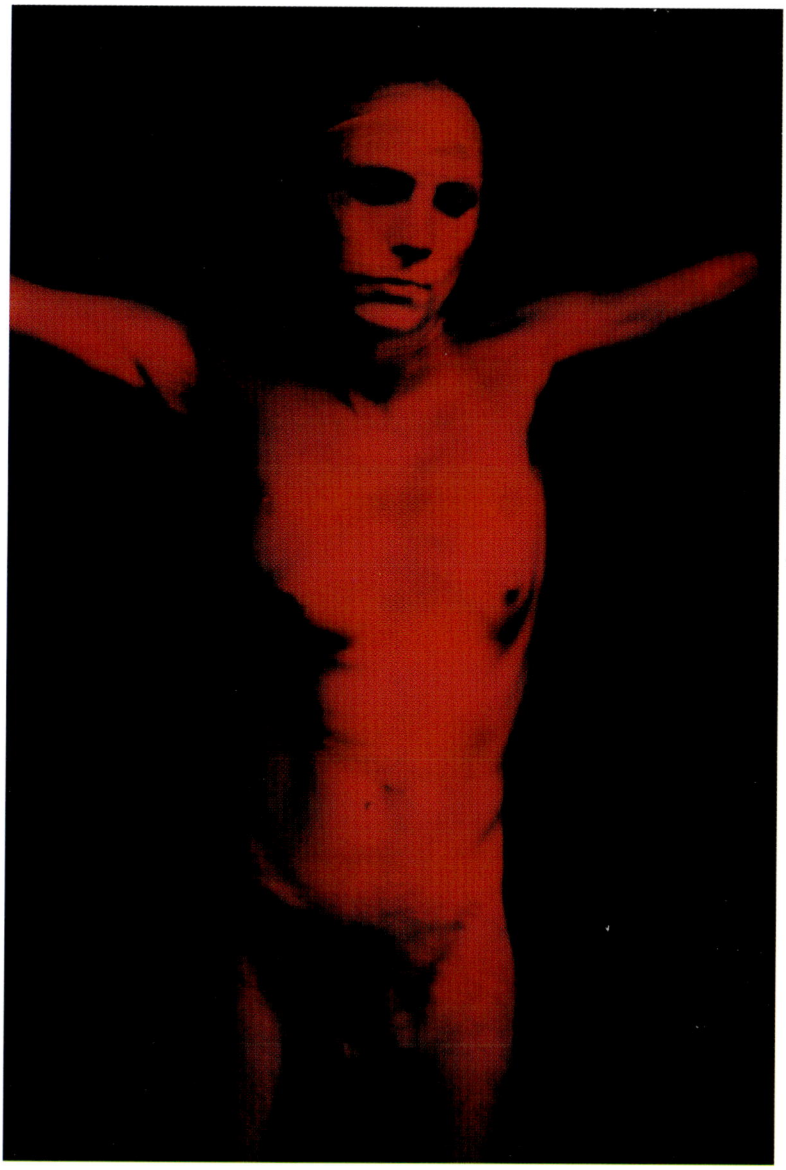

Fig. 117. Dennis Del Favero *La Linea Sfumata (The Blurred Line)* (1993) Cat. 40

resolved new whole, without the edgy uneasiness of the Del Favero, nor the sense of truncated form of Gober. Despite the sense of wholeness, it is not sufficiently 'like us' to enable much more than the most rudimentary identification: a sense of animate, tactile, carnal flesh.

The 'hole' images of Anish Kapoor (Fig. 23) have a similarly reduced identificatory effect. They evoke an attenuated, abstracted sense of a body; a body etherealised, stretched and thinned out into simple surfaces and depths, with rich dark orifices that draw the gaze into their measureless depths.

Finally, the third category of works are those that thwart the scopic economy of identification and objectification through a kind of suspension. These works, like the Salcedo with which I began, draw one in (move one, so to speak), in a manner not unlike identification, and yet there is an insistent otherness that refuses merger – the work has an objecthood that asserts itself. This suspended state between objectification and identification could be described as a kind of 'syncope.' Catherine Clément uses this term to describe the pauses or breaths, that suspend masterful being. These suspensions stretch from the everyday cough, to fainting and rapture.[9]

Ana Mendieta's *Silueta Works in Iowa* (1976–78) provide another example of such a suspension (Figs. 24 and 118). This series of works holds in suspension, not just identification and objectification, but also presence and absence and other seemingly contradictory states. For example, the photographs stand as documentation, testifying to the fact that 'Mendieta was there,' while also recording her total absence – they are but traces of traces, photographs of Mendieta's silhouette dug out of the earth. These images thus manage to balance a sense of the concrete and the enduring with an equally strong sense of the ephemeral and the evanescent.

Nowhere is this fine balance more evident than in the evocation of the body; there is a sense of the weight, constancy and materiality of the body and yet also its fragility, mobility and changeability. We cannot objectify this shape and force that moves across the landscape, it totally eludes us, yet it has an insistence and a materiality to which we cannot help attend. Identification is clearly engaged, we have a strong sense of an embodied 'fellow-traveller' moving through time and leaving her mark upon space, but we are given no body to objectify.

The imposition of her form on the earth is not an exercise in sovereignty over the landscape. On the contrary, it is a light touch that leaves no permanent impress. Her body is not thereby merged with nature. Mendieta draws herself upon the landscape, suggesting a different kind of affinity with the environment, a continuity that does not outlaw individuation. Figure and ground intermingle.

Yet 'oneness with the landscape' is not the predominant feeling evoked by these images. The locations are deserted, and often desolate, suggesting a challenge, if not a threat, to human dwelling and existence. Yet despite the suggestion of extinction, the traces of the solitary figure survive, evoking a strong sense of isolation, aloneness, even loneliness. In this last 'contradictory' combination of extinction and survival, life and death, Mendieta reminds us of Heidegger's notion of the wholeness of life being only achieved in death, when we are no longer 'there.'[10] It is thus not through our presence but through our passing, that we are finally individuated and complete. So too, it is in the suspension of our lived scopic regime – the suspension of syncope, the withdrawal of life in the little death of the sneeze or the cough – that the whole contradictory experience of the lived body is most fully evoked.

This formulation might seem to suggest that life and the life-like lie beyond viewing conventions. This is not what I want to suggest, all of the works discussed can be placed firmly within the debt or legacy of Realism; herein lies the possibility of legibility, recognition, and the

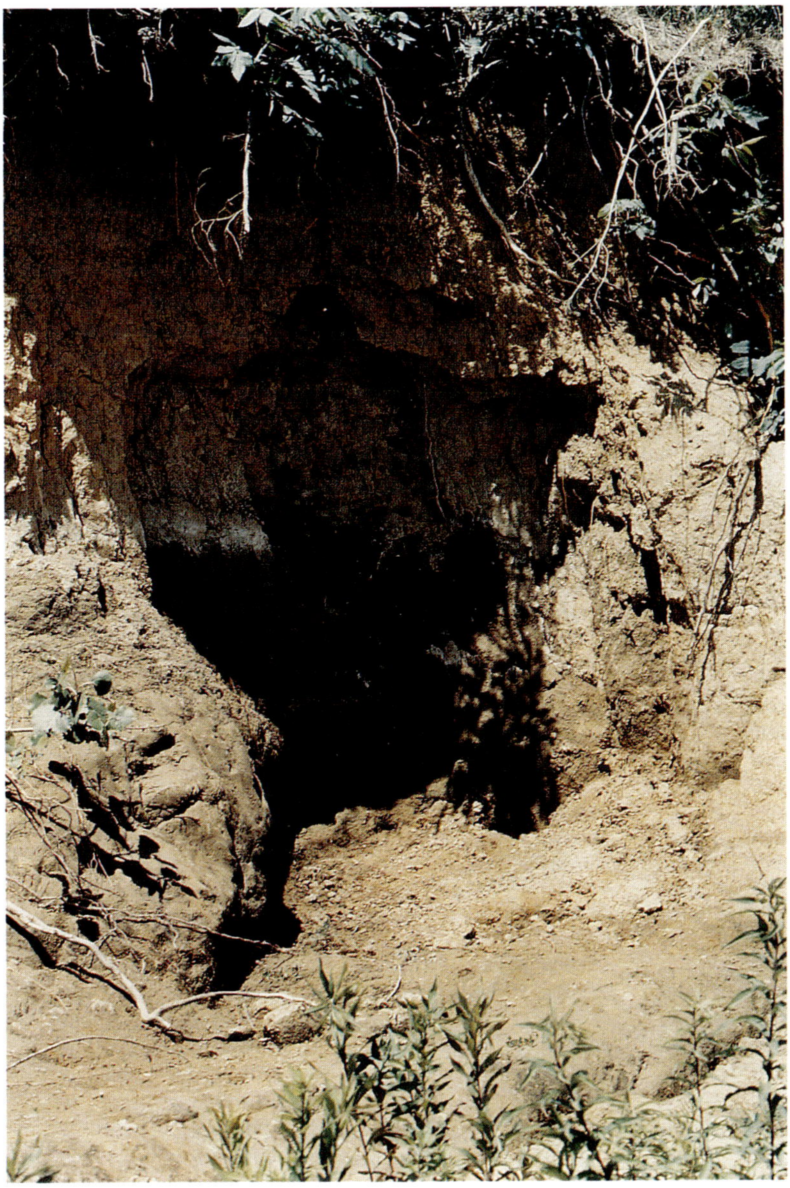

Fig. 118. Ana Mendieta *Silueta Works in Iowa*
earth/body work with carved earth, Carved Clay Bed, Iowa (1976–78) Cat. 95.

capacity to trigger the familiar push-pull of objectification-identification. Rather, what I want to emphasise is the unravelling of Realism that is internal to it. We saw this unravelling clearly manifested by Duchamp's reworking of *The Origin of the World*, a reworking which revealed a nascent regard for the unrepresentable within the heart of Realism. Within Realism itself there is thus a resistance to the very gaze it is said to constitute or presuppose.

It is when works of art both rely upon and push up against (or past) our viewing conventions in this fashion, that we are perhaps most disposed to being moved. We are drawn into the picture, so to speak, just as we are pushed out. The capacity to hold in tension contradictions – such as in/out, identification/objectification – such that both 'pulls' are equally felt, may well represent one of the key structures of aesthetic 'movement' in the late twentieth century. The suspense of syncope is thus not the absence of conventions, but rather the space of their fullest expansion. In this expansion or unfolding we may find the space to speak, once again, of affect and visual pleasure.

Notes

[1] Aristotle, *De Anima (On the Soul)*, trans. H. Lawson-Tancred (Harmondsworth: Penguin, 1986) 150. Thanks to Suzannah Biernoff for this reference.

[2] Hal Foster, Postmodernism: A Preface, *The Anti-Aesthetic: Essays on Postmodern Culture*, ed. H. Foster (Washington: Bay P, 1983) xv–xvi.

[3] Christine Battersby, "Situating the Aesthetic: A Feminist Defence," *Thinking Art: Beyond Traditional Aesthetics*, ed. A. Benjamin and P. Osborne (London: ICA, 1991) 35.

[4] Laura Mulvey, "Visual Pleasure and Narrative Cinema," *Screen* 16.3 (Autumn 1975).

[5] Innumerable writers have extended the literature on the gaze. See, for example, Mulvey's further comments, "Afterthoughts on 'Visual Pleasure and Narrative Cinema' Inspired by *Duel in the Sun*," *Framework* 15/16/17 (1981): 12–15. See also Mary Anne Doane, *The Desire to Desire: The Woman's Film of the 1940s* (Bloomington: Indian UP, 1987); Griselda Pollock, *Vision and Difference: Femininity, Feminism and the Histories of Art* (London: Routledge, 1988); Kaja Silverman, *The Threshold of the Visible World* (London: Routledge, 1996).

[6] Immanuel Kant, *Critique of Judgement*, trans. W. S. Pluhar (Indianapolis: Hackett, 1987) 54.

[7] See Craig Adcock's commentary on the male/female inversions of the erotic sculptures (*Female Fig Leaf* and *Object Dard*) in "Duchamp's Eroticism: A Mathematical Analysis," *Marcel Duchamp: Artist of the Century*, ed. R. E. Kuenzli and F. M. Naumann (Cambridge, Mass: MIT P, 1990) 161–2.

[8] Doane, *Desire to Desire* 15.

[9] Catherine Clément, *Syncope: The Philosophy of Rapture*, trans. V. A. Conley (Minneapolis: U of Minnesota P, 1994) 1–21.

[10] Martin Heidegger, *Being and Time*, trans. J. Macquarrie and E. Robinson (Oxford: Basil Blackwell, 1962) 281.

Sarah Faunce

Courbet: Feminist in Spite of Himself

As the title of this essay implies, it is my premise that there is, with respect to Courbet's conception of woman, a noticeable gap between the life and the art. Much critical attention has been given, ever since the artist's lifetime, to his personality and behaviour: his so-called vanity or narcissism, his propensity for self-promotion, his deliberately unpolished personal style. Only in recent years has it become apparent how little relevance these traits have to the significance of his painting; or rather, where there is relevance, as in the case of his self-promotion, this has been newly understood as an aspect of the modernity of his Realist project to develop a new public for his work. In all this history of focus upon his personal behaviour, little attention has been given to his private attitudes towards women. In part this is because he so seldom expressed himself on the subject; even now, with the welcome publication by the American scholar Petra Chu of his complete Letters, we know little in detail about his private life, feelings and opinions. What we do know does not give a very promising picture; yet I will argue that while in his life he expressed an attitude of offhand exploitation and disparagement of women that was typical of his time, in his art Courbet revealed something very different. In examining the work, particularly in relation to the predominant female imagery of his time, we will find a deeply positive conception of woman across a wide range of subject matter, some of which has in the past presented difficulties for feminist thinkers.

Courbet's most lasting and affecting relationship with a woman appears to have taken place in his late twenties and early thirties. Virginie Binet was a local woman who bore him a son in 1847 and who left for Dieppe with her child in 1852. Learning of her departure, he responded in a letter of early 1852 to his friend Champfleury: "May life be good to her, if this is what she thinks she ought to do . . . to me, a married man is a reactionary."[1] By the age of 32 he had arrived at the conviction that in order to devote all his energy to the founding of a new kind of art he must not engage in what was, from the conventional perspective of his time, a bourgeois manner of life. In that patriarchal framework, marriage meant, for the man, the taking on of the full responsibility of home, household, children and wife as possession and upper servant. It meant becoming hostage to fortune and property; it meant establishing a position, however modest, in conventional society. All of this ran counter to Courbet's idea of what his real responsibilities were. His culture provided him with no alternative conception of sexual partnership; and so he wrote to his fellow countryman Francis Wey in July 1850 the well-known phrase, ". . . I have just embarked on the great wandering and independent life of the bohemian."[2] This was at a time when the word 'bohemian' still carried its full strength of meaning as gipsy and nomad, and was only beginning to be used to refer to the 'vie de Bohème' of the artists who lived a marginal existence at the edges of bourgeois society. Courbet's positive valuation of this life can be seen in one of his best-known paintings, *The Meeting*, also known under the title of *Bonjour, Monsieur Courbet*, painted in 1854 for his Montpellier patron Alfred Bruyas and now in the Musée Fabre in that city. Here we see the image of the artist as a proud male figure, moving freely in a world of men, with his life packed on his back. In such a group in that time, the figure of a woman could only have been an inferior, an encumbrance, or a complete outsider.

As a matter of practice, the bohemian and the bourgeois conceptions of woman were not so different. The bohemian accepted the bourgeois view of woman as property: he did not quarrel with it; he only rejected it for himself. For both, sexual encounters outside of marriage were taken for granted, and were for the most part casual or superficial. In his letters Courbet gives few details of his relationships; with the exception of Laure Bourreau, who belonged to the idyllic year of the stay in Saintonge in 1862–63, his best women friends were not his sexual partners. Though he is voluble in his letters in matters of art and politics, he speaks little of private, especially sexual feelings. One of his few specific comments about women is not one that is apt to endear him to an audience of our own day. He wrote in 1863 to his friend the social philosopher Pierre-Joseph Prudhon, "Woman, who has neither aesthetic nor dialectic faculties, must be subject and faithful to man."[3] Even taking into consideration the context – a long memorandum to Prudhon full of social-political aperçus, many of them quite valid, and written to a man who held the most drastic patriarchal, not to say misogynist views – this is hard to take. But in an age when only the most independent and well-financed women were able to be educated in any way that would truly develop their aesthetic faculties, let alone their dialectic ones, such views were not exceptional. In his private life and opinions in this area, Courbet was very much a man of his time.

But if in the written record we find no real evidence of anything that might be called a feminist tendency of thought, some very different conclusions emerge from the examination of Courbet's paintings. It is my argument that over the course of the 1850s and 1860s Courbet frequently turned to the female figure, in various contexts, to bear the crucial content of the new kind of art that he was trying to bring into being. In his insistence on the primacy of the real, on the tangible life of this earth, he was declaring war on that long tradition of the Ideal, in which the subtext always was that the Ideal (the lofty sky, the source of light, the intellect: the positive) represented the male principle, while the Real (the lowly earth, the fertile darkness, the body: the negative) represented the female. In the process of achieving his Realist project he created a number of powerful, memorable images of women, images that were notably at odds with the gender conventions of his time, just as they were at odds with the stylistic conventions which so effectively encoded those gender messages.

I take as a starting point for this argument Courbet's great manifesto painting, *The Painter's Studio* (Fig. 119). It was painted to be shown at the first *Exposition Universelle* in 1855; when it was not accepted for the Exhibition itself, Courbet went to work to create his own Pavillion of Realism, where this vast work together with 39 others were shown in one of art history's earliest independent one-man shows. This painting, with its immensely impressive, enigmatic groupings of figures drawn from all aspects of his own experience of life, makes very clear the strongly *public* nature of Courbet's art: the fact that he conceived of art as a means of addressing a large public, and that both his imagery and his way of painting were the embodiment of ideas about the role of art in society. This public character is something which Courbet takes from the very tradition that he is also opposing: the classical academic tradition, the tradition that had the full backing of the state and that was most prominently exemplified by Jean-Auguste-Dominique Ingres. Ingres' major pictorial statement about that tradition, *The Apotheosis of Homer* (Fig. 120)– shown at the 1855 Exhibition as the centrepiece of an official retrospective of his work – provided Courbet with a model in two ways. It is an example of public art with large public meanings about the nature of art, and it is composed symmetrically, with groups of figures on either side of the central figure of

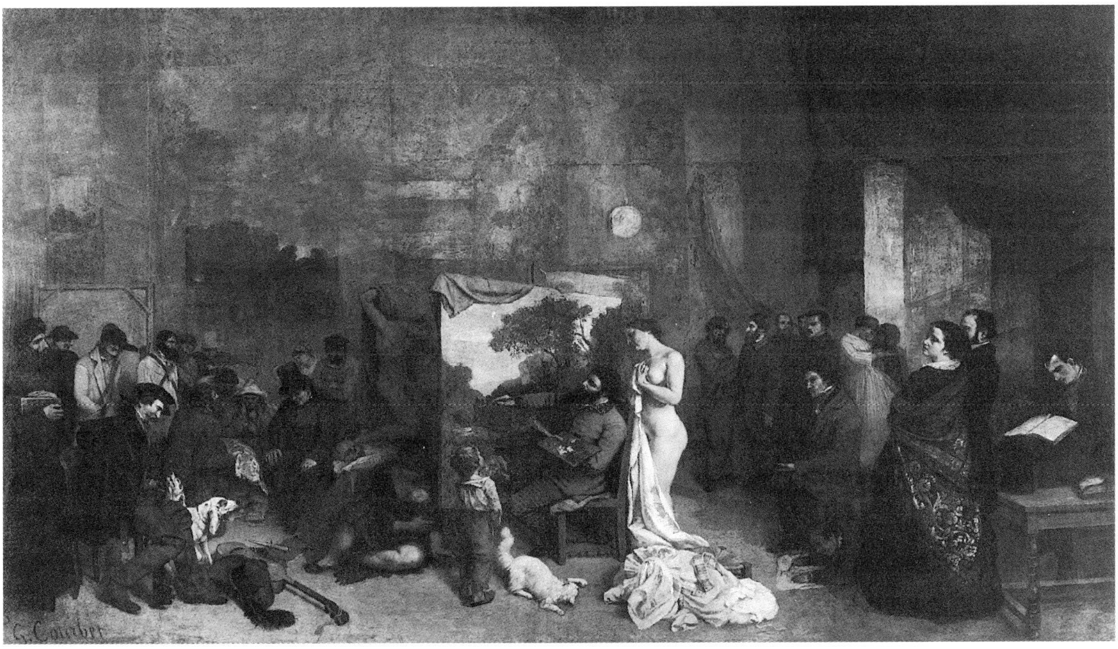

Fig. 119. Gustave Courbet *The Painter's Studio* (1855) Ref. 13

the artist – in Ingres' case Homer, the poet of ancient Greece; in Courbet's case himself, the painter from Ornans.

With this last difference we begin to see the much more important ways in which *The Studio* differs radically from *The Apotheosis*. Ingres' painting is concerned with the fixed canon of classical art, a tradition of high idealism in which the most recent figures are those of Poussin and Corneille, taking their places among the much larger number of poets from the world of Greece and Rome. These personages (regardless of what their own historical circumstances or varieties of expression may have been) are conceived by Ingres in terms of the values of perfection, closure, and hierarchy. The pyramidal composition leads up to the topmost figure of Homer, at the moment of being crowned as the father of classical narrative poetry. The whole structure is spatially placed at a distance from the viewer, whose position is assumed to be that of a worshipper of the virtues of this rigidly structured ideal world.

Courbet's painting stands as a powerful critique of all of this. He conceives of the artist as a living being within the real world, and of the artist's studio as a microcosm of that world. The artist is at the center, but he is not raised, he is not receiving homage; he is a worker, making a

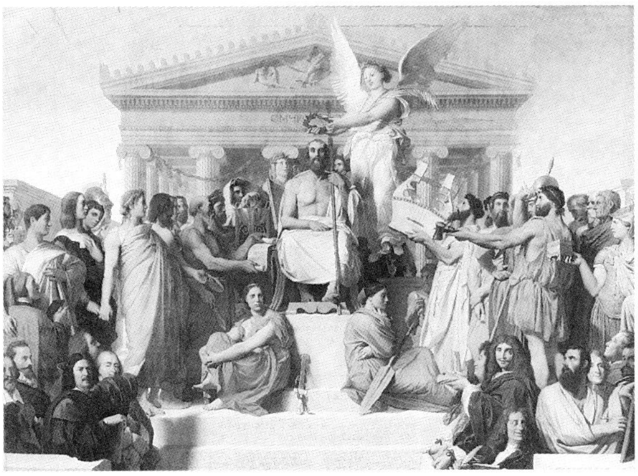

Fig. 120. Ingres *The Apotheosis of Homer* (1827) Ref. 23

painting. He is at the center because, according to the Fourierist beliefs held by Courbet, the arts are central to human society – not as a distant ideal but as a way of understanding the life of one's own time. The viewer of *The Studio* is not kept at a distance: Courbet constructs a pictorial space that his audience can experience as being fully commensurate with their own, and he fills it with figures entirely of his own time.

At the center of this living world Courbet represents himself as a painter at his easel, painting a landscape. To his right stands a partially draped nude model; to his left a small boy gazes up at his work. By this time in the nineteenth-century the presence of a nude woman in an artist's studio was taken for granted as an emblem of his authenticity as an artist – a kind of symbol of professional status in a visual culture in which the display of the female body played a major role. But in *The Studio* the nude woman is not on display in the usual sense; rather she operates as a partner in several dualities: male/female, artist/subject, model/painting. The image represented on the canvas, the work in progress, is not that of a nude but of a landscape, recognisably one from Courbet's native province. But the close presence of the model links her with the painting, thus setting up a parallel between woman and nature. Such a parallel has normally been seen by feminist thinkers as a denigration of the female, as indeed it was in the ancient hierarchal tradition according to which the female is equated with the passivity of nature, while the active

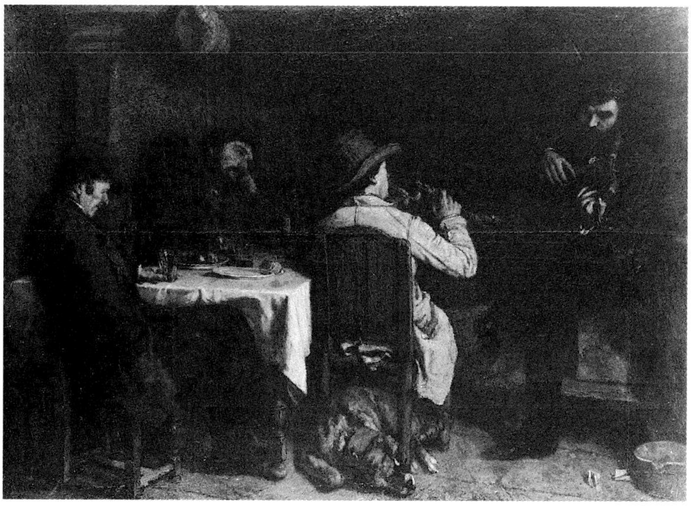

Fig. 121. Gustave Courbet *An After-Dinner at Ornans* (1848–49) Ref. 5

world of culture is the province of the male. But for Courbet, to whom the natural environment of his boyhood in the Franche-Comté represented the highest positive value, this gendered hierarchy was invalid. The earth was not in any way inferior to the sky. The very realism which led him to create a new imagery born of the actual life and landscape of his own country people represented a profound critique of this age-old kind of thinking about nature and woman, in which primacy was given to constructing a distance from both, and to inventing a realm of intellect and idealism from which to look down upon both as being beneath the level of culture. Courbet, on the contrary, was immersed in the Real: its representation *was* culture.

Seen in this light, Courbet's subtitle for *The Painter's Studio* – "A real Allegory, summing up a period of seven years of my artistic life" – appears as a statement of fact rather than the pretentious phrase it has often been taken to be. From the late 1840s onward his driving ambition had been to create "a living art" by means of the representation of the people of his own class and region, shown for the first time in their actual, unvarnished character, and given by the painter's

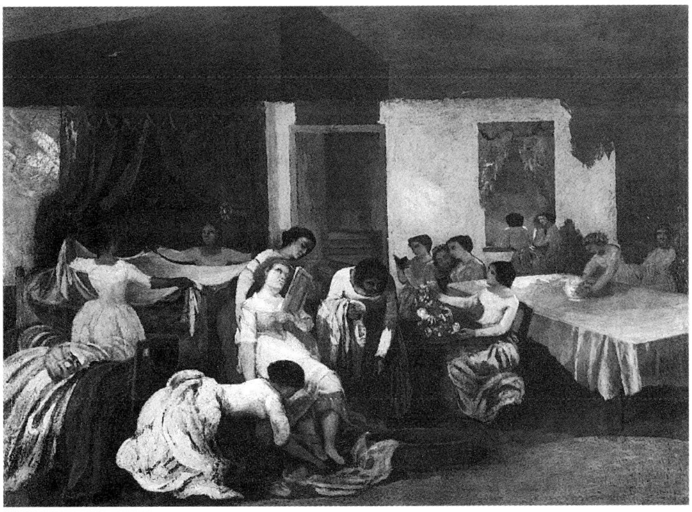

Fig. 122. Gustave Courbet *The Preparation of the Dead Girl* (mid-1850s) Ref. 14

work the dignity of high art. Unlike the typical provincial artist of his time, whose talents drew him to Paris where he could learn the skills that would enable him to rise above his origins, Courbet followed the same path but with the purpose of using those skills to enable him to represent the reality of his origins. His first large major painting, *An After-Dinner at Ornans* (Fig. 121), was also the most successful, having been shown in the Salon of 1849 during the brief interval of the Second Republic. In it he creates for the first time the kind of wholly accessible pictorial space that is present on a grander scale in *The Studio*. Within it he represents four countrymen in their private lives, dining, smoking, and contemplatively listening to the music played by one of their own circle. Very different in subject but equally masculine in theme is *The Stonebreakers*, shown at the Salon of 1850–51 along with *The Burial at Ornans*, and to the same hostile critical reception. *The Burial*, like *The Studio* later, was a kind of summation, taking in as it does a large group of citizens, equally black-clad but strongly gendered in the separate groupings of men and women.

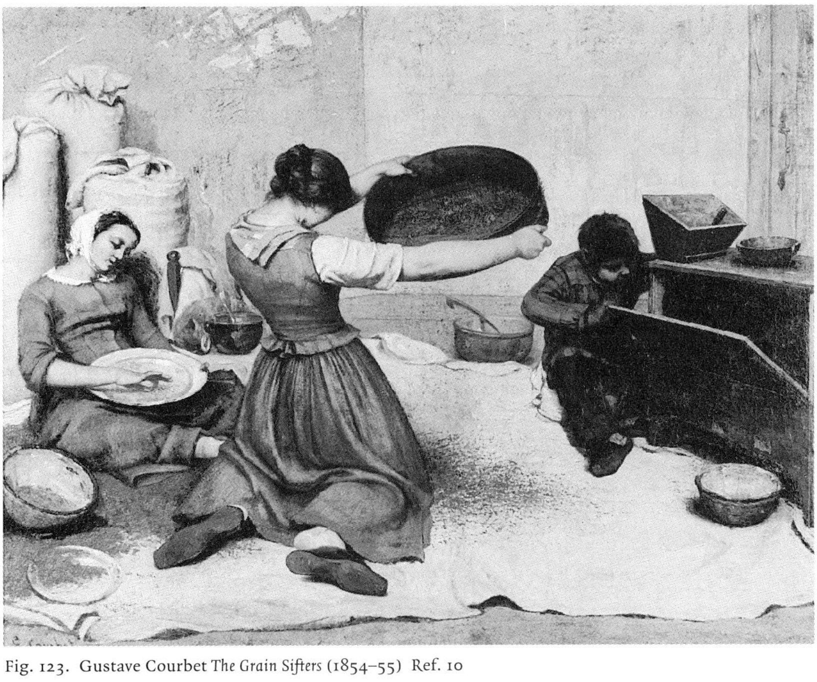

Fig. 123. Gustave Courbet *The Grain Sifters* (1854–55) Ref. 10

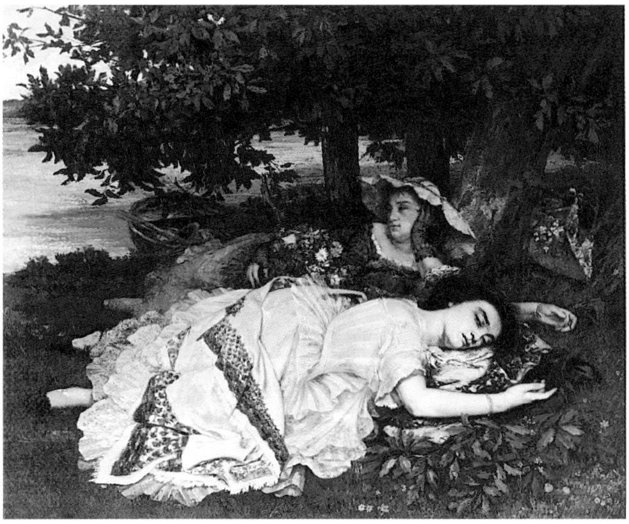

Fig. 124. Gustave Courbet *The Young Ladies on the Banks of the Seine* (1856–57) Ref. 22

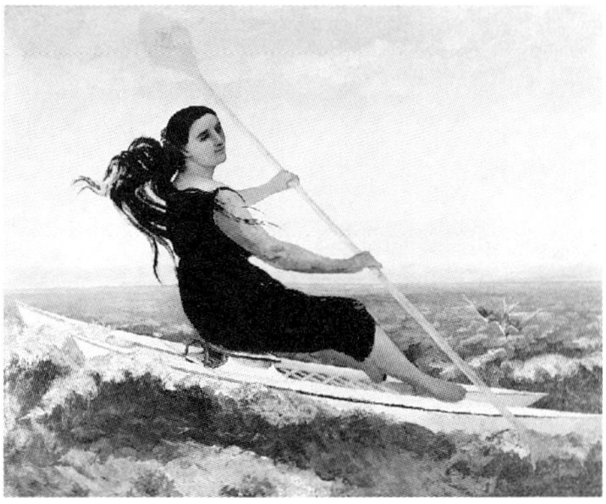

Fig. 125. Gustave Courbet *The Woman in a Podoscaphe* (1865) Ref. 18

During the early years of the 1850s, the focus of these paintings began to shift toward figures of women. In such works as *The Sleeping Spinner*, *The Young Ladies of the Village*, *The Preparation of the Dead Girl* (Fig. 122) and *The Grain Sifters* (Fig. 123), the female figure assumes the primary content of Courbet's Realist project. He used the phrase "moeurs de campagne" – "customs of the country" – to describe the theme of these paintings of women who play essential economic and social roles in the rural community. The most striking of these from the point of view of Courbet's feminism is *The Grain Sifters*. The figure that dominates the composition is heroic without being thereby masculinised, in the manner of the traditional imagery of female heroes. She is young, healthy and strong, with a narrow waist and broad hips, and her heroism consists not of military victory but of work, which sustains the life of the family and the community. Her right arm is raised in a gesture reminiscent of the warriors in David's *Oath of the Horatii*; but these are figures of men who are vowing to go to war, while opposite them sit their wives and sisters-in-law, drooping in impotent mourning at the prospect of death and destruction, true to the gender conventions of neoclassical art. *The Grain Sifters* is an image of woman that challenges these conventions and makes of this female figure a statement of action, modernity and power.

A very different kind of working woman is the subject of *The Young Ladies on the Banks of the Seine* (Fig. 124), one of the few paintings in which Courbet drew his imagery from contemporary urban, rather than provincial life. In typical fashion, he went straight for an aspect of that life which the Parisian bourgeoisie would very much rather not have had brought to their attention. Represented in the painting are two women of a type increasingly found in the Paris of that time: country women, in fact, but women whom the long term shift from a rural to an industrial economy was bringing to the city in ever greater numbers. There they found what work they could, in the harsh struggle to avoid the twin pitfalls of beggary and professional prostitution. Whether the two figures in the painting have already succumbed to the second of these fates, or whether they are simple *grisettes* – women who toiled at manual work during the week and willingly allowed men to pay for their favours on weekend jaunts – cannot be determined and does not really matter. It is clear that they are represented here in their role as sexual companions, and thereby as women who in their worldly experience are not passive in relation to men. The issue of 'the male gaze' is thrust back at the viewer by the heavy-lidded, knowing gaze of the foreground figure, whose sexual display is essentially a matter of petticoat, bodice and thinly gloved hands. In his title to this painting Courbet used the word *demoiselles* in an even more pointed way than he had done in his Ornans painting of young women on a country walk, *Young Ladies of the Village*. The ironic reference to the status of 'ladies' is directed not at either the rural or the urban women represented in the two paintings, but against the rigidities of class and the fixed assumption that neither the indigenous or the displaced countrywomen were valid subjects of serious art.

In yet another context, that of the Normandy coast in the mid 1860s, Courbet invented an extraordinary image of a woman that ran counter to all the gender conventions of his time. The resort towns of Trouville and Deauville, where Courbet worked in the summers of 1865 and 1866, were flourishing as part of the new seaside culture of Second Empire Parisians. Though Courbet painted several portraits of society people staying there, he did not, like Boudin, take as a subject the actual life of the visitors promenading on the beach; most of his work at Trouville is pure seascape. But from his observations of one unusual seaside visitor he constructed an image unlike any that emerged from those years during which the life of leisure on the Channel coast became an important theme in French painting. He and others had noted a woman who was remarkable for going out on the water on her own in a newfangled catamaran-type vessel powered by a double-ended oar. *The Woman in a Podoscaphe* (Fig. 125) is an image of woman as adventurer and free spirit, a woman totally self-propelled, whose loose hair, bare arms and legs and spirit of autonomy run counter to the period's very firm conventions of feminine attitude and deportment. Courbet called the painting his *Modern Amphitrite*,[4] with this classical reference to the goddess of the sea clearly placing the work in ironic reference to all the Venuses and Dianas that regularly filled the galleries of the Paris Salons. These were images, like that of the *Birth of Venus* shown in 1863 by Alexandre Cabanel (Fig. 2), which used the classical themes in order to display to viewers the qualities of the female they most desired to see: smooth rosy flesh, pliant curving forms, passive accessibility. Against this soft porn standard, Courbet's painting stands as an antithesis powerful enough to be seen as a counterattack upon prevailing norms both in painting and in the conception of woman.

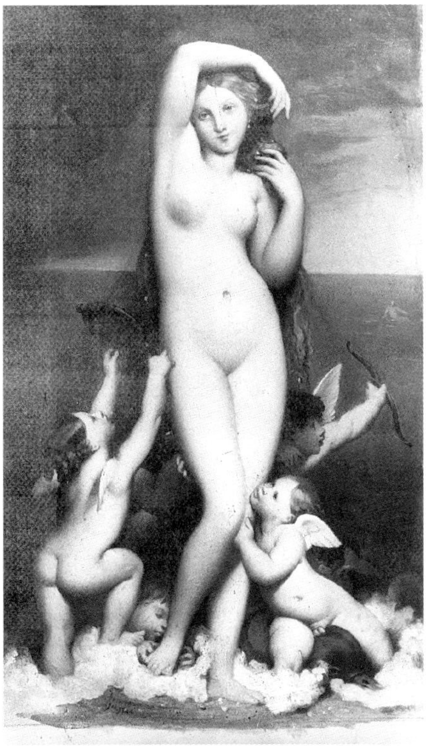

Fig. 126. Ingres *Venus Anadyomene* (1848) Ref. 26

The artist to whom Cabanel, Bouguereau, Gerôme and the others looked as their ideal and master of this mode was of course Ingres, whose conception of the female nude is at its heart. His *Venus Anadyomene* (Fig. 126) was first conceived as early as 1808, though not completed and shown until 1848. This was a period during which the representation of the female nude came be seen as central to the academic tradition, and Ingres was a major contribution to this development. In this tradition the female nude figure is conceived in terms of an ideal of perfection, as an *exemplum* of completely controlled form, which can by definition possess no further potential and therefore moves away from the direction of life. Ingres' figure of Venus is perfectly contained within her linear silhouette and her smooth surfaces; her attributes are suavity, pliancy and objectification. Ingres' mastery puts a check on the soft porn qualities that appear in the work of

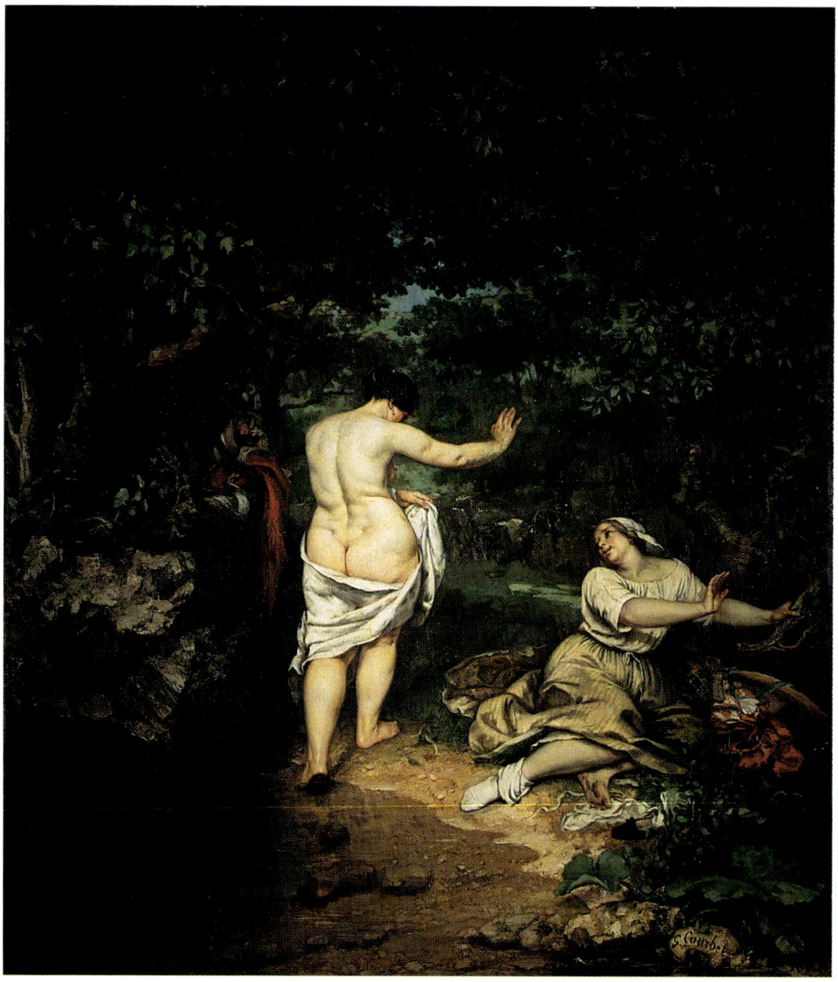

Fig. 127. Gustave Courbet *The Bathers* (1853) Ref. 7

his less gifted followers, but a figure such as this is nonetheless a powerful statement of a certain kind of male fantasy of female perfection: soft, smooth, passive and as malleable as a doll.

The theme of Venus, born of the sea, is also part of a larger idea of the relation of the female nude to nature, of which the theme of Diana bathing in the forest is another example. The image of the female nude as Bather in a landscape setting, without specific classical reference, was emerging during this period as a significant subject in the academic tradition. Courbet's first important statement of this subject was *The Bathers* (Fig. 127), shown in 1853, only five years after Ingres' *Venus*. Without doubt it was composed as a kind of principled insult to the tradition of ideal perfection represented by Ingres. The painting has for so long been lampooned and laughed at that people have tended to lose sight of this fact, thus granting continuing life to the conventional view of the time, that Courbet was only capable of painting vulgarity and awkwardness. Instead, the painting is a powerful statement of the problems inherent in the theme of the Bather: the issue of linking woman and nature through the use of the artificiality of the ideal nude; and the even wider issue of the traditional meaning of that linkage, to which Courbet's work represents a continuing challenge. For the age old assumption of the greater closeness of the female to the natural world was only part of the larger hierarchical notion of the intrinsic lowness of all things earthly and concrete, as opposed to the higher realm of intellect and the ideal, always associated with the male. Courbet's primary challenge to these hierarchies was empirical and social, not sexual; but in the course of building an oeuvre which insisted on the primacy of the actual, the world of ordinary people, of animals and natural environments, he displayed an understanding of the degree to which these hierarchies signified a lack of respect both for the female and for the natural world.

Despite what might be called the definitive put-down embodied in the Montpellier *Bathers*, Courbet continued during the following decade or so to struggle with this conflicted theme of the female nude in the landscape. True to his sense of the contradictions inherent in the theme, he neither aimed for nor achieved the sense of the easy relationship between the figures and the natural setting that critics required and that less complex artists could succeed in accomplishing. In *The Young Bather* in the Metropolitan Museum (Fig. 128), the figure of the nude is not fully integrated with the landscape, and one's sense of her as a naked and probably chilly young woman testing the temperature of the water runs counter to the symbolic demands intrinsic to this theme. Her discomfort seems both physical and existential, as though she asks herself, What am I doing here? In the Petit Palais' *Three Nudes* (Fig. 129), the tension has become aggressive. The pose of the central figure is a kind of parody of the pose of Ingres' *Venus*, in which the raised arm and the bent knee, attributes of grace and fluidity in the Ingres, become elements of torsion and anxiety. A strange interpersonal narrative seems to grip these women, as the central figure is torn between the poles of the solid, long-haired seated figure at the right and the more active, black haired figure at the left (a clothed figure, not a nude, despite the title). In the *Seated Bather* we see a greater integration of the figure with the setting, but in an unconventional way. Here the nude figure assumes the massiveness and strength of the rock on which she is seated. The way in which her body is constructed, and the way in which it dominates the pictorial field imparts a powerful sense of energy, equal to that of the natural forces surrounding her. We are very far indeed from the cool and totally controlled world of the perfect Ingres nude.

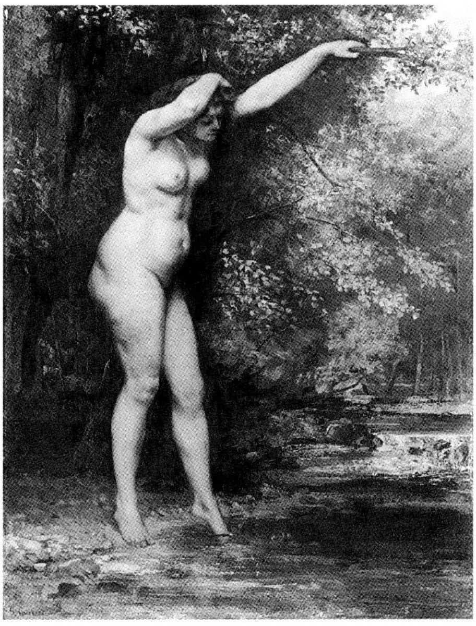

Fig. 128. Gustave Courbet *The Young Bather* (1866) Ref. 21

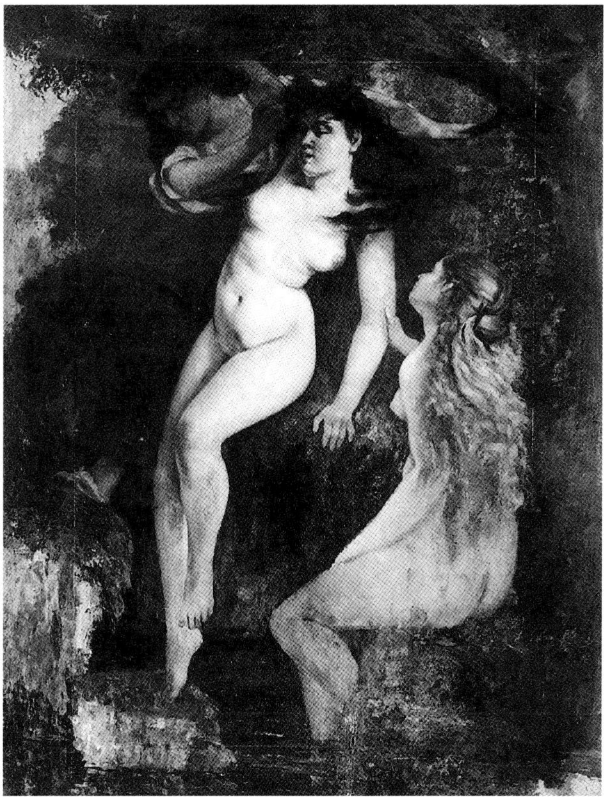

Fig. 129. Gustave Courbet *Three Nudes* (1868) Ref. 17

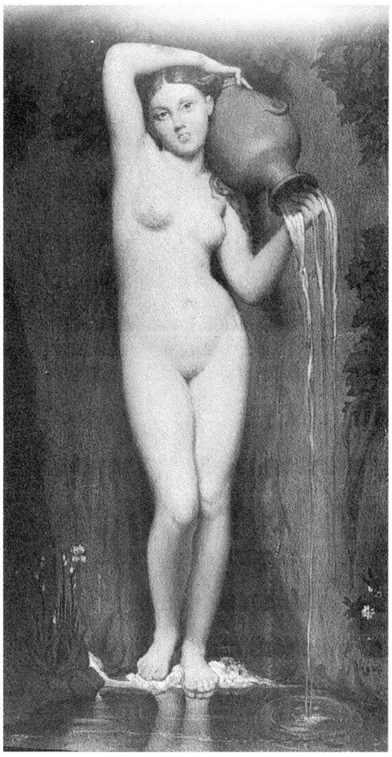

Fig. 130. Ingres *The Source* (1856) Ref. 24

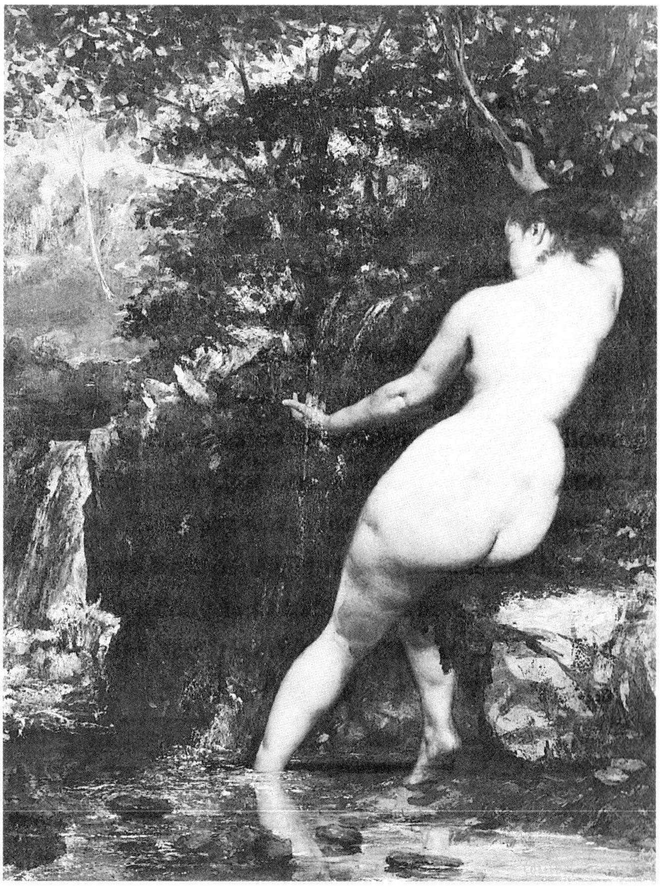

Fig. 131. Gustave Courbet *The Source* (1868) Ref. 16

In the theme of 'The Source' one can explore the great contrast between Ingres, the solidly established hero of the Academy, and Courbet, the younger man who is struggling to achieve a new interpretation of reality. The word 'source' has the same specific meaning in French as in English: that is, a place where water rises out of the earth to become a stream or pool, thereby giving rise to the metaphor of origin or fountainhead. Its concrete referent, the emergence of life-giving water, is a natural phenomenon of great significance to human beings. In Ingres' painting *The Source* in the Louvre, dated 1856, the theme is given form by a female nude figure which combines the cool clarity of marble with the rosy glow of flesh (Fig. 130). She stands in a classic pose closely related to that of the *Venus Anadyomene*; here the raised arms that display the curves of her torso are holding an amphora out of which pours water into the shallow pool at her feet. Behind her, like a niche, stands a wall of rock with touches of vegetation. This fragment of natural background is subsumed into the purely symbolic statement, in which both the figure and the stream of water can be admired from a distance for their beauty, with no risk of feeling the force of either. Courbet's painting of the same title of 1868 (Fig. 131), now in the Musée d'Orsay, is perhaps the most successful of his attempts to reconcile what were for him the intrinsic contradictions of the theme. Here too a female nude is placed in the context of a source of water, but in a very different way. The figure has the irregularities and disproportions of an actual woman, and the act of putting out her hand under the water as it pours forth from the ground establishes a direct connection between her own physical being and that of the springing water. Though a sizeable figure, she is surrounded by the activity of nature: the stream at her feet, the rocky bank, the trees and the small fall of water in the middle-ground. But Courbet's sense of reality is too great for such a theme, in which the female nude is called upon to take on so much symbolic baggage; he has not got Ingres' traditional certainties, and has not yet achieved his own solutions in this particular area.

Something different is happening in the series of paintings Courbet made in the mid 1860s, all titled *The Source of the Loue* (Fig. 17). The Loue is the small river that runs through Ornans, passing closely by the house where Courbet was born. Its source is in the hills not far away from the town. Like the other sources in the region of the Doubs, its waters are the foundation of human cultivation. The site of its source, a deep cave in a rocky cliff, is an impressive one; Courbet makes it more impressive by transmuting it into a work of art. The viewpoint he constructs is close enough for the viewer to feel the magnetic pull of the dark cave, the rushing water, and the powerful rocks, their mineral forms endowed by the action of the brush with an almost animal force. Even before the noted painting *The Origin of the World* (Fig. 15) was as well known as it now is, these paintings of the Source of the Loue could be experienced as metaphors of female sexuality, in their structure and in their theme of the life-giving energies of the flowing waters. Now that *The Origin of the World* is happily settled in the Musee d'Orsay, the rhyming between the two paintings is readily available to the eye. Both paintings speak of the positive forces of nature, expressed alike in the site of female sexuality and procreation and in the origin of the productive rivers. Each is linked to the other, not symbolically but analogically. The subject of *The Origin of the World* has been called the "site of castration anxiety," in classic Lacanian manner; but for Courbet it was not the site of fear but of female sexual energy, as natural and positive as the energies of the river's source. Thus his linking of the natural world with the female body is not a denigration of either; Courbet's representation of each of them endows them with abundant meaning and vitality.

Another kind of analogy between the positive force of flowing water and the female body can be found in those paintings in which a woman is depicted with long, curling, waving hair that flows energetically down her back. Probably the best known of these paintings is the *Portrait of Jo, the Beautiful Irish Girl*, a composition that exists in four versions. Jo Heffernan, the model and mistress of Whistler whom Courbet had met in Trouville, was Courbet's model for the painting. He shows her gazing intensely into a mirror, a format drawn from traditional *Vanitas* paintings. But she is not composed as an image of warning. All around her face and shoulders springs the electric energy of her dark red hair, flowing with the natural abundance of a waterfall. Knowing from Courbet's landscape paintings how highly he valued the moving waters of rivers, streams and the waves of the sea, we can be confident – as we would in any case from the way it is painted – that the lively flowing hair of women was given the same high value. As in the case of *The Origin of the World* and *The Source of the Loue*, the rhyming of the two natural elements reinforces the metaphorical link between them. Another way to measure Courbet's positive feeling for the sexual energies of the female is to compare the image of Jo with the characteristic imagery of the long flowing hair of women as we see it in the Symbolist tradition, from Rossetti to Munch, where the motif carries a fierce charge of entrapment and threat to the male. That figuring of male sexual terror, so predominant in Symbolist art, is totally foreign to the imagery of Courbet.

With the painting called *The Sleepers* (Fig. 132) in the Petit Palais in Paris we come to Courbet's highest achievement in the painting of the nude female body. As in *The Origin of the World*, the body is seen for its own sake. The symbolic connection with nature disappears, giving way to the real connection, constructed in terms of the sexual energies of the female body. The setting is not nature but a Paris bedroom. The lesbian theme was of course transgressive; while it was widely available in Paris in literature and in popular prints, it was far from being acceptable in high art. Courbet's treatment of the theme in this instance arose through the circumstances of the commission of the painting by one Khalil Bey, a wealthy and somewhat notorious Turkish diplomat living in Paris, who had asked Courbet for a second version of his *Venus and Psyche*, a subject calling for two female nudes (it was he who also commissioned *The Origin of the World*).[5] Courbet chose instead to paint an entirely new composition in which the subject exists on its own without justification in classical narrative. Eventually of course it made trouble for him; when Khalil Bey went bankrupt and had to sell his collection after the Franco-Prussian war, the appearance of this painting in a shop window in 1872 brought a flurry of denunciations of Courbet's immorality to the police. It is not the subject, however, that gives the painting its quality or its significance as an image of woman; these come from the force and character of the painting as a work of art.

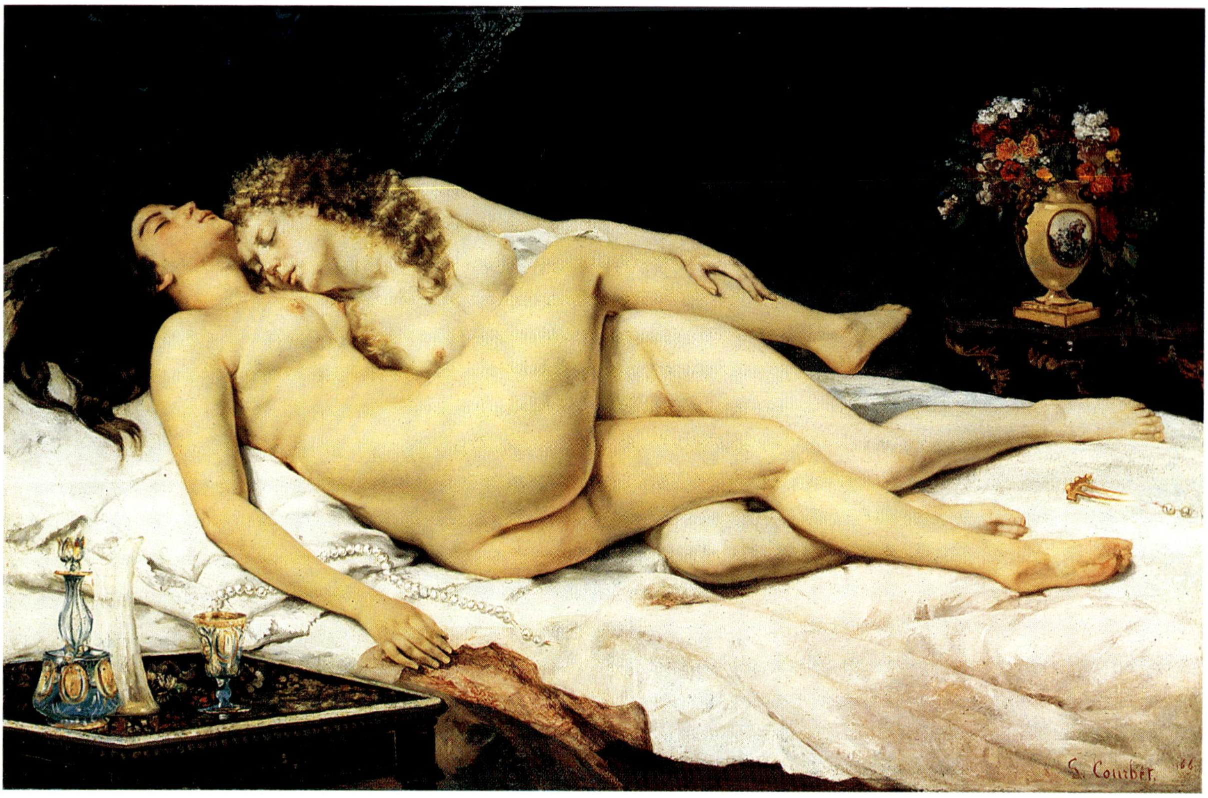

Fig. 132. Gustave Courbet *The Sleepers* (1866) Ref. 15

One way of assessing the power of this painting from the point of view of Courbet's conception of woman is to compare it with an important painting of his own, made during the same year: *The Woman with a Parrot* at the Metropolitan Museum (Fig. 133). While *The Sleepers* was unknown to the public before 1872, *The Woman with a Parrot* was shown in the Salon of 1866, to critical and public acclaim. And strong as the painting is, it is possible to see in it some of the aspects of style that belonged to the Salon tradition of the nude: the smooth, almost shiny flesh and the sense conveyed of a woman who is engaged in a conscious, voluntary act of self-display. Although *The Sleepers* has often been discussed in terms of erotic display, and though certainly this was a motivation for Khalil Bey's commission, such is not the primary experience one has in the

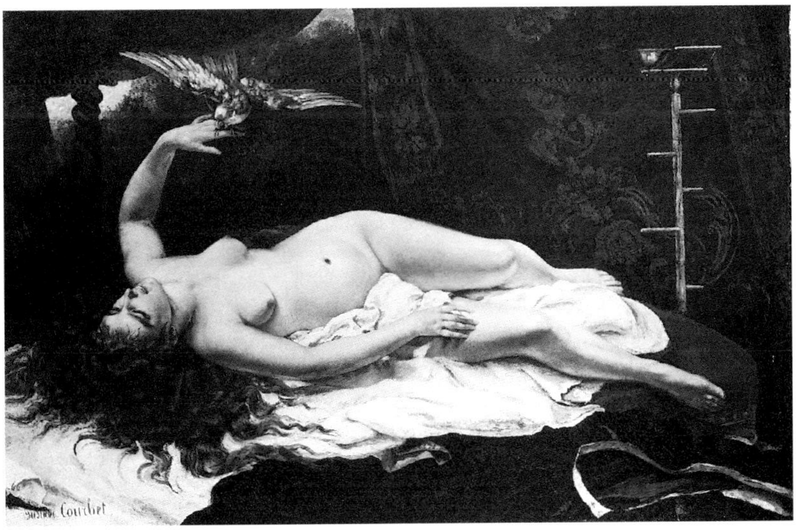

Fig. 133. Gustave Courbet *The Woman with a Parrot* (1866) Ref. 19

presence of the painting itself. In part this is a result of the fact that the figures are profoundly unself-conscious in their experience of passionate absorption with one another. Courbet has achieved something rare and remarkable in this painting: the depiction on canvas, through the painting of the flesh and the facial expressions of these women, of an image of consummated desire.

A final comparison further illuminates the deep gulf between Courbet's conception of woman and that of the prevailing neoclassical tradition exemplified by Ingres. *The Turkish Bath* (Fig. 134) – completed only a few years earlier than *The Sleepers* and also a part of the Khalil Bey collection – is an erotic fantasy constructed out of conventions of painterly style which themselves can be read as a complex of gender conventions. The pictorial space is filled to bursting with female flesh, curves upon curves of smooth surfaces and intertwining limbs which in their extreme smoothness and linear containment are an invitation less to passionate caress than to a kind of cool lust. The indolent bodies fall into poses that suggest the passivity and infinite malleability of bodies that act only under the motivation of another being, not of their own. Ingres constructs this enclosed world, itself based on the Orientalist motifs of the period, by means of figures often derived from

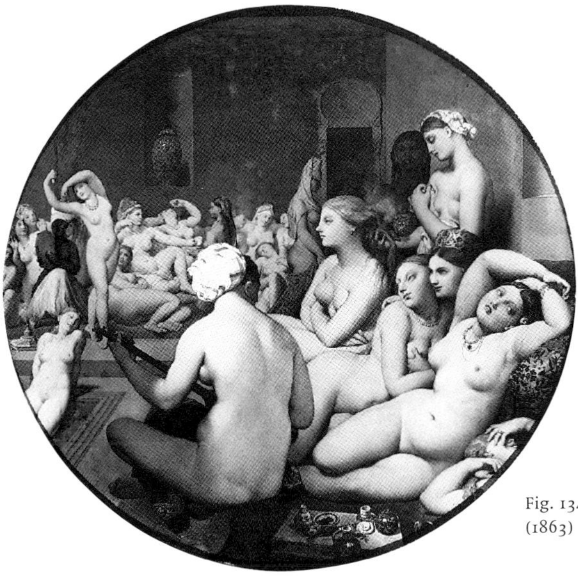

Fig. 134. Ingres *The Turkish Bath* (1863) Ref. 25

his own earlier works, such as the *Odalisque with Slave* and the *Valpinçon Bather*, a painting that dates back to fifty years earlier. With *The Sleepers*, we are not in an exotic world, nor in a library of reliable poses, but thrust into the reality of the here and now, and of the sexual energies of the female body as observed and constructed with a fresh eye. Courbet's lifelong battle for painting's engagement with reality makes it possible for him to paint flesh that is erotic in the actual, not the voyeuristic sense of the term. These are women with blood vessels, muscles and nerve endings, who are capable of being motivated by desire, and whose flesh can experience passion. *The Sleepers* is a painting with which, once the lesbian subject is put into perspective, a female viewer can identify, as she can with *The Origin of the World*. Whatever the role of the 'male gaze' here, it is does not exclude the female viewer, because these are figures that provide an image of the subjectivity of passionate women. Such an image takes its place among the varied number of paintings by Courbet in which, as he worked to forge a new kind of art, he demonstrated the depth of his respect for a new kind of woman.

Notes

1 Petra ten-Doesschate Chu, *Letters of Gustave Courbet* (Chicago: Chicago UP, 1992) 106.

2 Chu, *Letters of Gustave Courbet* 99.

3 Chu, *Letters of Gustave Courbet* 231.

4 Chu, *Letters of Gustave Courbet* 267.

5 *Venus and Psyche* was destroyed in Berlin during World War II. A modified version of it is in the Kunstmuseum in Berne. For the details of the Khalil Bey collection, see Francis Haskill, "A Turk and His Pictures in Nineteenth-Century Paris," *Oxford Art Review* 5.1: 40-47.

Jill Beaulieu and Mary Roberts

Courbet's Corporeal Realism: The Phenomenological Body and the Anti-Theatrical Tradition[1]

> . . . my readings will be grounded in a consideration of the relationship between painting and beholder in Courbet's art; but what distinguishes that relationship from its antecedents in the art of Greuze or David or even Gericault is that beholding in Courbet so profoundly implicates the body, goes by way of the body, that all discussion of the issue of theatricality as it pertains to his work will necessarily be concerned with questions of embodiedness and corporeality, including, so to speak, the corporeality of painting (it will prove impossible to separate the issue of beholding from questions of the physical making of his pictures).[2]

Michael Fried's reading of Courbet's art is a profound and radical reinterpretation of his realism. Fried displaces the centrality of a mimetic model of Realism through an exploration of the metaphorical reading of Courbet's relation to the process of painting.[3] According to Fried Courbet's model of realism is a corporeal mode of self-representation which diminishes the role of vision and favours the tactile and bodily relation of the painter to the act of painting. We will focus on two important ramifications of Fried's model of corporeal realism: linkages between genres in Courbet's art that had previously been considered quite distinct; and the subversion of the distancing gaze. The crucial role of the body and its relation to this new model of self-representation in Fried's reading of Courbet's art can be specified through a comparative analysis of Courbet's self-portraits and his images of women.

Embodied Self-Portraits

Fried analyses Courbet's self-portraits not from the perspective of psychological or autobiographical studies of the artist, or as a reflection of the sitter's likeness, but as Courbet's "desire and compulsion" to depict his own embodiedness – "to evoke within the painting his intense absorption in his own live bodily being."[4] Fried arrives at this premise by noting a number of "peculiar characteristics" across several of Courbet's early self-portraits. Characteristics such as excessive tension evident in the sitter's hands, an emphasis on the proximity of the figure represented to the surface of the canvas and the predominance of states of sleep, reverie or semi-consciousness, have either previously gone unnoticed or been dismissed as merely awkward. We would argue that an important consequence of Fried's phenomenological reading of Courbet's self-portraits, which focuses on the artist's internal sensations rather than observing his external characteristics, is the subversion of the distancing gaze.[5]

What is most striking in the painting *Man with the Leather Belt* (Fig. 135) is the sitter's hands, which convey much more tension than seems warranted by their activity. Similarly in *Country Siesta* (Fig. 136) the positioning of Courbet's right hand with his palm facing upwards, prominently placed on top of his thigh, exhibits a tension that is extraordinary given his relaxed state. Fried claims that the tension evident in Courbet's hand "makes us aware of the hand as a potential locus of sensation and hence as a sign of the male sitter's possession from within his own body."[6] The sitter's left hand is also given prominence in *Wounded Man* (Fig. 137), due to the contrast of flesh tone against his brown cloak and the encompassing white of his sleeve. The man leans against a tree with his eyes closed in a semi-conscious state while his hand grasps a fold in the cloak. Fried interprets this hand as having a metonymic relation to the body, resulting in the hand signifying both "his body as *object*" and "his body *as actually lived*, as possessed from within."[7] Fried's interpretation of the wounded man's hand is applicable to all three self-portraits: that "the hand functions as a visual metaphor for the . . . (non visual) experience of his embodiedness."[8] What Fried refers to as the "double gesture" of the hand – "directed simultaneously outward towards the world and inward towards its own lived physicality,"[9] thereby denoting the body as both subject and object – is similar to Merleau-Ponty's concept of corporeal reflexivity. Merleau-Ponty's premise is that one cannot touch an object without being touched by it, so that the act of touching an object invokes an awareness of oneself.[10] The body is not only the means of knowing and communicating with the world but also the means of knowing oneself.[11] More explicitly, Merleau-Ponty claims that subjectivity is not divorced from the body: "my existence as subjectivity is one with my existence as body and with the existence of the world . . ."[12]

Fried extends this reading to associate the tension in the sitter's hands in *Man with the Leather Belt* with the physical act of painting. Besides the tension of the sitter's right hand, Fried notes that it is twisted around to face into the canvas, physically coinciding with the painter-beholder's

Fig. 135. Gustave Courbet *Man with the Leather Belt* (c.1845–46) Ref. 11

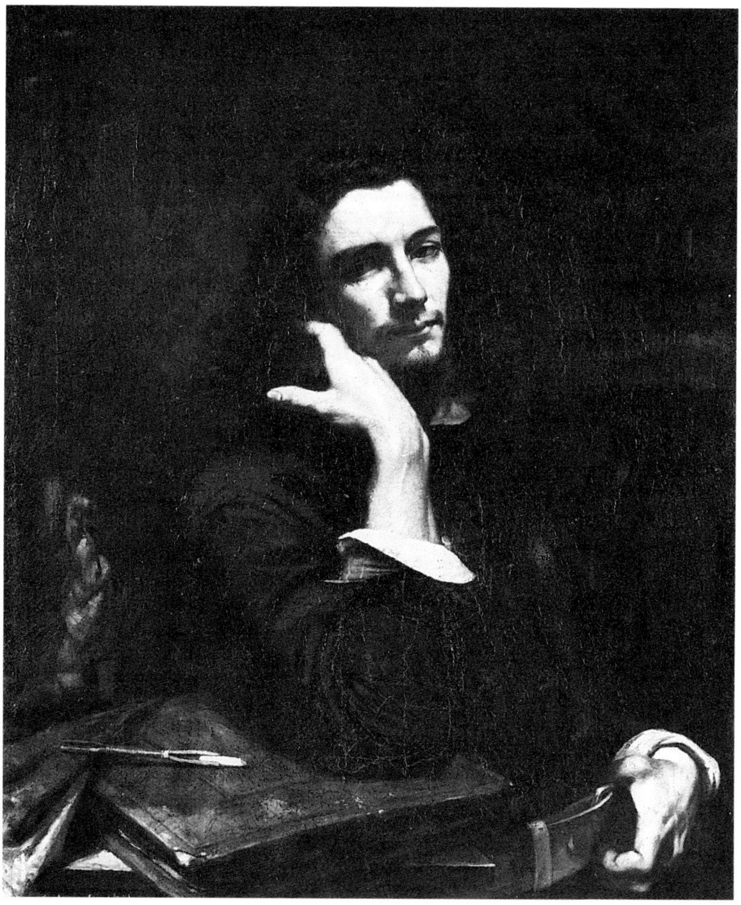

hand, despite the fact that the sitter faces the viewer in this painting. The evident tension and the positioning enacts a "positional and actional congruence"[13] between the figure and painter that he was later to discover in the central sifter of the *The Grain Sifters* (Fig. 123), which is discussed below. Pursuing the analogy, Fried interprets the sitter's left hand actively gripping his belt as expressing the effort involved in holding a palette and brushes. Establishing a connection between Merleau-Ponty's phenomenology and Courbet's pictorial concerns, Fried states that the "act of painting . . . [is] a vehicle of the painter-beholder's determination to be 'true' to the lived actuality of his embodiedness for as long as was required to produce the painting before him."[14]

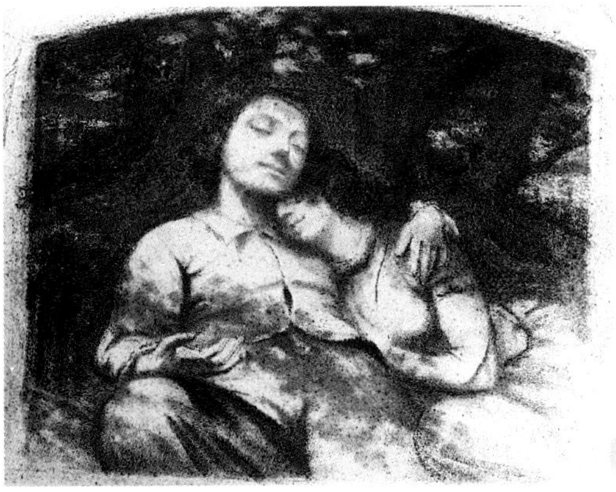

Fig. 136. Gustave Courbet *Country Siesta* (early 1840s) Ref. 8

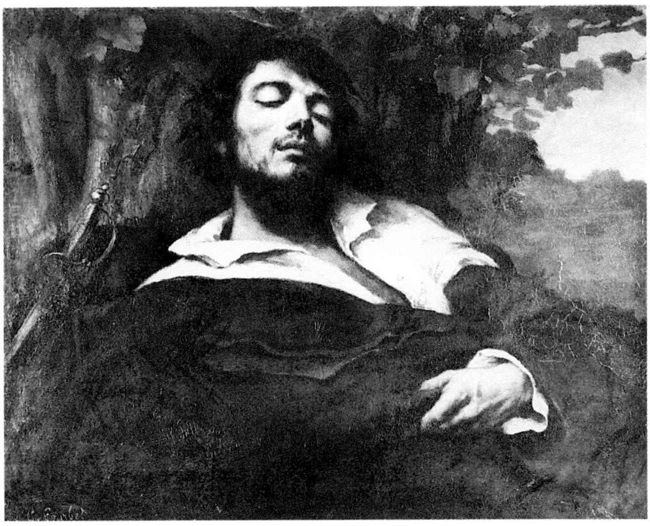

Fig. 137. Gustave Courbet *Wounded Man* (c.1844–54) Ref. 20

Another remarkable feature of Courbet's self-portraits is the consistency with which he represents his figures extremely close to the front of the picture plane. This proximity can be read as continuing to destabilise the fixed positions of subject and object by attempting to overcome that distance which divides the viewer from the viewed – in other words, the distance that is necessary to look at the things that surround us. Looking again at *Wounded Man*, the upper half of the man's body is depicted in the immediate foreground of the canvas, which gives the sensation of his legs extending past the frame and into the viewer's space. Fried claims that this presumed extension into the viewer's space "calls into question the impermeability of the bottom framing-edge, the capacity of that edge to contain the representation, to bring it to a stop, to establish it at a fixed distance from both picture surface and beholder."[15] This preoccupation with nearness is evident also in Courbet's extraordinary self-portrait *Man Mad with Fear* (Fig. 65), which depicts Courbet in medieval costume in the act of jumping off the edge of a cliff. The man stares outwards while his right hand thrusts forward, as if into our space. Because the painting is unfinished and the figure of the man is not clearly delineated, there is an even greater sense of the instability of his position. This act of leaping forward, as if into the viewer's space, is interpreted by Fried as a desire "to cancel or undo all distance not merely between image and picture surface but also, more importantly, between sitter and beholder, to close the gulf between them, to make them one."[16] This attempt to annul all distance between sitter and beholder is, in phenomenological terms, the attempt to regain undifferentiated oneness, the primordial perception which preceded division into seer and seen, subject and object. Explaining the desire to regain unity, Merleau-Ponty discusses the way in which the subject experiences a form of alienation in relation to the other's gaze which he describes as the "'confiscation' of the subject by the others who look at him."[17]

The devaluation of sight is a consistent feature of Courbet's self-portraits. Even in those portraits in which the sitter gazes outwards, the figure is not actually looking at the viewer. This is evident for instance in *Man with the Leather Belt* where the man's gaze, which is directed to the viewer's left, does not indicate vision but an absorption in his own thoughts. A much more dramatic example of this unseeing gaze, which Fried refers to as a type of blindness, is evident in *Man Mad with Fear*. Although the man gazes directly out, he is as if blinded by his fear. His blindness in the act of jumping off the cliff reinforces the reading that the portrait expresses a desire to annul the distance between sitter and viewer whereas a confrontational gaze would enforce a separation between the two. Manet's *Olympia* (Fig. 139) is an excellent example of the confrontational gaze. Olympia's gaze immediately makes the viewer feel as if they are the intruder, conveying an uncomfortable feeling of being studied and assessed in return.[18] By contrast, the motif of blindness in Courbet's paintings is a means of avoiding confrontation between the sitter and beholder.

According to Fried, Courbet's desire to escape this confrontational gaze explains the predominance of sleep, reverie or semi-conscious states in Courbet's self-portraits and in his later images of women. It is in these states, Merleau-Ponty suggests, that we have a privileged relation to the experience of embodiedness. While the man's hand in *Country Siesta* invokes a "body liveness," the reclining pose establishes his "primordial" relation to the world because he has relinquished the upright posture that "establishes human beings in perceptual opposition to the world."[19] What is also significant is that sleep, semi-consciousness and reverie can be seen to be about "surrendering all control of bodily functions as if to a power or rhythm outside oneself."[20] Moreover the woman resting against the man seems to meld into his body, an effect conveyed by the lack of delineation of her right upper torso and head, thus underlining the indistinct boundaries between self and world experienced in sleep.

At the end of his chapter on the self-portraits, Fried associates his phenomenological reading of these images (and the issues they raise about the relation between painter and painting), to the anti-theatrical tradition. Emerging in the mid-eighteenth century, this was a tradition motivated by the concern to offset a false, decorative or overly sentimental 'theatrical' style of art. Absorption was called upon to defeat theatricality yet strategies to achieve absorption had to keep changing in order to forestall theatrical excess and exaggeration.[21] In order that the artist depict a "convincing image of the world,"[22] it was necessary that the artist not be seen to be painting for an audience, thus effectively ignoring the viewer by absorbing the figures in their actions and states of mind. It was therefore necessary that the painter establish the fiction that the beholder did not exist, that there was no one standing before the picture.[23] By the mid-nineteenth-century defeating theatricality became increasingly difficult and more extreme measures were required. In Courbet's art, the issue of defeating theatricality centred on the artist as first beholder, making it necessary that Courbet merge with the painting before him. Given the impossibility of literal merger, Fried refers to the desire for merger as the quasi-corporeal merger. Courbet's desire for merger is both metaphorically indicated and enacted in the process of painting itself. Courbet's mode of attempting to defeat theatricality was, according to Fried, his own unique form of corporeal realism.

It was initially the conventions of self-portraiture that brought into focus issues of Courbet's own spectatorhood. As Fried explains, "by calling for the depiction of a figure that would at once double and, at least approximately, face its maker, the conventions in question provoked in

Courbet both as painter and as beholder – that is *as painter-beholder* – a heightened intuition (I don't quite want to say awareness) of his physical separateness from and opposite orientation to the painting before him."[24] Although Fried does not specifically discuss merger in relation to the self-portraits, the various motifs discussed in his reading are crucial signifiers of the desire for merger. For instance, where the hands invoke embodiedness, thereby emphasising internal sensations; where proximity questions the impermeability of the bottom edge of the canvas annulling the distance between the sitter and the painter-beholder; where blindness and sleep-states are means of avoiding the confrontational gaze that would theatricalise the painter-beholder's relation to the painting.

While the painter-beholder's desire for merger is only implicit in Fried's reading of the self-portraits, it is the central focus in Fried's reading of the images of women. In this chapter the experience of corporeality is focused on the act of painting which is read through a series of gender metaphors. What will become apparent in juxtaposing Fried's analysis of the self-portraits and images of women is that the self-portraits make evident the phenomenological basis of Fried's reading of Courbet's images of women. By the same token reading the images of women in relation to the self-portraits makes explicit the implied connections between embodiedness and merger in the self-portraits.

Gendering Merger

Although unconscious on Courbet's part, Fried argues that the artist's desire for merger is articulated in his images of women. Given that the quasi-corporeal merger is a striving to eliminate the distinction between seeing and being seen, Courbet's paintings of women are not, according to Fried, exclusively about a distanced gaze which objectifies the representation of woman. This reading has significant consequences for our understanding of the artist's relation to these images of women. Conventional gendered hierarchical distinctions are reconfigured through a number of important strategies that displace the distancing gaze. These include bigendering, which combines masculine and feminine traits, thus relocating sexual difference *within* the painter-beholder; an emphasis on internal body sensation rather than exteriority; the concept of the absorptive continuum which conveys a unifying mood between painter-beholder and figures thereby signifying the desired merger; and finally, the "blindness of sexual union" as a metaphor for the painter's immersion in the process of painting which also designates the extreme limit of Courbet's project.

Fried argues that the central sifter in the *The Grain Sifters* invokes metaphors for the act of painting through an emphasis on bodily productivity (menstruation)[25] and agricultural labour (sifting). According to Fried, the shower of grain suggests the flow of menstrual blood as well as the fall of pigment onto the canvas from the sieve. The central sifter's exertion in the act of sifting is linked to the physical act of painting and the metaphor of menstruation construes painting as a bodily process. Fried notes the similarities between this metaphor for engagement in the physical process of painting in the *The Grain Sifters* and the procedures for applying paint to canvas employed by Jackson Pollock and Morris Louis a century later.[26] As evident in Namuth's film, Pollock's physical immersion in the process of painting entailed stepping onto the canvas, in effect moving inside his painting. Pollock's relationship to the process of painting has been described as 'painting blind.'[27] For Fried the central sifter is also read as a surrogate for the painter-beholder because her positioning is congruent with his: she faces into the canvas with her back to the viewer; her kneeling position and her arms extended out in the act of sifting are analogous to the painter's position in the physical act of painting. She thereby *embodies* the painter-beholder rather than being the object of his controlling gaze.[28] Further evidence for the dissolution of the boundaries between sifter and painter-beholder is the coexistence of masculine and feminine traits evident in the central sifter which Fried terms bigendering.[29] Bigendering transforms the masculine and feminine binary by resituating sexual difference 'within' the painter-beholder, rather than between him and the object of his desire. Similarly in *The Sleepers* (fig. 132) Fried argues that the bigendered painter-beholder is signalled by the masculine traits of the woman with the darker hair and tanned skin. Implicit in this reading of the painting is the notion that the bigendered painter-beholder is so implicated *within* the painting that he no longer has a distanced command of the pictorial field.

Focusing on internal bodily relations rather than on the external visibility of the feminine body, Fried's reading, which emphasises touch and proximity, differs from a more familiar feminist psychoanalytic reading of the female nude. For example with *Sleeping Blonde Girl* Fried states that "the body's integrity of outward form is sacrificed to an evocation of its sensuous presence to itself."[30] This reading has striking parallels with his phenomenological reading of *Country Siesta* which emphasises the male sitter's "possession from within."

What also disrupts the distancing gaze is the notion of the painter-beholder's "absorptive continuum" which implies a dissolving of the differences between figures in a painting and between those figures and the painter-beholder by means of the predominance of a unifying mood. A thematics of absorption for instance pervades *The Grain Sifters* in which each of the figures are so absorbed either in sifting, sleeping or peering into the tarare that they are oblivious to all else. A different strategy for breeching the boundaries is evident in *The Sleepers*. The entwining of the two women enacts a "virtual merger," implying "a single (bigendered) female body, embraced by a single pair of arms."[31] This "virtual merger" of the two women ensures that there is neither one figure, nor two, and that they are neither completely subject nor object, feminine nor masculine. An analogy between the sleepers and their surroundings is implied by the vaginal motif, the exposed underside of the rose-pink coverlet on which the sleeper's hand rests (this body metaphor is given prominence because it is on the edge of the bed that is closest to the front of the picture). *The Sleepers* is read as evoking a "fantasy of total corporeal presence."[32] Fried extends his reading of the feminisation of the pictorial field to Courbet's paintings of caves. *The Source of the Loue* (Fig. 17) for instance invokes not only a morphological resemblance to the vagina, but also a reciprocal movement through the outward flow of water and the implied inward movement of the painter-beholder into the painting.[33] The eye moves into this painting by following the cave wall, a visual metaphor for the painter-beholder's corporeal merger.

In Fried's reading of *The Sleepers* and of Courbet's other female nudes the sexual act is read as a metaphor for the painter-beholder's desire for merger. Feminist art historians and literary theorists have alerted our attention to the fact that an erotic metaphor for the act of painting or writing is a familiar masculinist strategy, for instance, the metaphor of the "brush/pen/penis writing the virgin page."[34] Fried's model is different from these more familiar masculinist metaphors because it is motivated by a desire for the dissolution of the distinction between subject and object. (Although we are not suggesting that Fried's model is unproblematic for feminism.)[35] This desire places emphasis on a prolongation of the *experience* of painting which stresses the *process* of painting rather than the product. Thus Fried's readings emphasise the immersion in the act of painting rather than the object-status of the women depicted. In the case of Courbet's erotic nudes, *Nude with White Stockings* and *The Origin of the World* (Fig. 15) this immersion in the act of painting is read as the "blindness of sexual union" – that moment of "the complete undoing of distance and hence spectatorship."[36] The blindness of merger is also evoked by the dark interior of the caves which for Fried signifies the extreme limits of this project of merger, "the undoing of spectatorhood – that would be concomitant with the absorption of the painter-beholder into the painting on which he was working."[37]

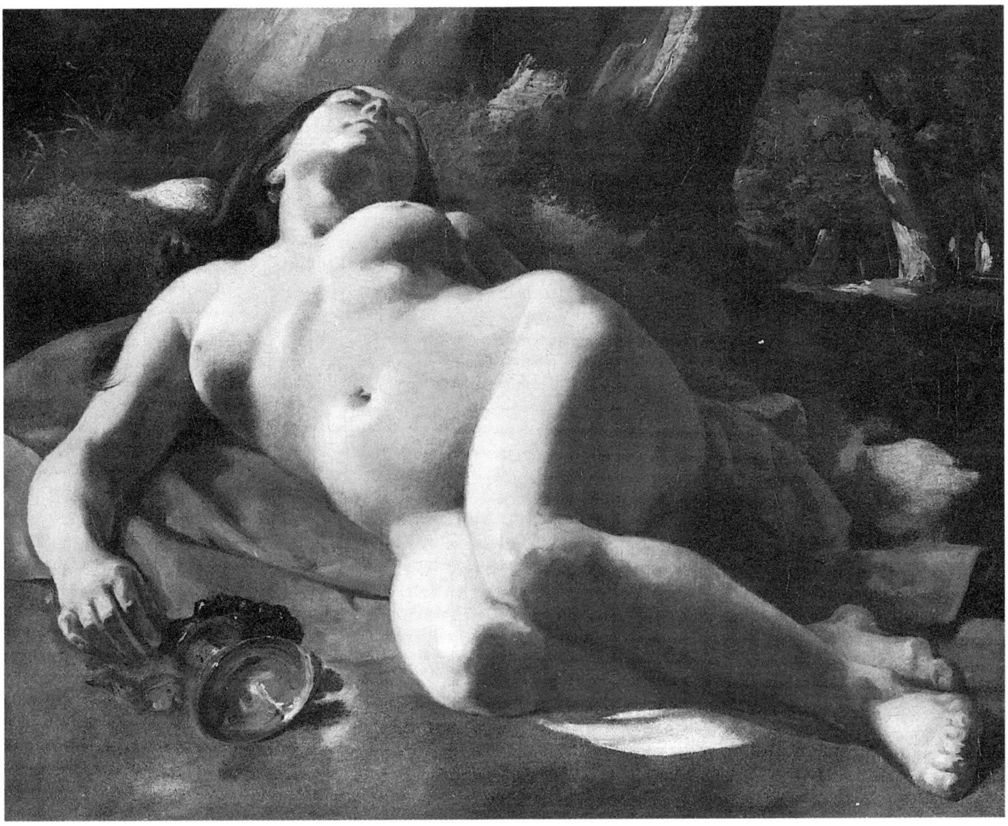

Fig. 138. Gustave Courbet *The Bacchante* (1844–45) Ref. 6

Fried is compelled to acknowledge that this extreme limit – the desired merger – is an impossibility and his analysis of Courbet's images of women seems to force this acknowledgment.[38] For example Fried recognises that the signifiers of the painter-beholder's merger in *Sleep* could easily be appropriated as a "new and powerful technology for the production of erotic, even semipornographic effects . . . [for] the masculinist public at large."[39] Fried makes one last attempt to forestall the failure of the merger in his reading of *The Bacchante* (Fig. 138). He negotiates the inevitability of the 'pornographic effect' through a temporal strategy. Whereas Fried interprets the sexual act in *Origin* and *Nude* as a metaphor for the corporeal relation between painter-beholder and painting, *The Bacchante* depicts its aftermath, the mutual falling back of painter and painting into separate realms. The female figure's transition back into the painting is suggested by her unusual positioning: her legs, right hand and lower torso are at the very front of the picture plane while her upper body is further back. Fried argues that *The Bacchante* implies an intermediate moment rather than a complete reversal back to the distinction between subject and object because the tangibility of the woman's body is "less a provocation to possession than the form of a memory" of the merger.[40] Memory establishes the merger but also its inevitable failure through a temporal process that implies the merger retrospectively.

By focusing on Fried's reading of the embodied self-portraits and the gendered metaphors of merger in Courbet's images of women we've highlighted some of the key methodological foundations of his project and made explicit the connections between embodiedness and merger. Fried's reading of Courbet's art is valuable not only because it provides new ways of thinking about the role of the body in Courbet's art, but also because it calls into question the relationship between artist and image. His model is significant precisely because it doesn't locate the meaning of Courbet's images in the conscious intentions of the artist, nor does it assume that the artist's relationship to the image is identical with that of subsequent spectators. Fried does not construct an idealised notion of the painter's unmediated relation to the process of painting – not only is the project unconscious, it is also impossible. It is precisely the impossibility of literal merger that motivates the quasi-corporeal merger. One is tempted to think about how this model might apply to a reading of embodiedness in the work of other painters and in particular other realists. Yet that which resists an easy transfer also accounts for its richness. Fried's method is grounded in an astute understanding of the historical and pictorial specificities of Courbet's art which puts into question the axiom that 'paintings are made to be beheld'.

Notes

1 We would like to thank Anthony Bond and Caroline Butler-Bowdon for the opportunity to bring together our respective interests in Fried's complex project in the context of the *BODY* exhibition. We would also like to thank our respective institutions and colleagues for their support (University of Western Sydney, Nepean and Canberra School of Art, ANU), in particular Jill would like to acknowledge the support of a Publication Time Release Grant from UWS, Nepean.

2 Michael Fried, *Courbet's Realism* (Chicago: U of Chicago P, 1987) 49–50.

3 Assessing the use of realism in Art History – most commonly either subscribing to the mimetic model or the demystification of the "reality effect" – Fried claims "that commentaries on Courbet's art . . . have often focused on questions of subject matter, either narrowly or broadly construed. And it has also meant that discussion has tended to proceed on the unexamined assumption that a realist painting's representation of a given scene was to all intents and purposes determined by the 'actual' scene itself, with the result that features of the representation that ought to have been perceived as curious and problematic, as calling for reflection and analysis, have either been made invisible (the usual outcome) or, if registered at all, have been attributed to reality rather than to art." Fried, *Courbet's Realism* 3.

4 Fried, *Courbet's Realism* 64.

5 Fried qualifies his use of phenomenology by stating that his notion of the body is culturally coded: "the body in question . . . must be understood as culturally coded, even culturally produced, in the most intimate recesses of its 'primordialness.'" Fried, *Courbet's Realism* 50.

6 Fried, *Courbet's Realism* 66.

7 Fried, *Courbet's Realism* 65.

8 Fried, *Courbet's Realism* 65.

9 Fried, *Courbet's Realism* 65.

[10] See in particular Maurice Merleau-Ponty, "The Experience of the Body and Classical Psychology," *Phenomenology of Perception*, trans. Colin Smith (London: Routledge, 1992) 90–97.

[11] As Merleau-Ponty states, "it is through my relation to things that I know myself." *Phenomenology of Perception* 383.

[12] Merleau-Ponty, *Phenomenology of Perception* 408.

[13] Fried, *Courbet's Realism* 227.

[14] Fried, *Courbet's Realism* 81.

[15] Fried, *Courbet's Realism* 59.

[16] Fried, *Courbet's Realism* 61.

[17] Merleau-Ponty, "The Child's Relations with Others," *The Primacy of Perception and Other Essays on Phenomenological Psychology, The Philosophy of Art, History and Politics*, ed. James M. Edie (Chicago: Northwestern UP, 1964) 137.

[18] It is precisely this distinction between the absorptive effects in Courbet's paintings and an acknowledgment of theatricality (facingness) in Manet's art that distinguishes Courbet's role in the pre-modernist anti-theatrical tradition and Manet's modernism.

[19] Fried, *Courbet's Realism* 67.

[20] Fried, *Courbet's Realism* 67. Merleau-Ponty refers to "that quasi-stupor to which we are reduced when we really try to live at the level of sensation." *Phenomenology of Perception* 215.

[21] For Fried theatricality and absorption are not static, universal categories, but historically located critical judgements. For an analysis of the distinction between the concept of absorption in Diderot's art criticism (specifically the notion of entry), and Courbet's more radical project of merger see Jill Beaulieu's essay in *The Opacity of Vision*, eds, Jill Beaulieu, Mary Roberts and Toni Ross [Forthcoming Power Publications].

[22] Fried, *Courbet's Realism* 7.

[23] In Chapter One of *Courbet's Realism*, Fried traces the evolution of absorption and theatricality.

[24] Fried, *Courbet's Realism* 80.

[25] Fried establishes that menstruation is a sign of bodily productivity by citing advanced scientific thinking in Courbet's day which held that menstruation was an indicator of woman's fertility, equivalent to heat in animals. See *Courbet's Realism* 336 n.16 in which he cites Thomas Lacquer's "Orgasm, Generation, and the Politics of Reproductive Biology," *Representations* 14 (Spring 1986): 27.

[26] Fried, *Courbet's Realism* 153.

[27] For an analysis of this notion of Pollock painting blind, which considers the relationship between Fried's *Three American Painters*, Derrida's *Memoirs for the Blind* and Lacan's gaze as *objet a* see Keith Broadfoot's essay "Before and After Pollock" in *The Opacity of Vision*. Also James E. Breslin's comparative analysis of the relation of the painter's body to 'organic abstraction' in the work of Rothko and Pollock, "Out of the Body: Mark Rothko's Paintings," ed. Kathleen Adler and Marcia Pointon, *The Body Imaged: The Human Form and Visual Culture Since the Renaissance* (Cambridge: Cambridge UP, 1993) 43–52.

[28] Fried, *Courbet's Realism* 227.

[29] Bigendering is distinct from bisexuality because the latter term "implies a doubleness of object choice," whereas the former addresses the problematics of self-representation. Fried, *Courbet's Realism* 191.

[30] Fried, *Courbet's Realism* 207.

[31] Fried, *Courbet's Realism* 207.

[32] Fried, *Courbet's Realism* 207.

[33] Although Fried notes the similarities between Hertz's psychoanalytic reading of the cave paintings and his own interpretation, he observes that while Hertz emphasises specularity, his argument stresses corporeality: "where I perhaps still differ from him, (Hertz) or at least wish to assert a different emphasis, is the weight I give to the notion of a double movement into and out from the painting, and more broadly in my insistence on the importance of corporeal as distinct from specular and/or psychoanalytic considerations in my reading of Courbet's pictures." *Courbet's Realism* 341 n.45.

[34] See Lisa Tickner, "Art History and Sexual Difference," *Genders* 3 (Fall 1988): 109.

[35] For a more in depth analysis of the relationship between Fried's model and feminism see Mary Roberts' essay in *The Opacity of Vision.*

[36] Fried, *Courbet's Realism* 217.

[37] Fried, *Courbet's Realism* 217.

[38] In a succinct explanation for the impossibility of the merger, Stephen Melville states: "The paintings are *visual* just because this continuity of the self and its activity [the activity of painting] cannot be realized without remainder: there will always be, in the end, not *painting* but a *painting* . . . because paintings exist, initially and finally to be beheld, and even painting blind, a metaphorical description that tempts Fried repeatedly, cannot deliver the process from vision. Stephen Melville, "Compelling Acts, Haunting Convictions," *Art History* 14.1 (March 1991): 118.

[39] Fried, *Courbet's Realism* 209.

[40] Fried, *Courbet's Realism* 220.

Alan Krell

Fearful Desires: 'Embodiments' in Late Nineteenth-Century French Painting

> . . . the image of the body should be understood as itself a historical matrix, marked and moulded in a crucible of social, cultural and psychosexual circumstance.
>
> — Abigail Solomon-Godeau, 1993[1]

In the preface to his second edition of *Thérèse Raquin*, a novel widely accused of pornography when it was first released in 1867, Zola claimed that his "object [had] been first and foremost a scientific one." Thérèse and Laurent, his two central characters, "are human animals, nothing more. . . . I had only one desire: given a highly-sexed man and an unsatisfied woman, to uncover the animal side of them and see that alone, then throw them together in a violent drama and note down with scrupulous care the sensations and actions of these creatures. I simply applied to two living bodies the analytical method that surgeons apply to corpses."[2]

Zola's formulation of the Naturalist novelist as someone akin to a scientist or surgeon was consistent with the prevailing assumptions of scientific determinism, which held that human conduct was explainable solely in terms of physiological factors and the material environment.

Fig. 139. Edouard Manet *Olympia* (1863) Ref. 28

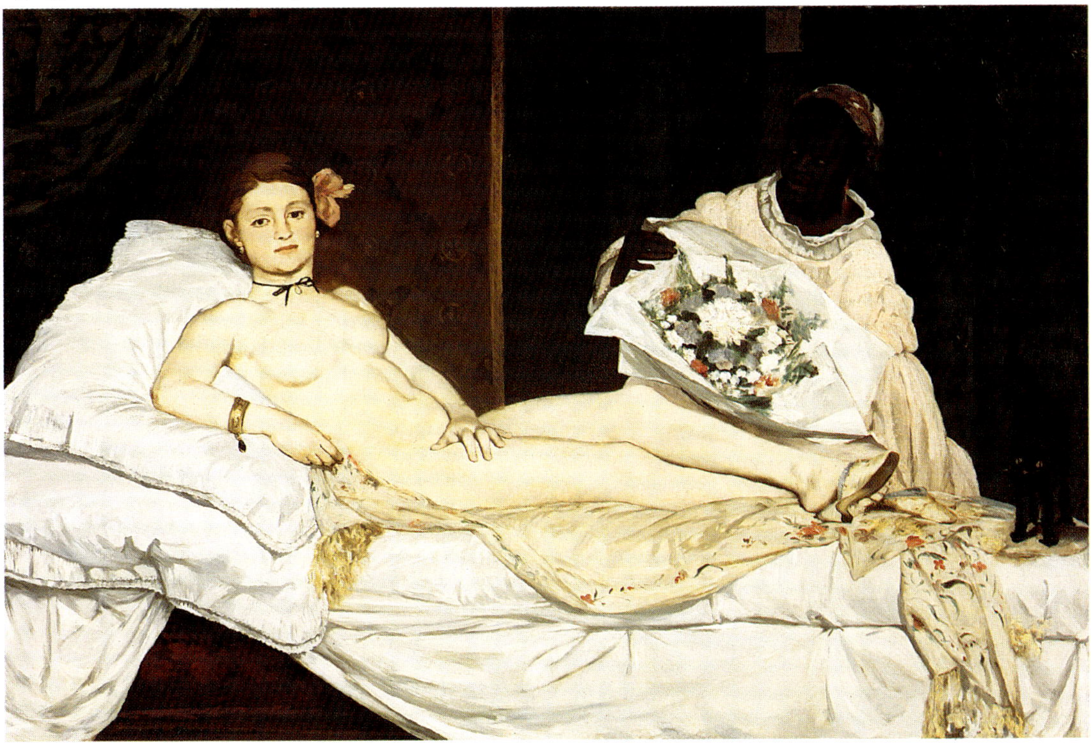

That such beliefs are resonant in *Thérèse Raquin* is true, but the story is far more than a "scientific demonstration."[3] Nowhere is this more evident, paradoxically, than in Chapter 13, where Zola details Laurent's visits to the morgue to see if Thérèse's husband, Camille, whom he had murdered by drowning, was "well and truly dead." The "murmur of running water," the "sickly smell, the smell of washed flesh" layed out naked on "rows of grey stone slabs" repulse Laurent, but disgust and fear give way to "a strange pleasure in looking violent death in the face. . . . naked bodies spattered with blood, sometimes with holes in them, held him spell-bound."[4] (Portentous, as it so happens, of that haunting world of carnage and 'lethal obsessions' represented in David Cronenberg's current, and hugely controversial film, *Crash*.)[5] Fascination quickly turns to lust, when Laurent sees a "girl who had hanged herself out of unrequited love. He lingered over her face for a long time, running his eyes up and down her body, lost in a sort of fearful desire."[6]

The phrase "fearful desire" brings to mind that anxious world of bodily odours, miasmas, decomposition and sexuality so vividly evoked and critiqued in Alain Corbin's brilliant study, *The Foul and the Fragrant: Odour and the French Social Imagination.* Fundamental to the work of medical scientists of the nineteenth century, "the golden age of osphresiology (the science of smells)"[7] was the belief, advanced a century before, that "every animal species, every individual organism . . . had its distinctive odour."[8] The humours (bodily fluids), in particular, lent themselves to much speculation. And in this discourse, gender assumed a defining role. So, for example, male and female blood was thought to be distinguished by odours; while in men, the seminal humour guaranteed "the individual's animality;" it produced "that fetid odour which vigorous males exude," wrote Johann Philipp Withof.[9] Through coitus, woman was impregnated by the *aura seminalis* and thereby acquired her ideal smell. "In every sphere," observes Corbin, "sexual intercourse was held to complete femininity."[10] But immoderate sexual intercourse supposedly left women with a repugnant fetor; hence the emergence of the French slang word for prostitute, 'putain', from 'puanteur' (stench).[11]

Small wonder, then, that the naked woman (Victorine Meurent) in Edouard Manet's *Olympia* (Fig. 139), a canvas exhibited at the Paris Salon of 1865, was considered to be unwashed and stinking.[12] Widely recognised at the time as a picture of a contemporary prostitute/courtesan, *Olympia* evoked such intense hostility that it was removed from its "place of honour" and repositioned "at a height where even the worst daubs had never been hung, above the huge door of the last room, where you scarcely knew whether you were looking at a parcel of nude flesh or a bundle of laundry."[13]

Represented in this current exhibition (Fig. 140) by one of the small etchings Manet did of his painting in 1867 (and used to illustrate the critic Emile Zola's study of him published in the same year, one which, incidentally, emphasised the purely formal aspects of the picture), *Olympia* seems anything but inflammatory. Indeed, even when looking at the original painting in the Musée d'Orsay (it should be noted that the etching differs from the oil in some important respects), it is difficult to comprehend the scandal of 1865. But contexts, of course, change, and so do perceptions. For the critic Geronte (pseud. of Victor Fournel), Olympia was a street-walker who had come from the rue Mouffetard. And the rue Mouffetard was definitely not a salubrious locale: "this squalid street, stinking in summer, muddy in winter and filthy throughout the year," was how the writer Charles Virmaître described it.[14] Stench and filth were precisely the terms of reference for Bertall's outrageous cartoon of *Olympia* published in the *Journal amusant* on 27 May 1865. Olympia is pictured in a grubby interior: the bed linen is unkempt; the mattress is shabby; and there is a chamber-pot under the bed. Clearly this is not the boudoir of a prosperous courtesan, but rather the ramshackle dwelling of an impoverished prostitute. Olympia's body is grotesque: she appears to be wearing a body stocking and a clown's mask; her right arm is ungainly and her feet ridiculously large. The extended caption to this cartoon in part reads: "This picture by Manet is the bouquet of the exhibition. . . . The great colourist has chosen the moment when the lady is about to take a bath, something which she certainly seems to need."[15] So that would explain the steam clouds Bertall has included to the one side of Olympia's black maid. Or perhaps they represent the foul smell rising from Olympia's absurdly large feet.

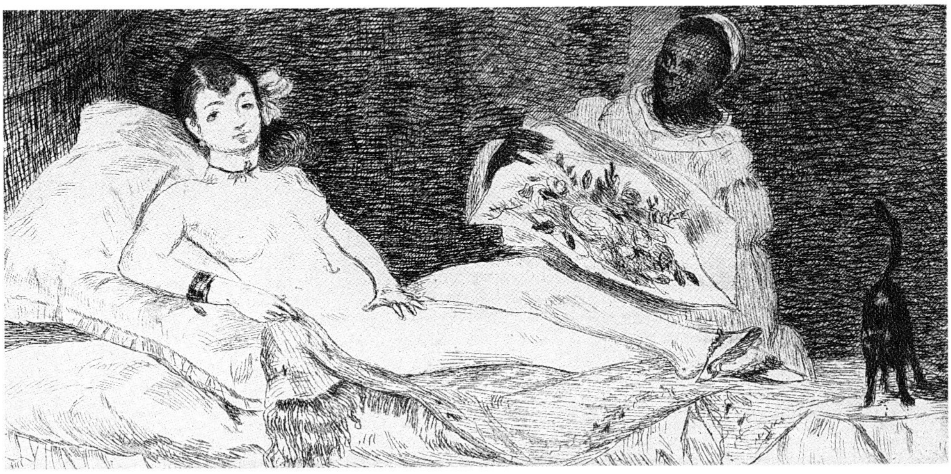

Fig. 140. Edouard Manet *Olympia* (small plate) (1867) Cat. 89

The maid's expression in this image can best be described as a wide-eyed grimace, one that mimics the look of the agitated cat at the foot of the bed. Cartoon after cartoon played on this affinity, and in the process incriminated both Negress and *chat noir* in some frenzied erotic sub-plot. Critics, too, were quick to comment on the animal. "At the foot of the bed crouches a black cat," wrote Ernest Filloneau, "who probably doesn't like flowers since it cuts such a pathetic figure."[16] With its arched back and tail raised to resemble a question-mark in reverse (and vice-versa in the etching), the animal doubtless brought to mind thoughts of an unbridled and potentially dangerous sexuality, a view given credence by the writings of the influential eighteenth-century naturalist, Georges-Louis Leclerc, le comte de Buffon. For Buffon, as quoted by Kathleen Kete in her recent study of the relation between animals and culture in nineteenth-century Paris, cats had "an innate malice, a falseness of character, a perverse nature. . . . They take easily to the habits of society, but never to its moral attitudes; they only appear to be affectionate."[17] Buffon, like many other writers, made special mention of the creature's sexual predilections. He maintained that the female of the species was sexually far more active than the male: "she invites it [sex], calls for it, announces her desires by her piercing cries, or rather, the excess of her needs . . . when the male runs away from her, she pursues him, bites, and forces him, as it were, to satisfy her . . ."[18]

If the critics' responses to Olympia in 1865 signal anything, it is this: she embodied a rampaging sexuality at once desirable yet threatening, fetid but seductive. Olympia was unpossessable. Significantly, Manet has her left hand spread spider-like across her genitals, a gesture that removes them from sight, declares a no-go zone, but at the same time emphasises their presence. They are also, of course, figuratively present in the cat, the 'chatte' (pussy) as the female genitals were euphemistically called. Here, though, the exaggerations of caricaturists again prove revealing. Time and again these emphasise the phallic nature of the cat's tail, thereby investing the animal with an hermaphroditic significance.[19]

Androgynous is perhaps an apt description of the figure in Auguste Renoir's extraordinary and little known *Young Boy with Cat* (Fig. 30), painted a few years after *Olympia*, in 1868–69. Originally owned by the musician Edouard Maitre, a friend of Renoir and Frédéric Bazille, the work was recently purchased from a Berlin collection by the Musée d'Orsay.[20] In contrast to the deodorised female nudes that would later become the staple of Renoir's production, *Young boy with cat* locates itself within the realist enterprise of Gustave Courbet and Manet. Unique, as far as I am aware, in Renoir's oeuvre, this image of the male nude looks back, in part, to those "ideal but androgynous incarnations of masculine beauty" discussed by Abigail Solomon-Godeau in her absorbing essay, "Male Trouble: A Crisis in Representation."[21] Setting out "to account for the eclipse of the male nude and the ascendancy of the female nude" in the course of the nineteenth-century in France, she focuses on works by artists such as David, Ingres, Fabre and Granger produced mostly in the first three decades of the century.[22] In them she discerns symptoms of a wider crisis in masculinity and its representations; a crisis brought about by massive social, political and cultural change.

The male nude, though, did not simply disappear, as evidenced by *Young boy with cat* and others I shall consider shortly. That Renoir chose not to send his painting to the Salon, however, may suggest he attached little importance to it. Alternatively, his refusal to do so may support the claim that "new visual regimes of pleasure and desire" were in the ascendancy.[23] Let's take a closer look at this picture. When the solitary male nude appeared in the work of contemporary academic artists it was always in the context of classical and mythological themes. The popular story of the Trojan boy Ganymede, for example, gave rise to numerous paintings, such as that by J.-P. Granger (1812, Musée des Beaux-Arts, Bordeaux). Singled out by Solomon-Godeau to illustrate a homoerotic strand within the thematic of a "feminized masculinity,"[24] the Granger shows a full-frontal, naked youth standing, legs crossed, amidst a swirl of clouds. His glacial, too-beautiful-by-half features contrast sharply with the fleshy, somewhat clumsy figure of Renoir's. No cup-bearer to the gods this, but clearly a flesh-and-blood young man posed in a studio setting. Yet "male trouble" is discernible in his feminized facial features; his languor bordering on effeteness. Like Granger's Ganymede he stands cross-legged but, unlike the former, he presents us with a view of his back and backside. Leaning slightly forwards, he wraps his hands around a large, docile tabby who looks passively out at the spectator. Both appear lost in reverie. In the light of our earlier comments on the place of cats in the French social imagination, what are we to make of Renoir's portrayal? Certainly this is no cat on heat, nor is it suggestive of a promiscuous sexuality. If anything, the sexuality flagged may best be described as a subdued, almost inactive one; domesticated, if you like. The creature's black tail curls up, reluctantly, complementing the shadowed area in the drapes below which, angled sharply downwards, temptingly suggests the boy's flaccid penis.

If Renoir's young man is the antithesis of an heroic masculinity – little vigorous male animality here, to paraphrase the words of Withoff quoted earlier – what then of the naked male in Pierre Bonnard's *Man and Woman* (Fig. 141) painted some thirty years later? A self-portrait of the artist himself, he is the tall, lanky figure separated by a partition from the undressed women, his companion and model, Marthe de Méligny (Maria Boursin), whom he would marry in 1925.[25] She appears by herself, also naked, in two other canvases done close in time, *Indolence* and *Siesta* (Fig. 5), which, grouped together with *Man and Woman*, constitute a highly charged essay on sexuality. The shadowed, somewhat uneasy figure of Bonnard is set apart from the illuminated Marthe. On

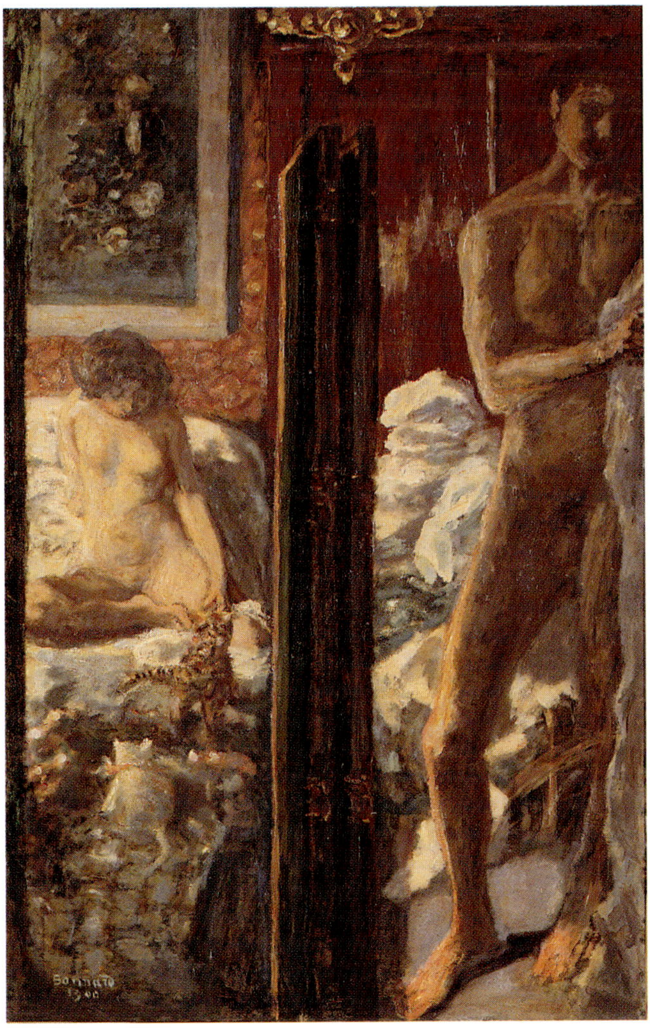

Fig. 141. Pierre Bonnard *L'Homme et la Femme (Man and Woman)* (1900) Cat. 24

one obvious level, this tonal division may be taken to signify the predatory, evil male (whose sexuality is emphasised by the rigid screen dividing the canvas in half) and the unwilling, innocent woman who lowers her head as if in remorse. Yet in other respects the picture speaks of a shared duplicity. If sexual intercourse has or is about to take place, then Bonnard has situated it in a hot-house atmosphere of mutual distrust and subterfuge. The presence, therefore, of a playful pair of cats on the bed, sporting delicate pink bows and staring at Marthe, seems incongruous. Much closer in spirit to Renoir's feline than Manet's, they invite comparison with the similarly beribboned dog in *Siesta*. In that picture Marthe lies face down, eyes closed, on a crumpled bed; the dog, asleep on the floor, mimics her pose but faces in the other direction. Mimics is the operative word. As Kete has shown, the fictive worlds the bourgeoisie formulated around the family dog collapsed the distinction between humans and animals. But if in this process the dog became a type of 'doppelganger', it also became the site on which the fantasy of an ideal nature could be constructed: canines could be taught, trained and manipulated, like children and women. Above all else, the dog was considered to embody devotion and loyalty,[26] attributes, as we've seen, absent from its feline counterpart which personified an aggressive individualism and sexuality. Yet by the end of the nineteenth-century the cat had been 'rehabilitated', becoming, like its rival, a good pet, reliable and trustworthy.[27] Bonnard's creatures seem to function figuratively in this reassuring manner, suggesting a compliant female sexuality.

Yet in *Siesta* it is also an equivocal sexuality. Lying on her front, the woman's dramatically foreshortened left leg, bent at the knee, contrasts with her relaxed, undulating pose. A grey shadow creeps up this limb, moves over the thigh and terminates in the buttocks, thereby emphasising the fissure of her anus. By contrast, in *Man and Woman*, Marthe's one leg bends sharply at the knee and its heel, caught in a yellow light, points directly at her genitals. That the antique sculpture *Sleeping Hermaphrodite* provided the pose for *Siesta* simply reinforces its sexual open-endedness.

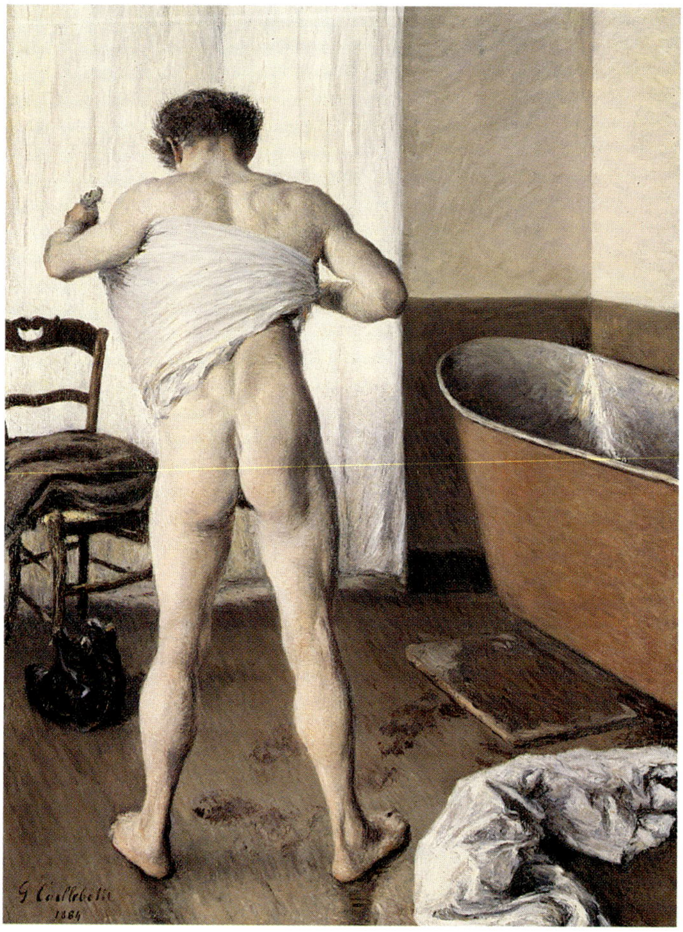

Fig. 142. Gustave Caillebotte *Man at his Bath* (1884) Ref. 2

We have already encountered the male rump in Renoir's sexually ambiguous *Young Boy with Cat*, an image that oscillates between realist matter-of-factness and fanciful artifice. In Gustave Caillebotte's near life-size *Man at his Bath* (Fig. 142) from 1884, the male rear is treated in a startlingly different way. Unique in the context of nineteenth-century French 'nudes', the painting is an uncompromising representation of a strapping male vigorously drying himself after a bath.[28] The subject – personal ablutions – was itself at the cutting-edge of modernity. Entangled in a complex network of taboos and constraints, washing and immersion gradually gained respectability following Pasteur's discoveries of microbes and bacteria in the 1870s. To accommodate this growing interest in bodily hygiene, "The bathroom finally won space for itself, and appeared in some apartment houses after 1880."[29] (New hygienic practices were exclusive to a moneyed few.) The prosperous Caillebotte possessed a bathroom in his home on the rue de Miromesnil, Paris, with a cast-iron bathtub no doubt like the one depicted at the right of his painting. Off to the left some clothing lies neatly on a wooden chair, with a pair of boots nearby.

Wet footprints conspicuous on the floor emphasise the singularity of the person: it is *his* mark, on *this* surface. Unlike Renoir's young boy whose genitals are concealed, or, for that matter, Paul Gauguin's bizarre Breton youth (Fig. 28) whose genitals have been erased, Caillebotte's man has his scrotal sac revealed between parted thighs. The vulnerability suggested here is reinforced by his left leg which, in a movement barely detected at first, bends inwards slightly at the knee.[30] The heavily impastoed, rather grotesque form at the bottom right (another towel or smock?), reminiscent of the similarly painted shape behind Bonnard in his *Man and Woman*, further adds to the aura of insecurity.

Caillebotte sent *Man at his Bath* to Brussels in 1888 for the exhibition of *Les XX*. If what a commentary at the time implied is correct, the painting was removed from public view and placed in a closet-like chamber[31] – out of sight, out of mind. Not so with François Sallé's equally remarkable *The Anatomy Class at the École des Beaux-Arts* (Fig. 143), which was displayed in the Paris Salon of the same year. Secured by Eliezer Montefiore for what was then the National Art Gallery of New South Wales,[32] this provocative painting has remained in relative obscurity since then: publicly on show, but receiving little if any scholarly comment.[33]

Born in Bourges in 1839 and a pupil of Luminais, Sallé was represented by this single work in the 1888 Salon where it was titled *Un cours d'anatomie*.[34] Notwithstanding the picture's award of a third-class medal and its selection for purchase by the French government, the volumes of contemporary art criticism had nothing to say about it. With one exception, as far as I am aware, and I will return to this later.[35]

It's a huge canvas, some 222 x 300cm, recalling those earlier 'history paintings' of modern life by the likes of Manet (*Execution of Maximilian*, 1867), and more academic painters such as Adolphe Yvon (*Capture of the Malakoff Tower, 8 September* 1855, *[Crimea]*, 1857). Its immediate subject, though, has nothing to do with executions or warfare: it is a lecture and presentation by Mathias-Marie Duval to students and staff at the École des Beaux-Arts, where Duval, a highly respected professor of histology at the Faculty of Medicine of the University of Paris, taught from 1873 until 1899.[36]

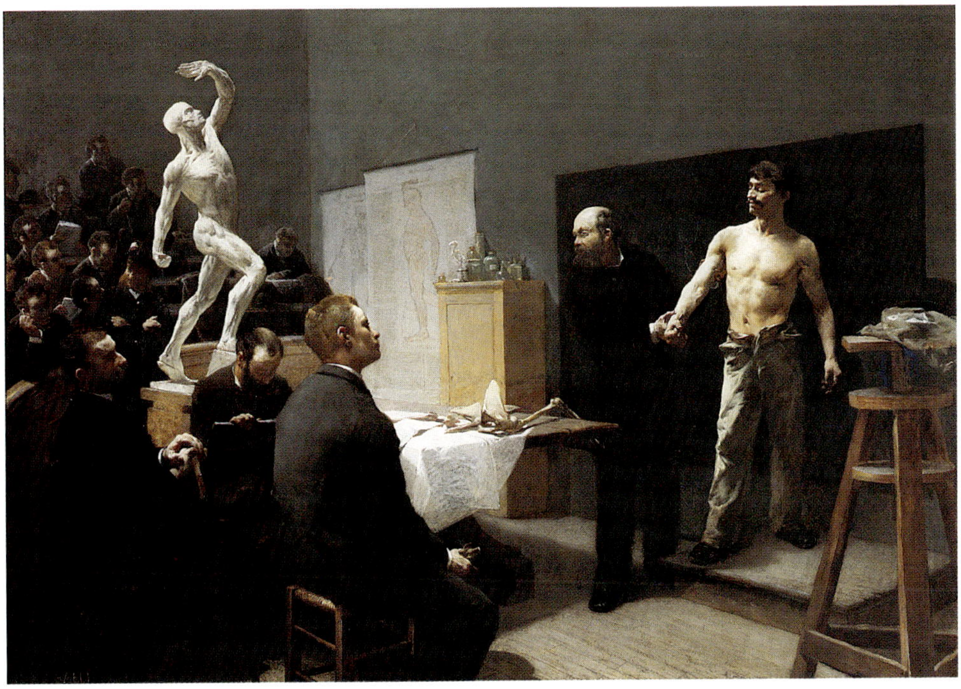

Fig. 143. François Sallé *The Anatomy Class at the École des Beaux-Arts* (1888) Cat. 136

So much for the picture's obvious theme – an anatomy lesson for art students at the prestigious National school. A closer analysis, however, invites other more pointed readings, ones which involve considerations of sexuality, class and their representations. Let's consider first the male model, at whom the two seated figures in the foreground, carefully realised in profile, gaze. The epitome of virile masculinity, his trousers, rugged features and tousled hair would signify working-class origins. By contrast, the 'refined' features and apparel of the two gazing men (invitees to the lecture and/or teachers) suggest quite different social roots and inclinations. But back to the model. Stripped down to reveal a powerfully built torso, his top trouser button is unfastened and the garment hangs suggestively open at, or just below, the waist; above is the large indentation of his navel. Duval 'holds' the man's right arm, turns his back on him, and presents the limb to his audience. I place 'holds' in scare quotes, because the movement is not exactly that; there's a tentativeness to it, as if Duval was handling something offensive, perhaps even unclean: no female prostitute here (Olympia), nor a naked man (by implication, well-off) bathing himself (in *Man at his Bath*), but rather a labourer, one of 'the great unwashed'. Significantly, the only critic in 1888 to comment on the painting singled out Duval's action. In a short paragraph in the evening journal, *Paris*, Ch. Laurent wrote:

> M.P [sic] Sallé has painted a solidly made *Anatomy Lesson*, in the middle of which a fine piece of nude (*un beau moreceau de nu*) stands out: the model obligingly allowing a professor to knead (*pétrir*) his biceps.[37]

"Knead" is a revealing word, denoting in this context a very physical, manipulative exercise:[38] the worker's arm and, by extension, his body, is there to be shaped, like dough or perhaps even clay, signified by the modelling stand at the bottom right of the picture (on which rests the man's blue scarf, shirt and hat). Yet everything about his stance and demeanour suggests the opposite of malleability. Although shorter than Duval, his position on the raised platform places him well above the professor. Striking an assertive pose (which interestingly recalls that of the central male figure in Daumier's polemical lithograph, *Don't Meddle with the Press*, 1834), he looks down proudly at his extended arm, the object of Duval's (and the class's) attention. Here the model (subject) looks at himself being looked at. No longer simply the object of scrutiny, he is also an active spectator. That this dual role is played out by a working-class, half-naked male, of course, raises the stakes.

Which brings us to the two soberly dressed men who gaze intently at this figure. Of particular interest is the younger of the two, the man nearest to us, whose expression can best be described as one of awe. Given the explicit sexualising of the model's body, discussed previously, it's not too fanciful to suggest an underlying homosocial desire bordering on the erotic. And here I use the term 'homosocial' in the sense that it's employed by Eve Kosofsky Sedgwick and Solomon-Godeau, to designate "a network of relationships that are themselves derivative of patriarchal social and sexual organization."[39] Needless to say, *The Anatomy Class* shows men in the company of men; men functioning in a patriarchal institution (the École des Beaux-Arts) with its own inherent hierarchical structure (pupil, teacher, master, model). One final observation on the wonder-struck young man, whose right hand rests on his groin clasping a glove and a hat: the highlighted, shaft-like shape of the glove temptingly suggests the implicit – but 'hidden', of course, because it is proscribed – phallus.

Paintings and other forms of visualisation embody – ideas, concepts, etc. They may also embody in another sense, that of picturing the body. In respect of the *The Anatomy Class*, however, 'embodiment' understood in this latter sense is taken one step further: there are the bones on the table (shoulder joints, arms and forearm bones, they refer to that section of the model's anatomy considered by Duval); the anatomical charts on the back wall ('fleshed' and skeletal respectively); and the ghostly, nude sculpture, oscillating between the animate and the inanimate (its flexed right pectoral muscle a mirror image of the same section of the 'real' model's anatomy).[40] This demystification, if you like, of the body; this stripping it bare and then building it up (a quintessentially nineteenth-century project; Zola's surgical strategies come to mind) contrasts with the painting's 'unspoken' narratives, those of sexuality and class and power. Which perhaps may help explain – if that is the right word – why critics in 1888, with the one exception I'm aware of, said nothing about it. Why it was awarded a third class medal, and why it was acquired for the (now) Art Gallery of New South Wales, is another story

*My thanks to Martin Sims, Fay Brauer and Graham Forsyth for their comments, and to students for their feedback.

Notes

1 Abigail Solomon-Godeau, "Male Trouble: A Crisis in Representation," *Art History* (June 1993): 286. This is also the title of her recently released book published by Thames and Hudson (1997), which I have not had the opportunity to read.

2 Leonard Tancock, preface to the second edition (1868), *Thérèse Raquin* by Emile Zola, trans. Tancock (London: Harmondsworth, 1962) 22–23.

3 Tancock, preface to *Thérèse Raquin* 15.

4 Zola, *Thérèse Raquin* 106-118.

5 Evan Williams, "The Weekend Review," *The Sydney Morning Herald* 1–2 Feb. 1997: 11.

6 Zola *Thérèse Raquin* 109.

7 A. Corbin, *The Foul and the Fragrant: Odour And The French Social Imagination* (London and Basingstoke, 1994) 36.

8 Corbin, paraphrasing Johann Philipp Withof (1756), *The Foul and the Fragrant* 35.

9 Quoted in Corbin, *The Foul and the Fragrant* 36.

10 Corbin, *The Foul and the Fragrant* 46.

11 See Corbin, *The Foul and the Fragrant* 246, n.75.

12 See T. J. Clark, *The Painting of Modern Life: Paris in the Art of Manet and his Followers* (London: Thames and Hudson, 1985) 96–7; A. Krell, *Manet and the Painters of Contemporary Life* (London: Thames and Hudson, 1996) 65–6.

13 Jules Claretie (pseud. of Jules Arsène Arnaud), *Le Figaro* 20 June 1865, quoted in G. H. Hamilton, *Manet and his Critics* (New York: W. W. Norton, [1954] 1969) 73.

14 C. Virmaître, *Les Curiosites de Paris* (Paris, 1868) 17.

15 Illustrated in Krell, *Manet* 57.

16 Ernest Filloneau, *Moniteur des Arts*, quoted in Hamilton, *Manet and his Critics* 72.

17 Buffon, quoted in K. Kete, *The Beast in the Boudoir: Petkeeping in Nineteenth-Century France* (Berkeley, U of California P, 1994) 118.

18 Kete, *The Beast in the Boudoir* 118-19.

19 See Krell, Manet 58-62.

20 See A. Distel, *Revue Du Louvre*, April 1993: 82.

21 Solomon-Godeau, "Male Trouble" 286.

[22] Solomon-Godeau, "Male Trouble" 287.

[23] Solomon-Godeau, "Male Trouble" 287.

[24] Solomon-Godeau, "Male Trouble" 301.

[25] See N. Watkins, *Bonnard* (London: Phaidon, 1994).

[26] Kete, ch. 2: "The Notion of Fidelity in a Bourgeois World," *The Beast in the Boudoir* 22-38.

[27] Kete, ch. 7: "Cats and Categorization," *The Beast in the Boudoir.*

[28] Reproduced with comment by Gloria Groom in *Gustave Caillebotte Urban Impressionist*, exh. cat. (Paris: La Réunion des Musées Nationaux Musée d'Orsay and Chicago: The Art Institute of Chicago with Abbeville Press, 1995) 216. I discuss *Man at his Bath* in an essay in *Impressions of Modernity*, ed. Richard Hobbs, soon to be published by Manchester UP. See also my poster, *Gazing at Caillebotte: Reflections on recognition, removal and relocation*, XXIXth International Congress of the History of Art, Amsterdam, September 1996. A synopsis and image appears on the World Wide Web at the following address: http://www.let.ruu.nl/CIHA/posters/. Tamar Garb deals with questions of masculinity and modernity in Caillebotte's male figures in a forthcoming book, *In Visible Touch: Modernism and Masculinity*, ed. Terry Smith (The Power Institute of Fine Arts, University of Sydney). See also A. Callen, *The Spectacular Body: Science, Method and Meaning in the Work of Degas* (New Haven: Yale UP, 1995) esp. 147, 150-1.

[29] G. Vigarello, *Concepts of Cleanliness: Changing Attitudes in France since the Middle Ages*, trans. Jean Birralee (Cambridge: Cambridge UP, 1988) 218.

[30] My thanks to Malcolm Park, a postgraduate student at the University of New South Wales College of Fine Arts, for pointing this out to me.

[31] See Groom, *Gustave Caillebotte.*

[32] This information appears in *Le Télègraphe* 23 June 1888: 1. Montefiore, we are informed, also purchased Gaston Latouche's *The First-Born*. Eliezer Montefiore (1820-1894) was one of the founding trustees of the gallery.

[33] See the article by Anthea Callen published shortly before this essay went to press: "The Body and Difference: Anatomy training at the Ecole des Beaux-Arts in Paris and the later nineteenth century," *Art History* 20.1 (Mar. 1997): 41–5 and notes 9, 69-70.

[34] The painting, no. 2230, was hung in salle XXXI, in the company of works by artists such as Edmond Picard, Joseph Saint-Germier, Fernand Pelez and Jean-Paul Sinibaldi.

[35] The 1888 Salon was widely covered by the Parisian press. My observation is based on an examination of reviews in some sixty publications (daily newspapers, journals, satirical magazines) held in the Bibliothèque Nationale, Paris. A Special Studies Programme granted by the University of NSW College of Fine Arts allowed me to pursue this research.

[36] See the entry on Duval in Charles Coulston Gillispie, ed., *Dictionary of Scientific Biography* cited in the Sallé dossier, Art Gallery of New South Wales, Sydney. Also *Les Hommes d'aujourd'hui*, 6.273, n.d., unpaginated, devoted to "Professeur Mathias Duval." Characteristic of this publication, a drawing of the celebrity appears on the front cover; here it's a caricature of Duval by Roc. Although the journal is undated, it can be established that the issue came out close in time to the Salon of 1888; this makes the scarcity of references to Sallé's picture, at least to the identity of the learned professor, a 'man of today', all the more unusual.

[37] Ch. Laurent, "Le Salon de 1888," *Paris*, 1 May 1888.

[38] The phrase "un beau morceau de nu" is also tantalising. In colloquial French it means a "nice bit of skirt." See for example R. J. Herail and E. A. Lovatt, *Dictionary of Modern Colloquial French* (London, 1984) 199. My investigations so far, however, have not shown that the phrase was used in this manner in the late nineteenth-century. I am grateful to Richard Hobbs for drawing this matter to my attention.

[39] Solomon-Godeau, "Male Trouble" 288; E. K. Sedgwick, *Between Men: English Literature and Male Homosocial Desire* (New York: Columbia UP, 1985).

[40] My thanks to Dr George Weisz for this observation.

Jill Bennett

Kama and Eroticism: The Five Senses in the Work of Francesco Clemente and Pierre Klossowski

In two enigmatic paragraphs of *The History of Sexuality* Michel Foucault summarily rejects the idea that the west possesses an *ars erotica*.[1] Unlike China, Japan, India, Ancient Rome, and the Arab-Muslim societies, he argues, we have displaced the erotic arts in favour of scientific discourse. We have looked to medicine, biology, psychiatry and sexology to provide us with knowledge about sex. These disciplines have obliged by constructing a set of norms based around the taxonomic identification of perversions and the pathologising of sexual deviants. To our great cost we have as a culture ignored the potential value of an *ars erotica* in which sex acts are catalogued for their own sake; where "pleasure is not considered in relation to an absolute law . . . but first and foremost in relation to itself."[2] We have not allowed ourselves to learn about the body, to develop a knowledge of sexual practice, through the use of literary, visual and performative arts. We thus have no equivalent of the *Kama Sutra*, for example – an ancient text written for the instruction of men and women in sexual arts – and nothing rivalling the rich tradition of Indian miniature painting and temple carving that documents an extensive range of sexual activity.

To flesh out Foucault's thesis, it could be argued that two features of the western visual arts tradition have militated against the development of an *ars erotica* on the non-western model. The first is the privileged status accorded to visual experience relative to other forms of sensory experience. The second – and this is linked to the first – is the decline of the convention of using art as a teaching aid, stimulus, or model for action. By way of contrast, these aspects are central to the spirit of the *Kama Sutra* which tells us:

> Kama is the enjoyment of appropriate objects by the five senses of hearing, feeling, seeing, tasting and smelling assisted by the mind together with the soul. The ingredient in this is a peculiar contact between the organ of sense and its object, and the consciousness of pleasure that arises from that contact is called Kama. Kama is to be learned from the Kama Sutra (aphorisms on love) and the practice of citizens.[3]

The five senses have traditionally been hierarchised in western societies. The senses which operate over distance – sight and hearing – have generally been regarded as superior to the close contact senses of touch, taste and smell (smell is conventionally included here as it covers only limited distances). In modern societies, social relations are largely mediated through the distant senses; we see and talk to one another in the public realm but for fully socialised adults, most activities involving touch, taste and smell are either confined to private, intimate settings or subject to taboo.[4] In the field of art history this division has been entrenched since at least the European Renaissance when modes of spatial perception underwent a profound shift from the *haptic* (tactile, bodily mode of perception) to the optic.[5] An index of this shift is the increasing concern of the visual arts with the simulation of appearance or with the constitution of a unified space over which visual mastery is possible. In terms of erotic art we see this in the tradition of the

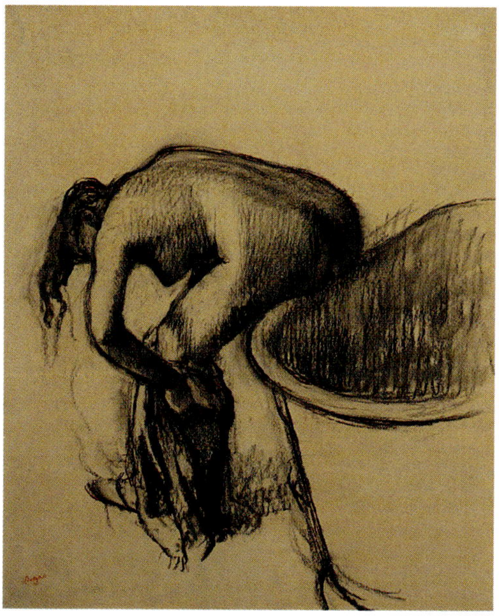

Fig. 144. Edgar Degas *After the Bath* (c.1900) Cat. 37

nude, a genre which from the Renaissance has privileged the voyeuristic experience of a spectator over an engagement with corporeal subjectivity. Feminist analysis has highlighted the spectatorial 'gaze' as the structuring feature of works such as Degas' *After the Bath* (Fig. 144). Such 'keyhole' images emphasise the experience of perception at a distance; one can observe a girl bathing without being physically compromised, without in fact being physically present. One can argue that scant attention is paid to the sensory experience of the woman depicted here, but indeed, equally little concern is given to the body of the spectator. Kenneth Clark offers a rationale for this in his monograph on the nude.[6] The (female) nude in art, Clark argues, is not arousing in the way that its pornographic counterpart is, for it operates not on the body but on the mind. The pleasures that it yields are sublimated – aestheticised – so that the experience is purely visual.

The attitude which underpins Clark's distinction between pornography and art has its roots in the Renaissance classification of painting and sculpture as 'liberal' arts. Unlike medieval imagery, which operated in more bodily terms, eliciting a mimetic response from viewer, the 'liberal' arts of the Renaissance were conceived as both *originating in*, and *operating upon*, the intellect; and in so far as they invoked a sensory response their primary appeal was to the eye. In this respect, art ceased to be 'used' (as stimulus, as model) and came to be 'viewed'. From this point, the notion that erotic art might spur one to action would always sit uneasily with the western idea of art as an intellectual practice.

There are, however, moments in which these cultural limits have been actively transgressed through the reinstating of a kind of haptic understanding of the body and its encounters. The work of the Italian born artist Francesco Clemente is a case in point, particularly as the sources for his iconography are precisely the *ars erotica* of India (Hindu and Tantric imagery) and the pre-Renaissance Italian (Catholic) medieval painting tradition.

Clemente's *Testa Coda* (1988–90) (Fig. 145), a series of 27 oil paintings each titled either *Heart*, *Head*, *Foot* or *Oblation*, and in one instance *Lover*, incorporate several references to crucifixion imagery. In one image called *Foot*, two feet ooze viscous blood from large red holes – a reference to the nail wounds in the crucified body of Christ.[7] These feet, cut off above the ankle by the frame, appear to hang in space; they have no narrative context, yet seem to tell a story. The toes are splayed, rigorised as if in fright; the only movement is the flow of blood from the intense red gashes on the prominently displayed soles, forcing their way towards the picture plane.

This kind of focus on the detail – particularly the intense scrutiny of the wound – is a feature of late medieval Italian painting, the aim of which was to convey the horror of Christ's Passion through a mnemonic which imprinted itself upon the spectator. A haptic rather than optic art, Italian painting of that period offers the spectator not a unified visual field to be perceived at a distance, but a symbolic system in which figures and forms are enlarged according to their narrative significance, and in which *the part* is therefore more significant than the whole. Operating on the principle of contact, such painting seeks not to engage the eye at a distance but to bring the spectator into proximity with the body of the holy figure depicted. Graphic detailing and repetition of the wound functioned as a kind of agitation, stirring the body and emotions. The relationship between such imagery and the body of the spectator was not so much semiotic as "ballistic"; the image was, in a very palpable sense, 'felt' rather than merely observed.[8]

An ovoid form recurs throughout Clemente's *Testa Coda* series as wound, as chest opening, as vagina and also as a negative space formed in between feet or cupped hands. It is, of course, a pornographic signifier, as graphic and as engaging as the red foam vagina in Cindy Sherman's *Untitled* (1992) (Fig. 97). Whether the deep red gash is read as vagina or wound is immaterial; holes in bodies are always sexy.[9] They violate the integrity of the individual, constituting a point of entry as well as seepage. Thus they are always erotically charged. Because they excite us, there is no space between stimulus and response in which to reflect. The violent and the pornographic act upon the sensory body before it has a chance to process information, to 'read' the image. The body is, in effect, contacted or touched, so that the distance between the eye and the object of its

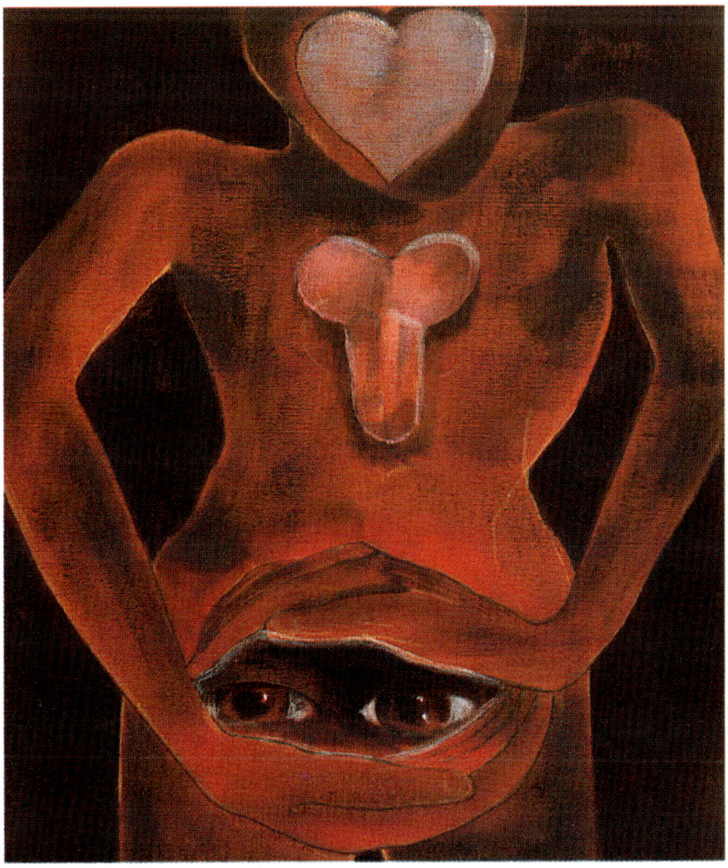

Fig. 145. Francesco Clemente *Heart (XVI)* (1991–92) Ref. 4

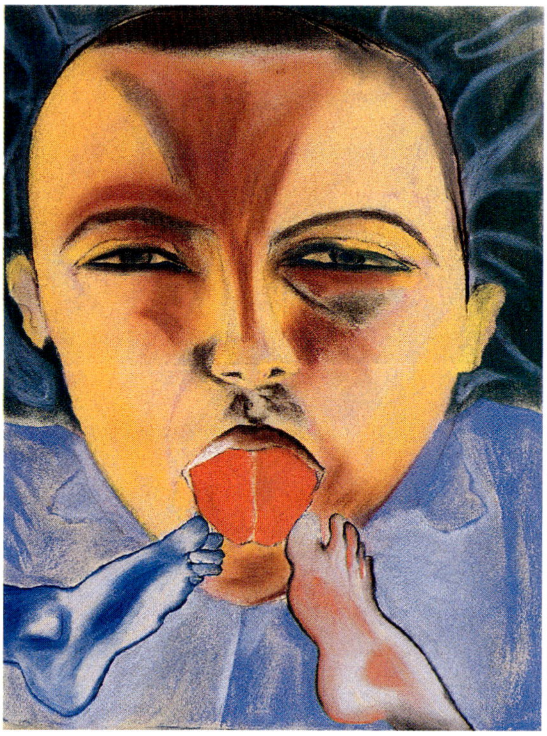

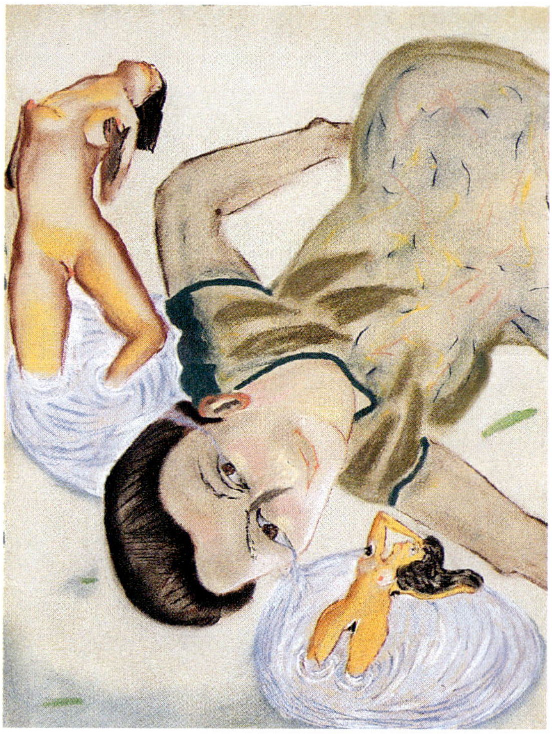

look is eradicated. Rather than attaining a mastery of the visual field, the eye is brought into collusion with the contact senses.

The medieval eye that gazed upon the wound in Christ's side did not maintain its distance from the wound but sought to touch it (like St Thomas) and to enter inside (like the medieval mystic St Catherine who imagined herself climbing into the wound and hiding). In a similar spirit, Clemente depicts the tactile eroticism of fingers penetrating a chest cavity and of hands touching the edges of a large red gash in a chest as someone pokes a stick at the tiny heart shape within it.[10]

In these paintings one is not presented with an organised body – a body to make sense of – but with bodies that can only be sensed; moved in and out of rather than observed from the outside. Clemente's corporeal signifiers, like those of the medieval Italian painters, speak "the language of the body" – an untranslatable idiolect. To enter into dialogue one must interpret through the body, or through the five senses. This requires of the viewer a propensity to feel an image on the body; it implies the kind of 'openness' that appears to have characterised the medieval body.[11] The 'open' body is marked not only by wounds but by orifices in general: a multiplication of mouths, lips, holes and rims, the function of which may be ambiguous and interchangeable. It consumes and is consumed in a feast that invokes not just touch but the other exclusively 'contact' sense of taste (mystics like St Catherine, for example, drank from Christ's wound and tasted his blood). A culture in which devotees express their love for Christ through touch and taste is a culture with a profound *ars erotica*, for it is a culture which gives full vent to an art of affective oral expression.

Clemente's organs do not always function as they should in the fully socialised adult subject; they are desiring and rapacious and hence oblivious to social inscription. If they are tutored at all it is in the language of the body – the language of mystics and medieval theologians and of the

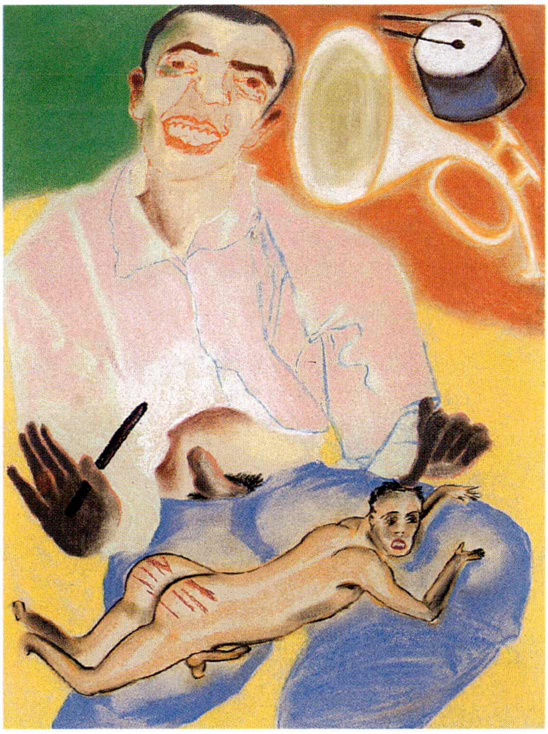

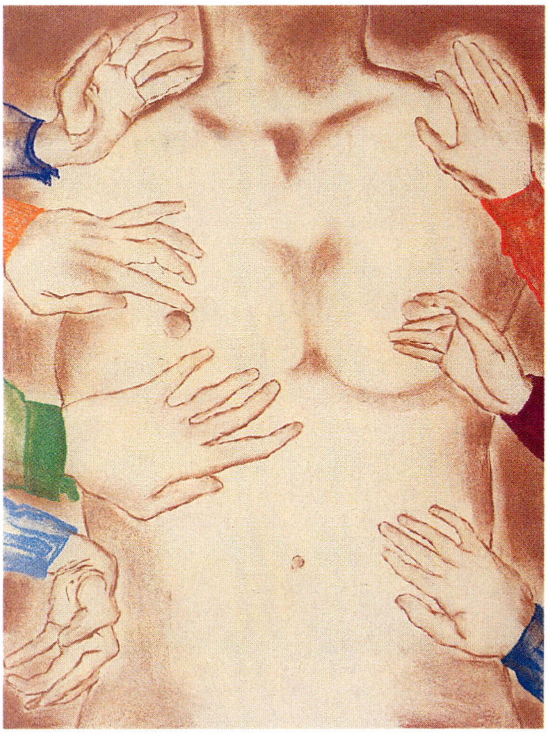

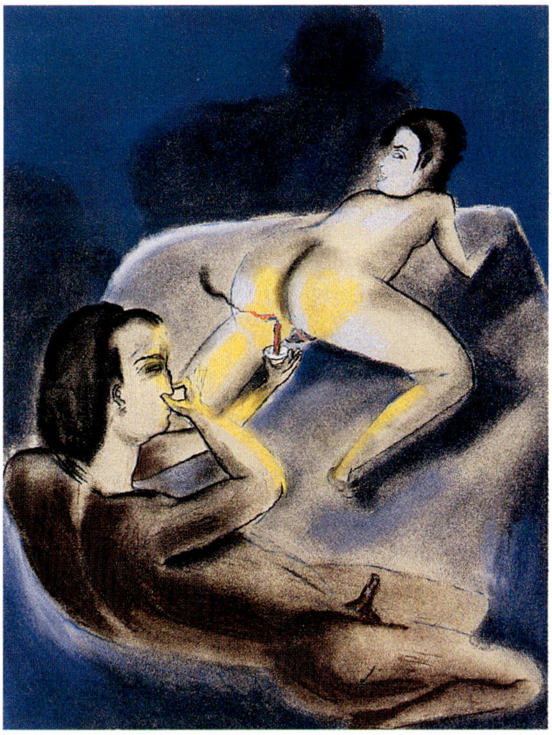

Fig. 146. Francesco Clemente
The Five Senses (1981) Ref. 3

Kama Sutra. In the *Five senses* (Fig.146) hearing is signified by the erotically charged sound of a slap – realised in an image which once again insists upon tactility, bringing a distant sense into collusion with a contact sense. Sight and smell are equally reified in images which play upon the ancient (Aristotelian) association of sight with the element of water and smell with that of fire.[12] By rendering sensory contact palpable, Clemente evokes in a material way the pleasure that arises from the contact between the sensing organ and its object.

The eye is not a privileged organ in Clemente's world. In *April: Left Eye* (Fig. 147), seeing is referenced only at the most tactile, visceral level. The eye is constituted by an ant hill, surmounted by a tortoise – apparently mating with a naked woman – whose convex shell serves as an eyeball. Where the pupil might be located, the 'eyeball' is pierced by a crucifix. Perception here is not a question of immaterial images imprinting themselves onto the retina, but of actual penetration – a tactile convergence in the fullest sense. The eye is simply an opening – an orifice on the open body. Images do not leave it unscathed; they enter it. In this respect *April: Left Eye* recalls the thirteenth-century Italian image of Christ implanting the Cross into the body of St Clare of Montefalco. That image represents not simply a metaphor but a "ballistic" encounter of the kind reiterated by Clemente in *May: Right Eye* (Fig. 148). Here the eye is penetrated from an entry point in the back of the skull. Light rays appear to pass through the hole, through the head itself and then the eye, to illuminate the image of an apple in the palm of a hand. The palm is literally touched by the beam that emanates from outside the picture frame, in a manner clearly reminiscent of the stigmatisation of St Francis of Assisi.

Clemente's bodies are always in the act of touch or in some way already touched or penetrated. Sometimes objects can be found inside organs; a heart contains a phallus, for example (another echo of the story of Clare of Montefalco whose heart was autopsied in 1308 and found – literally –

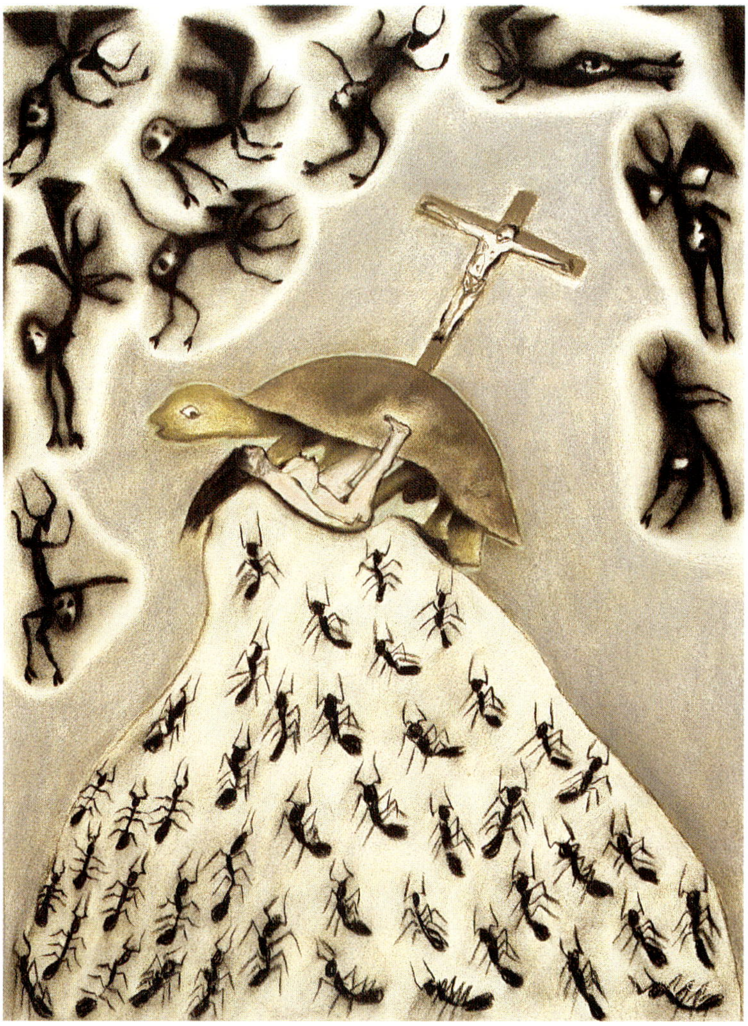

Fig. 147. Francesco Clemente *April: Left Eye* from *The Purification of The Twelve (A Calendar for 1988)* (1987) Cat. 32

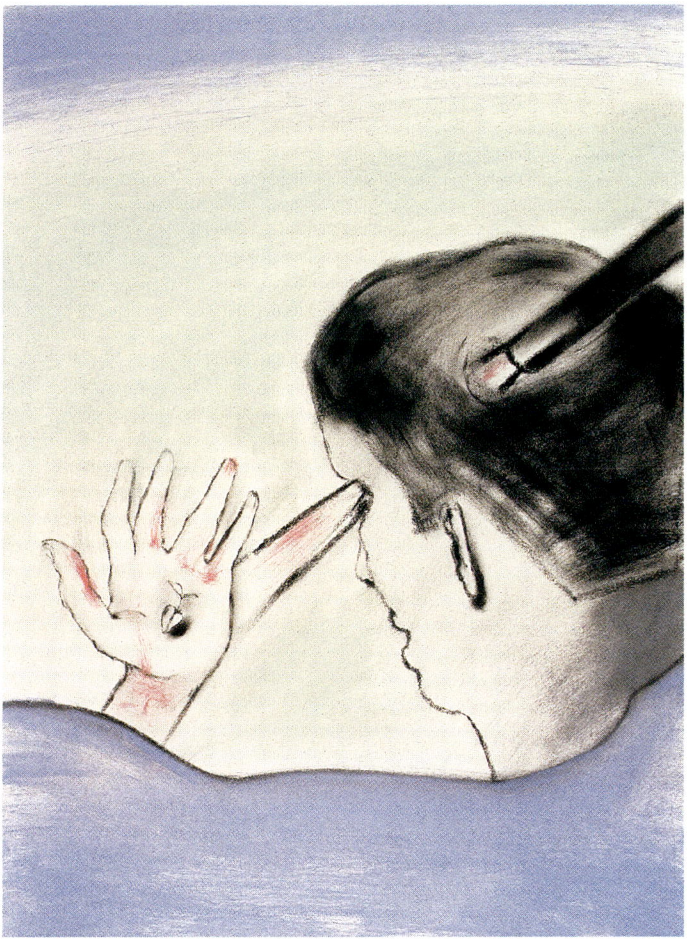

Fig. 148. Francesco Clemente *May: Right Eye from The Purification of The Twelve (A Calendar for 1988)* (1987) Cat. 32

to contain the instruments of Christ's Passion). The redistribution of organs around the body is further reminiscent of Hindu Tantric imagery. The disembodied phallus, for example, appears inscribed upon the bodies of the Tantric goddesses along with crescent moons, emblems of the sacred vulva or yoni, and other dismembered parts. The abstraction of genitalia is of course, fundamental to Hindu iconography in general. Every temple dedicated to Lord Siva has in its sanctum a Siva lingam, or phallus, set within a yoni, and the ritualistic anointment of the lingum (with curd and ghee and so forth) emphasises the tactile nature of this iconic form. When Clemente approaches Hindu iconography it is as pure tactile convergence. Two images from *Testa Coda* (titled *Oblation*) evoke the Siva lingam in the form of a central white phallus, touched by a nipple, a penis, a finger. These abstracted body parts are not articulated as belonging to a cohesive whole; they simply collide as parts. Bodies are pared down so as to signify only contact – only the event of touch.

The ultimate absurdity of subjecting the sensory body to the rigour of scientific classification is demonstrated by Clemente in his ironic titles for the images that make up the series *Purification of the Twelve*. Here, twelve body parts are distributed according to the calendar months. But if the mapping of anatomy onto a timescale seems arbitrary, the system is further confused as parts do not always correspond to labels. In this respect they elude identification and understanding except at the level of corporeal affect. The actuality – the viscerality – of experience inevitably exceeds the bounds of taxonomy.

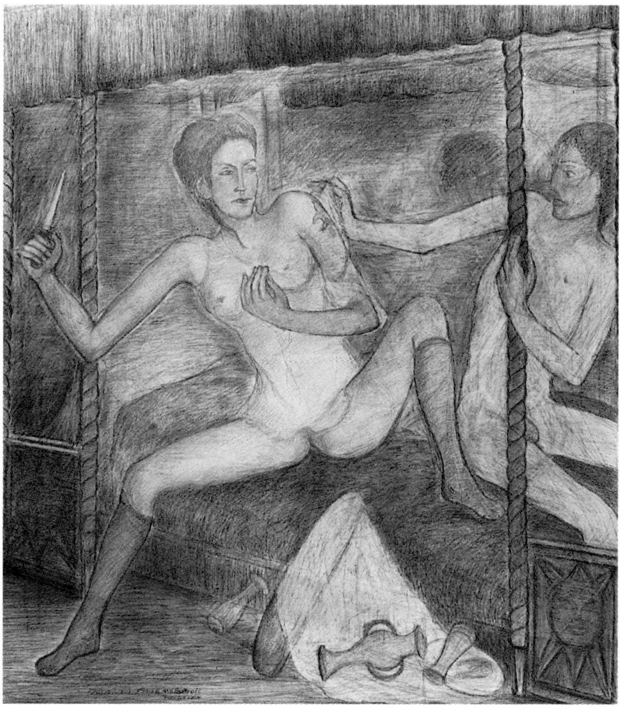

Fig. 149. Pierre Klossowski *Milady and D'Artagnan* (1986) Ref. 17

Like Clemente, Pierre Klossowski is concerned with an asystematic production and with sensation rather than with orderly appearance. He seeks not to reproduce the object of emotion but "to reproduce this emotion itself."[13] Passions, Klossowski says, are "incompatible with established order," therefore always exceeding their designation. If one animates the body with passion, feeling and sensation, one necessarily ruptures the social boundaries of the body. It is therefore impossible to produce an *ars erotica* that operates within the law of sociality, that conforms to social norms or pre-set rules.

In many ways Klossowski's work appears the antithesis of Clemente's. The 'open' or 'pornographic' body, filled with holes or fragmented into parts through which Clemente effects a kind of haptic address is far removed from the relatively genteel spirit of Klossowski's large scale coloured pencil drawings. These works are usually narrative scenes involving identifiable characters. They cannot be said to operate upon the body by the same means as Clemente's more violent, more pornographic images. They are not *exciting* in the same way.

But like Clemente, Klossowski operates through metonym or what Clemente calls "ideogram." His *modus operandi* also invites comparison with medieval narrative painting. Although he creates a *mise-en-scène* he is not concerned with optical realism. Figures are flattened, lacking in volume (their sketchy rendering and pale colouring also recalls the light palette and thin application of tempera and fresco paintings). If these ineffable, weightless bodies are organic and psychic unities, it is only to demonstrate the flow of emotions beyond, across the body. These emotions coalesce at nodal points – usually where hands attach one body to another. Where there is no evocation of depth one reads surface pattern; the points of intensity are established through the detail and through symbolic enlargement.

The tactility of Klossowski's erotica is encoded in the emblem of the hand – the signifier of process as well as of emotion and sexual intensity. The hand stands as an emblem for the whole body, and like Christ's wounds it tells a story.[14] In *The Improbable Understanding of Tadzio and*

Aschenbach II (Fig. 35), a scene based on Thomas Mann's *Death in Venice*, the grasped wrist and the thumb ensconced in the palm knot together the two weightless bodies. In Mann's novel there is no physical contact between the two protagonists, it remains "improbable." Here the symbolically charged space of the palm, clasping the thumb, signifies a point of entry, realising a fantasy of impossible union.

In Klossowski's well-known Parallel Bars series, the palm is even more pronounced as a sexual signifier, stroked and licked in the most unlikely of social settings. The sensory inversion, whereby taste and touch emerge within the visual field, has something in common with Clemente. But the animation of the palm – as in Clemente's *May: Right Eye* – takes us back to the wound, the hole on the body of Christ or the stigma on the body of his great imitator St Francis of Assisi. It is ultimately (the experience of) a moral stigma or punishment, and its manifestation of the body, that interests Klossowski. He speaks about this in relation to the scene from the Three musketeers where Milady brandishes a dagger and D'Artagnan grabs her to reveal the compromising fleur-de-lys on her shoulder (Fig. 149). In Klossowski's rendering of the scene, gesture encodes experience or feeling. Milady's hand is cupped as if to denote concealment, but the gesture is somewhat redundant as it is formed not at the site of mark, but across the body and a moment too late. It serves rather as a formal echo of D'Artagnan's own hand gesture, referring at one remove to the revelation of the "mark of infamy." The gesture – with medieval grandiloquence – impresses itself upon the viewer as a symbol encapsulating the full meaning of the event. (The same excessive, incongruous kind of gesture can be seen in the painting *The Room* by Klossowski's brother Balthus (Fig. 150)). Once inspired to copy the frescoes of Piero della Francesca and Masaccio, Balthus

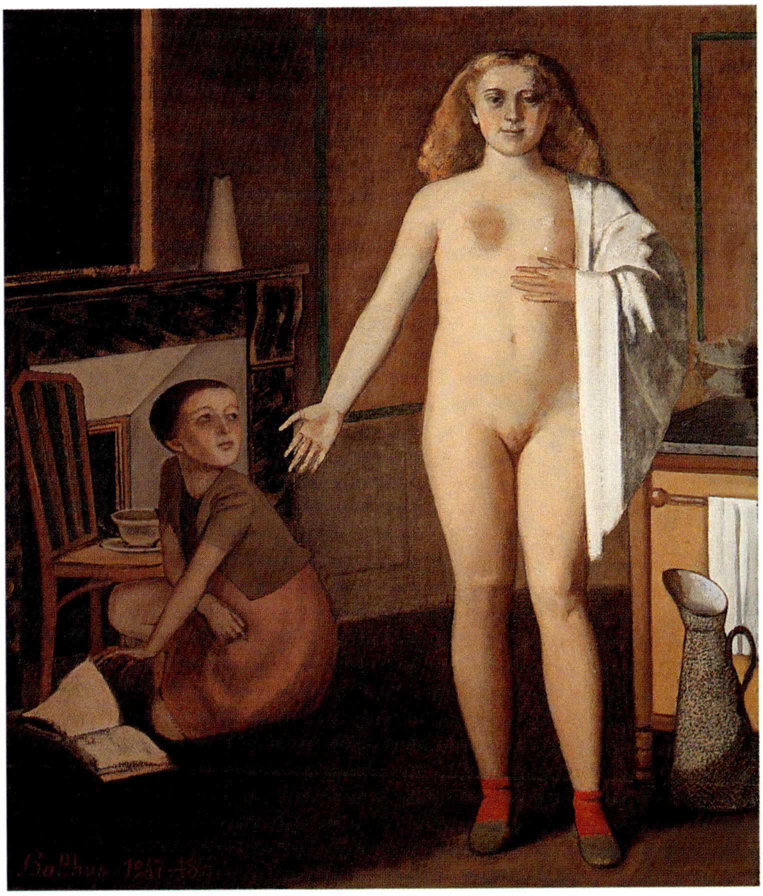

Fig. 150. Balthus *The Room* (1947–48) Cat. 7

seems to return to these artists for the source of this apparently overcoded gesture which undercuts the narrative of the domestic nude, disrupting continuity but focussing attention.)

The hand gesture for Klossowski signifies the subjective experience of bearing the stigma. Hence it is metonymic in precisely the terms of the medieval wound image, and because it conveys a feeling – like Passion imagery – it must be felt, understood with the body. Klossowski says that in an image of his fictional character Roberte he portrayed the fingerprints on the raped Roberte to show that she *knew* the feeling of stigma and shame mixed with pleasure. This, he says, is a sensation that exceeds moral sense and social identity. If *Milady and D'Artagnan* is about *knowing* the feeling of stigma, it is not about D'Artagnan *seeing* or Milady *appearing*, so much as about the impact of a sensation in the body. The stigma – like the gesture – is a mnemonic of pain, encoded onto the body. To this extent one cannot know these characters except as sensations. They do not operate within the boundaries of a determinate identity but always fall beyond the social. They are not representative of a given order but are what Klossowski calls "phantasms."[15] They – like medieval passion images – teach us the feeling of stigma and shame and offer the pleasure that accompanies it. Like medieval images, too, they do not teach us through letters but through a corporeal understanding.

Tantrism teaches that "There is no gnosis without pain. It is no good simply accepting that the . . . world which appears so real is actually composed of phantasms: one has to feel it. *One must know it not with the mind but with one's flesh.*"[16] St Thomas Aquinas, the great Italian Dominican theologian of the Middle Ages, also knew this for he never solved problems through the mind alone. Whenever he was stuck on a point of logic he would resort to bodily mortification. For Aquinas and for the tens of thousands of his contemporaries who practiced ritual flagellation, knowledge was attained through a mimetic identification with Christ's Passion. Similarly knowledge of the truth came to St Francis when God imprinted him with the wounds of Christ. Through literally bearing and feeling – like Milady – a stigma (or in his case five *stigmata*); through being touched and imprinted, came understanding. The most famous technology imagined in modern times for communicating through the body in this way is the machine that writes punishment into the flesh in Kafka's story *In the Penal Colony*. It is difficult for a witness to read the bloody message the machine inscribes but that is not the point; as the officer in charge of the machine explains, the victim "deciphers it with his wounds."[17] Understanding is an effect of feeling; likewise for the witness of the barbaric practice whose response is not intellectual but visceral – a 'gut' response.

Klossowski's work does not make the spectator wince as would a barbaric incision. His bodies do not leak and bleed like Clemente's. But the work is about sensation which exceeds classification; about an understanding that can only proceed from the embodied experience, an untranscribable event. In this sense it is not scopic; the exploration of sensory experience can never restrict itself to the field of the visual and can never operate entirely through a visual language.

In as much as Klossowski evokes the feeling of "shame" mixed with pleasure, his erotica is amoral. His characters oscillate like medieval devotees absorbed in the image of Christ; they feel the suffering and humiliation, but this is accompanied by the sweetest pleasure – something that might in fact be close to *kama*. As with Clemente's bodies, there can be no moral order imposed upon all this, no separation of pleasure and pain, violence and pornography. An *ars erotica* in the full sense is an art of the body and an art of the senses. It offers not the possibility of containment within a visual field – a mastery by the eye – but pure bodily sensation: an encounter based on *affect* or the transformation of bodies through contact. *Ars erotica* breaches the distance between the eye and the image to apply direct pressure upon the body. Its images are material and they affect (stir, agitate) the body through their presence; its ideas are communicated in a corporeal language.

Foucault suggests to us that this is the only way to an expansive knowledge of pleasure and of senses. We cannot trust science to provide a disinterested account of these things, and since we have not encouraged artists to provide knowledge in this way, we need to look hard at – and value – work which may nevertheless provide us with an art of the senses – an art which proceeds from the sensory body rather than from social body. We need, as Francesco Clemente says, to learn to ". . . *trust all of those who have 'thought' through their bodies.*"[18]

Notes

1 Michel Foucault, *The History of Sexuality, Volume 1: An Introduction*, trans R. Hurley (New York: Vintage Books, [1978] 1980) 58.

2 Foucault, *The History of Sexuality* 58.

3 *The Kama Sutra of Vatsyayana*, trans. R. Burton (New Delhi: Penguin, 1993) 64.

4 See for example, Georg Simmel, "Sociology" (1908), discussed in P. Falk, *The Consuming Body* (London: Sage Publications, 1994).

5 See Alois Riegl in M. A. Holly, *Panofsky and the Foundations of Art History* (Ithaca: Cornell UP, 1984) 73.

6 K. Clark, *The Nude: A Study of Ideal Art* (London: John Murray, 1956).

7 This image is reproduced as Foot number xiv in *Francesco Clemente Testa Coda*, Gagosian Gallery (New York: Rizzoli, 1991).

8 Walter Benjamin uses the term "ballistic" in this sense to describe the operations of the cinematic image. W. Benjamin, *Illuminations* (1955), trans. H. Zohn (London: Fontana, 1973) 240.

9 See Alfonso Lingis, "Savages" in *Excesses: Eros and Culture* (New York: SUNY 1984).

10 *Francesco Clemente*, plates labelled *Heart* xxiv and *Heart* ii respectively.

11 See M. Bakhtin, *Rabelais and his World* (Cambridge, Mass.: MIT P, 1968).

12 See Aristotle, *De Sensu* and *De Anima*, especially the volume *Aristotle's De Anima Books II, III*, trans. D. W. Hamlyn, Clarendon Aristotle Series (Oxford: Clarendon P, 1963) 116.

13 P. Klossowski, "The Decline of the Nude" (1967), trans P. Foss, *Art & Text* 18 (July 1985): 20.

14 This point is discussed in relation to the *Parallel Bars* series (and specifically in reference to an image of Roberte in which Klossowski says "one hand lies while the other admits to a crime which she feels in her fingers.") in C. Francblin, "Pierre Klossowski: The Voyeur and his Counterpart," *Flash Art* 107 (May 1982): 22–27.

15 *Phantasm and Simulacra: The Drawings of Pierre Klossowski*, spec. issue of *Art & Text* 18 (July 1985).

16 I. Sinha, *The Great Book of Tantra: Translation and Images from the Classic Indian Texts with Commentary* (Rochester: Destiny Books, 1993) 129 (my italics).

17 F. Kafka *The Judgement* and *In the Penal Colony*, trans. M. Pasley (London: Penguin 60s Classics, 1992) 31.

18 Quoted in "Francesco Clemente," interview by G. Politi, *Flash Art* (Apr.-May 1984): 1.

David Bromfield

Posing the Question: Rodin's *Iris* and the Modern Body

Je hais le mouvement qui déplace les lignes,
Et jamais je ne pleure et jamais je ne ris.

Les poètes, devant mes grandes attitudes,
Que j'ai l'air d'emprunter aux plus fiers monuments,
Consumeront leurs jours en d'austères études.

— *La Beauté*
from Charles Baudelaire's *Les Fleurs du Mal*, 1857
but written earlier.[1]

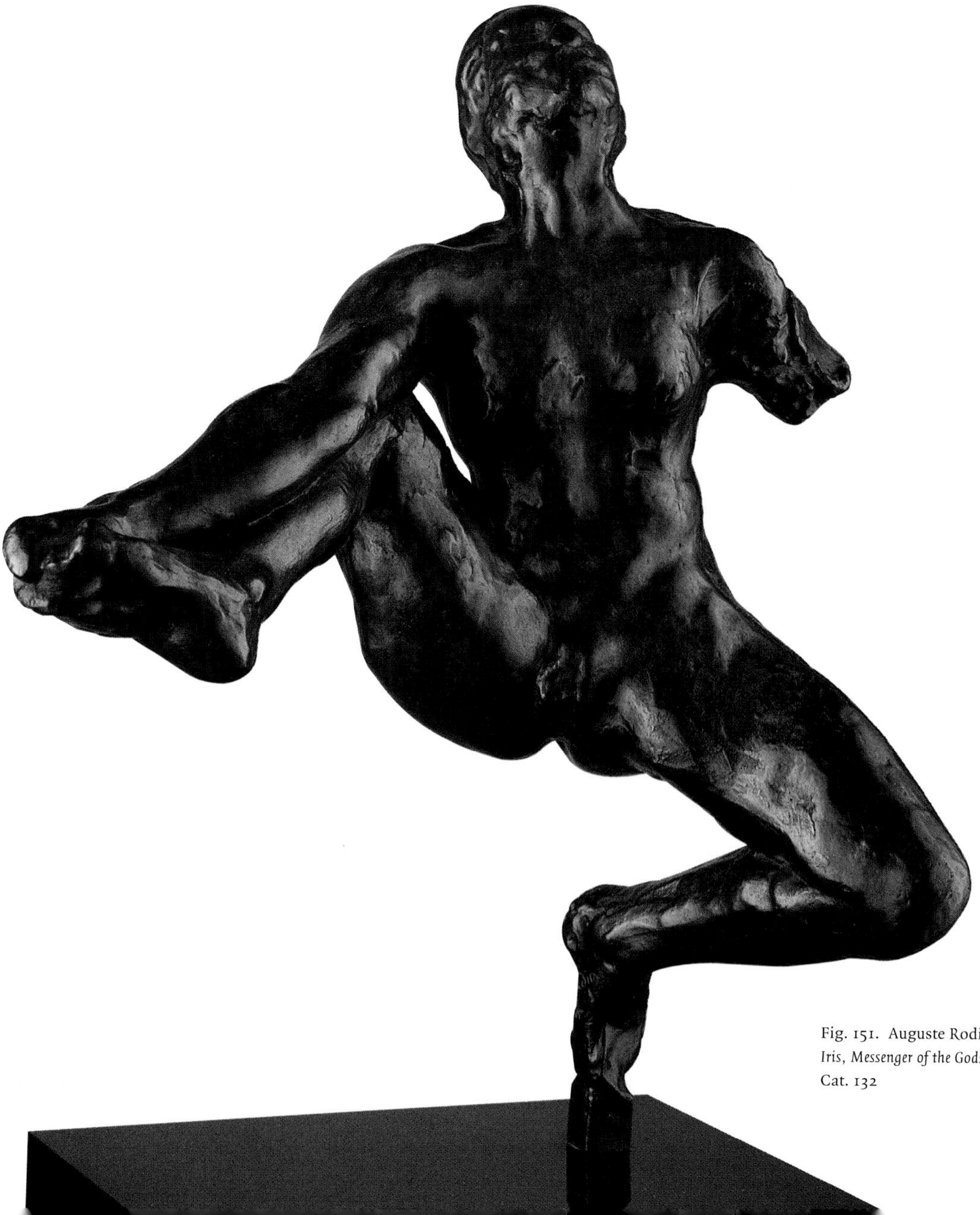

Fig. 151. Auguste Rodin
Iris, Messenger of the Gods (1890–91)
Cat. 132

. . . et j'aime à la fureur
les choses où le son se mele à la lumière

Elle était donc couchée et se laisser aimer,
Et du haut du divan elle souriait d'aise
A mon amour profond et doux comme la mer
Qui vers elle montait comme vers sa falaise

Les yeux fixés sur moi, comme un tigre dompté,
D'un air vague et reveur elle essayait des poses,
Et la candeur unie à la lubricité
Donnait un charme neuf à ses metamorphoses;

Et son bras et sa jambe, et sa cuisse et ses reins,
Polis comme de l'huile, onduleux comme une cygne,
Passaient devant mes yeuxs clairvoyants et sereins;
Et son ventre et ses seins, ses grappes de ma vigne

S'avancaient plus calins que les Anges du mal,
Pour troubler le repos où mon ame était mise
Et pour le déranger du rocher de cristal
Où calme et solitaire, elle s'était assise.

— *Les Bijoux*
from *Les Fleurs du Mal*, 1857.[2]

I waited until we stopped again, and adjusted the driving mirror so that I could see into the rear seat. Vaughan had moved his thumb into the girl's vagina, forefinger into her rectum, as she sat back with her knees against her shoulders, drawing mechanically at the second of the cigarettes.

His left hand took the girl's breast, his ring – and forefingers propping up the nipple like a miniature crutch. Holding these elements of the girl's body in his formalised pose, he began to rock his hips back and forth, driving his penis into the girl's hand. When she tried to move his fingers from her vulva Vaughan knocked her hand away with his elbow, holding the fingers securely in her body. He straightened his legs, rotating himself around the passenger compartment so that his hips rested on the edge of the seat. Braced on his left elbow, he continued to work himself against the girl's hand, as if taking part in a dance of severely stylised postures that celebrated the design and electronics, speed and direction of an advanced kind of automobile.

This marriage of sex and technology reached its climax as the traffic divided at the airport overpass and we began to move forwards in the northbound lane. As the car travelled for the first time at twenty miles an hour Vaughan drew his fingers from the girl's vulva and anus, rotated his hips and inserted his penis in her vagina. Headlamps flared above us as the stream of cars moves up the slope of the overpass. In the rear-view mirror I could still see Vaughan and the girl, their bodies lit by the car behind, reflected in the black trunk of the Lincoln and a hundred points of the interior trim. In the chromium ashtray I saw the girl's left breast and erect nipple. In the vinyl window gutter I saw deformed sections of Vaughan's thighs and her abdomen forming a bizarre anatomical junction. Vaughan lifted the young woman astride him, his penis entering her vagina again. In a triptych of images reflected in the speedometer, the clock and revolution counter, the sexual act between Vaughan and this young woman took place in the hooded grottoes of these luminescent dials, moderated by the surging needle of the speedometer. The jutting carapace of the instrument panel and the stylised sculpture of the steering column shroud reflected a dozen images of her rising and falling buttocks. As I propelled the car at fifty miles an hour along the open deck of the overpass Vaughan arched his back and lifted the young woman into the full glare of the headlamps behind us. Her sharp breasts flashed within the chromium and glass cage of the speeding car. Vaughan's strong pelvic spasms coincided with thudding passage of the lamp standards anchored in the overpass at hundred yard intervals.

— from J. G. Ballard, *Crash*[3]

It has become fashionable to regard the body as a construction, a product of description and discourse, a mirage of social and economic mores, which falls apart the minute one questions its role as a vehicle for desire. In fact the imaginative and cultural coherence of the body, like the nature of desire itself, has been a central dilemma for artists (and most others) for more than a century. Those who talk of the disappearance of the body as something about to happen, evidenced by the profound banality of virtual sex, have only grasped one small facet of a complex situation that underpins the continuing relevance of the body to contemporary art. What I shall call the modern body still provides artists with resistant raw material. It still marks the space where they find their most important questions.

The modern body exists beyond discourse, at the borderline between presence and absence, the moment just before its fragments fall into the abyss. It is best thought of as a sequence of continually dislocated poses and re-presentations, moving stillness rather than frozen motion. As Baudelaire found, in *Les Fleurs du Mal*, eternal Beauty is embodied as a dream in stone, with marble breasts, a body that detests motion. There are, however, other versions of the beautiful for which moving stillness is essential. In opposition to the unbroken line of Beauty, Baudelaire discovered a kaleidoscope of poses, like glittering reflections in the facets of polished stones. This essay sketches the emergence of some of the factors which have formed this predominant modern version of the body in the visual arts.[4]

Every visitor to the Musée Rodin is struck by the bronze cast of *Iris, Messenger of the Gods* displayed on a pedestal at chest height amongst a number of other bronze figure studies. Only *Iris* is uncomfortable on its plinth. The works close to it are easily grasped, frontally oriented, male and female torsos. Across the room, variously phallic studies of Balzac testify to Rodin's irreconcilable difficulties with presence in the male nude.

The headless *Iris* is disturbingly unlike all the others, at once a whirlwind of potential movement and rigidly constrained, bound tight by her mass and pose. The right arm reaches out so that the hand can grasp and flex the toes of the right foot, holding the thrusting limb tensely compressed just beyond the normal limit of its flexing. The outstretched arm is parallel to the right calf, their joints lock rigid against each other. The left leg is tightly bent downwards, ready to spring open. It appears to support the weight of the entire body.

In fact a thick square metal bar, more like an orthopaedic brace than an armature, runs up close behind the figure to keep it from toppling over. The left arm is absent so that the entire work presents only the logic of tension with no relaxed counterbalance. It can never be still. Between the junction of the explosively tense lower limbs the vagina is wide open to view, a powerful if graceless punctuation mark. The rough surface of the straining belly and breasts catch the light like stones in a cliff face.

For some time an alternate title for *Iris* was *Endless Tunnel*,[5] which is immediately reminiscent of Courbet's *The Origin of the World* (Fig. 15). Yet its significance is completely other. The railways had given tunnels firm associations as passages of unknowing darkness of indeterminate length. Tunnels, like sculpture, were inescapably associated with hard manual labour. Rodin's lost title, if indeed it was Rodin's, suggests something more than vague vaginal mysteries. It declares that the body itself is akin to a tunnel. To be precise the body defines that through which we must always pass and that passage will be hard work.

Iris was conceived as testimony to the emergence, through Rodin's practice, of an unrelenting need to refigure and reconstruct the body that remains central to contemporary culture. During the 1880s, in response to the demands of the commission for *The Gates of Hell*, he had developed a tactile method of composition which made use of pre-formed body fragments – limbs, hands, heads, torsos – which he juxtaposed to produce new figures and new groupings. This procedure required his finished figures, his bodies, to move from provisional states to a fixed form. Ultimately, traces of the provisional overwhelm the fixed finished form.

Iris resists the unifying touch of hand or eye. Unlike the other works in the room at the Hotel Biron its 'awkwardness' inevitably sets the viewer in motion, constantly shifting in a fruitless attempt to grasp an absent line. The missing head and arm intensify this search. Most sculptures of the moving body, such as Degas' *Dancer Looking at the Sole of her Right Foot* (Fig. 4), rely on the presence of a head and its implied gaze to motivate their actions and to locate the viewer. However introspective Degas' sculpture may be, it does not place the viewer at the very limits of coherence, it throws out a grace line to follow.

Rosalind Krauss has commented at length on the implications of Rodin's method for the authenticity of avant-garde art.[6] It also has implications for the disappearance of the 'authentic' eternal body of Beauty and the re-production of that body as a sequence of poses. *Iris* marks the moment when Rodin's stratagem fails, when the facility of his constructions breaks down to reveal the void at their centre, the endless tunnel.

The least regarded, but most promising explanation for the pose of *Iris* is the suggestion, by Keisch, that it is derived in whole or part from the experience of Can-Can dancers that Rodin apparently drew in the mid to late 1890s.[7] At one moment in the dance the dancers seize their right foot in their right hand to prolong the effect of the kick and either hop or rotate on the spot. The Can-Can is the first of a series of spectacular modern dances intended to display the female body as a sequence of standing waves of flesh and clothes, one pattern following another. Its popular status and mechanical format link it directly to striptease and even to contemporary 'soft' pornography which are both composed from partial, unresolved images, assemblages of bodily fragments.[8]

There is evidence that Rodin was directly affected by the powerful but increasingly incoherent versions of the modern body first experienced by Baudelaire in *Les Fleurs du Mal*. *Beauté*, one of Rodin's illustrations for *Les Fleurs du Mal*, commissioned in 1887 by the publisher Gallimard, bears no resemblance to Baudelaire's austere, monumental stone breasted, figure. Her veiled body shimmers under cross hatching suggesting any number of poses.[9]

In her study of the history of Rodin's failed *Monument to Victor Hugo* Jane Mayo Roos has shown that the figure, but not the final pose of *Iris*, evolved from one of the muses which Rodin wished to place around the figure of Hugo.[10] The monument was commissioned from Rodin in 1889 as a part of the programme for the newly secularised Pantheon. Rodin conceived a private meditative work, barely taking into account its public function.

Iris, Messenger of the Gods was probably conceived and completed in the mid to late 1890s in response to the failure of the Hugo monument. Its paradoxical, shifting but highly powerful erotic presence is a response to Rodin's failure to invent a public embodiment for the muses or for the democrat Hugo himself. It must surely have taxed Rodin to find an eternal, monumental pose for the ever fickle voice of the people. Like Baudelaire before him Rodin abandoned an austere public eternal beauty for a private modern mistress of many poses.

Most features of the modern body first emerged in *Iris*. There is a clear homology between Rodin's use of preformed fragments to assemble his bodies and the academic technique of constructing the eternal ideal figure through the aggregation of prescribed poses in the Academic life class, shown in François Sallé's *The Anatomy Class at the École des Beaux-Arts* (1888) (Fig. 143). In *Iris*, however, a frustrated Rodin freed his body fragments to exist as a sequence of poses in potential motion with no expectation that they should later converge into a single idealised state. Later Rodin required his models also to be in state of constant movement dancing and rolling round the studio while he drew them.[11]

The modern body, then, is accessed as a series of fixed poses in perpetual motion. Because of this it cannot be located clearly within a public space. It offers no external point of view; it can only exist while travelling an endless tunnel. Fredric Jameson has pointed out that in post-modern space there are no external coordinates, that this space can only be experienced in motion from the inside, preferably from the interior of a moving vehicle, such as the car driven by Ballard's fictional alter ego.

> . . . this latest mutation in space – post modern hyperspace – has finally succeeded in transcending the capacities of the individual human body to locate itself, to organise its immediate surroundings perceptually, and cognitively to map its position in a mappable external world.[12]

For art, at least, this problem began well before 1900. It grew in intensity throughout the century. Vaughan's systematic rearrangement of the limbs of the prostitute in *Crash* is an attempt to get his bearings while in motion.[13]

The modern body is always on the edge of flight. Because it is perpetually in motion all sculpture which engages it seeks to escape from the plinth. The modern body tends to lose its head. Decapitation, concealment or cancellation of the head and face offer themselves as the most logical artistic solution to the problems it presents. The late appearance of African masks in *Les Demoiselles D'Avignon* could be considered as Picasso's response to the headless monsters he had discovered.

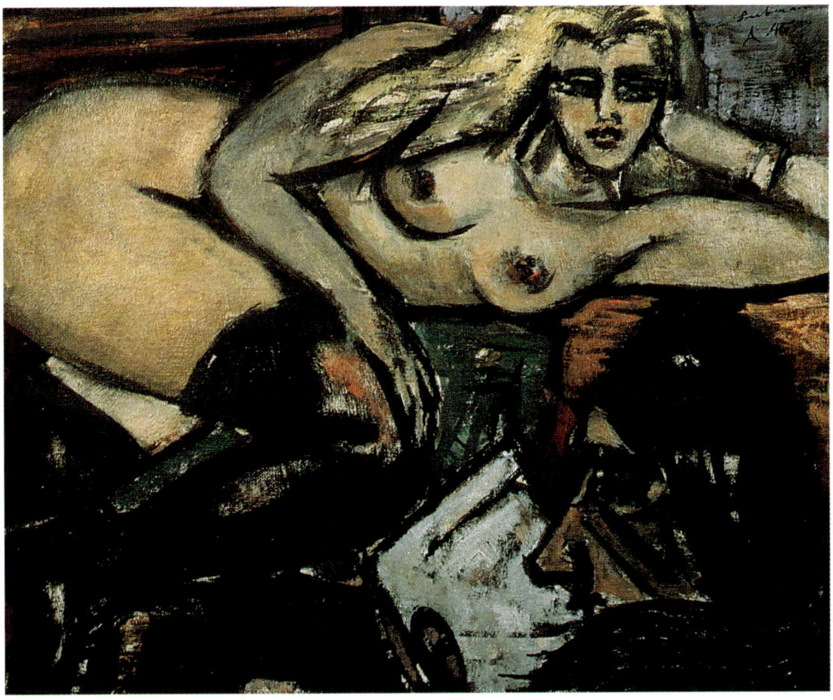

Fig. 152. Max Beckmann *Der Brief (Liegender Halbakt) (The Letter (Reclining Nude)* (1945) Cat. 11

The modern body is always caught up directly with the erotic as spectacle. The erotic forms the hinge between one pose and the next, the punctuation mark between absence and presence which allows the body's constant re-formation. It is the erotic which enables the modern body to cover the abyss. Each new construction, every new pose interrogates the emptiness beyond it. The modern body represents our century's best attempt at immortality. Its endless shifting poses seek to deny or rather ignore death. It 'embodies' a dream of absolute alienation. Its fragmentary existence is closely related to the division of labour. It emerges with the advent of industrial production, technology and spectacular entertainment. It is endlessly re-assembled through a complex division of labour, produced and reproduced through cycles of fashion fetishism and style. It is negotiable in every sense but, unlike every other negotiable item, can never be fully alienated from its origins. This exhibition presents many different responses to the perpetual re-emergence of the modern body.

Some artists, such as Otto Dix, rerun the paradigmatic experiences of Baudelaire. His *Odd Couple* (1925) (Fig. 47) belong in *Les Fleurs du Mal*. The old bald man clutches with his shrunken claws of hands at the over ripe buttocks and back of the distracted blonde whore on his knee. Her plump calf and black high-heel boot contrast sickeningly with his carbuncled foot and the varicose veins across his shin; through the open window the breeze bears the corrosive smoke and fumes from the infernal factoryscape beyond.

Only our memory of the long lost possibility of the body as evidence of eternity saves *The Odd Couple* from becoming an unbearable moral cliché. Its residual tragedy emerges if it is compared with Rodin's compositions of couples such as *The Eternal Idol* or with Baudelaire's description of his prostrate worship of his mistress in *Les Bijoux*. The old man is attempting to force a modern body to yield an eternal presence.

The modern body has also given rise to particular fetishised versions of the sensual nude. Max Beckmann's *The Letter (Reclining Nude)* (Fig. 152) is typical of these representations in which covering and uncovering of parts of the body by stockings or lingerie reduce it to a schema of

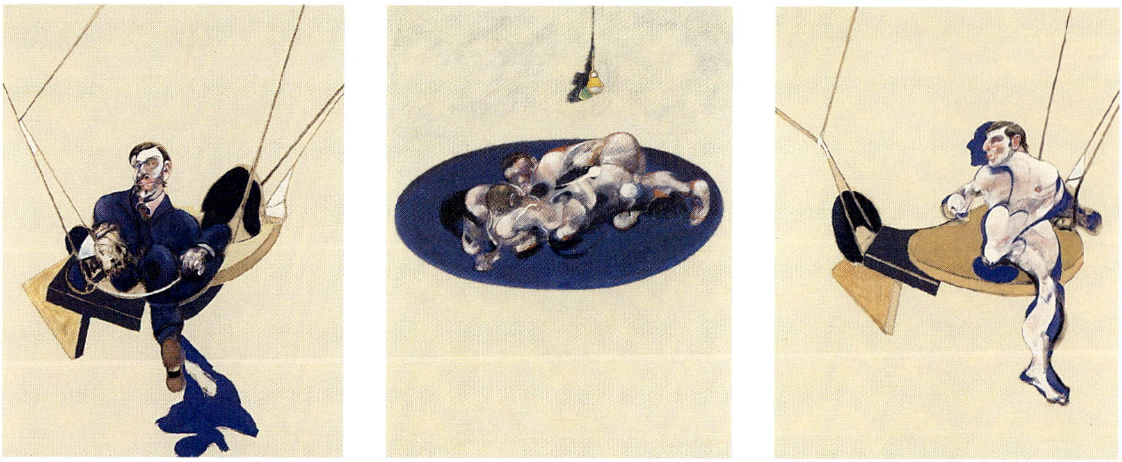

Fig. 153. Francis Bacon *Triptych* (1970) Cat. 5

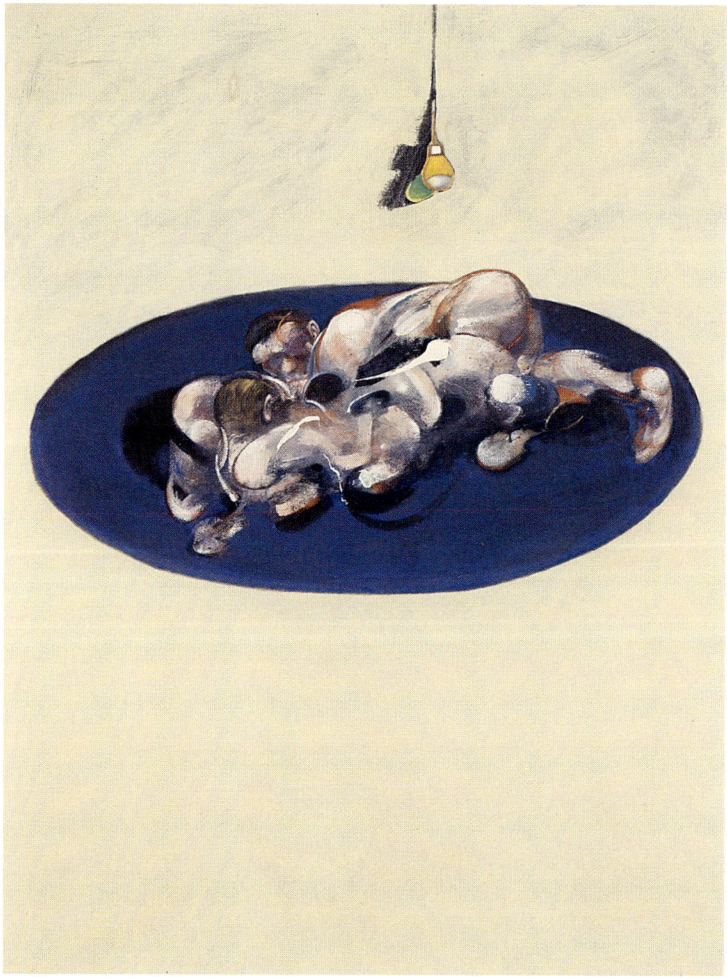

Fig. 154. Francis Bacon *Triptych* (1970) (detail) Cat. 5

forces and fragments. The direct delight of Beckmann's highly visible but tightly tuned brush work carefully amplifies this effect. Egon Schiele's drawing of a half naked girl (Fig. 32) is much closer to the primary elements of the modern body, even to Rodin's *Iris* itself. A dark shirt, stockings and high-heels frame bare upper thighs; midriff and pudenda are indicated only by lines which allow their spatial placement and volume to remain ambiguous, potentially in motion. How, for instance, is the belly disposed against the backbone?

Much has been said about this particular version of the modern body as intrinsic to the representation of femininity, as an instrument of male vision and power. It is very difficult to link questions of power and gender so directly to the body. Egon Schiele's *Eros (Self-portrait Masturbating)* (Fig. 31), which shows the artist with his hand at the base of a plainly visible full erection, also accesses the body via a system of implied poses, presences and absences. He is naked, except for a dressing gown round his shoulders which creates a partial separation between his head and body. It frames his legs and genitals, forming an empty background for the erection so that it also recalls the abyss.

Some artists whose work is inconceivable without the modern body have found gender barely relevant. In 1963 Francis Bacon commented:

> With Nietzsche I believe that man must remake himself. We must woo the doctors and scientists in the attempt to renew and alter ourselves, but there will be a lapse of time before their religious hangover will allow them to act freely. . . . The division between the sexes has to a large extent been invented. Only a comparatively small number of people are active within this division. The rest are waiting for something to happen or be done to them. But society has attempted to make moral differences. We must have the freedom to drift and find ourselves again.
>
> I have deliberately tried to twist myself, but I have not gone far enough. My paintings are, if you like, a record of this distortion. Photography has covered so much: in a painting that's even worth looking at, the image must be twisted if it is to make a renewed assault on the nervous system.[14]

Bacon's *Triptych* (Figs. 153 and 154) demonstrates this 'twisting' in terms of the successive sequence of poses required by the modern body. Bacon's painting method always involved reconstitution of the body from photographs, illustrations, the live model or memory. He refigures the body from the wind-blown dross that has all but covered it.

The two merging, melting figures spread across the blue disc in the central panel of *Triptych* are one of Bacon's favourite motifs, an image of wrestlers taken from the photographic studies of human and animal motion by Muybridge (Fig. 155). Their bodies are 'twisted' almost to the point of dissolution by their passionate engagement. Their dissolution is staged as a spectacle for the two figures, one besuited, one nude, who swing in hammocks in the right and left panels. The hammocks invoke an unstable space which amplifies the tendency to see each figure as a shifting

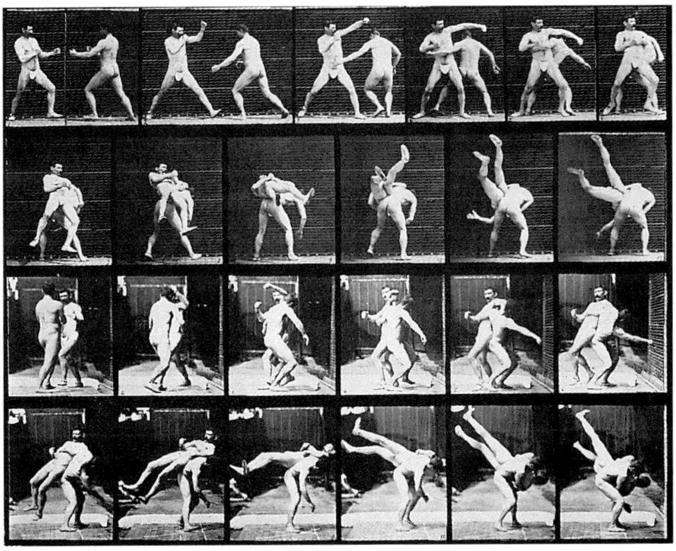

Fig. 155. Eadweard Muybridge *Animal Locomotion. Plate 332 (Wrestling)* (1875–85) Cat. 110

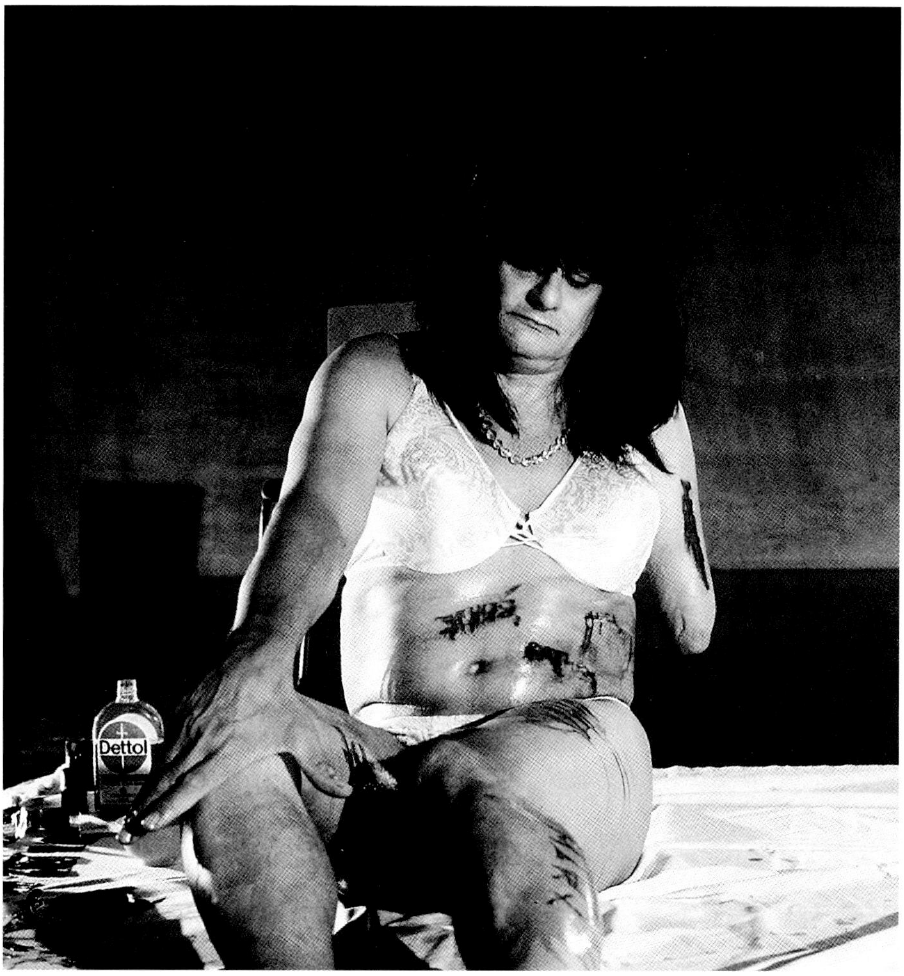

Fig. 156. Mike Parr *The Unword Performances* (1996) Cat. 119

sequence of poses. The brushmarks, stains and 'arbitrary' marks which make up Bacon's figures are nearly always self-referential and linear: one moves from one mark to the next. Indeed the 'arbitrary' marks serve to emphasise the impossibility of 'fixing' them with external coordinates.[15]

A major strategy employed by contemporary artists to confront and critique the modern body is performance. The legendary Schwarzkogler fragmented the body directly, through technology, in such a way as to circumvent the dilemmas of representation (Fig. 74). This permanent sacrificial strategy sought to reveal the body's inalienable residual resistance by testing it to destruction. Even the photographic relics of his work on show here escape any sense that they are posed alternatives.[16]

Another less permanent, though equally aggressive strategy, is to remake one's own body in direct collaboration with an audience in the face of the very technology normally used to multiply its poses. Mike Parr has worked in this way since 1971. His best known pieces of this kind are associated with his film *Rules and Displacement Activities Part 3*, completed in 1983. The most famous of these performances is *Cathartic Action, Social Gestus No 5* in which he severed a false arm filled with offal, then attempted to engage his audience in discussion. Although they were aware that he only had one arm, his carefully staged attack on the integrity of his body reduced them to silence for 20 minutes during which the artist delivered a fugue like monologue. In *Blue Movie* (1977), Parr screened a pornographic film to members of his extended family and filmed their increasingly hysterical reactions.

In *Unword* (Fig. 156) Parr, dressed as a bride, complete with wig and elaborate make up, incised a group of key words (Mother, Father, Marx, Sister and others) into his flesh with a scalpel so that his blood welled up to form the letters.[17] The event was filmed and photographed in detail and will be presented to the public in both versions. While *Unword* was largely concerned to free the body from the tyranny of verbal language it also destroyed the possibility of seeing or photographing the body as a system of poses, which is always another form of arbitrary linguistic order. Unlike Schwarzkogler, Parr has an extraordinary ability to return the body to a pre-signifying state without staging it's complete absence.

Others have concentrated on reducing the resistant body to nothing but arbitrary significance by circumventing it. In 1963 Bacon's suggestion that "We must woo the doctors and scientists in the attempt to renew and alter ourselves . . ." appeared reasonable. By the 1980s it was clear that he had underestimated the power of the technicians (especially the photographers he so much envied) and capital to reassemble the modern body so that no substantial renewal need ever take place.

Helmut Newton's *Self-portrait with June and Models* (1981) (Fig. 3) is best understood as a picture of a mechanic's workshop, akin to a panel beaters where the damaged and disintegrated fragments of the modern body are reassembled in hyperspace. Newton's sparse technical workshop is alien to the traditional conception of an artist's studio. Newton's model is no muse, she is a co-worker whose body presents as a sequence of fragmentary and isolated poses, the product of their joint labour. Her full length pose reflected in the mirror alludes to nineteenth-century attempts to retain the body as an eternal ideal, notably Ingres' *The Source* (Fig. 130). It is, however, made provisional by the appearance of a second pair of shapely legs in high-heels. They belong to a model seated out of sight to the right, waiting to take up her pose in the frame. In order to retain credibility for his smoothly engineered images Newton has been forced to re-present the body as an allegory of his working practice. The games he plays with double viewpoints, the mirror, the return gaze of the wife to the left, merely serve to emphasise the hermetic closure of his workshop, its commitment to predestined outcomes.

The photographic work of Parr and Newton marks the opposite limits of artistic response to the modern body. It is important, however, to see both as outcomes of one situation, to grasp that this work of reassembly takes place throughout our culture. It is possible that technology and capital may one day succeed in completely appropriating the body to themselves. If so that day is further away than current critical fashion may wish to believe. Until then artists will continue to pose the question, while the modern body simply poses.

Notes

1 ". . . movement I hate, that disturbs the ideal line, and never do I weep nor ever smile. Before the grandeur of my poses – seemingly inspired by the noblest monuments – poets will consume their days in austere research." This translation and original from Francis Scarfe, ed., *Baudelaire*, The Penguin Poets Series (Harmondsworth: Penguin, 1961) 26.

2 ". . . and I madly love those things in which sound and light commingle. So she reclined and let herself be loved, and high on the divan she smiled for joy upon my love, as deep and gentle as the sea, which rose towards her as to a cliff. With her eyes intent on me like a tame tigress, with vague dreamy look, she tried this pose and that and candidness and wantonness together

gave a novel charm to her variations. Her arms and legs, her thighs and loins, glistening like oil, rippling swanlike, passed before my clairvoyant and serene eyes; and her belly and her breasts, those clusters of my vine, thrust themselves forward more alluring than the angels of evil, to trouble the rest my soul had found and cast it down from the crystal rock whereon it had settled, calm and solitary." Francis Scarfe, *Baudelaire* 41–42.

3 J. G. Ballard, *Crash* (London: Vintage Books, 1995) 142–143.

4 A recent study by Eugene W. Holland discusses *La Beauté* and other related poems so as to bring out the multi-layered complexities of the poet's exploration of this issue. See Part 1, *Baudelaire and Schizoanalysis: The Sociopoetics of Modernism*, Cambridge Studies in French No. 45 (Cambridge: Cambridge UP, 1993) 43 ff.

5 See for instance Ginger Danto Rodin, "Erotic Inspiration in Nature" in *Rodin, Eros and Creativity*, ed. Rainer Crone and Siegfried Salzmann (Munich: Prestel, 1992) 198.

6 See Rosalind E. Krauss, "The Originality of the Avant Garde" and "Sincerely Yours" in *The Originality of the Avant-garde and other Modernist Myths* (Cambridge, Mass.: MIT P, 1985) 151, 171 ff.

7 See Claude Keisch, ed., *Auguste Rodin: Plastik Zeichnung Graphik* (1979), cited in Mary L. Levkoff, *Rodin in his Time*, (London: Thames and Hudson, 1994) 210 n4.

8 There are also equally spectacular dances which present the male and female bodies as fragmentary poses, notably the Tango. See note 15.

9 For a discussion of these illustrations see Albert E. Elsen, *The Gates of Hell by Auguste Rodin* (Stanford, Ca.: Stanford UP, 1985) 112 ff.

10 Jane Mayo Roos, "Rodin's *Monument to Victor Hugo*: Art and Politics in the Third Republic," *Art Bulletin* 68.4 (Dec. 1986): 653–655.

11 See Alain Kirili, "The Scandal of Rodin and his Models" in *Rodin, Eros and Creativity*.

12 Fredric Jameson, *Postmodernism or the Cultural Logic of Late Capitalism* (London: Verso, 1991) 44.

13 There is no space in this essay to discuss the work of other artists in which the modern body first appears, notably Cezanne. See for instance Mary Louise Krumrine, *Paul Cezanne: The Bathers* (Basel: Museum of Fine Arts, 1989).

14 See "From a conversation with Francis Bacon," *Cambridge Opinion*, 1964. Michael Peppiat quotes this conversation with Bacon in *Francis Bacon: Anatomy of an Enigma* (London: Weidenfeld and Nicholson, 1996) 395.

15 Interestingly the title frames for the film *Last Tango in Paris* – another central document for the various manifestations of modern body – feature paintings by Bacon. Bertolucci was filming in Paris at the time of Bacon's retrospective in the Grand Palais. He revisited the show with Marlon Brando and kept a copy of the catalogue by him while directing. See Peppiatt, *Francis Bacon* 244, and Enzo Ungari, *Bertolucci by Bertolucci* (London, 1987).

16 The relationship of Schwarzkogler to Mike Parr is dealt with elsewhere in this catalogue. For a more detailed discussion of the works covered in this essay, see D. Bromfield, *Identities, a Critical Study of the Work of Mike Parr 1970-1990* (Perth: UWA P, 1991) and Graham Coulter Smith, *Mike Parr: The Self Portrait Project* (Melbourne: Schwarz City P, 1994).

17 This closed event took place at the School of Fine Arts and Architecture, The University of Western Australia, Perth. A brief account of this event and an interview with Parr will appear in the first issue of *RE-Vision* magazine published by the Centre for the Creative Eye at the School.

Charles Merewether

The Unspeakable Condition of Figuration

To speak of body is to refer to its primary materiality, its corporeality and substance as that which is expended. As such it presupposes little that is irreducible except matter. Following Heidegger's question "How is there something rather than nothing," we may ask what it is for matter to make its way, to be made visible as the contours of the body: a coming into being of the subject, its naming, its inhabitation and place within the world.

One of the earliest images of the Americas was that of Jan Van der Straet's view of Amerigo Vespucci who, as he stepped upon the shores of the Americas, discovered before him a naked indigenous woman lying in a hammock. Michel de Certeau commenting on the image writes that it is the "unnamed presence of difference," in which "the conqueror will write the body of the other and trace there his own history." From this body he will make a "historied body – a blazon – of his labors and phantasms. She will be 'Latin' America."[1] It is an inaugural scene that initiates the "colonization of the body by the discourse of power . . . a will to write and a written body."[2] The body of woman as nature becomes the womb to be occupied and from which the Americas will be borne.

The scene is one of wonder, of discovery, but a wonder that is both erotic and warlike. This wonder would be for Luce Irigaray, "the passion of the encounter between the most material and most metaphysical, of their possible conception and fecundation one by the other."[3] It is this encounter, this exposure of matter to light that gives body its naming, a corporeality that gives woman a place: woman as land, its foundation. And as Irigaray observes:

> the female lover waits for light – the light that shines through discourse, that filters through words, that bestows a sense of the cosmos, but also that which is illuminated in the grace of regeneration and transfiguration. Giving herself to nature to be reborn from there, made fertile – within herself. . . . Fecundity of a love that gives itself over, on this side of and beyond reason – to the source of light.[4]

Woman comes into being through light. But if there is exposure, there is also place. In the following essay, I will suggest how woman as the subject of visibility, that is of naming and recognition, and of emplacement become central issues to the artistic practice of three women artists: Frida Kahlo, Ana Mendieta and Doris Salcedo.

What is the place given the body? To where does it belong? How do we understand its being in and of this world? Irigaray suggests the body of woman is place itself. The body of woman performs place insofar as it is itself an envelope that contains a receptacle. The boundaries are porous. "Woman, insofar as she is a container, is never a closed one. Place is never closed. The boundaries (of her body) touch against one another while still remaining open."[5] However, as both mother and woman and therefore double, she is doubly emplaced.

> The maternal-feminine remains the place separated from "its" own place, deprived of "its" place. She is or ceaselessly becomes the place of the other who cannot separate himself from it. Without her knowing or willing it, she is then threatening because of what she lacks, a "prope " place.[6]

Woman is given an unaccountable materiality that is systematically eliminated in the adoption of a metaphysics of presence. She is "never anything but the still undifferentiated opaqueness of sensible matter, the store (of) substance for the sublation of self, or being as what is, or what he is (or was), here and now."[7] The 'phallogocentric economy' as Judith Butler commenting on Irigaray argues, produces the 'feminine' as its constitutive outside in which the distinction between matter and form underscores 'matter' as the site at which the feminine is excluded from philosophical binaries.[8]

Following Irigaray, one needs to site the feminine as the "unspeakable condition of figuration, as that which, in fact, can *never* be figured within the terms of philosophy proper, but whose exclusion from that propriety is its enabling condition."[9] The feminine is set under erasure as the impossible necessity that enables ontology. She is then outside, other, at once interior and exterior. Exclusion is achieved in the differentiation between form and matter, in which matter is the site of inscription.

The violent exclusion of woman from the social is a concept that resonates strongly in the conception of the sacrificial and expenditure as the sacred moment of figuration and hence, the formation of the social. In his book *The Labyrinth of Solitude*, Octavio Paz argues that the promise of communion is achieved only through sacrifice.[10] For Paz, the religions of pre-Columbian and colonial Mexico were both founded on the idea of a sacrificial economy, economies that entailed death of a member of the community through sacrifice. This represented the release of a surplus vital energy and the possibility of community.[11]

> Everything merges, loses shape and individuality and returns to the primordial mass. . . . Ritual death promotes a rebirth . . . the orgy, sterile in itself, renews the fertility of the mother or of the earth. The fiesta is a return to a remote and undifferentiated state, prenatal or presocial. It is a return that is also a beginning, in accordance with the dialectic that is inherent in social processes. The group emerges purified and strengthened from this plunge into chaos. It has immersed itself in its own origins, in the womb from which it came.[12]

When and where women are represented within this economy is precisely the site of their erasure. Woman as the womb of the earth, the telos and origin of man's desire and redemption, *her* sacrifice as the foundation of representation and *his* promise of continuity. Essentialised as maternal body and therefore as a natural resource, culture places her outside, within the natural realm. An economy of excess depends, in other words, on a recognition and disavowal of difference. Paz's book was indebted to the work of the French anthropologist Marcel Mauss and, in turn, to both Georges Bataille and Roger Caillois, whose elaboration of a theory of sacrifice was based on a concept of excess or *expense*.[13] As Bataille proposed:

> Death, and death alone, constantly ensures the renewal of life. The law given in nature . . . life is effusion, it is contrary to equilibrium. It is tumultuous movement that bursts forth and consumes itself. Its perpetual explosion is possible on one condition: that the spent organisms give way to new ones, which enter the dance with new ones.[14]

Like Bataille's idea of spent organisms, Caillois also noted that just as with festival where waste and destruction are rightfully part of the festival's excess, so death by sacrifice is a ceremony of renewal or generation of the socius.[15]

Dis/embodiment

Both Frida Kahlo and Ana Mendieta produce images of themselves that explore this relation of inside/outside. Figuration reveals how "the subject's exterior is psychically constructed; and conversely, how the processes of social inscription of the body's surface construct a psychical interior: i.e. looking at the outside of the body from the point of view of the inside, and looking at the inside of the body from the point of view of the outside . . ."[16] There is no outside, except by transforming oneself into the object of sacrifice. However, having said as much, its impossible condition is that the body appears in Kahlo's work by virtue of an experience already of dislocation or dehiscence. The appeal to be seen in Kahlo's work and the act of embodiment belong to this economy, an economy of rupture within the woman as body that precedes and impels the movement of figuration.

In paintings *My Birth* (1932), *My Nurse and I* (1937) and *The Broken Column* (1944) Kahlo appropriates Catholic imagery with which to represent the sacrificial. She is the body of the martyr, the mother of Christ, the Virgin Mary, the prostitute and defiled woman who is the object of exchange. Kahlo played with the duality given woman. She plays out the role, appropriating through mimetic identification the body of Christ in *The Broken Column*. In *My Nurse and I* and *My Birth*, she is respectively the child of the indigenous mother and the mother who dies, in *A Few Small Snips* (1935), she becomes the object of crime. Again the sacrificial body. Her work also reveals the relation between nature and death as the constitutive condition given to woman. In a state of exile, her body finds its place outside the social, a place where the dead are buried. The subject is condemned to its own erasure. For Julia Kristeva, this exclusion produces what she names the abject. The paintings of Kahlo, we can say, are haunted by Kahlo, insofar as she can never be present. For, the condition of presence, as we see in these paintings demands a violent rupture with the body, of giving herself up, of absenting herself in order that the image can make its way. This absence, this dereliction of the self, is precisely what gives the work its powerful iconic presence. Kristeva writes of the abject that:

> The one by whom the abject exists is thus a *deject* who places (herself), *separates* (herself), situates (herself), and therefore *strays* instead of getting her bearings, desiring, belonging, or refusing. . . . Instead of sounding herself as to her 'being', she does so concerning her place: "Where am I?" instead of "Who am I?" For the space that engrosses the deject, the excluded, is never *one*, nor *homogeneous*, nor *totalizable*, but essentially divisible, foldable, and catastrophic . . .[17]

For Judith Butler the subject of feminine difference is "constituted through the force of exclusion and abjection, one which produces a constitutive outside to the subject, an abjected outside, which is, after all, 'inside' the subject as its own founding repudiation."[18] Against this dereliction, Irigaray seeks to view the materiality of the body from a different place, so that one might say "she is indefinite, infinite, *form is never complete in her*. . . . No metaphor completes her. Never is she this, then that, this and that."[19] Critical to her enterprise has been Merleau-Ponty's concept of an ontology that is founded within alterity, providing as constitutive of one and another, the interrelations between the inside and outside, the subject and object, the presence of the other in the same, the subject's own selfhood. In the essay "The Body as Expression and Speech" Merleau-Ponty locates the fundamental obscurity at the site at which living flesh seeks to understand itself through its objectifications, through its history and *écart* which is the temporal self-differentiation of flesh. For Merleau-Ponty, the body writes itself, "it is characteristic of every human gesture to signify beyond its simple existence, to inaugurate a meaning."[20]

> The body not only flows into a world whose schema it bears within itself but possesses this world at a distance rather than being possessed by it.[21]

From the late 1930s on, one can perceive in Kahlo's paintings an increasing shift away from the mimetic appropriation in which she feminised the figure of sacrifice. Paintings such as *Roots* (1943) and *The Earth Itself* or *Two Nudes in the Jungle* (1939) (Fig. 25) or her self-portraits, construct a different image of the self, a porousness of the body as woman that links her intimately to the world. This interconnectedness breaks down the dichotomies between animate and inanimate, human and animal, the body of the other. Following Merleau-Ponty, flesh is, as Elizabeth Grosz described it, the "shimmering of a *différance*, the (improper) belongingness of the subject of the world, and the world as the condition of the subject."[22] Kahlo represents the body and earth as both fertile and barren, suggesting that finally the body will die if the earth does not give it succour nor receive her fertility. This kind of dichotomy in Kahlo's work resonates with certain principle beliefs surrounding the Virgin Guadalupe. For Mexican Creoles (Spanish born in Mexico) Guadalupe was the dark Virgin who offered the possibility of striking roots in the soil of Anahuac, and so give validation to their relation to the land.[23] She was both the womb and the grave: to strike root is to bury oneself in the earth. In this regard, *My Nurse and I* provides a critical instance of this dichotomy. However, Kahlo offers also an amorous dialogue with nature, a reciprocity between the body as woman and nature, this porousness that draws upon and gives itself to the world. This flowing of bodily fluids – of blood and of milk – should be seen as a continuation of the earlier paintings, but no longer as the sacrifice of the body. Unlike Paz or Bataille/Caillois, in which the regeneration of the social, as founded on an erotic expenditure, requires woman to be object in order that transgression (and dereliction or erasure) be possible, Kahlo's paintings point towards a corporeal erotics of the body that is not given to figuration. This is what Irigaray calls for in her desire to find a place for woman and to conceive again the body as the site of sexual difference. The flesh, the organs, the sensations of the body, an open, connecting fertile tissue that cannot be contained or occupied, a subject who comes into being through her emplacement. She is both mother and other internally divided. She exceeds the figure of mother and nurse, as in *My Nurse and I*. The feminine of woman exceeds the maternal function. She is irreducible to the womb, to nature, to the form that occupies her as place. Rather the materiality of her flesh, an underground of organs, an eros of surfaces is restored. And, as we see in Kahlo's later paintings, there is a certain mystical relation to and continuity with the world, a radiant assenting to life, the body flows into the world.

As Merleau-Ponty conceived the concept of lived experience, in his final unfinished book *The Visible and the Invisible*, "one can say that we perceive the things themselves, that we are the world that thinks itself – or that the world is at the heart of our flesh."[24] Flesh is an inherent intertwining of subject into the object world, a body-world relationship. The flesh is the trace of the other, and therefore the presence of the other in the same. The subject is for itself an other and alterity is folded into the very definition of subjective self-sameness. However, Irigaray appropriates Merleau-Ponty's definition as a way of postulating how the body is both the object of interpretation or inscription and that which does the interpretation. Central to this is the maternal function of woman, not as the 'essence' of woman, but as belonging to the heterogeneous alterity of sexual difference:

> the woman and mother are not mirrored in the same fashion. A double specularization in and between her/them is already in place. And more. For the sex of woman is not one. And, as jouissance bursts out in each of these/her "parts," so all of them can mirror her in dazzling multifaceted difference.[25]

Dissolution

Ana Mendieta grew up in Iowa, North America, after leaving her homeland of Cuba at the age of 13 years without her parents. The significance of this experience of displacement and exile can be seen in an artistic statement she used throughout the '70s. Mendieta presented, in a rewritten form, a passage from Octavio Paz's *Labyrinth of Solitude*: "All detachment or separation provokes a wound . . . a feeling of aloneness (that) identified itself as a form of orphanhood. . . . The penalties and shame of separation caused me necessary sacrifices and solitude as a way of purifying myself."[26] Following her early performance and film work of 1972–75, Mendieta began to make autonomous pieces, beginning with a series she would call *Silueta* (silhouette) (Figs. 24 and 118). Creating a template replicating the contour and scale of her own body, Mendieta was able to remove herself as the material object of her art, and work directly in the landscape. The silhouette served as a surrogate form of her body, a surface of inscription that could be transformed or be destroyed leaving only a residue or trace.

Mendieta's decision represented two decisive shifts in her work. It freed her from a polarity between a form of essentialism and the idea of all things being a social construction. And, although she had explored the idea of the subject as originating within the locus of relationships, and therefore always already alienated through its inscription into the symbolic order, the issue of separating the body and self had, until this point, remained unresolved. For, while her work sought to address the idea of the social as founded on an identification of woman as nature and the excluded other; the very fact of using her body made it less than clear whether the *materiality* of the body was already exterior to language. By moving her work into the landscape with her *Silueta* series, Mendieta raised the question of how one might imagine an outside that was not only a figuring of a "utopian beyond," but exposed, as Judith Butler argues, the "constitutive categories that seek to keep gender in its place by posturing as the foundational illusions of identity."[27] Moreover, it raises, in this context, again the question of figuration, and the function of the trace to precede the possibility of recognition (naming) and therefore the object of sacrifice.

For Mendieta matter was the body as woman and the violent erasure which she performs on her work distantiates this body from the possibility of recuperation, a recuperation which naturalised the outside or heterogeneous as other than cultural. As such, the work represents a profound critique of the social sphere and an attempt to think the outside, the heterogeneous as the site at once of restitution and dissolution. The challenge was to create an art that was not an aesthetics that 'naturalised' woman as other. Equally, if figuration's power was its ability to break down the boundaries of containment, of going outside of the self, this power was also potentially threatening, a movement of transgression that did not return as the same. By assuming forms of embodiment and disembodiment, the ephemeral character and unstable condition of the work became critical to the identity of the subject. She exposed the body's limits and excesses, working against its constraints, its proximities to the organic, to animal, and closest of all to the concept of death as always the border across which the horizon of exteriority could be viewed. The return to earth not only stood for a return to the womb of birth, but the grave of death, a lease on and release from life, a pro-jective and de-structive movement. It is evident from the work of this time that Mendieta recognised the power that could be achieved both through the process of the body's replication and its direct interaction with materials and the environment.[28]

The risk was dissolution, a yielding or "trend to lose oneself in the environment instead of playing an active role in it; the tendency to let oneself go and sink back into nature."[29] In such terms, there is the threat of not-belonging, of being *of* but not *in* the world. Such is the danger of reproduction, where the embodiment, the doubling, becomes fixed in its place, outside of one, by another, a victim if you will, and therefore a kind of fetish, an object, disembodied, dead.

Mendieta's work articulates what may be called the negative dialectics of exile. It occupies a borderland, homelessness, wandering, a solitude that yearns for an imagined community, yet yields to living out a community of absence. The landscape is no longer the paradisiacal, the womb of culture. Rather it is the spectral land of absence and a place of a certain freedom. Such is the landscape of modernity, in which the language of culture and community is poised on the fissures of the present: shuttling between residual and emergent signs, seeking recovery in a repetition of the same or threatening to disrupt violently in incommensurate otherness. Rather than the association of women with the home and with the 'earthbound mother', associations which contain woman, the place of exile is defined by what is missing, not by what it contains. Mendieta's work displaces the location of meaning and identity from the fixity of the image or place onto the performative and the marks of inscription. Identity is always in the making and Mendieta radically disturbs its perpetual positioning by laying waste to its idealisation and authorising an image of difference founded within a space of absence, a *mise-en-abime*. The disembodied silhouette marks the trace of the body. It is what remains, the trace that appears by virtue of the disappearance and absence of the body. She continued, as in her early work with blood, with a notion of expenditure, as in Bataille's theory of *expense*, but it now appears as the trace of the body. What is constitutive of the trace is the erasure of the body, a lack of origin or originary presence. Inscription occurs only by effacing it. The trace never refers back to an original marking. This nothing was what remained after the sacrifice of matter.

To inscribe and erase at the same time represents the movement of the trace. Throughout this work of the 1970s, Mendieta moved towards reinscribing Robert Smithson's concept of the *non-site*: a place where there had been something, but once excavated, had left nothing. The trace has no place. Like the body as woman, it is always lacking. As Derrida writes :

> Since the trace is not a presence but the simulacrum of a presence that dislocates itself, displaces itself, refers itself, it properly has no site – erasure belongs to its structure. . . . Still legible; and to be read. . . . Proposing *all at once* the monument and the mirage of the trace, the trace simultaneously traced and erased, simultaneously living and dead, and, as always, living in its simulation of life's preserved inscription . . . a text without a voice.[30]

With the disappearance of the work itself, the photographic reproduction now displaces the real altogether. As actions that were never seen by a public, reappropriated by the landscape, their appearance is by virtue of the photograph. The photograph then dramatises the distance between Mendieta's body and her work. It marks a play of rupture and repetition, a space between experience and representation. And, while the photographs carry something which is in excess of this distantiation, of a place of origin, they bear within the same movement its ephemerality, displacing the original work by an 'after-life' of the image. As Barthes writes of the ghostly nature of the photographic sign: "I am neither subject nor object, but a subject who feels he is becoming an object . . . I am truly becoming a specter."[31] Photography, as itself a trace of something else, serves only then to heighten the sense of her work itself being about the trace, only able to capture its 'spirit.'

The power of the image is its ability to usurp the real, leading us to a place where there is nothing, a void, a place which is the essential condition of the real, but which the real seeks to turn away from. This would be Barthes's concept of the *punctum*, but more radically so. For

Mendieta's work puts on notice the visible, the visible is itself the object of sacrifice, and the photograph becomes a commemoration of its passing.

Abandonment

From her earliest work on in the mid-80s onwards, Doris Salcedo has used domestic objects, furniture and belongings as the raw material with which to address the subject of disappearance and absence as the effect of violence in Colombia.[32] Rather than *sighting* the body, it bears testimony to its radical separation. To do so is to recognise the existence of a non-site, a place that is subject to erasure by dominant forms of representation and institutions of circulation. In a manner that resonates with Mendieta, Salcedo's work elaborates too the concept of the non-site. But she begins with abandonment and erasure. Nothing precedes. There are no traces; vestiges, reliquaries perhaps, but no traces. It is exposure, but to a place that reveals that there is no outside, no infinity that is not already marked by the fragility of finitude: the "motionless time of destitution."[33]

In the ongoing series of *Atrabiliarios* (Fig. 107), it is the empty shoe, and in *La Casa Viuda (The Widowed House)* (1993–95), the abandoned home. In each the body has been removed. What is left is the container. The body as woman is the absent subject. *Atrabiliarios* is composed of a row of niches along the wall as repositories for shoes either owned by persons or their families who had suffered violence, together with a series of empty boxes made of transparent animal skin placed on the floor. In addition, the niches are covered by pieces of rough and opaque skin taken from animal bladders, stitched with thick black thread to the wall, like a provisional gauze over a gaping wound.

Salcedo's niches immediately recall those in the cemetery as the site and support for the body's remains after cremation. Transposed into a museum space, the shoes attain the status of both relic and a fetish. As a relic they stand in for the remains of the deceased; and as a fetish, they become a substitute object of both identification and disavowal. The shoe is both intensely personal and a discrete material object independent of the individual. They both belong to and are separate from their referent, the body. The intervention on the part of Salcedo is to resist making visible that which is absent, to accommodate loss. The masking of the niches with the animal skin not only makes it difficult to see the shoes inside, but acts as an interruption of vision. It disturbs our visual relation to the image. At the same time, by using such intimate and visceral materials as a person's shoe and animal skin, the work draws its audience closer to the locality and affective dimension of an experience of loss. Perception is informed by the non-visual, the tactile, be it the viscerality of the skin, the coarseness of the thread and by the lack of the visuality, the emptiness of the shoes. The coarse, visceral texture of the skin alters the character of some of the shoes. The shoes in some niches can barely be seen, in others they appear more like the bare bones of the foot, and in others the thin membrane of skin. By acting as a material signifier of that which is absent, the object arrests death yet, as a metonymic displacement, it also stands as a sign of the radical difference and separation death brings to the world of the living. Yet, such an act of gathering together in one place is not with a view to representing violence but rather its effect and its overcoming.

Critical to this work is the issue of how to address the very structuring of memory, that is itself strongly contingent upon the social formation in which it is founded. In countries such as Colombia, dominant forms of cultural modernity have exploited the strong substratum of

Catholicism with its belief in the notion of sacrificial violence and redemption as the foundation of emancipation. What this creates is a cultural climate of having to live with violence. This has produced communities which, faced with death, seek a mystical communion with the dead, their dead, as a way to overcoming the enforced separation and violence of loss.

What Salcedo puts on public view are the traces, relics and fragments of the subject of violence: those vanquished, the fallen, the forgotten. These are stories of abandonment, the fissures, silences and oblivion of history and her work a re-collection of that which represents the repressed archive of a nation, that which has been silenced and buried. It belongs in the space of the family, the 'feminine' which serves as a sanctuary of refuge and shelter from the State and public space for those who live in terror and the memory of the disappeared.[34] The intimate, sensuous space created by the work points to a hidden dimension, a place in which rituals of remembrance and mourning for the dead are performed. They become personal reliquaries that stand for a life taken away, a family or widow's story.

Such art not only reclaims the public sphere as a space of commemoration but an ethics based on collective memory and continuity as a future with sacrifice. The installation forces us to recognise this absence over which history has been constructed. Testifying to private experience, the work makes its audience bear witness to that which has passed. The objects become mute witnesses and yet in their insistent presence of that which is absent, they are a testament to a violence against the body. They remain unquiet objects that represent the excess of memory. However, this excess is not of the order of the visual, but rather of the absent body. What is painful is not the sight of the image, but the impossibility of remembering and yet one's desire to remember the skin of another, the caress, the voice that mingles with mine. There is a luminosity that the skin gives to the niches. They become precious sites and, yet, they illuminate not a form but the memory of the lived corporeality of the body.

Like Kahlo and Mendieta, Salcedo's work begins with the impossible yet necessary condition of figuration to which the body as woman is exposed. Each artist designates what it means to speak of Mexico, Cuba, North America or Colombia. Identity is inscribed, it inscribes itself by way of what it excludes. The work of each artists, in different ways, risks repeating the ceaseless demand to become the object of sacrifice: disembodiment, dissolution and abandonment. It addresses the condition of this exposure, seeking to turn away from the light, from the visible, to a place where the flesh is the trace of the other, and therefore the presence of the other in the same. It is an openness that leads away from self-identity towards the other, a movement away from continuity by appropriation and sacrifice: a body founded within alterity, an always already fragile space of difference.

Notes

1 Michel de Certeau, *The Writing of History* (New York: Columbia UP, 1988) xxv.

2 de Certeau, *The Writing of History* xxv/xxvi.

3 Luce Irigaray, *An Ethics of Sexual Difference*, trans. Carolyn Burke and Gillian C. Gill (Ithaca, NY: Cornell UP, 1993) 82.

4 Irigaray, *Ethics* 197. Yet, for Irigaray, "When the beloved woman presents herself or appears to the male lover as a paradise to be referred back to infancy and animality, then the act of love leads not only to profaning, but also to destruction, a fall. The beloved woman would be cast down to the depths so that the male lover could be raised to the heights." *Ethics* 198.

5 Irigaray, *Ethics* 51.

6 Irigaray, *Ethics* 10-11.

7 Luce Irigaray, *Speculum of the Other Woman*, trans. Gillian C. Gill. (Ithaca, NY: Cornell UP, 1985) 224.

8 Judith Butler, *Bodies that Matter* (New York: Routledge, 1993) 35.

9 Butler, *Bodies that Matter* 37.

10 Octavio Paz, *The Labyrinth of Solitude*, (New York: Grove P, 1961).

11 Within Aztec society, each person had "tonalli" or an energy source that gave them a vital autonomy. Christian Duverger, "The Meaning of Sacrifice" in *Fragments for a History of the Human Body*, vol. 3, Zone 5 (New York: Zone, 1989) 367–385.

12 Paz, *Labyrinth* 51–52.

13 Paz, *Labyrinth* 50ff and 332. See also Bataille's discussion of this concept in "The Notion of Expenditure" in *Visions of Excess: Selected Writings 1927–1939*, ed. and trans. Allan Stoekl with Carl R. Lovitt and Donald M. Leslie Jr. (Minneapolis: U of Minnesota P, 1985) 116-129.

14 Georges Bataille, *Eroticism: Death and Sensuality* trans. Mary Dalwood (San Francisco: City Lights Books, 1986) 129.

15 Roger Caillois, "Festival" in *The College of Sociology 1937-1939*, ed. Denis Hollier (Minneapolis: U of Minnesota P, 1988) 281.

16 Elizabeth Grosz, *Space, Time and Perversion* (New York: Routledge, 1995) 104.

17 Kristeva, *Powers of Horror*, trans. Leon S. Roudiez (New York: Columbia UP, 1982) 8. I have taken the liberty of changing the gender of this text where possible in order to bring it into closer proximity to Mendieta.

18 Butler, *Bodies that Matter* 3.

19 Irigaray, *Speculum* 229.

20 Maurice Merleau-Ponty, *Signs*, ed. and trans. Richard C. McCleary (Evanston: Northwestern UP, 1964) 68.

21 Merleau-Ponty, *Signs* 67.

22 Elizabeth Grosz, "Merleau-Ponty and Irigaray in the Flesh," *Thesis 11* 36 (1993): 43.

23 Octavio Paz, "The Flight of Quetzalcoatl and the Quest for Legitimacy," foreword to Jacques Lafaye, *Quetzalcoatl and Guadalupe: The Formation of Mexican National Consciousness*, trans. Benjamin Keen (Chicago: U of Chicago P, 1976).

24 Maurice Merleau-Ponty, *The Visible and the Invisible* (Evanston: Northwestern UP, 1968) 136.

25 Irigaray, *Speculum* 239.

26 These remarks first appeared in my essay on Mendieta's early performance work, "From Inscription to Expenditure: An Essay on Expenditure in the Work of Ana Mendieta" in *Ana Mendieta: A Retrospective*, Centro Galego, Santiago de Compostela, Spain, 1996). See also my forthcoming book: *What Remains* (New York: Routledge, 1998).

27 Judith Butler, *Gender Trouble, Feminism and the Subversion of Identity* (New York: Routledge, 1990) 34.

28 In making a copy of herself, she was also able to introduce Afro-Cuban religious beliefs and pract ices that she had not only been aware of in her childhood, but had begun to read about through the writings of anthropologists, notably the work of Fernando Ortiz and Lydia Cabrera. Interview with Hans Breder by author, November 1993. According to Afro-Cuban religious principles the replication of the body could be, through its mediation with the human form, imbued with a deity or spirit's power, and therefore reunited with the forces of nature.

[29] Max Horkheimer and Theodor Adorno, *Dialectic of Enlightenment* (New York: Continuum Books, 1991) 227. For reference to Caillois' ideas on mimeticism, see his "Mimicry and Legendary Psychaesthenia," *Minotaure* 7 (1935): 4–10. Reprinted in *October* 31 (Winter 1984): 17–32.

[30] Jacques Derrida, *Margins of Philosophy* (Chicago: U of Chicago P, 1982) 24.

[31] Roland Barthes, *Camera Lucida*, trans. Richard Howard (New York: Hill and Wang, 1981) 14.

[32] See my essay: "Naming Violence in the work of Doris Salcedo," *Third Text* 24 (Autumn 1993) and also "The Anonymity of Violence: Re-elaborating the non-site" in *Propositions*, Musee Departmental d'art contemporain, Rochechouart, France, 1996.

[33] Avital Ronell, *Finitude's Score* (Lincoln: U of Nebraska P, 1994) 5.

[34] Jean Franco, "Killing Priests, Nuns, Women, Children" in *On Signs*, ed. Marshall Blonsky (Baltimore, Maryland: John Hopkins UP, 1985).

Anthony Bond, Mike Parr

A Conversation

AB I'd like to ask you about your early involvement with some of the European and American performance artists included in this exhibition, but to begin with, tell me how you began working with body art.

MP The earliest pieces were done in 1971 with Peter Kennedy. They were derived from my earlier poems, some of which took the form of instructions. One which I never performed would have been like a Saint Vitus dance. I was to sit in the bush on a very windy day, strings would be attached to all parts of my body, which would in turn be attached to the trees in the environment and as the wind blew I would be turned into a kind of Marionette, and I would be jerked up and down by the ferocity of nature. These simple sorts of transmissions were much more like poetry but by the end of 1971 I found myself doing things like *Hold Your Breath for as Long as Possible*, and *Hold Your Finger in a Candle Flame*.

AB But holding your breath or holding your finger in a flame are about your control whereas the tree piece would have been about abandonment.

MP Yes, and it's probably interesting that it was never performed. It began to dawn on me that these limits raised the problem of negotiation in a really acute way. I'll never forget my experience of the piece where Peter Kennedy bit into my shoulder. I remember you asking me the other day whether I had been aware of Acconci's biting action at the time. I recall now that we probably would have known that because I had a copy of the *Avalanche* Magazine with all of his pieces in it and I was interested in the way in which he would propose an action and then he would speculate about its meaning. And he would speculate about it in this rather impersonal way, which interested me.

I think that my 'arm-biting' on the other hand was quite different. What I was interested in was precipitating an absolutely concrete situation with the audience, where in a sense the issue of content was immediately re-inscribed in terms of interaction. You might say that the performance was the audience's response.

AB When you started working with Peter Kennedy did it ever occur to you that there is a 'biter' and a 'bit'? Was it always clear to you that it was going to be your body that was the site of any actions?

MP Yes, it was actually (Parr seemed surprised by this question).

AB That was never even an issue for you?

MP No, it follows the solipsism of my impulses at that time. I was using Peter in a way to define my body in an interactive situation: there's this crucial relationship with Peter Kennedy then the relationship with the audience, so I'm presenting a two person interaction in the most sado-masochistic and regressive sense. There's the biter and the bitten and the sense of a relationship based on a kind of primitive devouring. It's very close to being eaten. It's very strange when I think about it. Peter and I only had a relationship as long as we were doing these kinds of performances.

AB You had read about Acconci in *Avalanche* so you were aware of some of those actions. Was that how you began to be aware of what was happening in Europe?

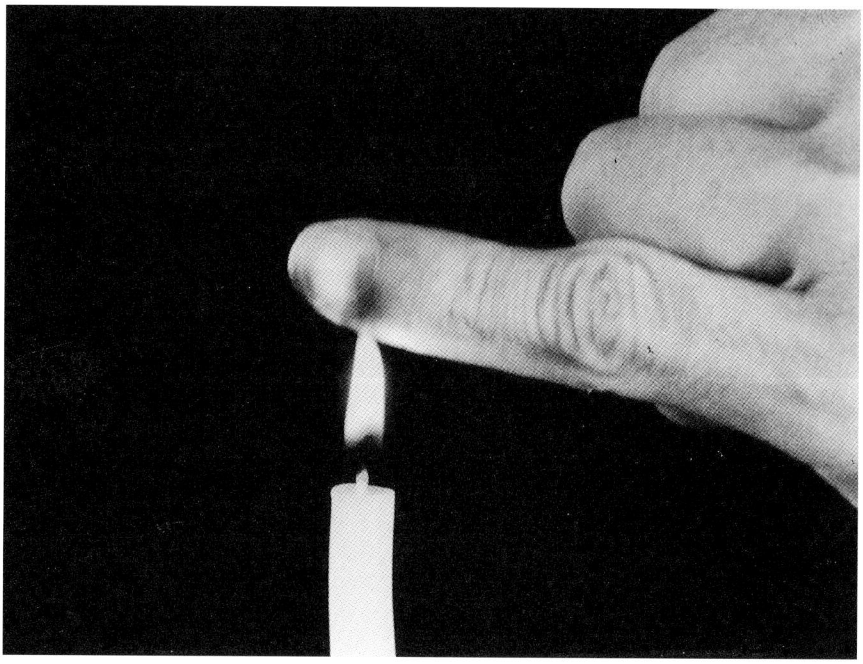

MP The other source of being aware of what was happening in Britain was Tim Johnson's trip to London in 1970. He met people like Ian Breakwell and John Hilliard. He then went on to New York and came back with some of Sol Le Witt's instructions for works. We considered performing one of these at Inhibodress in the *Activities* show. The instruction was to fire a shotgun at the gallery wall. I found that a very interesting idea. In our first serious show at Inhibodress (1971) we performed instruction pieces by artists like Medalla, Ben Vautier, Breakwell, Hilliard, Sol Le Witt and Richard Long.

AB When did you first get to Europe and how did you make contact with artists there?

MP We went to Poland, Hungary and Western Europe in 1973 and I also met Klaus Groh who lived up in Oldenberg in Northern Germany. He ran the International Artists Co-operation. He was a key influence for a lot of the 'mail art'—it hadn't become 'mail art' then, there was something called the *Eternal Network* that was being put together. He had many hundreds, maybe thousands of artists' names and addresses from all around the world. It was an early, primitive form of the internet.

AB Was this network political coming at the end of the 1960s, or was it just about communication between artists?

MP It was about communication primarily but joint actions and exhibitions were also organised. But I think the notion of communication was seen as political in its own right and of course there was the 'iron curtain', the division between East and West, and this network facilitated a dialogue with the East. Through this network I met Arnulf Rainer in 1973, I went to his studio on Mariahilfstrasse and we spent an hour or so together. He was really only interested in getting hold of my mailing lists but it was a useful meeting because he told me that Nitsch would be doing something out at the Castle that July.

AB Were you already familiar with the direction that the Vienna artists were taking in 1973?

MP I had no knowledge of Wiener Aktionismus in 1973. It wasn't until later when I was working with Albe Thoms who had filmed and photographed them in Vienna. I can remember Rainer talking about what was happening in Austria and I asked him about Schwarzkogler and he was completely derisive, he said to me "Schwarzkogler was simply a little student of Hermann Nitsch, the man was inherently unstable and he jumped out a window." It was he who told me all about Robert Hughes getting it wrong and perpetrating the myth in the English speaking world that Schwarzkogler had died by shaving off his penis.

AB Tell me about your response to Nitsch's performance. Did you find that the audience was half embarrassed going through with it or were people throwing themselves into it with great gusto?

MP No, there was a definite divide between Nitsch and his cohorts doing the thing, and the audience. People were cringing.

AB So the people participating in the actions are not the audience.

MP No, they're not. He has his entourage of people and they do these things together.

AB That is very different from your performances in Switzerland in 1972 where you engaged the audiences directly.

MP Yes, I did a whole series of new performances in Lausanne. That was when I first began to think about video feedback systems. I sited monitors in the audience, performed the works and put the audience in a situation where they could see their own response to works as they were occurring. I was very interested in somehow transferring the autism of these instruction pieces to the audience, by demonstrating that their role as audience was also autistic. Their ambivalence made them as culpable, or it made them as involved as I was. I did a great deal of analysis and talking about that.

AB And when you came back the performances you did in Central Street and in Newtown continued that process of audience interaction. As I recall it you pushed the audience pretty close to their limits.

MP I did and I didn't. I filmed *Rules III* in Newtown, and seeing it again now I find it particularly decisive, whereas, seeing *Rules II* again really irritated me. Although I think the performance elements are often good, I've got grave doubts about things like "Touching" and so on, I think they were a bit wanky. There's this magisterial quality about me, it was very irritating in *Rules II*. So these were the inherent limitations to that kind of interactive situation with friends, where we all sat around smoking dope, touching one another up.

AB A lot of that material was in a way predicated on the fact the camera was running, providing instant feedback. Did that give the events a theatrical quality? Perhaps we should discuss the question of photo-documentation and film in relation to performance. What do you think about the authenticity or otherwise of that kind of process?

MP I have been looking again at *Rules I and II* and I became very excited at the sheer primitive concentration of performances like *Tack Line Up the Leg* or the one where Noel Sheridan is cutting into my right arm and smearing the blood onto my face—the primitive revulsion. And pieces in *Rules II* when I'm eating the red bread ferociously and when I vomit red while they're trying to find a vein in my arm and they're cutting into my arm, the camera is crucial to these pieces. It's crucial in an absolutely fundamental way because it becomes a linguistic component if you like. This business of framing takes the place of language. By 1973 the process of filming has moved on, the camera becomes an incredible experience for me and I think what happens is that it becomes the eye of God, and performances become absolutely specific in relation to the camera. I begin forcing the camera to look, it's like an accusation. I set the camera up there and it's like the ideal audience.

AB To what extent is your documentation determining the form of the actions? Can we distinguish between the photographic image as a literal record of real events and the simulation of an experience for a viewer in a theatrical sense?

MP I begin the action, the camera stares at me intently and it records the action, and then the action ends. That piece of film for me remains absolutely congruent with the intention of the action, in fact the intention of the action has everything to do with confronting the camera in the most literal way possible. So instead of sitting there simply staring at the camera, I return to my own body and inflict my limits the limits of the recording situation.

There is also the problem of still photography and it's one of the things now that is really worrying me, that more and more my performances come to be represented through still photography. That is a debacle because it presents the image of an action as iconic. It doesn't represent this excruciating dimension of duration, which is essentially my confrontation with the camera. That's why I'm using the limits of the body: it's to exacerbate duration to the point where people close their eyes or walk out of the cinema, they can't look at this stuff. It's different with the photographs from the 1970's. They're like Catholic trophies or residues, it really disturbs me to compare the reality of the film over and against the kind of re-representation that goes on through the photograph.

AB Talking of photographs as residues or relics, people like Beuys and Nitsch have also collected other material residues of performances and installed them as a vitrine, or as a painting in the case of Brus and Nitsch and so on. You have never done this, have you?

MP No, I haven't done that and it's a measure of my obsession with the problem of meaning, the relationship between the act and its visibility. It seems extraordinary that performance art has degenerated, in the case of Beuys and the Wiener Aktionismus artists, into poetry, a collation of traces. The importance of the aesthetic becomes paramount.

AB There are other artists in the exhibition whose work comes closer to your own position. I'd like to hear what you think about them. Gina Pane's *Azione Sentimentale*, for instance, is very autobiographical and very direct.

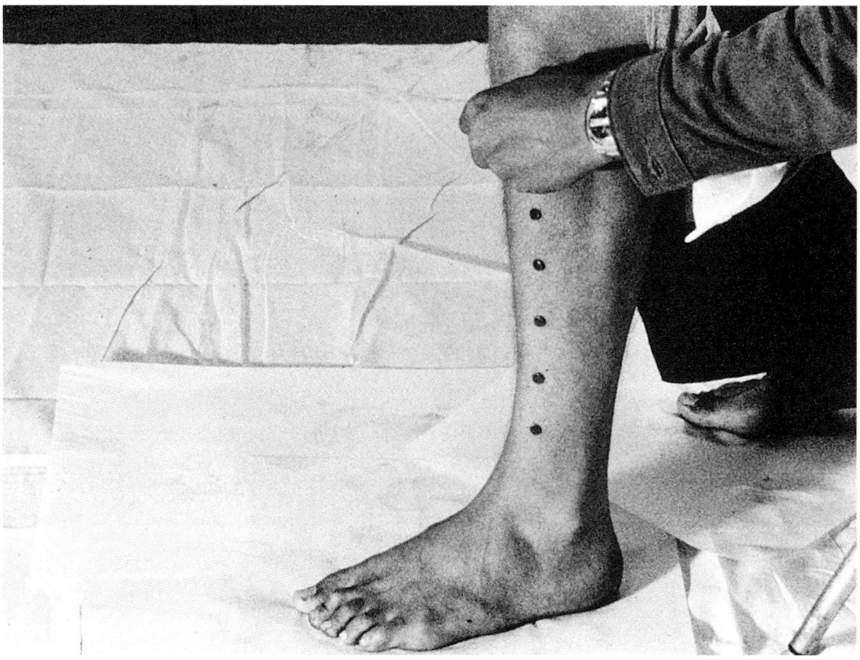

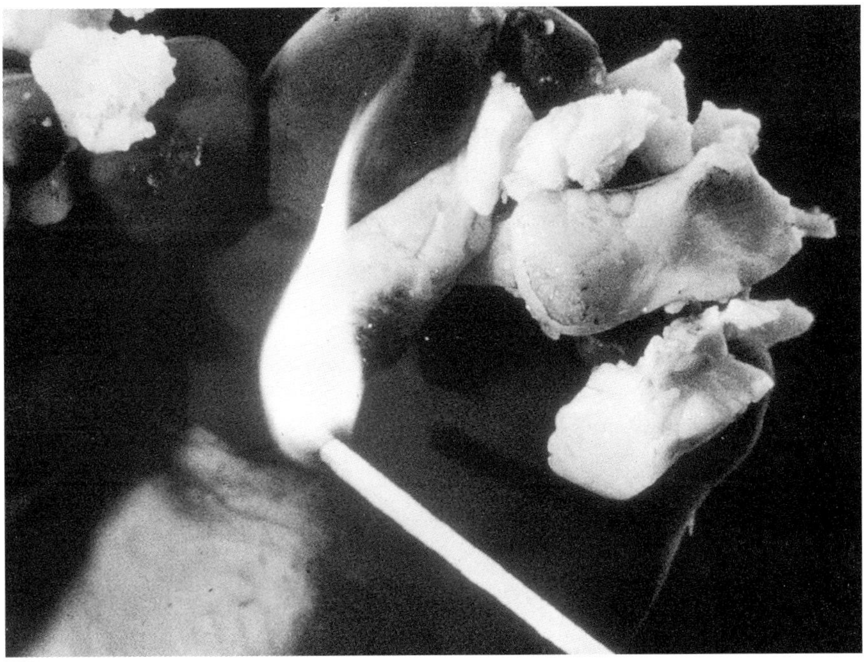

MP Her actions have a direct component but then they're very Catholic too aren't they? Instead of the thorns going into the brow they're pushed into other parts of Pane's anatomy. It's a sort of scarification of the most symbolic kind. You see there's no religion in my work, contrary to what people might imagine they see there. My literalites are much more congruent. The tack line which you could compare to the thorns in her arm is really the corrosive form of minimalist measurement. What it really exacerbates is the problem of figure and ground.

AB Gina in that particular case seems to be enacting an extreme ritual of preparation. I wouldn't have said particularly Catholic, but a preparation for a wedding, for the bride. It's dysfunctional, just as her own sexuality in relation to the notion of the sacrament of marriage is dysfunctional.

MP Its parodic in a way.

AB Yes, I would see it more in that light. Then one thinks about the autobiographical comparison.

MP Yes, it's interesting, you can make that comparison to my work, and my use of 'the bride' now.

AB I wondered about that.

MP I take the bride as an ultimately linguistic unit: the congruent form of symbol and meaning. I thought this 'bride' was very interesting, it recurs from Duchamp forward, all through the 20th Century, appearing in the work of Schwarzkogler, Klein and others. This recurrence of 'the bride' really interested me and the sense in which she is now an archaic institution. It's manifestly shambolic, a kind of commercial unit. It's this shambolic aspect that interests me, the fact that it has no identity, that its kind of left over.

AB One of the elements in Duchamp's *Bride* is the oculist's witness to her stripping bare. It just occurred to me that there are witnesses incorporated into many works in this exhibition. The witness in art is an interesting notion and I wonder whether it is an alter ego of the artist in some sense.

MP I think it is, I think artists set up the scene primarily for their own edification, a sort of self voyeurism, damn the public. Yes, it's very revealing. In my case the camera becomes my witness in a crucial way. It becomes the double. The show will be filled with all these clandestine witnesses, won't it.

AB We have not discussed Chris Burden and Marina Abramovic who are also more concerned with facts. In Burden's case I am thinking of things like *Shoot* where he had someone shoot him through the arm in 1972. They seem to be very straight forward and literal.

MP They remind me of Neil Evans swallowing the tape worm in 1975, and those reported things of his, *coprophilia* where he eats his own shit as he's leaving the art world. It doesn't last very long, there's a few events like that in 1976. They were important actions too.

AB Abramovic is somebody else who is very interesting in this context. Particularly the relentless nature of those performances. Can you relate your work to what she was doing?

MP Yes, certainly at the level of task. The idea of pursuing an action to an absolute limit and allowing an image to emerge over which you have no control. I really appreciate that aspect of Abramovic's work. I can remember one of her earliest actions from 1973 where she took psychiatric drugs, psychotropic drugs that control schizophrenic outbursts or catatonia and she induced these extraordinary states. The photographs have this amazing authenticity. You know she's not acting, she's going into these spasms. That concreteness is very important and there are only a few performance artists in the 1970s that were prepared to take task to that extreme. There's Chris Burden, and I think Acconci to some extent too.

AB I think Acconci's autobiographical work is very relevant, *Seedbed* in 1972 for example.

MP Yes, that is the masturbation one. It is very interesting and there's another extraordinary one, *Trappings*, that he did in 1971. He sat under a stair surrounded by dolls' clothes, it's a really regressive piece, dressed his penis in dolls' clothes and talked to it like a child. This is one of the interesting things about '70s performance art, this fanaticism of the idea and the task is the crucial thing, and I think at its most powerful there's this connection again back to *art brut* and psychotic art. It has the same qualities you get in psychotic drawings and paintings.

AB There is a section of the exhibition which connects Bacon to Dubuffet and Arnulf Rainer in something akin to *art brut*, there is a sense of urgency about the mark making.

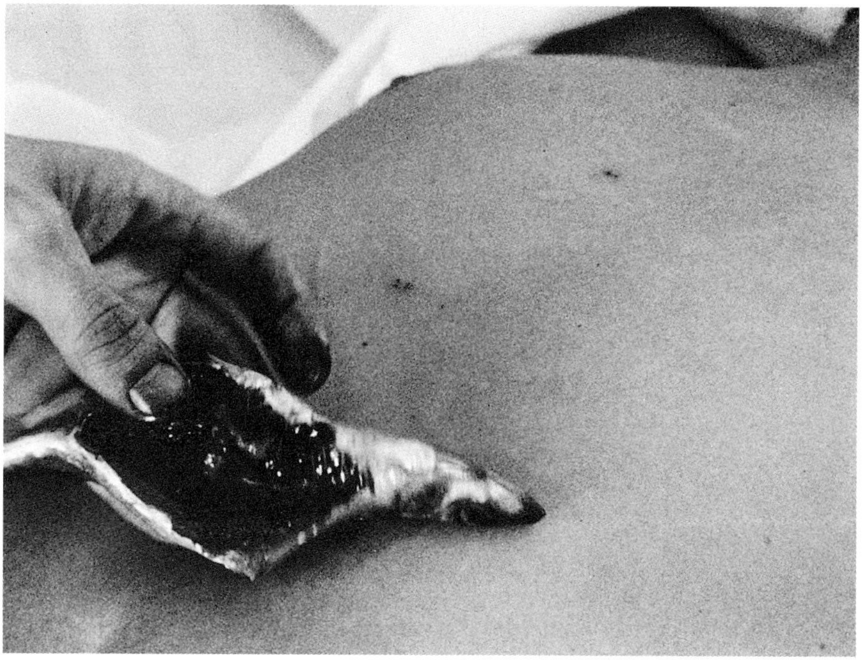

MP There's some truth in that potency. Rainer's *Face Farces* are extraordinary, you can feel this sense of him trying to claw his way back into the photograph. It's such a primitive urgency of alienation and you get it again of course in the early '80s with Clemente. The best of the Transavantgarde shared this sense of urgency with 1970s performance art.

What suddenly comes to mind is the Australian movie called *Angel Baby*. It's about a schizophrenic girl, it has a tremendous ring of authenticity about it. She falls over and has an attack, she goes into a terrible disassociated state in a supermarket and she trips over, and she cuts herself and starts to bleed and her boyfriend is trying to help her and she promptly begins to lick her own blood up like mad because her bodily fluids are running out and she has to re-ingest them as fast as they're running out and she starts drinking and licking up her own blood in this frenzied fashion. That 'loop' could have been a '70s performance. You get that in Clemente, that same kind of violently short-circuiting loop back into the body even through the drawing. Marina and Ulay got this you see, and there's a sense in which Chris Burden gets it too. There's something extraordinary about that piece *Shoot*, arranging to be shot at. Just slipping to that edge and the bullet going through his arm.

Catalogue List, Artists' Biographies and Selected Bibliographies

Suzannah Biernoff and Caroline Butler-Bowdon

All details in the Catalogue list were correct and complete at time of printing
All measurements are given in centimetres, height x width x depth
and include framing unless otherwise indicated

Abramovic, Marina

1 *Rhythm 10* 1973
published 1994, edition of 16
black and white photograph, 75.6 x 100.3
26.0 x 18.4 text panel
Courtesy of Sean Kelly, New York

2 *Lips of Thomas* 1975
published 1994, edition of 16
black and white photograph, 75.6 x 100.3
26.0 x 18.4 text panel
Courtesy of Sean Kelly, New York

3 *Lips of Thomas (Star on Stomach)* 1975
published 1994
black and white photograph, 75.6 x 100.3
26.0 x 18.4 text panel
Courtesy of Sean Kelly, New York

Born, 1946, Belgrade
Lives Amsterdam
Abramovic has worked as a performance artist both in Belgrade and, more recently, in Amsterdam. International recognition followed her collaborative performance with the Dutch performance artist Ulay at the 1976 Venice Biennale. In much of their subsequent work Abramovic and Ulay have pursued a form of Body Art that at its most extreme verges on ritualised self-mortification. "You have to break your body before you can free your mind," Ulay has remarked, invoking comparison with religious asceticism (Kontova 4). Equally significant, however, is their emphasis on the interaction of the artists and viewer within the performative environment. Now separated, Abramovic has continued her career in performance, video installation and sculpture on her own.

- *L'Art au corps: le corps exposé de Man Ray à nos jours*. exh. cat. Marseille: Musées de Marseille, 1996
- *Fémininmasculin: le sexe de l'art*. exh. cat. Paris: Centre Georges Pompidou, 1995.
- Kontova, H. "Abramovic." Entry in *Contemporary Artists*. Ed. C. Naylor. Chicago: St James P, 1989.
- *Marina Abramovic*. exh. cat. Berlin: Neue Nationalgalerie, 1995.
- *Marina Abramovic: Objects, Performances, Video, Sound*. exh. cat. Oxford: Museum of Modern Art, 1995.
- McEvilley, T. "Marina Abramovic/Ulay." *Artforum* 22 (Sep. 1985): 52–5.
- Messchede, F. *Marina Abramovic*. Berlin: Editions Cantz, 1993.

Bacon, Francis

4 *Study of the Human Body* 1981–82
oil and pastel on canvas, 198.0 x 147.5
Musée National d'Art Moderne,
Centres Georges Pompidou, Paris

5 *Triptych* 1970
oil on canvas, 198.0 x 147.5 (each of 3 canvases)
National Gallery of Australia, Canberra
© National Gallery of Australia, Canberra

Born, 1909, Dublin
Died, 1992, Madrid
An Anglo-Irishman, Bacon was largely self-taught with no formal professional education. While he started exhibiting in London in the 1930s, it was not until 1945 that his signature style appeared and his reputation was established, eventually making him the most celebrated British painter of the twentieth century. Bacon's work was distinguished by its rich materiality, his distinctive expressive style and the confronting nature of his characteristic themes of violence and the alienation of the individual. Bacon used certain key images in his paintings such as the screaming Pope, the Crucifixion, isolated single figures and images of sexual coupling based on Eadweard Muybridge's photographs of wrestlers. It was the subject of the human body which became his life-long obsession providing endless opportunities for him to explore his belief that art is an obsession with life: "Only Bacon, among all the painters of his generation realised that . . . vast unexplored sinister territory was opening up in the representation of the human body" (Gowing 12).

- Brusatin, M. and J. Clair, eds. *Identity and Alterity: Figures of the Body 1895/1995*. XLVI Venice Biennale. exh. cat. Venice: Marsilio, 1995.
- Demetrion, J. and L. Gowing, eds. *Francis Bacon*. exh. cat. New York/London: Hirshhorn Museum and Smithsonian Institute, 1989.
- Oliva, A. B., ed. *Figurabile: Omaggio a Francis Bacon*. exh. cat. Milan: Venice Museo Correr La Biennale di Venezia, 1993.
- Peppiat, M. *Francis Bacon: Anatomy of an Enigma*. London: Weidenfeld & Nicholson, 1996.
- Sinclair, J. A. *Francis Bacon: His Life and Violent Times*. New York: Crown, 1993.

Balthus
(Balthazar Klossowski de Rola)

6 *Le Lever (Getting Up)* 1955
oil on canvas, 161.0 x 130.4
Scottish National Gallery of Modern Art, Edinburgh

7 *The Room* 1947–48
oil on canvas, 190.3 x 160.4
Hirshhorn Museum and Sculpture Garden, Smithsonian Institution
Gift of the Joseph H. Hirshhorn Foundation, 1966

8 *Nude with Cat* 1949
oil on canvas, 85.5 x 101.8
National Gallery of Victoria, Melbourne
Felton Bequest, 1952

Born, 1908, Paris
Lives France
The brother of Pierre Klossowski who is also included in this exhibition, Balthus is a French citizen of Polish descent. He was raised in an artistic environment in Switzerland which brought him into contact with Bonnard, Derain, Rainer Maria Rilke and André Gide. Presenting the ordinary banalities of contemporary urban life, Balthus's realism is classically inspired and yet retains a strong and highly identifiable personal style. Influences of Piero della Francesca, Paolo Uccello and Nicolas Poussin are evident in his work as is the inspiration he drew from the work of Cézanne and contemporary German Realists (Dix, Grosz, Beckmann). Balthus is best known for his depictions of adolescent girls awkwardly positioned in old fashioned bourgeois interiors. They pose languidly, absorbed in books or in themselves and are invariably illuminated by a late afternoon sun. He was Director of the Académie de France in the Villa Medici in Rome from 1961 to 1976 and has exhibited widely internationally.

- Bozo, D. and Lieberman, eds. *Balthus*. exh. cat. Paris: Centre Georges Pompidou, 1983.
- Brusatin, M. and J. Clair, eds. *Identity and Alterity: Figures of the Body 1895/1995*. XLVI Venice Biennale. exh. cat. Venice: Marsilio, 1995.
- Leymarie, J. and F. Fellini, eds. *Balthus*. exh. cat. Venice: Biennale, 1980.
- Leymarie, J. and J. Helfenstein, eds. *Balthus: Zeichnungen*. exh. cat. Basle: Berne Kunstmuseum, 1994.
- Rewald, S., ed. *Balthus*. exh. cat. New York: MOMA, 1984.
- Soby, J. T., ed. *Balthus*. exh. cat. New York: MOMA, 1956.

Baquié, Richard

9 *Sans Titre. Etant Donnés: 1° La chute d'eau 2° Le gaz d'eclairage (Untitled. Given: 1. The Waterfall 2. The Illuminating Gas)* 1991, installation
251.0 x 204.0 x 406.0
Musée d'Art Contemporain de Lyon
Photographs: J. B. Rodde, Blaise Adilon and C. Ganet

Born, 1952, Marseille
Died 1995
Baquié's work has its roots in the tradition of plastic art initiated by the bricolage artists, Duchamp, Rauschenberg and Tinguely. He became known in the 1980s for his assemblages of salvaged objects, from car parts and plastic containers to refrigeration systems and electrical conductors. The isolation of these objects from their original functions and their unlikely convergence in Baquié's sculptures acts as a prompt for the observer's individual imagination. Baquié's work in BODY differs from his other installations in that he has executed a faithful reproduction of another artist's work, Duchamp's *Etant Donnés*. Unlike the Duchamp however, which offers the viewer a seamless (if tantalisingly fragmentary) voyeuristic illusion from the front, Baquié also allows the viewer behind the scenes where the machinery of Duchamp's 'peep show' is laid disturbingly bare.

- *Fémininmasculin: le sexe de l'art*. exh. cat. Paris: Centre Georges Pompidou, 1995.
- Jouannais, J.-Y. "Richard Baquié: An Aesthetic of Doubt." *Art Press* 161 (Sep. 1991).
- Ottinger, D. "Marcel Duchamp: Revolution or Sabotage?" *Beaux Arts* 110 (Mar. 1993).
- Picazo, G. and J.-M. Avrilla, eds. *Collection for a Region: Fictional Places – Richard Bacquié, Jederermann N. A., Jeff Koons, Rombouts & Droste, Haim Steinbach*. exh. cat. Bordeaux: Musée d'Art Contemporain, 1993.
- Valebregue, F. "Richard Baquié: The Novel of Titles." *Artefactum* 18 (Apr.–May 1997).

Baselitz, Georg

10 *Akt Elke lll (Nude Elke lll)* 1976
oil on canvas, 200.0 x 162.0
Art Gallery of South Australia, Adelaide
South Australian Government Grant 1985

Born, 1938, Dentsuhbaselitz, Germany
Lives Holle, Germany
Baselitz (born Hans Georg Kern) is a contemporary German painter of significant reputation, highly prolific and widely known internationally. Having begun his studies in what after World War II became East Germany, Baselitz moved in 1958 to the Hochschule für Künste in West Berlin where he taught until 1988. A contemporary of A. R. Penck and Eugene Schönebeck, Baselitz was opposed to the dominance of abstract painting, choosing rather to explore an expressive figurative style influenced by psychotic art and *art brut*. With Schönebeck he wrote the apocalyptic Pandemonium manifestos. In 1969 Baselitz produced the first of his trademark upside-down paintings, a vehicle for minimising the illusion of pictorial depth and emphasising the materiality of the painted surface.

- Brusatin, M. and J. Clair, eds. *Identity and Alterity: Figures of the Body 1895–1995*. XLVI Venice Biennale. exh. cat. Venice: Marsilio, 1995.
- Calvocoressi, R., ed. *Georg Baselitz: Paintings 1960–1983*. exh. cat. Amsterdam: Stedelijk Museum, 1983.
- Gallwitz, K., ed. *Georg Baselitz*. exh. cat. Venice: Biennale, 1980.
- Gohr, S., ed. *Georg Baselitz: Retrospektive 1964–1991*. exh. cat. Munich: Munich Kunsthalle der Hypo-Kulturstiftung, 1992.
- Harten, J., ed. *Georg Baselitz*. exh. cat. Zurich: Kunsthaus, 1990.

Beckmann, Max

11 *Der Brief (Liegender Halbakt)*
(The Letter (Reclining Nude)) 1945
oil on canvas, 50.0 x 60.0
Von der Heydt-Museum, Wuppertal

Born, 1884, Leipzig
Died, 1950, New York
Schooled in traditional techniques at the Weimar Academy (1900–03), Beckmann drew inspiration from medieval and High Renaissance painting as well as being influenced variously by Symbolism (from 1904), Cézanne and later Cubism. Rejecting the trend towards abstraction, his paintings and prints imbue modernity with an apocalyptic and distinctly Gothic flavour. A dense, sculptural quality and fractured perspectivism characterises the work he produced during and after World War I, when he served for a year in the medical corps in Flanders. The chilling, anaemic tones of his wartime paintings gave way, in the 1920s, to brighter colours and an increasing use of black and white; but his existential preoccupations continued to be fuelled by the rise of Fascism. Branded a degenerate artist by the Nazis, Beckmann left Germany in 1937, eventually emigrating to the USA.

- Brusatin, M. and J. Clair, eds. *Identity and Alterity: Figures of the Body 1895/1995*. XLVI Venice Biennale. exh. cat. Venice: Marsilio, 1995.
- *Catalogo della XXV Biennale di Venezia*. exh. cat. Venice: Biennale, 1950.
- Gallwitz, K., ed. *Gemalde 1905–1950*. exh. cat. Stuttgart: Leipzig Museum der Bildende Kunste, 1990.
- *Max Beckmann: Gravures (1911–1946)*. exh. cat. Les Sables d'Olonne: Les Sables d'Olonne Musée de l'Abbay Sainte-Croix, 1994.

Bellmer, Hans

12 *La Demie-Poupée (Half-Doll)* 1971
wood, paint and assemblage, 90.0 h.
The Art Gallery of New South Wales, Sydney
Mervyn Horton Bequest Fund 1996
Photograph: Jenni Carter

13 *Erotic Drawing* 1948
pencil
Courtesy of Ivor Braka Ltd., London

14 *Variant from Les Jeux de la Poupée*
(The Doll's Games) c.1940
gelatin silver print, oil paint, 16.2 x 16.5
National Gallery of Australia, Canberra
© National Gallery of Australia, Canberra

Born, 1902, Kattowitz, Germany (now Katowice, Poland)
Died, 1975, Paris
Bellmer's highly controversial photographs of dismembered, deformed and provocatively erotic dolls are inevitably linked to the artist's hatred of his authoritarian father, and retreat into a secret childhood garden. Populated by toys and visited by local girls, this refuge from paternal tyranny became the nostalgic and erotic inspiration for Bellmer's first *Doll*. That this event coincided with the rise to power of National Socialism (welcomed by his father) in 1933 was no coincidence. In 1923 he had been sent to study engineering in Berlin, a course soon abandoned in favour of involvement in the Dada Movement. Following the enthusiastic reception of a series of photographs of *Die Puppe* in the Surrealist magazine *Minotaure* in 1934, Bellmer's work was included in the major exhibitions of Surrealism in Paris. Obsessively returning to what he described as the 'experimental poetry' of his dolls, after 1945 he also produced drawings and prints to accompany various erotic texts, including the writings of de Sade, Baudelaire and Bataille.

- *L'Art au corps: le corps exposé de Man Ray à nos jours*. exh. cat. Marseille: Musées de Marseille, 1996
- Brusatin, M. and J. Clair, eds. *Identity and Alterity: Figures of the Body 1895/1995*. XLVI Venice Biennale. exh. cat. Venice: Marsilio, 1995.
- Clair, J., ed. *l'âme au corps, arts et sciences, 1793–1993*. exh. cat. Paris: Gallimard, 1993.
- Duroux, F. "Hans Bellmer: photographies de l'irrepresentable." *La Recherch Photograph* 5, 1988.
- *Fémininmasculin: le sexe de l'art*. exh. cat. Paris: Centre Georges Pompidou, 1995.
- *Hans Bellmer*. exh. cat. Paris: Centre Georges Pompidou, 1971.
- Webb, P. *Hans Bellmer*. London: Quartet, 1985.

Beuys, Joseph

15 *Ohrschmuck (Goldenes Ohr mit Feotusform)* 1953
gouache on perforated paper, 13.7 x 21.0
Museum Moderner Kunst Stiftung Ludwig, Vienna

16 *Dickes Mädchen* 1955
watercolour, fat, 18.5 diameter
Museum Moderner Kunst Stiftung Ludwig, Vienna

17 *Mann mit den Goldenen Beinen* 1955
gouache on delivery docket, 15.0 x 10.3
Museum Moderner Kunst Stiftung Ludwig, Vienna

18 *Ohne Titel* 1949
gouache, 10.5 x 5.7
Museum Moderner Kunst Stiftung Ludwig, Vienna

19 *Springerin* 1953
pencil, 22.0 x 36.5
Museum Moderner Kunst Stiftung Ludwig, Vienna

20 *Am Schwimmbecken* 1954
pencil on cardboard, 27.9 x 15.8
Museum Moderner Kunst Stiftung Ludwig, Vienna

Born, 1921, Krefeld
Died, 1986, Dusseldorf
Drafted into the German Army at 19, Beuys found his plans to study thwarted by World War II. In winter 1943 his plane was shot down over the Crimea, and he was dragged from the deep snow by Tartars who treated his wounds with animal fat and wrapped him in felt against the Arctic winter. These materials, fat and felt, were to recur in many of his sculptural works. Pervasive throughout his oeuvre – which also includes drawings and prints, installations and performances – is a curative, redemptive sentiment: he referred to his art as a 'tablet' or 'ointment'. Biological metaphors are equally

ubiquitous: the creation of art, he insisted, was not an act of genius but rather an 'embryonic' process that dissolved the boundaries between the body, art objects, and the natural environment. Beuys's 'expanded concept of art' (first articulated around 1960) encompassed not only teaching, but involvement in Die Grünen (The Greens) and various groups seeking democratic social reform.

- Bastian, H., ed. *Joseph Beuys: Skulpturen und Objekte* and *The Secret Block for a Secret Person in Ireland*. exh. cat. Berlin: Gropiusbau, 1988.
- Brusatin, M. and J. Clair, eds. *Identity and Alterity: Figures of the Body 1895/1995*. XLVI Venice Biennale. exh. cat. Venice: Marsilio, 1995.
- Kuspit, D. "Joseph Beuys: The Body of the Artist." *Artforum* 10 (Summer 1991).
- Rose, B. and A. Temkin. *Thinking is Form: The Drawings of Joseph Beuys*. Philadelphia: Philadelphia Museum of Art; New York: MOMA, 1993.
- Tisdall, C., ed. *Joseph Beuys*. exh. cat. New York: Guggenheim, 1979.
- Zweite, A., ed. *Beuys, Nature, Materie, Form*. exh. cat. Munich: Dusseldorf Kunstsammlung Nordrhein-Westfalen, 1991.

Bomberg, David

21 *Nude* 1943
oil on canvas, 91.5 x 71.5
Tate Gallery, London

Born, Birmingham, 1890
Died, London, 1957
The fifth child of a Polish immigrant leather worker in Birmingham, Bomberg moved to the Whitechapel area of London. He studied under Walter Bayes and Walter Sickert before gaining acceptance to the Slade School of Fine Art, London in 1911. Fully immersed in the great changes in London with the arrival of Modernism, Bomberg soon became a Vorticist and one of the most talented painters of his generation in Britain. His highly energetic depictions of the human figure attracted greatest acclaim. Profoundly disturbed by his experience in the war, Bomberg's pre-war machine-inspired images were quickly replaced by more organic works, based on a direct experience of nature, of which *Nude*, 1945 in this exhibition is a good example. This later work indicates Bomberg's adoption after 1929 of a looser, more gestural brushmark. Leading artists of the London group, Frank Auerbach, Lucian Freud and Leon Kossoff all acknowledge Bomberg as a significant influence.

- Cork, R. *David Bomberg*. New Haven: Yale UP, 1987.
- —. ed. *David Bomberg*. exh. cat. London: Tate Gallery, 1988.
- Drew, J. and D. Sylvester, eds. *Bomberg: Paintings, Drawings, Watercolors, Lithographs*. exh. cat. London: Fischer FA, 1973.
- Forge, A. et. al., eds. *David Bomberg 1890–1957* London: Arts Council of Great Britain, 1967.
- Spurling, J., ed. *David Bomberg: The Later Years*. exh. cat. London: Whitechapel AG, 1979.

Bonnard, Pierre

22 *The Bath* 1925
oil on canvas, 86.0 x 120.6
Tate Gallery, London

23 *Nu de Dos à la Toilette (Nude at Toilette, Back View)* 1934
oil on canvas, 107.3 x 74.0
Musée National d'Art Moderne,
Centre Georges Pompidou, Paris

24 *L'Homme et la Femme (Man and Woman)* 1900
oil on canvas, 115.0 x 72.5
Musée d'Orsay, Paris
© photo RMN – Gérard Blot

25 *Siesta – The Artist's Studio* 1900
oil on canvas, 109.0 x 132.0 (unframed)
National Gallery of Victoria, Melbourne
Felton Bequest, 1949

Born, 1867, Fontenay-aux-Roses, nr. Paris
Died, 1947, Le Cannet
Bonnard was a member of the Nabis and labelled an 'intimist' for his mastery of the private or unguarded moment and emphasis on domestic settings: woman in post-coital sleep, woman bathing, a couple breakfasting. Known for his use of high-keyed colour which is loosely applied and yet tightly knitted together, his canvases are filled with light, his models caught up in a medley of colour and pattern. The woman in most of Bonnard's paintings is Maria ('Marthe') Boursin, his companion from 1893 to his death in 1942. Intensely loyal to her, Bonnard continued to paint her body as never ageing, slender and supple, in a range of domestic situations. It is the series of her in the bath that has earned Bonnard his reputation as one of the greatest painters of nudes in the twentieth century. After years of painting trips to the south, they settled at Le Cannet, near Cannes in 1925 where he continued painting canvases of immense size. Often combining several points of view, these compositions allow the viewer entry from the positions of the objects.

- Bell, J. *Bonnard*. London: Phaidon, 1994.
- Brusatin, M. and J. Clair, eds. *Identity and Alterity: Figures of the Body 1895/1995*. XLVI Venice Biennale. exh. cat. Venice: Marsilio, 1995.
- Clair, J., ed. *Bonnard*. exh. cat. Paris: Centre Georges Pompidou; Washington DC: Phillips Collection; Dallas: Dallas Museum Art; Zurich: Kunsthaus, 1984.
- —. ed. *Pierre Bonnard*. exh. cat. Milan: Milan Palazzo Reale, 1988.
- Rewald, J. and C. Terrasse, eds. *Pierre Bonnard*. exh. cat. New York: MOMA, 1948.

Bourgeois, Louise

26 *Janus Fleuri* 1968
bronze, with golden patina, 26.7 x 31.8 x 21.2
Courtesy of Robert Miller Gallery, New York

Born, 1911, Paris
Lives New York
Louise Bourgeois attended the École des Beaux-Arts in Paris prior to moving to New York in 1938, where she continued to

study painting and exhibited with the Abstract Expressionists. She gave up painting for sculpture in 1949, and during the 1960s began exploring the symbolic and biomorphic possibilities of a wide range of media, including plaster, latex rubber, cement, marble and bronze. A Surrealist sensibility informs much of her work, which has tended to be autobiographical in both motivation and content. The result has been an iconography of desire as well as anxiety, loneliness and vulnerability. Her interest in feminism dates back to the 1940s, although a greater degree of ambiguity and intimacy characterise her organic sculptures of the '60s and '70s. Awarded honorary degrees from Yale University (1977) and Bard College (1981), her first major retrospective was held at the Museum of Modern Art, New York, in 1982.

- Bernadac, M.-L. *Louise Bourgeois*. Paris: Flammarion, 1995.
- —. *Louise Bourgeois: pensées-plumes*. Paris: Centre Georges Pompidou, 1995.
- Brusatin, M. and J. Clair, eds. *Identity and Alterity: Figures of the Body 1895/1995*. XLVI Venice Biennale. exh. cat. Venice: Marsilio, 1995.
- Clair, J., ed. *l' âme au corps, arts et sciences, 1793–1993*. exh. cat. Paris: Gallimard, 1993.
- *Fémininmasculin: le sexe de l'art*. exh. cat. Paris: Centre Georges Pompidou, 1995.
- Gardner, P. *Louise Bourgeois*. Universe Series on Women Artists. New York: Universe, 1994.
- Weiermair, P. *Louise Bourgeois*. exh. cat. Zurich: Edition Stemmle, 1995.

Boyd, Arthur

27 *Figure in Landscape (Nude Washing in a Creek III)* 1961
oil, tempera on hardboard, 160.0 x 183.0
The Art Gallery of New South Wales, Sydney
Photograph: Ray Woodbury
Reproduced with the permission of Bundanon Trust

Born, 1920, Murrumbeena, Victoria
Lives Bundanon, New South Wales
Arthur Boyd was born in rural Victoria into a family of artists and writers, and was taught ceramics and landscape painting at home. While a member of the Army Survey Corps in World War II he became involved with the Contemporary Art Society, contributing to their Anti-Fascist Exhibition of 1942. It was during this period that he began to develop his distinctive expressive style, while remaining committed to the aims of social realism. By the end of the war, Boyd had turned his attention to the landscape, drawing on his religious upbringing and an idiosyncratic synthesis of Surrealism and Expressionism to explore the relationship between humanity and nature. A retrospective exhibition of his work was held at The Art Gallery of New South Wales in 1995.

- Dobrez, P. and P. Herbst. *The Art of the Boyds: Generations of Artistic Achievement*. Sydney: Bay Books, 1990.
- Pearce, B. *Arthur Boyd Retrospective*. exh. cat. Sydney: AGNSW, 1994.
- Robertson, B. *Arthur Boyd*. exh. cat. London: Whitechapel AG, 1962.

Brus, Gunter

28 *Selbstbemalung III (Body Painting III)* 1964–65
notebook, sequence of 9 pencil drawings
collage with vellum paper, clips and razor blade
29.7 x 21.0 (each)
Courtesy of Sammlung Friedrichshof

29 *Selbstbemalung (Body Painting)* 1964
photo portfolio, 29.3 x 22.0
Courtesy of Galerie Krinzinger, Vienna

30 *o.T.* 1960
emulsion paint on paper, 90.0 x 120.0
Courtesy of Sammlung Friedrichshof

Born, 1938, Ardning, Styria
Lives Graz, Austria
Brus trained in commercial graphic art in Vienna between 1957 and 1960. Inspired by visits to Spain and the Venice Biennale, Brus began to paint gestural abstractions. This practice was truncated in 1961 by his military service. He then found it difficult to resume this style, choosing instead to focus on the act of painting itself. With Muehl, Nitsch and Schwartzkogler he founded the Aktionismus group. The emphasis in his work was on portraying various acts of self-mutilation in his *Aktionen*. Throughout the '60s, Brus pushed his analysis of the body to the limit, publicly urinating, defecating and cutting himself with a razor. After *Breaking Test* in 1970, Brus returned to painting, drawing and making artist books.

- *L'Art au corps: le corps exposé de Man Ray à nos jours*. exh. cat. Marseille: Musées de Marseille, 1996
- *Aktions-malerei-Aktionismus 1960-1965*. exh. cat. Klagenfurt: Kassel Winterthur, 1988.
- Amanhauser, H. and D. Ronte, eds. *Gunter Brus: Der Uberblick*. exh. cat. Vienna, 1986.
- Brusatin, M. and J. Clair, eds. *Identity and Alterity: Figures of the Body 1895/1995*. XLVI Venice Biennale. exh. cat. Venice: Marsilio, 1995.
- Grenier, C., ed. *Gunter Brus: limite due visible*. exh. cat. Paris: Centre Georges Pompidou, 1993.

Dinos and Jake Chapman

31 *Doggy* 1997
fibreglass resin and paint, 82.0 x 6.0 x 60.0
Courtesy of Victoria Miro, London

Dinos Chapman
Born, 1962
Jake Chapman
Born, 1966
Both live in London
Both Chapmans studied at the Royal College of Art, with Dinos completing his first degree at Ravensbourne College of Art and Jake at North East London Polytechnic. The brothers began exhibiting together in 1992 and since then have forged a strong international reputation for their sculptural objects: mutant figures which are simultaneously disturbing, compelling and clever challenges to "the tired of seeing" (*Chapmanworld* n.p.). Drawing on psychoanalysis, ". . . these objects are *simulacra* or bad copies of the ideal, they are puerile, slippery and annoying. Here are entities with no fixed identity

or allegiance to the ideal, nomadically breeding in an unlimited becoming" (*Chapmanworld*).

- *Chapmanworld*. exh. cat. London: ICA, 1996; Graz: Grazer Kunstverein, Austria, 1996; Berlin: Kunste-Werke, 1997.
- Gillick, L. "Project." *Art & Text* 51 (1995).
- Morgan, S. "Rude Awakening." *Frieze* 19 (Nov./Dec. 1994).
- Rosenblum, R. "Dinos and Jake Chapman." *Artforum* 35.1 (Sep. 1996).

Clemente, Francesco

32 *The Purification of The Twelve (A Calendar for 1988)*
1987, set of 12 pastels on paper, 67.0 x 48.5 (each)
Courtesy of Anthony d'Offay Gallery, London

Born, 1952, Naples
Lives, New York
Clemente began studying architecture in Rome and concurrently established a studio to make drawings based on childhood memories and dreams. He became widely known in the mid-1970s with richly coloured, highly personal erotic images of body parts and contemplations on the naked self. Clemente was one of a group of figurative painters, including his compatriots Enzo Cucchi and Sandro Chia, to emerge in the early 1980s labelled *transavangardia* referring to an artistic attitude that combined images from high and low art and across avant-garde movements. Clemente has become well known for his passion for Indian folklore and mysticism. He now moves between three homes in Madras, New York and Rome.

- Auping, M. *Francesco Clemente*. New York: Harry N. Abrams, 1985.
- Brusatin, M. and J. Clair, eds. *Identity and Alterity: Figures of the Body 1895/1995*. XLVI Venice Biennale. exh. cat. Venice: Marsilio, 1995.
- *Fémininmasculin: le sexe de l'art*. exh. cat. Paris: Centre Georges Pompidou, 1995.
- *Francesco Clemente: Early Morning Exercises*. exh. cat. Paris: Centre Georges Pompidou, 1994.
- Oliva, A. B. ed. *Transavanguardia: Italia/rica*. exh. cat. Modena: Modena Galleria Civica del Comune, 1982.
- Percy, A. and R. Foyle, eds. *Francesco Clemente: Three Worlds*. exh. cat. Philadelphia: Philadelphia Museum of Art; Hartford: Wadsworth Atheneum; San Francisco: SFMOMA; London: Royal Academy, 1990.

Courbet, Jean-Désiré-Gustave

33 *The Source* 1862
oil on canvas, 120.0 x 74.3 cm (unframed)
The Metropolitan Museum of Art
H. O. Havemeyer Collection,
Bequest of Mrs. H.O. Havemeyer, 1929

34 *The Source of the Loue* c.1865
oil on canvas, 99.7 x 142.2 (unframed)
The Metropolitan Museum of Art
H.O. Havemeyer Collection,
Bequest of Mrs. H.O. Havemeyer, 1929

Born, 1819, Ornans, France
Died, 1877, Tour-de-Peliz, Switzerland
The rural setting of Courbet's early life, in the town of Ornans on the River Loue, contributed much to his artistic imagination as well as his political convictions. Although he lived in Paris from 1839 until four years before his death, Courbet produced not one painting of the city. His early works, many of them self-portraits, are markedly influenced by the quality of light and expressive brushwork of painters like Rembrandt and Frans Hals. During the 1850s Courbet's rejection of the slick, illusionistic style prescribed by the Academy was extended to subject matter, and the exhibition of three of his works at the Paris Salon of 1851 sparked a debate that is often associated with the beginning of modernism. Declaring that "art must be dragged through the gutter" (Riat 74), Courbet defended the coarse realism of his peasants and labourers against the offended sensibilities of his critics. Celebrated as a 'socialist painter,' his politics were also resolutely regionalist. From the late 1850s he turned his attention increasingly to landscapes.

- Clair, J., ed. *l' âme au corps, arts et sciences, 1793–1993*. exh. cat. Paris: Gallimard, 1993.
- Clark, T. J. *Image of the People: Gustave Courbet and the 1848 Revolution*. New Jersey: Princeton UP, 1980.
- Eisenman, S., "The Rhetoric of Realism: Courbet and the Origins of the Avant-Garde." *Nineteenth Century Art: A Critical History*. London: Thames and Hudson, 1994.
- Faunce, S. and L. Nochlin. *Courbet Reconsidered*. exh. cat. Brooklyn, New York: The Brooklyn Museum, 1988.
- *Fémininmasculin: le sexe de l'art*. exh. cat. Paris: Centre Georges Pompidou, 1995.
- Fried, M. *Courbet's Realism*. Chicago: U of Chicago P, 1990.
- Riat, G. *Gustave Courbet: Peintre*. Paris, 1906.
- Rubin, J. H. *Realism and Social Vision in Courbet and Proudhon*. New Jersey: Princeton UP, 1980.

De Andrea, John

35 *Allegory: After Courbet* 1988
oil on polyvinyl and mixed media
172.2 x 152.2 x 190.2 (installed)
The Art Gallery of Western Australia, Perth

Born 1941, Denver, Colorado
Lives Morrison, Colorado
John De Andrea was educated at the University of Colorado in Fine Arts. A Verist sculptor, De Andrea like Duane Hanson uses painted polyvinyl to simulate flesh. Producing the equivalent of 3-dimensional Photo Realism, he strives to arrive at total objectivity. De Andrea depicts all the details of the human body, including pores and broken capillaries, in his effort to hide nothing. The casts are taken from the living model in segments, then poured and painted. While his earlier figures are more like mannequins, the late figures look like they are capable of movement.

- Genauer, E. "Art in the Artist." *New York Post* Dec. 1971.
- Glueck, G. "A New Realism in Sculpture." *Art in America* (Nov./Dec. 1971).
- Kalina, R. "Real dead." *Arts Magazine*. (Dec. 1991): 48–53.
- Mashek, J. "The Verist Sculptors: 2 Interviews: Duane Hanson and John De Andrea." *Art in America* (Nov./Dec. 1972).

Degas, Edgar

36 *Dancer Looking at the Sole of her Right Foot* 1919–21
bronze, lost wax, 48.0
The Art Gallery of New South Wales, Sydney
Bequest of Paul Haefliger 1982
Photograph: Tim Marshall

37 *After the Bath* c.1900
black chalk, 73.7 x 59.8
The Art Gallery of New South Wales, Sydney
Margaret Hannah Olley Art Trust 1994
Photograph: Ray Woodbury

Born, 1834, Paris
Died, 1917, Paris
Although a founding and exhibiting member of the French Impressionists, Degas' preoccupation with the human figure and his intimate engagement with the minutiae of everyday life set him apart from the aims and methods of the group. "My art," he insisted, "has nothing spontaneous about it, it is all reflection" (Monnier 619). The distinctive linearity of Degas' work – a product of his classical training – evolved into a dynamic vocabulary of gesture and movement. His 600 or so variations on the theme of ballerinas have been compared to the photographic studies of animal and human locomotion undertaken by Eadweard Muybridge in the 1870s and '80s. Degas' fascination with the moving body was extended and developed through his sculptures, many of them produced as wax sketches and not cast until after his death.

- Brusatin, M. and J. Clair, eds. *Identity and Alterity: Figures of the Body 1895/1995*. XLVI Venice Biennale. exh. cat. Venice: Marsilio, 1995.
- Clair, J., ed. *l' âme au corps, arts et sciences, 1793–1993*. exh. cat. Paris: Gallimard, 1993.
- Kendall, R., ed. *Degas: Images of Women*. exh. cat. Liverpool: Tate Gallery, 1989.
- Lemoisne, P. *Degas et son oeuvre*. 4 vols. New York: Garland, 1984.
- Lipton, E. *Looking into Degas: Uneasy Images of Women and Modern Life*. Berkeley: U of California P, 1986.
- Loyrette, H. *Degas: Passion and Intellect*. London: Thames and Hudson, 1993.
- Monnier, G. "Degas." J. Turner, ed. *The Dictionary of Art*. 34 vols. London: Macmillan, 1996.

De Kooning, Willem

38 *Two Figures in Landscape* 1968
oil on paper, 122.5 x 154.0
National Gallery of Australia, Canberra
© National Gallery of Australia, Canberra

39 *Clamdigger* 1972–79
cast bronze, 151.0 x 75.0 x 61.0
Stedelijk Museum, Amsterdam

Born, 1904, Rotterdam
Died, 1997, New York
Willem De Kooning received basic training as a commercial artist and then completed a degree in Fine Arts in Rotterdam before moving to New York in 1925. He rose to prominence in the 1940s, becoming known as a pioneer of Abstract Expressionism, the style of the New York school whose other members included Jackson Pollock and Mark Rothko. His *Women* series (1950 to 1953) is widely considered his best, taking his Expressionist paint-handling to extreme. He said of *Woman I*, "it does one thing for me: it eliminates composition, arrangements, relationships, light – all those stupid discourses on line, colour and form" (Cummings). The violent *art brut* paintwork of his figure paintings gives way to more lyrical calligraphy in his later landscape and abstract compositions.

- Cummings, P. et. al., eds. *Willem De Kooning: Drawings, Paintings, Sculptures*. New York: Whitney Museum of American Art, 1983.
- *Fémininmasculin: le sexe de l'art*. exh. cat. Paris: Centre Georges Pompidou, 1995.
- Waldman, D. *Willem De Kooning*. London: Thames and Hudson, 1988.
- *Willem De Kooning: Paintings*. exh. cat. Washington: National Gallery of Art, 1994.
- Yard, S. "Willem De Kooning's Women." *Arts Magazine* 53.3 (Nov. 1978).

Del Favero, Dennis

40 *La Linea Sfumata (The Blurred Line)* 1993
3 Type C colour photographs
100.0 x 150.0 (triptych: each of 3 photographs)
The Art Gallery of New South Wales, Sydney
Purchased with funds provided by the Contemporary Collection Benefactors' Scheme, 1993
Photograph: Christopher Snee
Represented by Mori Gallery, Sydney and Galerie Andreas Weiss, Berlin

Born, 1953, Sydney
Lives Sydney
Del Favero began exhibiting in the mid-1980s; since then his photographs, videos and installations have been shown in Australia, Europe, Scandinavia, Canada and Israel. The interrelated themes of masculinity and violence recur through much of Del Favero's work, most recently in *Motel Vilina Vlas*, a series of photographs based on rape camps in former Yugoslavia; *Coming Apart*, a video installation recounting the suicide of a male porn star; and *Prima Facie*, the project from which *La Linea Sfumata* derives. In *Prima Facie*, within the narrative framework of a homicide, Del Favero plays on the multiple registers of forensic photography (the body as evidence of a violent crime), religious iconography (specifically Christ's passion), and the sexual indeterminacy of the male nude.

- Best, S. "Man, the Darker Continent." *Prima Facie*. exh. cat. Wollongong: Wollongong City Gallery, 1993.
- —. *Coming Apart*. exh. cat. Sydney: Australian Centre for Photography, 1997.
- Genocchio, B. "The Subject of Rape." *Third Text* 33 (Winter 1996).
- Rowley, S. "Prima Facie, Unravelling Masculinity." *Photofile* 43 (1994).
- Sommer, T. "Jenny Holzer: Kriegszustand und Dennis Del Favero: Motel Vilina Vlas: The Uses of Rape." *Das Kunst-Bulletin* (June 1996).

de Monchaux, Cathy

41 *Worried About the Weather?* 1996
brass, copper, leather and chalk, 33.0 x 40.0 x 7.0
Edition of 3 (Private Collection: Belgium;
Private Collection: Switzerland; Private Collection, UK)

Born, 1963, London
Lives London
de Monchaux completed an M.A. at Goldsmiths' College in London in 1987. She has continued to carve a significant reputation in Europe and now the US for her sculptural constructions. Simultaneously ornate, seductive and sexually charged her work utilises a variety of materials from glittery lamé to velvet and leather, often incorporating them on skeletal superstructures of brass. de Monchaux is best known for combining sophisticated formal accuracy with a nuanced commentary on sexuality.

- *Cathy de Monchaux.* exh. cat. London: Chisenhale Gallery, 1993.
- Renton, A. "Velvet Sex Trap." Interview with Cathy de Monchaux. *Flash Art* 154 (Oct. 1990).
- Koplos, J. "Cathy de Monchaux at Sean Kelly." *Art in America* 84 (June 1996).
- Schwabsky, B. "Cathy de Monchaux." *Artforum* 34.8 (Apr. 1996).
- Todd, S. "Cathy de Monchaux." *Art & Text* 49 (Sep. 1994).

Dix, Otto

42 *Drei Weiber (Three Women)* 1926
oil on wood, 181.0 x 105.5
Galerie der Stadt Stuttgart

43 *Ungleiches Liebespaare (The Odd Couple)* 1925
tempera on wood, 180.0 x 100.0
Galerie der Stadt Stuttgart

Born, 1891, Untermhaus, nr. Gera, Germany
Died, 1969, Singen, Germany
Dix's stylistic and ideological origins ranged from northern Renaissance painting to German Expressionism and Dada, but his imagination, like that of many of his contemporaries, was fuelled above all by the experience of war. "War," he once remarked, "is something so animal-like: hunger, lice, slime, these crazy sounds. . . It is necessary to see people in this unchained condition to know something about man." (*Otto Dix*, 1985, 280). A machine-gunner in the German army from 1914–18, and a conscript and prisoner of war in Word War II, Dix's harrowing depictions of the trenches and war cripples during the 1920s find a gruesome complement in his images of prostitutes and their clients of the same period. Both faces of human bankruptcy and cruelty are rendered with his characteristic unflinching and exaggerated realism. Censored by the Nazis after 1933, Dix retreated into empty, classically composed landscapes and religious allegory.

- Brusatin, M., and J. Clair, eds. *Identity and Alterity: Figures of the Body 1895/1995*. XLVI Venice Biennale. exh. cat. Venice: Marsilio, 1995.
- *Fémininmasculin: le sexe de l'art.* exh. cat. Paris: Centre Georges Pompidou, 1995.
- Hartley, K., ed. *Otto Dix 1891–1969*. exh. cat. London: Tate Gallery, 1992; Stuttgart: Galerie der Stadt, 1991; Berlin: Nationalgalerie, 1991/2.
- *Otto Dix 1891–1969*. exh. cat. Munich: Villa Stuck, 1985.
- Sabarsky, S., ed. *Otto Dix*. exh. cat. Milan: Genoa Villa Croce, 1986.

Drozdik, Orshi

44 *Body Self* 1983–93
rubber figure, steel table, six photos and six plates
dimensions variable
Ludwig Museum of Contemporary Art, Budapest

Born Hungary
Lives New York
Raised and educated in Hungary, Drozdik graduated from the Hungarian Art Academy in Budapest. The censored version of modern art did not fulfil her intellectual interests in conceptual art and contemporary ideas so she relocated temporarily to Amsterdam and then in 1980 to New York. There she began investigations into the scientific representation of nature and the human body. From 1983 she researched displays in 18th and 19th century science, medical and technological museums. These displays formed the basis of a series of installations using glass, iron, lead, plaster and porcelain accompanied by photographs and texts. In the 1990s she turned her attention to the idea of 'self' in its multiple configurations: historical, cultural, racial and gendered.

- Kravagna, C. "Orshi Drozdik." *Artforum* 33 (Apr. 1995).
- Mahoney, R. "Tom Cugliani Gallery, New York." *Arts Magazine* 64 (May 1990).
- Upshaw, R. "Tom Cugliani Gallery, New York." *Art in America* 82 (Jan. 1994).
- Welchman, J. C. "Orshi Drozdik: The Medical Venus." *Art & Text* 50 (Jan. 1995).

Dubuffet, Jean

45 *Gymnosophie* 1950
oil on canvas, 97.0 x 146.0
Musée National d'Art Moderne,
Centre Georges Pompidou, Paris

Born, 1901, Le Havre
Died, 1985, Paris
Known for his rebellious stance against traditional art and his persistent fight against accepted aesthetic values, Dubuffet has had a decisive influence on the course of 20th century art. He began his artistic career in 1942 and developed *art brut* in 1945. Literally 'raw art', the term refers to the work of non-professionals, children, Naive artists and the mentally ill. Dubuffet found inspiration in this kind of work because he considered it refreshingly authentic and direct. His distinctive style combines gritty and encrusted surfaces – he used materials such as asphalt, broken glass, newspapers and clay – and innovative methods such as scraping and slashing with a consciously simplified but expressive drawing style. *Gymnosophie*, 1950, in this exhibition clearly shows Dubuffet's dexterity of hand: the enlarged bodies are spread on the canvas, the background and figures sharing the same materiality.

- Brusatin, M. and J. Clair, eds. *Identity and Alterity: Figures of the Body 1895/1995*. XLVI Venice Biennale. exh. cat. Venice: Marsilio, 1995.

• *Fémininmasculin: le sexe de l'art*. exh. cat. Paris: Centre Georges Pompidou, 1995.
• Glimcher, M. *Jean Dubuffet: Towards an Alternate Reality*. New York: 1987.
• *Jean Dubuffet: A Retrospective*. exh. cat. New York: Solomon R Guggenheim Museum, 1973.
• Jean Dubuffet 1901–1985. exh. cat. Frankfurt: Frankfurt Schirnkunstalle, 1991.
• *Jean Dubuffet 1943–1963: Paintings, Sculptures, Assemblages*. exh. cat. Essays by Susan J. Cooke et. al. Washington DC: Hirshhorn Museum/Smithsonian Institution P, 1993.

Duchamp, Marcel

46 *A la Manière de Delvaux (In the Manner of Delvaux)* 1942
collage: tinfoil, cardboard, photograph, 34.0 x 34.0
Courtesy of Galleria Schwarz Collection, Milan
Photograph: S.A.D.E. archives

47 *Objet Dard* 1951–63
galvanised plaster, 7.5 x 20.1 x 6.0
Courtesy of Galleria Schwarz Collection, Milan
Photograph: S.A.D.E. archives

48 *Coin de Chasteté (Wedge of Chastity)* 1954–63
galvanised plaster and plastic, 5.6 x 8.5 x 4.2
Courtesy of Galleria Schwarz Collection, Milan
Photograph: S.A.D.E. archives

49 *Feuille de Vigne Femelle (Female Fig Leaf)* 1950–51
galvanised plaster, 9.0 x 14.0 x 12.5
Courtesy of Galleria Schwarz Collection, Milan
Photograph: S.A.D.E. archives

50 *The Lovers*
series of 9 etchings
i *Morceaux Choisis d'après Rodin (Selected Details after Rodin)* 1968
50.5 x 32.5
ii *Morceaux Choisis d'après Ingres, I (Selected Details after Ingres, I)* 1968
50.5 x 32.5
iii *Morceaux Choisis d'après Ingres, II (Selected Details after Ingres, II)* 1968
50.5 x 32.5
iv *Morceaux Choisis d'après Cranach et "Relâche" (Selected Details after Cranach and "Relâche")* 1968
50.5 x 32.5
v *Morceaux Choisis d'après Courbet (Selected Details after Courbet)* 1968
50.5 x 32.5
vi *King and Queen* 1968
50.5 x 32.5
vii *Après l'Amour* 1967
50.5 x 32.5
viii *The Large Glass and Related Works*
42.2 x 25
ix *Le Bec Auer* 1968
50.5 x 32.5
Courtesy of Galleria Schwarz Collection, Milan
Photograph: S.A.D.E. archives

Born, 1887, Blainville, Normandy
Died, 1968, Neuilly-sur-Seine
Born into an extended family of artists, Duchamp took classes at the Académie Julian in Paris (1904–05), and exhibited paintings at the Salon des Indépendants and the Salon d'Automne in 1909. The inclusion of his dynamic, Cubist-inspired *Nude Descending a Staircase* in the Armory show in New York (1913) established his name in the US, and upon arriving there in 1915 he was welcomed into avant-garde circles. He had, by then, embarked on a number of projects that were to span his career and have a profound influence on the course of 20th century art. His early fascination with the human form in motion, which had been inspired by the chrono-photography of Eadweard Muybridge, was extended in mechanomorphic studies for his major work, *The Large Glass*. At the same time, his reflections on the nature of art and the role of the artist led to the creation of his first Ready-Made in 1913, and ultimately prompted him to abandon painting altogether in the 1920s. Although he proceeded to direct much of his creative and intellectual energy into chess (becoming chess champion of Haute-Normandie in 1924), he continued quietly to pursue his ideas in forms other than painting. Literary puns were published under the pseudonym of Rrose Sélavy, Duchamp's female alter-ego (from *arroser*, 'to wet' or 'to moisten'). And ironically, given his insistence that art should go beyond the purely "retinal," he embarked on a study of optics and perspective in 1918 that was to occupy him for the next 20 years. During the occupation of Paris in 1942 Duchamp again left for New York, where he began work on *Etant Donnés*, his last major work that, characteristically, took 22 years to complete. He envisaged the installation as a continuation of the *Large Glass*, translating the abstract components of the latter into a more literal treatment of sexual desire and its frustration.

• D'Harnoncourt, A. and K. McShine, eds. *Marcel Duchamp*. exh. cat. New York: MOMA; Philadelphia: Philadelphia Museum of Art, 1973.
• D'Harnoncourt, A. and Walter Hopps. "*Etant Donnés: 1°La Chute d'eau, 2°Le Gaz d'éclairage*": *Reflections on a New Work by Marcel Duchamp*. Philadelphia: Philadelphia Museum of Art, 1987.
• Brusatin, M. and J. Clair, eds. *Identity and Alterity: Figures of the Body 1895/1995*. XLVI Venice Biennale. exh. cat. Venice: Marsilio, 1995.
• Caumont, J. and J. Gough-Cooper, eds. *Marcel Duchamp*. exh. cat. Venice: Venice Palazzo Grassi, 1993.
• Clair, J. ed. *l' âme au corps, arts et sciences, 1793–1993*. exh. cat. Paris: Gallimard, 1993.
• *Fémininmasculin: le sexe de l'art*. exh. cat. Paris: Centre Georges Pompidou, 1995.

Eakins, Thomas

51 *Wrestlers* 1899
oil on canvas, 101.6 x 127.0
Philadelphia Museum of Art
Bequest of Fiske and Marie Kimball

Born, 1844, Philadelphia
Died, 1916, Philadelphia
Eakins studied at the Pennsylvania Academy of the Fine Arts, the École des Beaux-Arts and in the studio of Jean-Léon Gérome. During this time Eakins pursued his studies of

human anatomy and dissection. Returning to Philadelphia in 1870, he embarked on a career of painting. He disliked the 19th century tradition of stylising and perfecting the nude, which he considered unfaithful to nature. Instead he focused on representing his subjects in powerful physical and psychological terms. A keen observer of human and animal movement, Eakins' subjects included rowing, wrestling, bathing, boxing as well as detailed surgical operations and commissioned portraits.

- Brusatin, M. and Clair. J. eds. *Identity and Alterity: Figures of the Body 1895/1995*. XLVI Venice Biennale. exh. cat. Venice: Marsilio, 1995.
- Homer, W. I. *Thomas Eakins: His Life and Art* New York, 1992.
- Johns, E. *Thomas Eakins: The Heroism of Modern Life*. Princeton, NJ: Princeton UP, 1983.
- Sewell, D. *Thomas Eakins: Artist of Philadelphia*. exh. cat. Philadelphia: Philadelphia Museum of Art, 1982.
- Wilmerding, J., ed. *Thomas Eakins (1844–1916) and the Heart of American Life*. London: National Portrait Gallery, 1993.

Fontana, Lucio

52 *Concetto Spaziale (Spatial Concept)* 1962
oil on canvas, 101.0 x 81.0
Courtesy of L. F. Toninelli

53 *Concetto Spaziale, Attese (Spatial Concept)* 1962
tempera on canvas, 100.0 x 81.0
Courtesy of L. F. Toninelli

Born 1899, Rosario, Santa Fé, Argentina
Died, 1968, Comabbio, Italy
An Italian of Argentine birth, Fontana lived and worked in Buenos Aires as well as in Milan, where he studied sculpture at the Accademia di Brera from 1928–30. By 1934 he had begun to produce abstract works that hovered between two and three dimensions. These early investigations were taken further in his concept of *Spazialismo* ('Spatialism'). In manifestos written between 1947 and '52 Fontana advocated a dynamic, invasive form of art, articulated in four dimensions (including time): ideas that foreshadowed the emergence of environmental art and related developments. *Concetto spaziale* ('spatial concept') became the generic title for most of his subsequent works, notably his *Buchi* ('holes') paintings (begun in 1949) and the closely related *Tagli* ('slashes') series (from the mid-1950s).

- Bois, Y. "Fontana's base materialism." *Art in America* 77 (Apr. 1989).
- Brusatin, M. and J. Clair, eds. *Identity and Alterity: Figures of the Body 1895/1995*. XLVI Venice Biennale. exh. cat. Venice: Marsilio, 1995.
- Crispolti, E., ed. *Fontana: Catalogo Generale*. 2 vols. Milan, 1986.
- *Fémininmasculin: le sexe de l'art*. exh. cat. Paris: Centre Georges Pompidou, 1995.
- Fossati, P., ed. *Lucio Fontana: Concetti Spaziali*. exh. cat. Turin: 1970.
- *Lucio Fontana*. exh. cat. Amsterdam: Stedelijk Museum; London: Whitechapel AG, 1988.

Freud, Lucian

54 *Naked Man with Rat* c.1977–78
oil on canvas, 91.5 x 91.5
Art Gallery of Western Australia, Perth

55 *Naked Girl Asleep II* 1968
oil on canvas, 55.8 x 55.8
Courtesy of Ivor Braka Ltd., London
Private Collection: Courtesy of Richard Nagy, London

Born, 1922, Berlin
Lives London
The grandson of Sigmund Freud, Lucian Freud moved to England at the age of 10 where he studied at the Central School of Arts and Crafts (1938) and later at Goldsmith's College (1943). He represented Great Britain with Ben Nicholson and Francis Bacon at the Venice Biennale XXVII (1954). While Freud executes cityscapes and highly detailed nature studies, his work – like that of his compatriot Bacon – is dominated by the human form. Freud is principally known for the precision of his brush combined with a clinical gaze, producing unsettling figure studies which manage to fulfil his stated aim of touching "the senses by an intensification of reality" (LF in *Lucian Freud, Dipinti* 23).

- Brusatin, M. and J. Clair, eds. *Identity and Alterity: Figures of the Body 1895/1995*. XLVI Venice Biennale. exh. cat. Venice: Marsilio, 1995.
- Gowing, L. *Lucian Freud*. London: Whitechapel AG, 1982.
- *Lucian Freud*. exh. cat. Sydney: AGNSW, 1992–93.
- *Lucian Freud: Paintings*. exh. cat. Intro. by R. Hughes. Washington DC: Smithsonian Institute; Paris: Centre Georges Pompidou; London: Hayward Gallery; Berlin: National Gallery, 1987.
- *Lucian Freud: Recent Drawings and Etchings*. New York: Matthew Marks Gallery, 1993. [includes interview with the artist]
- Mantura, B. and A. Cook, eds. *Lucian Freud: Paintings and Works on Paper 1990–91*. exh. cat. Milan: Castello Sporzesca; Liverpool: Tate Gallery, 1991.

Gauguin, Paul

56 *Breton Youth* 1889
oil on canvas, 93.0 x 73.5
Wallraf-Richartz-Museum, Cologne

Born, 1848, Paris
Died, 1903, Atuona, Marquesas Islands
Between his early childhood in Lima and his final, isolated years on an island in the Marquesas, Gauguin joined the Merchant Marine, succeeded and failed as a stockbroker, married (in 1873) and left his wife and children to live first in the Breton village of Pont-Aven (in 1886) and ultimately in Tahiti (on and off from 1891). His career as an artist was no less subject to vicissitudes. Despite his participation in Impressionist exhibitions from 1880, his later acclaim in Symbolist circles, and the extent of his stylistic influence on twentieth-century artists (including Picasso, the German Expressionists and the Fauves), he did not achieve official recognition until after his death. Characteristic of Gauguin's Pont-Aven period, *Breton Youth* prefigures the artist's later identification with the 'untamed' sensuality of Polynesian culture; and exemplifies the stylistic achievements of Synthetism.

- Bretell, R., ed. *The Art of Paul Gauguin*. exh. cat. Washington DC: National Gallery of Art; Chicago: Art Institute; Paris: Paris Grand Palais, 1988.
- Brusatin, Manlio and J. Clair, eds. *Identity and Alterity: Figures of the Body 1895/1995*. XLVI Venice Biennale. exh. cat. Venice: Marsilio, 1995.
- Cachin, F. et. al., eds. *Gauguin*. exh. cat. Paris: Paris Grand Palais, 1989.
- Gauguin, P. *The Writings of a Savage*. Ed. D. Guérin. Trans. E. Levieux. New York: Da Capo P, 1996.
- Sweetman, D. *Paul Gauguin: A Complete Life*. London: Hodder and Stoughton, 1995.

Geczy, Adam

57 *Invocation and Exorcism* 1997
photographs and text panels, 392.0 x 100.0
Courtesy of Mori Gallery, Sydney

Born, 1969, Sydney
Lives Sydney
Geczy has recently submitted a PhD in 19th century French art history at Sydney University. He combines this knowledge with training in fine arts at Sydney College of the Arts. Geczy works in photography, computer imaging and painting. His painting, reminiscent of Fascist Neoclassicism, is concerned with insidious visual stereotypes of style, genre, taste, beauty. His work in *BODY* derives from 'The Terror of Art' series inspired by the preparatory photographs Hitler used to reflect on his gestures for the Nüremberg rallies. This series interrogates the point of connection between personal and collective memory as well as the junctures of differing cultural histories.

- Curnow, B. "Co-existence." *Art Monthly* 69 (May 1994).
- Davies, S. "Adams." *Agenda* 32 (July 1993).
- —. "Coexistence." *Agenda* 37 (July 1994).
- Gibson, T. "Adam Geczy: The Wedding." *Eyeline* 18 (Autumn 1992).
- Hood, C. "Op Art: Nike Savvas and Adam Geczy, Ars Multiplicata." *Photofile* 37 (Nov. 1992).

Gober, Robert

58 *Man Coming Out of Woman* 1993–94
beeswax, hair, fabric and leather, 34.0 x 86.0 x 72.5
Fonds National d'Art Contemporain, Paris.

Born, 1954, Wallingford, Connecticut
Lives New York
From 1972 to 1976 Gober studied literature and then fine art at Middlebury College, Vermont and then at the Tyler School of Art, Rome (1974–75) before moving to New York in 1976. There he pursued carpentry, making dolls' houses and stretchers for artists before starting to produce his own objects: plaster figures and small-scale models of houses using real building materials. He became known also for his painting with *Slides of a Changing Painting*, 1982–83. The work which first brought him acclaim, however, were his replicas of domestic objects such as drains, sinks and playpens executed from 1984. More recently he has turned his attention to the human body and the domestic environment. Fragments of the human body, usually male legs or the lower body are found unnaturally poking out of walls or floors. Part of specific room installations, Gober "invests ordinary manufactured objects with an erotic power, a transformation he accomplishes by symbolically associating them with human anatomy" (Néret 36).

- Bordowitz, G. "Against Heterosexuality." *Parkett* 27 (1991).
- *Fémininmasculin: le sexe de l'art*. exh. cat. Paris: Centre Georges Pompidou, 1995.
- Néret, G. *20th Century Erotic Art*. Berlin: Taschen, 1993.
- *Robert Gober*. exh. cat. Rotterdam: Museum Boymans-van Beuningen; Berne: Kunsthalle, 1990.
- *Robert Gober*. exh. cat. London: Serpentine Gallery; Liverpool: Tate, 1993.
- Simon, J. "Robert Gober et l'Extra Ordinaire." *Robert Gober*. exh. cat. Paris: Galerie nationale du Jeu de paume, 1991.
- Spector, N. "Robert Gober: Homeward Bound." *Parkett* 27 (1991).

Gontcharova, Natalia

59 *Mermaid* 1908
oil on canvas, 104.0 x 74.0
Museum Ludwig Köln, Sammlung Ludwig

Born, 1881, Negayevo, Russia
Died, 1962, Paris
Born and educated in Moscow, Gontcharova gained international recognition during her lifetime both for her prolific contribution to avant-garde painting, and for her celebrated stage and costume designs produced for the Ballets Russes and other opera companies. Her stylistic evolution was determined in part by her participation in the Golden Fleece exhibition of 1908 with Gauguin, Cézanne, Matisse and Bonnard. But while she was impressed by the raw, vibrant colours and simplified forms of Fauvism, and went on to explore the formal and dynamic possibilities of Cubo-futurism in her abstract compositions of 1913, her work remained firmly rooted in Russian life and culture. After emigrating to Paris in 1919, she participated regularly in the Salons, as well exhibiting her works in New York (1922) and Tokyo (1923).

- Bowlt, J. "Natalia Goncharova and Futurist Theatre." *Art Journal* 1 (1990).
- Compton, S., ed. *Russian Futurism 1910–1916: Poetry and Manifestos*. Cambridge: Cambridge UP, 1978.
- Parton, A. *Mikhail Larionov and the Russian Avant-garde*. Princeton, NJ: Princeton UP, 1993.
- Tupitsyn, M. "Collaborating on the Paradigm of the Future." *Art Journal*. 52.4 (Winter 1993).
- Yablonskaya, M. N. "Natal'ya Goncharova." *Women Artists of Russia's New Age 1900 –1935*. New York: Thames and Hudson, 1990.

Gormley, Antony

60 *Bearing* 1987–95
cast iron, 245.0 x 98.0 x 83.0
Courtesy of Jay Jopling, London

Born, 1950, London
Lives London
Gormley studied archaeology, anthropology and art history at Cambridge (1968–70) after which time he spent 3 years in India. He turned his attention to sculpture in 1973, studying at

the Central School of Art and Design in London, then at Goldsmith's College and finally at Slade School of Fine Art (1977–79). Taking the human figure as his constant source of imagery, Gormley's practice raises issues about the correspondences and fractures between art, the body and the environment. He uses iron and lead figures, often cast from his own body, to investigate the sensory and cognitive aspects of embodiment: ". . . to Gormley the body is the articulation of meaning; it is that in which sense is given and out of which sense emerges" (Hutchinson 42).

- Bann, S. *Antony Gormley* exh. cat. Sweden: Kunsthall Malmo; Liverpool: Tate Gallery; Dublin: Irish Museum of Modern Art, 1993.
- Bond, A. *A Field for the Art Gallery of NSW: A Room for the Great Australian Desert.* Sydney: AGNSW, 1989.
- *The British Show.* exh. cat. Sydney: AGNSW, 1985.
- Calvocoressi, R. *Antony Gormley.* exh. cat. Louisiana: MOMA, Louisiana; Denmark: Humblebaek, 1989.
- Hutchinson, J. et. al. *Antony Gormley.* London: Phaidon, 1995.

Hamilton, Richard

61 *Study for Leopold Bloom ("He foresaw his pale body")*
1948, ink on paper, 26.3 x 39.4
Courtesy of the artist and Anthony d'Offay, London

62 *He foresaw his pale body* 1948
pencil and watercolour on paper, 57.0 x 39.5
Courtesy of the artist and Anthony d'Offay, London

Born, 1922, London
Lives London
Hamilton is best known for his prominent role in the British Pop Art movement of the late 1950s and '60s. His earlier work, however, is equally significant in its experimental engagement with aspects of 20th century modernism. After re-reading James Joyce's *Ulysses* in 1946–47, he made a series of drawings which, in their stylistic diversity, were conceived as a graphic interpretation of the "slow coming to birth of language" in Joyce's text (RH in Morphet 16). Central to this project – which Hamilton hoped would form the basis of an illustrated edition of *Ulysses* – are concerns that recur throughout the artist's oeuvre; notably his ongoing interest in the interchangeability of visual and verbal signs, and an equally pervasive preoccupation with the human body.

- Field, R. S. *Richard Hamilton, Image and Process: Studies, Stage, and Final Proofs from the Graphic Works 1952–82.* Stuttgart: Edition H. Mayer; London: Tate Gallery, 1983.
- Francis, M., ed. *Richard Hamilton.* exh. cat. Edinburgh: Fruitmarket Gallery; Oxford: MOMA, 1988.
- Maharaj, S. *Richard Hamilton: XLV Venice Biennale British Pavilion.* London: The British Council, 1993.
- *Richard Hamilton: Prints 1939–83.* London: 1984.
- Morphet, R., ed. *Richard Hamilton.* exh. cat. London: Tate; Dublin: Irish MOMA, 1992.

Hatoum, Mona

63 *Deep Throat* 1996
wood, glass, paint, metal, cloth, monitor
and disc player, 75.5 x 85.0 x 85.0
Courtesy of Alexander and Bonin, New York
Photographs: Orcutt and Van Der Putten

Born, 1952, Beirut
Lives Maastricht
Raised in a Palestinian family in Beirut, Hatoum remained in London after an outbreak of civil war in Lebanon. She gained degrees in fine art from Byam Shaw School of Art and the Slade School of Art in the 1970s. In the 1980s Hatoum's career developed quickly, and she established a name for herself as a politically committed video and performance artist. In the 1990s she has turned her attention to making installations, her work exploring themes of physical violence and imprisonment, truth and the structuring of power, and anxieties about the "fragility of life." She exhibits widely in the leading international contemporary art forums.

- Brusatin, M. and J. Clair, eds. *Identity and Alterity: Figures of the Body 1895/1995.* XLVI Venice Biennale. exh. cat. Venice: Marsilio, 1995.
- *Fémininmasculin: le sexe de l'art.* exh. cat. Paris: Centre Georges Pompidou, 1995.
- *Mona Hatoum.* exh. cat. Paris: Centre Georges Pompidou, 1994.
- Van Assche, Christine. *Video et apres: la collection video du Musée National d'Art Moderne.* Paris, 1992.

Henson, Bill

64 *Untitled 1994/95* 1994–95
Type C photographs, adhesive tape, pins, glassine
The Art Gallery of New South Wales, Sydney
Photograph: Christopher Snee
Represented by Roslyn Oxley9 Gallery, Sydney

Born, Melbourne, 1955
Lives Melbourne
Largely self-taught, Henson's initial passion for hyper-realist painting gave way, in his late teens, to experimentation with photography. His 'fieldwork' has often taken him into extreme situations: including, on occasion, assisting with forensic photography at accident scenes. Yet Henson insists that, for him, photography is not about 'capturing' or documenting human vulnerability: "the pictures which work for me," he explains, "are those which are intensely intimate but where you've managed to maintain that unbridgeable gap. So that people can get close to it on one level, but they can't really get close to it on another level" (Craven 3). He treads such a fine line – between emotive seduction and intellectual distance, between photo-journalism and fantasy, and between aestheticism and realism – that his work has, inevitably, provoked controversy. By the early 1980s Henson's reputation as one of Australia's most significant contemporary photographers was firmly established. He has exhibited widely internationally, participating in the 1988 Venice Biennale and the *Passages de l'Image* exhibition at the Centre Georges Pompidou in 1990.

- *Bill Henson.* XLVI Venice Biennale. exh. cat. Melbourne: Australian Exhibitions Touring Agency, 1995.
- *Bill Henson Untitled 1983–84.* exh. cat. Canberra: Australian National Gallery, 1987.
- *Bill Henson: Photographs.* Sydney: Pan Books (Australia), 1988.
- Heywood, M. "Bill Henson: *Untitled 1983–84.*" *6th Biennale of Sydney.* exh. cat. Sydney: Sydney Biennale, 1986.
- McGillick, P. "Cazneaux and Henson." *Art and Australia* 32 (Winter 1995).

Hilton, Roger

65 *Dancing Woman December* 1963
oil and charcoal on canvas, 152.5 x 127.0
Scottish National Gallery of Modern Art, Edinburgh

Born, 1911
Died, 1975
Hilton studied painting at the Slade School of Fine Art in London (1929–31) and from 1935 exhibited regularly with the London Group. By 1950 he had largely abandoned figurative painting for a form of hieroglyphic abstraction and by the mid-50s his work was being compared to that of the American Abstract Expressionists. While asserting his stylistic independence, Hilton did remark in 1958 that "the act makes the meaning" (exh. cat. London, ICA). Dissatisfied with abstraction, he determined in the late 1950s to "reinvent figuration." The female nudes of this period retain the energetic, expressive quality of his earlier work, lending a raw, even aggressive edge to their childlike playfulness.

- Compton, S., ed. *British Art in the 20th Century: The Modern Movement*. exh. cat. London: Royal Academy of Arts, 1987.
- Lynton, N. and R. Hilton. *Roger Hilton: Paintings and Drawings 1931–1973*. exh. cat. London: Serpentine Gallery, 1974.
- *Roger Hilton*. exh. cat. London: Hayward Gallery, 1993–94.

Hopper, Edward

66 *Nude Crawling into Bed* c.1903–05
oil on board, 31.1 x 23.2
Whitney Museum of American Art, New York
Josephine N. Hopper Bequest

Born, 1882, Nyack
Died, 1967, New York
Hopper worked as an illustrator in advertising before moving to New York to pursue art classes with Robert Henry, a member of the group known as 'the Eight'. After a highly inspirational trip to Paris and London, he returned to New York never to move again. A pioneer of realism in the US, Hopper is best known for his depictions of human figures in isolation, sitting or standing, staring out of windows or loitering on the streets of New York. In spite of his reclusiveness he has been the subject of several retrospectives: in 1933, Barr organised Hopper's first retrospective for MOMA, the second being held in 1950 at the Whitney and the third at the Whitney in 1964. He is also distinguished by the fact that in 1925 *House by the Railroad* became the first painting by any artist acquired for MOMA in New York.

- Brusatin, M. and J. Clair, eds. *Identity and Alterity: Figures of the Body 1895/1995*. XLVI Venice Biennale. exh. cat. Venice: Marsilio, 1995.
- Levin, G., ed. *Edward Hopper: The Art and the Artist*. exh. cat. New York: Whitney Museum of American Art, 1980.
- Levin, G. *Edward Hopper: A Catalogue Raisonne*. New York: 1995.
- Lyons, D. et. al. *Edward Hopper and the American Imagination*. New York: Whitney Museum of American Art, 1995.

Horn, Rebecca

67 *Pendulum with Emu Egg* 1987–94
aluminium, emu egg, electric motor
300.0 x 70.0 x 50.0 (variable)
The Art Gallery of New South Wales, Sydney
Mervyn Horton Bequest Fund 1994

68 *Thermomètre d'Amour (Love Thermometer)* 1988
glass thermometer in a tailored leather case with silk
Edition 12 (of 12), 76.0 x 5.0
The Art Gallery of New South Wales, Sydney
Mervyn Horton Bequest Fund 1996
Photograph: Jenni Carter

Born, 1944, Michelstadt, Germany
Lives Berlin
Rebecca Horn studied in Hannover (1964–70) and London (1971–2) before moving to New York. She began documenting her 'body sculptures' on film in 1970, and has also used video for this purpose since 1972. She has also produced a number of feature films that extend the temporal concerns of her sculptures. Her sculptures, installations and performances have made Horn a leading contributor to contemporary performance art. The experience of human embodiment – particularly our sensory relationships with our environment and with each other – has been a central theme in much of her work. From as early as 1968 she was using objects and instruments to extend, amplify and disrupt the sensory limits of the body. In her subsequent work she has emphasised the psychological and physical inclusion of the viewer, so that our responses become an integral element of the work. To this end she has described her ongoing project as the creation of "new models of interaction rituals" (RH in *Contemporary Artists* 433).

- Durand, R. "Rebecca Horn: Danger Imminent." *Art Press* 181 (June 1993).
- *Fémininmasculin: le sexe de l'art*. exh. cat. Paris: Centre Georges Pompidou, 1995.
- Horn, R. Artist's Statement. *Contemporary Artists*. Ed. C. Naylor. Chicago: St James P, 1989.
- *Rebecca Horn*. exh. cat. Paris: Galerie de France, 1988.
- *Rebecca Horn*. exh. cat. New York: Solomon R. Guggenheim Museum, 1993.
- *Rebecca Horn: Diving through Buster's Bedroom*. exh. cat. Los Angeles: MCA; Milan: Fabbri Editori, 1993.

Kahlo, Frida

69 *Frida and The Abortion* 1932
lithograph
Private Collection, U.S.A.

Born, 1907, Mexico City
Died, 1954, Mexico City
Kahlo began painting in 1925 following a tram accident in which she sustained a shattered pelvis and broken spine. Her injuries left her crippled, unable to bear children, and in need of over 30 operations during the course of her life. "My painting," she once said, "carries within it the message of pain" (Chadwick 134). In 1929 she married Diego Rivera, whose commitment to Communism and Mexican indigenous culture she shared. The union was famously turbulent. Though suffering, violence and mortality are recurrent themes in

Kahlo's work, the intimate scale, naive style and fantastic quality of her numerous self-portraits recall Mexican popular art. Despite André Breton's description of her as a 'self-invented Surrealist', Kahlo insisted that her work dealt not with dreams or the unconscious, but with the reality of her life.

- Chadwick, W. *Women Artists and the Surrealist Movement*. New York: Thames and Hudson, 1985.
- *Fémininmasculin: le sexe de l'art*. exh. cat. Paris: Centre Georges Pompidou, 1995.
- *Frida Kahlo 1907–1954*. Madrid: Ministerio de Cultura, 1985.
- Herrera, H. *Frida Kahlo: The Paintings*. London: Bloomsbury, 1991.
- Kettenman, A. *Frida Kahlo 1907–1954: souffrance et passion*. Paris: Benedikt Taschen, 1992.
- Merewether, C. *The Art of Frida Kahlo*. exh. cat. Adelaide: Adelaide Festival of Arts, 1990.
- Mulvey, L. et. al. *Frida Kahlo and Tina Modotti* exh. cat. London: Whitechapel AG, 1982.
- Zamora, M. *Frida Kahlo*. Paris: Herscher, 1992.

Kapoor, Anish

70 *Untitled* 1989
gouache, emulsion, ink and pencil on paper, 83.0 x 63.0
Lisson Gallery, London

71 *Untitled* 1988
varnish and ink on paper, 83.0 x 63.0
Lisson Gallery, London.

72 *Untitled* 1989
oil and emulsion on paper, 83.0 x 63.0
Lisson Gallery, London

73 *Untitled* 1986
gouache and pencil on paper, 50.0 x 50.0
Lisson Gallery, London

Born, 1954, Bombay
Lives London
Born in Bombay, Anish Kapoor is one of a number of contemporary British-based artists to have gained international recognition as 'New Sculptors' during the 1980s. Informed both by Western and Indian traditions, his sculptures and drawings have a mystical presence at once contemplative and dynamic in their suggestion of ritualistic gesture. Using materials like slate, marble and sandstone and natural or vibrantly coloured pigments, often in raw powdered form, Kapoor's works have an elemental but deeply sensuous quality that is reminiscent of Indian religious art and ritual. This organic materiality is frequently extended (and sexualised) through references to the female body, evoking the biological and cosmological processes of birth and regeneration. Yves Klein is a European artist whose metaphysical project has had a profound influence on the art of Kapoor. His void fields and the use of Yves Klein Blue are acknowledged references.

- Ammann, J. C., ed. *Anish Kapoor*. exh. cat. Basle: Kunsthalle, 1985.
- *Anish Kapoor*. exh. cat. Villeurbanne: Le Nouveau Musée, 1983.
- *Anish Kapoor*. exh. cat. Venice: XLIV Venice Biennale, 1990.
- *Fémininmasculin: le sexe de l'art*. exh. cat. Paris: Centre Georges Pompidou, 1995.
- Forsha, L., ed. *Anish Kapoor*. exh. cat. La Jolla, CA: MCA, 1992.

Kirchner, Ernst Ludwig

74 *Two Nudes* 1907
oil on canvas, 196.1 x 65.4
National Gallery of Art, Washington

Born, 1880, Aschaffenburg, Germany
Died, 1938, Frauenkirch, Switzerland
The most prominent member of the German Expressionist group, Die Brücke (1905–13), Kirchner in many ways embodied the anxiety and idealism of his generation. Drawing inspiration from sources as diverse as German mysticism, the Fauves, and Oceanic sculpture, his paintings, sculptures and prints are, perhaps above all, shaped by the course of World War I. While the early period of Die Brücke produced fluid, intensely coloured and often exuberant works strongly influenced by the Fauves, Kirchner's wartime images of the streets of Berlin, executed in his distinctive compressed and jagged style, translate the psychological violence of wartime Europe into a drama of sexual aggression and desire. Discharged from military service on the grounds of physical and mental breakdown, Kirchner spent his remaining years in and out of sanatoria. His recurring illness, along with the confiscation of over 600 of his works from public collections by the National Socialists in 1937, led him to commit suicide the following year.

- *Ernst Ludwig Kirchner: Werke 1917–1923*. exh. cat. Davos Platz: Ernst Ludwig Kirchner Museum, 1988–89.
- Grisebach, L. and W. Henze, eds. *Ernst Ludwig Kirchner: Zeichnungen, Aquarelle, Pastelle*. exh. cat. Nuremberg: Kunsthalle, 1991.
- Herbert, B. *German Expressionism: Die Brücke and Der Blaue Reiter*. London: Jupiter Books, 1983.
- Lloyd, J. *German Expressionism: Primitivism and Modernity*. New Haven: Yale UP, 1991.
- Moeller, M. M. *Ernst Ludwig Kirchner: Die Strassenszenen 1913–1915*. Munich: Hirmer Verlag, 1993.

Klein, Yves

75 *ANT. 118* c.1960
monochrome blue dry pigment and synthetic resin on paper on canvas, 205.0 x 155.0
Galerie Gmurzynska, Cologne

76 *The Leap* 1960
photo by Harry Schunk
Courtesy of Harry Schunk

Born, 1928, Nice
Died, 1962, Paris
At the age of 18 Klein had begun to develop a theory of colour, something that was to fascinate him throughout his career as a painter, sculptor, performance artist and writer. His first monochrome paintings were purportedly exhibited in 1950 in London, and in Tokyo in 1953; the latter coinciding with the announcement of his "manifesto of the monochrome." Inspired by Giotto's use of blue and Delacroix's notion of the 'undefinable' quality of colour, as well as by Max Heindel's version of Rosicrucianism and spiritualist theories of cosmic resonance, Klein described monochrome as an "open window to freedom, as the possibility of being immersed in the immeasurable existence of colour" (Wember 9, 11). In 1960 he

staged his first *Anthropométries*, performances in which three female models, smeared in blue paint, pressed and rolled themselves against paper to the accompaniment of Klein's 'Symphonie Monoton.' In the same year he performed the Leap, launching himself from the 2nd floor of Iris Clert's studio into the void which he so passionately desired to possess – the domain of the immaterial.

- Brusatin, M. and J. Clair, eds. *Identity and Alterity: Figures of the Body 1895/1995*. XLVI Venice Biennale. exh. cat. Venice: Marsilio, 1995.
- *Fémininmasculin: le sexe de l'art*. exh. cat. Paris: Centre Georges Pompidou, 1995.
- Restany, P. *Yves Klein*. Trans. J. Shepley. New York: Abrams, 1992.
- Stich, S., ed. *Yves Klein*. exh. cat. Cologne: Cologne Museum Ludwig and Dusseldorf Kunstsammlung Nordrhein-Westfalen; London: Hayward Gallery 1994–95.
- *Yves Klein*. exh. cat. Paris: Centre Georges Pompidou, 1983.
- *Yves Klein 1928–1962: A Retrospective*. exh. cat. Houston, TX: Institute for the Arts, Rice University, 1982.

Klossowski, Pierre

77 *La Réalisation Invraisenblable de l'Entente de Tadzio et Aschenbach II (The Improbable Understanding of Tadzio and Aschenbach II)* 1987
colour pencil drawing on paper, 170.0 x 150.0
Museum Moderner Kunst Stiftung Ludwig, Vienna

Born, 1905, Paris
Lives Paris
Pierre Klossowski and his brother Balthus spent their childhood in Paris, Poland, and Geneva, where in 1919 they were introduced to Rainer Maria Rilke. While living in Paris between the wars, Klossowski became involved with the Surrealists, particularly through his friendships with André Masson and George Bataille. Like Bataille, Klossowski's writings, drawings and sculptures are both erotically loaded and inflected by Catholicism: he went as far as to study for the priesthood during the Second World War. Reminiscent of pre-war cartoon illustrations, Klossowski's narrative drawings are characterised by their childlike quality – combining awkward innocence with a sexual charge.

- *Fémininmasculin: le sexe de l'art*. exh. cat. Paris: Centre Georges Pompidou, 1995.
- Francblin, C. "Pierre Klossowski: The Voyeur and his Counterpart." *Flash Art* 107 (May 1982): 22–27.
- Greiner, C. et. al. *Pierre Klossowski*. Paris: ELA La Difference/CNAP, 1990.
- Henric, J. *Klossowski*. Paris: Adam Biro, 1989.
- *Phantasm and Simulacra: The Drawings of Pierre Klossowski*. Spec. issue of *Art & Text* 19 (July 1985).

Kokoschka, Oskar

78 *Zrani (High Summer)* 1938–40
oil on canvas, 68.3 x 89.2
Scottish National Gallery of Modern Art, Edinburgh

Born, 1886, Pöchlarn, Lower Austria
Died, 1980, Montreux

Kokoschka studied at the School for Applied Arts in Vienna (1905–9); then a centre of Viennese Jugendstil, and went on to create Art Nouveau objects for the Wiener Werkstätte. With the encouragement of Adolf Loos ("Ornament is Crime"), he turned his back on the decorative, gained access to the Viennese avant-garde and focused on executing highly expressive portraits. Adopting a strong individual style he strove to manifest the immaterial forces active behind the external appearance of his subjects. Well known for his cityscapes and portraits, the hallmark of Kokoschka's work is his highly painterly style, the nervous quality of his brushstroke coupled with incredibly vivid colour. Kokoschka also produced a large body of written work. In 1937 the Nazis confiscated 417 of his paintings, many of which were exhibited as 'Degenerate Art'.

- Brusatin, M. and J. Clair, eds. *Identity and Alterity: Figures of the Body 1895/1995*. XLVI Venice Biennale. exh. cat. Venice: Marsilio, 1995.
- Calvocoressi, R., ed. *Oskar Kokoschka 1886-1980*. exh. cat. London: Tate Gallery; New York: Guggenheim, 1986.
- *Klimt, Schiele, Kokoschka: Drawings and Watercolours*. exh. cat. London: Thames and Hudson, 1981.
- Werkner, P. *Austrian Expressionism: The Formative Years*. Trans. N. T. Parsons. Palo Alto, CA: Society for the Promotion of Science and Scholarship, 1993.

Lambert, George

79 *Chesham Street* 1910
oil on canvas, 60.0 x 49.5
National Gallery of Australia, Canberra
© National Gallery of Australia, Canberra

Born, 1873, St Petersburg
Died, 1930, Cobbity, New South Wales
George Lambert was educated in England before emigrating to Australia at the age of 14. Working initially as a station-hand on the property of his maternal grand uncle, he started taking evening classes with Julian Ashton in the 1890s, and turned his hand to commercial illustration. In 1900 he left to study in Paris on a scholarship and, although he did not return to Australia for 21 years, he served in Egypt and Gallipoli as an official war artist. The dark tones and painterly style characteristic of his pre-War paintings attest to the artist's particular regard for Velázquez (of the European masters) and Manet (of the moderns).

- Jose, A. et. al. *The Art of George W. Lambert*. Sydney: Art in Australia, 1924.
- Lambert, A. *The Career of G. W. Lambert: Thirty Years of an Artist's Life*. Sydney: Society of Artists Australian Artists Editions, [1938] 1977.
- Motion, A. *The Lamberts: George, Constant and Kit*. London: Chatto & Windus, 1986.

Leonard, Zoe

80 *Wax Anatomical Model Shot Crooked From Above* 1990
gelatin silver print, edition of 6
77.8 x 116.8
Courtesy of Paula Cooper Gallery, New York

Born, 1961, New York
Lives New York
Leonard's black and white photographs are comprised of inconsequential things, the residue of everyday life. Although these objects are easily overlooked, by placing them together and making them form the entire content of the image, Leonard produces photographs which are both evocative and suggestive. While her earlier work was more programmatic, addressing issues of sexual identity, her later work has become increasingly eclectic. Her interest in the grotesque however is consistently pursued, in the form of exquisitely detailed assemblages of mannequin busts with wigs, someone's false teeth, and similar objects. The anatomical model shown in this exhibition connects the classificatory systems of science with this interest in the grotesque.

- *L'Art au corps: le corps exposé de Man Ray à nos jours*. exh. cat. Marseille: Musées de Marseille, 1996
- Amman, J-C. "Vaginas." *Rogue* 16 (1992).
- *Fémininmasculin: le sexe de l'art*. exh. cat. Paris: Centre Georges Pompidou, 1995.
- Kandel, S. "Zoe Leonard." *Arts Magazine* (May 1991).
- Koether, J. "Zoe Leonard." *Flash Art* (Summer 1990).
- Lambrecht, L. "Zoe Leonard." *Forum International* 9 (Sep./Oct. 1991).

Lichtenberg-Ettinger, Bracha

81 *Eurydice*, no.2 1992–94
oil and photocopic dust on paper
mounted on canvas, 38.3 x 23.1
Courtesy of Elisabeth and Claude Samuel

82 *Eurydice*, no.6 1992–95
oil and photocopic dust on paper
mounted on canvas, 39.3 x 26.8
Courtesy of the artist

83 *Eurydice*, no.7 1992–95
oil and photocopic dust on paper
mounted on canvas, 36.0 x 24.2
Courtesy of the artist

84 *Eurydice*, no.8 1994–96
oil and photocopic dust on paper
mounted on canvas, 37.0 x 26.0
Courtesy of the artist

85 *Eurydice*, no.13 1994–96
oil and photocopic dust on paper
mounted on canvas, 34.0 x 27.3
Courtesy of Philippe Samuel

86 *Eurydice*, no.16 1994–96
oil and photocopic dust on paper
mounted on canvas, 41.7 x 22.0
Courtesy of the artist

87 *Eurydice*, no.19 1992–96
oil and photocopic dust on paper
mounted on canvas, 37.0 x 25.5
Courtesy of the artist

88 *Eurydice*, no.20 1994–96
oil and photocopic dust on paper
mounted on canvas, 38.5 x 27.0
Courtesy of the artist

Born, 1945, Tel Aviv
Lives Paris and Tel Aviv
Lichtenberg-Ettinger is both an artist and a writer on art. She has a PhD in aesthetics, a D.E.A. in Psychoanalysis, and an M.A. in Clinical Psychology. Her paintings provide a visual and tactile expression of her theoretical "matrixial borderspace." The works are based on photocopies of archival material and are not fixed, consequently they lose their definition only to be re-discovered by the brushstrokes which lay on the white, pink and purple paint that predominates in her palette. This appearing and disappearing has parallels with the way memory gives a name to an event and then allows it to slip back into the shadows in a play of presence and absence. Lictenberg-Ettinger's exhibition history includes: *Fâce a l'histoire* at the Centre Georges Pompidou, *Kabinet* at the Stedelijk Museum, and *Inside the Visible* at the ICA Boston, Whitechapel Art Gallery in London and the Art Gallery of Western Australia.

- De Zegher, C., ed. *Inside The Visible*. exh. cat. Boston: ICA; London: Whitechapel; Perth: AGWA 1996.
- Lichtenberg-Ettinger, B. "Matrix and Metamorphosis." *Differences* 4.3 Bloomington, IN: Indiana UP, 1996.
- —. "Metramorphic borderlinks and matrixial borderspace." *Rethinking Borders*. Ed. J. Welchman. London: Macmillan, 1996.

Manet, Edouard

89 *Olympia* (small plate) 1867
etching with needle and aquatint background, 8.8 x 17.7
Courtauld Institute Galleries, London
The Samuel Courtauld Trust

Born, 1832, Paris
Died, 1883, Paris
Manet's career was marked by public vilification and critical acclaim in fairly equal measures. The former, a response to his unconventional style as well as frequently provocative subject matter, erupted into scandal during the exhibition of *Olympia* in 1865. In this picture, which is typical of his early period, tradition (in this case Titian's *Venus of Urbino*) is played off against references to contemporary urban life in a way not dissimilar to mid-nineteenth century pornography. Stylistically, too, Manet combines tonal qualities reminiscent of 17th-century Spanish Masters with spatial and compositional disjunctions. His figures, 'flattened' through the absence of consistent perspective or modelling, are often unsettlingly isolated, relating more to the viewer than to each other. An important contributor to modernism, Manet's recognition during his life came from within avant-garde circles, including such luminaries as Zola and Mallarmé.

- Adler, K. *Manet*. Oxford: Phaidon, 1986.
- Bataille, G. *Manet*. Trans. A. Wainhouse and J. Emmons. London: Skira/Macmillan, 1983.

- Clark, T. J. *The Painting of Modern Life: Paris in the Art of Manet and his Followers.* London: Thames and Hudson, 1985.
- Krell, A. *Manet and the Painters of Contemporary Life.* London: Thames and Hudson, 1991.
- Hamilton, G. H. *Manet and his Critics.* New York: W. W. Norton, 1969.
- *Manet 1832–1883.* exh. cat. Paris: Galeries nationales du Grand Palais; New York: MOMA, 1983.

Man Ray

90 *Minotaur* 1933
gelatin silver print, 15.0 x 23.3
Courtesy of Ubu Gallery, New York

Born, 1890, Philadelphia
Died, 1976, Paris
A prominent figure in the New York avant-garde during the 1910s, in 1920 Man Ray co-founded, with Duchamp and Katherine Dreier, the Société Anonyme with the aim of promoting contemporary art. Though he always considered himself an American, Man Ray lived in Paris from 1921, returning to the US only temporarily during World War II. Achieving commercial success in the 1920s and '30s with his portraits and fashion photography for magazines such as *Vogue* and *Harper's Bazaar*, he was also one of the luminaries of Paris Dada and Surrealism. While he continued to work in various media (including painting, sculpture and film), his experimental photographic techniques – particularly the Sabattier (solarisation) process – were particularly influential in Surrealist circles.

- Brusatin, M. and J. Clair, eds. *Identity and Alterity: Figures of the Body 1895/1995.* XLVI Venice Biennale. exh. cat. Venice: Marsilio, 1995.
- *Fémininmasculin: le sexe de l'art.* exh. cat. Paris: Centre Georges Pompidou, 1995.
- Foresta, M., ed. *Perpetual Motif: The Art of Man Ray.* exh. cat. Washington DC: National Museum of Art/Smithsonian Institute, 1989.
- Janus, ed. *Man Ray: The Photographic Image.* Trans. M. Baca. London: Gordon Fraser Gallery, 1980.
- *Man Ray 1890–1976.* exh. cat. Ghent: Ludion P; New York: Abrams, 1994.

Matisse, Henri

91 *Le Modèle (The model)* 1900
oil on canvas, 99.0 x 72.5
Musée d'Art Moderne de la Ville de Paris
© Photothèque des Musées de la Ville de Paris

92 *Reclining Nude* 1919
oil on canvas, 33.3 x 41.2 (unframed)
National Gallery of Victoria, Melbourne
Felton Bequest, 1952

93 *The Serf* 1900–03
cast bronze 1903–50, 91.4 x 37.8 x 30.8
Hirshhorn Museum and Sculpture Garden, Smithsonian Institution
Gift of Joseph H. Hirshhorn, 1966

Born, 1869, Le Cateau-Cambrésis, nr Cambrai, Picardy
Died, 1954, Nice
Like Picasso, Matisse succeeded in radically redefining painting in the 20th century. Coming to art comparatively late in life, Matisse is renowned for his ability to work across a range of media. He took part in the Salon d'Automne of 1905 with the Fauves. The first avant-garde movement at the turn of the century, Fauvism was distinguished by its vividness of colour. In addition to his expressive manipulation of colour, Matisse is best known for the decorative quality of his art and his ground breaking treatment of the human figure. Throughout his life he emphasised the primacy of drawing from the human figure. In *BODY*, Matisse is represented by 3 works: *Le Modèle* and *The Serf* from his earlier period – in which an emphasis on structure and modelling suggests the craggy mass of the body – and *Reclining nude* of 1919, manifesting the linearity for which he is consistently championed.

- Brusatin, M. and J. Clair, eds. *Identity and Alterity: Figures of the Body 1895/1995.* XLVI Venice Biennale. exh. cat. Venice: Marsilio, 1995.
- Elderfield, J., ed. *Henri Matisse: A Retrospective.* exh. cat. New York: MOMA, 1992.
- Güse, E.-G. *Henri Matisse: Drawings and Sculpture.* Munich: Prestel, 1991.
- *Henri Matisse: catalogue raisonné de l'oeuvre sculpte.* Paris, 1994.

McCarthy, Paul

94 *Grand Pop 1977, Los Angeles California* 1977
gelatin silver prints, 40.5 x 50.4 (each)
The Art Gallery of New South Wales, Sydney
Mervyn Horton Bequest Fund, 1996
Photograph: Christopher Snee

Born 1945, Salt Lake City, Utah
Lives, Altadena, California
McCarthy began his career of making transgressive and subversive work as a student at the University of Utah (1966–68) where he burnt the surfaces of paintings, calling the charred remains 'black paintings'. He has always pursued a combined interest in photography, painting-as-action, performance, drawing and installation. Raiding American culture for references and using debased materials such as concoctions of food and artificial body parts, McCarthy's works are at once humorous and actively violent in execution, for instance when the male protagonist gives birth to a ketchup-smeared child. McCarthy has exhibited widely: in 1995 at the Whitney Biennial; in 1992 in *Helter Skelter – LA Art in the 1990s* and in a MOMA project in 1995.

- Brusatin, M. and J. Clair, eds. *Identity and Alterity: Figures of the Body 1895/1995.* XLVI Venice Biennale. exh. cat. Venice: Marsilio, 1995.
- Cohen, M. "Leap into the Void: Abjection and Survival in the Work of Paul McCarthy." *Flash Art* 26.170 (May-June 1993).
- McEvilley, T. "Art in the Dark." *Artforum* 21.10 (June 1983).
- Rugolf, R. "Deviations on a Theme: Paul McCarthy." *Artforum* 33.2 (Oct. 1994).
- Selwyn, M. "Paul McCarthy: There's a Big Difference Between Ketchup and Blood." *Flash Art* 26.170 (May–June 1993).

Mendieta, Ana

95 *Silueta Works in Iowa* 1976–78
suite of 12 colour photographs each documenting earth/body works with earth. Sharon Center, Iowa City
paper: 50.8 x 40.6, edition of 20
Courtesy and © of the Estate of Ana Mendieta and Galerie Lelong, New York

96 *Untitled (Silueta Series)* 1980–92
black and white photograph of earth carving executed at Montaña de San Felipe, Mexico
154.9 x 121.9
Courtesy and © of the Estate of Ana Mendieta and Galerie Lelong, New York

Born, 1948, Havana, Cuba
Died, 1985, New York
Mendieta was sent to the US at the age of 13, where she lived in orphanages and foster homes in Iowa. Her oeuvre includes sculpture, performance art, video art and painting, but the works for which she is best known are the 'earth body installations'. Executed in the Iowa landscape, these installations incorporated the primal materials of blood, earth, fire and water. The *Silueta Series* in this exhibition consists of powerful tracings of the image of her body on the ground, using a variety of materials including ignited gunpowder, grass, mud, stones, and leaves. A frequent visitor to Mexico and her native Cuba, Mendieta maintained her connections with Latin America.

- *Ana Mendieta: A Retrospective.* exh. cat. New York: New Museum of Contemporary Art, 1988.
- De Zegher, C., ed. *Inside The Visible.* exh. cat. Boston: ICA; London: Whitechapel AG; Perth: AGWA.
- *Fémininmasculin: le sexe de l'art.* exh. cat. Paris: Centre Georges Pompidou, 1995.
- Mendieta, A. *A Book of Works.* Miami: Grassfield P, 1993.
- Raine, A. "Embodied Geographies: Subjectivity and Materiality in the Work of Ana Mendieta." *Generations and Geographies in the Visual Arts: Feminist Readings.* Ed. Griselda Pollock. London: Routledge, 1996.
- Spero, N. "Tracing Ana Mendieta." *Artforum* 30.8 (Apr. 1992).

Mirò, Joan

97 *The Tightrope Walker* 1970
sculpture in bronze and steel, 53.0 x 28.0 x 13.0
Tate Gallery, London

Born, 1893, Barcelona
Died, 1983, Palma de Mallorca
Mirò studied contemporary art and went to business school in Barcelona. He gave away a career as an accountant (1910) to concentrate fully on his art practice. Mirò became a leading figure in the development of abstraction and Surrealism, carving out a position of enormous influence on twentieth-century art. He frequently incorporated references to the human figure in his work, though his private symbolic language reduced the human form to lines, signs and coloured areas. Mirò's exceptional ability to work with diverse media and artforms including paintings, prints, sculptures and ceramics was always underpinned by a debt to Surrealism. His later sculptural works, of which *The Tightrope Walker* is an example, embody the wry sense of humour and abstracted figurative concerns for which he is renowned. From 1966 Mirò's art practice was dominated by small sculptures, based principally on small, often found objects, joined together in quirky ways.

- Brusatin, M. and J. Clair, eds. *Identity and Alterity: Figures of the Body 1895/1995.* XLVI Venice Biennale. exh. cat. Venice: Marsilio, 1995.
- Dupin, J. Mirò. Paris: Flammarion, 1993.
- *Fémininmasculin: le sexe de l'art.* exh. cat. Paris: Centre Georges Pompidou, 1995.
- *Joan Mirò: A Retrospective.* exh. cat. New York: Solomon R. Guggenheim Museum; New Haven: Yale UP, 1987.
- *Joan Mirò 1893-1993.* exh. cat. Boston: Little, Brown, 1993.

Modersohn-Becker, Paula

98 *Kleiner Mädchenakt (Nude Girl)* 1906
oil on canvas, 35.3 x 28.5
Kunstammlungen Böttcherstraße, Bremen

99 *Nacktes Mädchen mit Apfel (Nude Girl with Apple)* 1906
oil on canvas, 45.4 x 23.2
Kunstammlungen Böttcherstraße, Bremen

Born, 1876, Dresden
Died, 1907, Worpswede
Paula Becker studied in Bremen, London and Berlin, where in 1897 she met members of the Worpswede artists' colony which was to become her home, on and off, from 1898. Attracted to the group's commitment to simplicity, both in their lifestyle and their art, it was at Worpswede (a farming village near Bremen) that she married and collaborated with Otto Modersohn. Equally influential, however, were her trips to Paris in 1899, 1903, 1905 and 1906, coinciding with a growing discontent with the Worpswede community. In Paris she continued her training, and encountered the work of Cézanne, Gauguin and the Symbolists (including Bonnard). These influences contributed to her pursuit of formal simplification and her interest in the ritual and symbolic aspects of art. Her most compelling works of this period, which deal with maternity, childhood and mortality, tragically prefigure her untimely death at 31, three weeks after her daughter's birth.

- Behr, S. *Women Expressionists.* Oxford: Phaidon, 1988.
- Slatkins, W. "Maternity and Sexuality in the 1890s." *Woman's Art Journal* (Spring/Summer 1980).
- Whitford, F. *Expressionist Portraits.* London: Thames and Hudson, 1987.

Molinier, Pierre

100 *Le Festin de Manès* (no.37) 1968–70
gelatin silver print, 20.0 x 16.2
Courtesy of Ubu Gallery, New York

101 *Le Festin de Manès* (no.34) 1968–70
gelatin silver print, 18.7 x 14.3
Courtesy of Ubu Gallery, New York

102 *Hanel No.1* c.1969
gelatin silver print, 19.7 x 14.6
Courtesy of Ubu Gallery, New York

103 *Le Stylite* 1968–70
gelatin silver print, 21.6 x 14.6
Courtesy of Ubu Gallery, New York

Born, 1900, Agen
Died, 1976, Bordeaux
By virtue of the fact that his birth date is April 13, 1900 – a lucky and significant religious date – Molinier was selected by representatives of the Dalai Lama in 1936 to paint a series of esoteric drawings for an unknown temple. From there

followed a period of revelation which led consistently to esoteric and autoerotic themes in his body performances and photo-documentation. By the 1950s he had befriended Hans Bellmer and André Breton who shared Molinier's interest in using photography to capture one's image and fantasies, but later rejected his notions of the "psychosexual theatre" for being superficial and unacceptably fetishistic. The self-portrait photographs taken from the mid 1960s until his suicide in 1976 combine transvestism and fetish objects. Frequent motifs include black stockings, garters, plaster casts of female legs in silk stockings, with Molinier in make-up or feminine masks abandoned to fetishistic narcissism.

- *Fémininmasculin: le sexe de l'art.* exh. cat. Paris: Centre Georges Pompidou, 1995.
- Gorsen, P. "Hans Bellmer – Pierre Molinier: Eine Archaologie der Erotik gegen die technologische Paranoia." *Real Text* (1993).
- *Pierre Molinier.* exh. cat. Winnipeg: Plug in Editions, 1993.
- Petit, P. *Molinier: une vie d'enfer.* Paris: Ramsay/Jean-Jacques Pauvert, 1992.

Muehl, Otto

104 *Materialaktion 31* 1966 (printed 1994)
cibachrome on plexiglass, 125.0 x 130.0
Courtesy of Hubert Klocker, Vienna

105 *Materialaktion 10* 1964 (printed 1994)
cibachrome on plexiglass, 125.0 x 130.0
Courtesy of Hubert Klocker, Vienna

106 *Materialaktion 33* 1966 (printed 1994)
cibachrome on plexiglass, 125.0 x 130.0
Courtesy of Hubert Klocker, Vienna

107 *Materialaktion 23* 1965 (printed 1994)
cibachrome on plexiglass, 125.0 x 130.0
Courtesy of Hubert Klocker, Vienna

108 *Materialaktion 29* 1966 (printed 1994)
cibachrome on plexiglass, 125.0 x 130.0
Courtesy of Julius Hummel, Vienna

109 *Materialaktion 12* 1964 (printed 1994)
cibachrome on plexiglass, 125.0 x 130.0
Courtesy of Julius Hummel, Vienna

Born, 1925, Grodnau, Burgenland
Lives Austria
Muehl's career as a performance artist, film maker, writer and a founding member of the Aktionismus group took root in post World War II Austria. His approach to art as a means of personal and social transformation was intended to erode the distinctions between art and life; or, as Muehl put it: "It is the assignment of the artist to destroy art and come closer to reality. The artist has the responsibility to change himself and society as well" (OM in Wilson 257). As with the other members of the Wiener Aktionsgruppe, the sexually explicit and violently confrontational *Aktionen* choreographed and documented by Muehl enraged the Austrian authorities, and on one occasion resulted in arrests. After the disbanding of the group in the late 1960s, Muehl turned his hand to the direct crafting of an alternative society based on communal ideals.

- *L'Art au corps: le corps exposé de Man Ray à nos jours.* exh. cat. Marseille: Musées de Marseille, 1996
- Klocker, H. *Otto Muehl: Ausgewahlte Arbeiten 1963–1986.* Zurndorf, 1987.
- Wilson, A. "Muehl." J. Turner, ed. *The Dictionary of Art.* 34 vols. London: Macmillan, 1996.

Muybridge, Eadweard

110 *Animal Locomotion – An Electrophotographic Investigation of Consecutive Phases of Animal Movements. Plate 332 (Wrestling)* 1875–85
collotype plate
The Art Gallery of New South Wales, Sydney

Born, 1830, Kingston-on-Thames
Died, 1904, Kingston-on-Thames
Edward James Muggeridge emigrated from England to the US around 1852 and by 1867 was promoting himself in California as 'Eadweard Muybridge, artist-photographer'. In 1872 he embarked on a project that was to have a decisive effect on his own career as well as on the history of photography. Leland Stanford, a former governor of California, engaged him in the hope of confirming a hunch that, while trotting, his horse Occident had all four legs in the air simultaneously. Although Muybridge's early results were inconclusive, he went on to refine and modify his equipment for studying motion. In the 1880s he toured Europe with a new invention, by means of which a series of images were synthesised and projected to create a crude 'moving image'. From 1883 his ongoing investigation of animal and human movement was funded by the University of Pennsylvania, leading to the publication of a remarkable 11 volume study entitled *Animal Locomotion.*

- Braun, M. "Muybridge's scientific fictions." *Studies in Visual Communication* 10.1 (1984).
- Brusatin, M. and J. Clair, eds. *Identity and Alterity: Figures of the Body 1895/1995.* XLVI Venice Biennale. exh. cat. Venice: Marsilio, 1995.
- *Eadweard Muybridge: The Stanford Years 1872–1882.* exh. cat. Stanford, CA: Dept. of Art, Stanford University, 1972.
- Hendricks, G. *Eadweard Muybridge: The Father of the Motion Picture.* London: Secker and Warburg, 1975.

Neel, Alice (Hartley)

111 *Joe Gould* 1933
oil on canvas, 99.0 x 78.7
Courtesy of Robert Miller Gallery, New York

Born, 1900, Merion Square, Pennsylvania
Died, 1984, New York

After graduating from the Philadelphia School of Design for Women in 1925 Neel settled in New York with her husband, the Cuban artist Carlos Enrìquez. Her career was not fully launched until the 1930s, because of the premature death of her daughter and the nervous breakdown she endured after the break-up of her marriage. During the reign of abstraction in the US, she steadfastly pursued a career in figurative art, her favourite subject being people. Neel's distinctively expressive style was used to depict a range of sitters from friends to strangers whose appearance and character interested her. Because they were not commissions, Neel was free to use an expressive manipulation of colour and highly idiosyncratic characterisations of her sitters' physiognomy and personality traits. Although she was honoured with a retrospective at the Whitney Museum in 1974 which brought her renown, she failed to sell her works because few collectors liked the highly individualised studies of her largely unknown models.

- *Alice Neel*. exh. cat. New York: Robert Miller Gallery, 1986.
- *Alice Neel: Paintings Since 1970*. Pennsylvania: Pennsylvania Academy of the Fine Arts, 1985.
- Bauer, D. "Alice Neel's Female Nudes." *Woman's Art Journal* (Fall 1994/ Winter 1995).
- *Fémininmasculin: le sexe de l'art*. exh. cat. Paris: Centre Georges Pompidou, 1995.
- Hills, P. *Alice Neel*. New York: Abrams, 1983.
- Princenthal, N. "About Faces: Alice Neel's Portraits." *Parkett* 16 (May 1988).
- Saltz, J. "Painter Laureate: Alice Neel's Symbols." *Arts Magazine* 66.3 (Nov. 1991).

Newton, Helmut

112 *Self-portrait with June and Models* 1981
black and white photograph
Permanent loan, Rheinisches Landesmuseum Bonn

Born, 1920, Berlin
Lives Paris

After serving an internship with the photographer Yva in Berlin, Newton worked for English *Vogue* in 1956 before moving to Paris in 1957. There he worked with fashion magazines, establishing his name and his signature style. It was not until 1975 that he had his first one-man show at the Nikon Gallery in Paris. He is best known for the multiplicity of meanings he gives his work and the presence of a second photograph, his double-image structure. These stylistic characteristics coupled with his carefully composed models and detailed construction of the scene intentionally encourages intense voyeurism on the viewer's part.

- Brusatin, M. and J. Clair, eds. *Identity and Alterity: Figures of the Body 1895/1995*. XLVI Venice Biennale. exh. cat. Venice: Marsilio, 1995.
- *Helmut Newton*. exh. cat. Intro. by K. Lagerfeld. New York: Pantheon; Paris: Centre national de la photographie, 1987.
- *Helmut Newton: Special Collection*. 24 photo lithos. London: Quartet, 1980.
- *Helmut Newton: Nuevas Imagenes*. exh. cat. Madrid: Madris Sala de Exposiciones de la Fundacion Caja de Pensiones, 1989.

Nitsch, Hermann

113 *Altar Piece* 1984–96
mixed media (blood on canvas), 250.0 x 300.0
Courtesy of the artist

Born, 1938, Vienna
Lives Prizendorf, Austria

One of the founding members of the Vienna based Aktionismus group in 1964, Nitsch shared with his collaborators (including Rudolf Schwarzkogler, Günter Brus and Otto Muehl) a commitment to the cathartic potential of art. Influenced by American action painting via the work of Arnulf Rainer, Nitsch began by spontaneously 'performing' paintings in 1960, but subsequently incorporated himself into the 'works' or *Aktionen*. The religious flavour of these performances was enhanced through the use of live animals and carcasses, quasi-liturgical garments, and crucifixion imagery. His participation, with Muehl and Brus, in the Destruction in Art Symposium in London (1966) drew legal condemnation on the grounds of "indecency," and the group disbanded a few years later. Nitsch, however, continued to work on his longstanding performance project, entitled the *Orgies-Mysteries Theatre*.

- *L'Art au corps: le corps exposé de Man Ray à nos jours*. exh. cat. Marseille: Musées de Marseille, 1996
- *Hermann Nitsch: Das Orgien Mysterien Theater 1960–1987*. exh. cat. Naples: Villa Pignatelli, 1987.
- Vujica, P. and I. Rein, eds. *Hermann Nitsch*. exh. cat. Innsbruck: Gallery Krinzinger; Vienna: Galery Krinzinger, 1991.

Oursler, Tony

114 *Stuck* 1996
cloth doll life size, LCD projector
2 parts – doll: 24.0 x 162.0 x 32.0
Courtesy of Lisson Gallery, London.

Born, 1957, New York
Lives New York

Tony Oursler started working with camcorders while a student at the California Institute for the Arts in the late 1970s, and during the '80s produced a series of feature-length videos. His dolls or "pseudofigures" as he calls them, of which *Stuck* is an example, began to attract international attention in 1994. Inspired by photos of New England scarecrows, the blank, stuffed heads of these crudely assembled figures function as screens onto which the face of actress Tracy Leipold is projected. The effect is a disturbing disjunction between the dolls' deflated, lifeless bodies and animated faces that express emotions ranging from fury to rapture. Like many of the contemporary performance and installation artists in *BODY*, Oursler's aim is to create works that are "in dialogue with the viewer" (Landi 23).

- Cooke, L. "Tony Oursler: Alters." *Parkett* 47 (1996).
- "In the Green Room: Tony Oursler and Tracy Leipold in Conversation with Louise Neri." *Parkett* 47 (1996).
- Landi, A. "Tony Oursler: The Vision Thing." *ARTnews: The Cutting Edge* (1996).
- Morrissey, Simon. "Tony Oursler." *Creative Camera* 339 (Apr./May 1996).
- Welchman, J. "Tony Oursler: Angels of the Techno-Grotesque." *Art & Text* 51 (May 1995).

Pane, Gina

115 *Aktione Sentimentale* 1973
photo portfolio
Courtesy of Galerie Krinzinger, Vienna

Born, 1939, Biarritz
Died, 1990, Paris
Gina Pane studied at the École des Beaux-Arts in Paris. She started to attract critical attention – and controversy – with her 'body art' in the 1970s. By puncturing and cutting her own body with nails, tacks and razor blades Pane draws attention to the body's status as both object (artistic medium) and subject (the locus of feeling). The emotional response elicited by her actions is similarly complex, ranging from fascination to repulsion, alienation and even empathy. Her performances, photographic and video documentation and, more recently, installations are as much about the relationship between her body and the viewer as they are about femininity, masochism, or the multiple symbolic significances of the wound.

- *L'Art au corps: le corps exposé de Man Ray à nos jours*. exh. cat. Marseille: Musées de Marseille, 1996
- *Gina Pane: Travail d'action*. exh. cat. Paris: Gallery Isy Brachot, 1980.
- Lippard, L. "The Pains and Pleasures of Rebirth: Women's Body Art." *Art in America* (May–June 1976).
- O'Dell, K. "The Performance Artist as Masochistic Woman." *Arts Magazine* 62 (Summer 1988).
- *Polar Crossings*. exh. cat. Los Angeles: ICA; San Francisco: Art Institute Galleries, 1978.
- Verzotti, G. "Richard Long, Salvatore Scarpitta, Gina Pane." *Flash Art* 117 (1986).

Parr, Mike

116 *Cathartic Action: Social Gestus No.5* 1977
colour photograph
The Art Gallery of New South Wales, Sydney
Photograph: John Delacour

117 *The Emetics (I Am Sick of Art) Primary Vomit (Red, Yellow and Blue)* 1977
colour photograph
The Art Gallery of New South Wales, Sydney
Photograph: John Delacour

118 *Portrait of M and F* 1977
black and white photograph
The Art Gallery of New South Wales, Sydney
Photograph: Paul Green

119 *The Unword Perfromances* 1996
black and white photograph
The Art Gallery of New South Wales, Sydney
Photograph: Peter Moody

Represented by Sherman Galleries, Sydney
and Anna Schwartz Gallery, Melbourne

Born, 1945, Sydney
Lives Sydney
Parr began his career as a poet, but through a process of reduction to the 'facts' behind language he arrived at poems that were instructions for tasks, some of which he later carried out as performance art. In the early '70s he made contact with European artists and exhibited at several venues in Europe and Canada. His performances at Impact Gallery in Lausanne, Switzerland provided a base for his later experiments with audiences in Sydney. Parr co-founded the Inhibodress Co-operative gallery (1970–73) with Peter Kennedy. Since 1984 he has been working on a self-portrait series using drawing and engraving to produce single and large modular works. Recently he has returned to performances which cause great physical discomfort and are of gruelling duration. Parr has represented Australia in many major exhibitions and Biennales including Venice in 1980, 10th Biennale des Jeunes, Paris, 1977, Havana Biennale in 1997, and has exhibited in innumerable exhibitions in Australia.

- Bromfield, D. *Identities: A Critical Study of the Work of Mike Parr 1970–1990*. Perth: UWA P, 1991.
- Coulter-Smith, G. *Mike Parr: The Self Portrait Project*. Melbourne: Schwarz City P, 1994

Pisani, Vettor

120 *La Tempesta (The Storm)* 1990
photograph, 180.0 x 120.0
Courtesy of Giovanni and Ana Rosa Cotroneo, Naples.

Born, 1938, Bari
Lives Rome
Pisani is associated with Arte Povera although his work often takes the form of painting or photography. Marcel Duchamp has been a key influence in his work since his first one-person exhibition in 1970 in La Salita Gallery in Rome. The perverse sexuality of *Etant Donnés* finds an echo in Pisani's *La Tempesta* and *The Virgin of the Waters* which he exhibited at the Venice Biennale in 1990. This work consisted of an enclosed painted steel container with peepholes in one side like the holes in the door of *Etant donnés*. The view through the holes was of a pubescent girl, her vagina exposed. A fountain was playing in a pool at the base of the container and the jet of water coincided provocatively with the girl's body. The paintings often exploit mythological characters, for example the sphinx. He has exhibited very widely internationally, participating in several Biennales and in *Arte Italiana 1960–1982* at the Hayward gallery in London in 1982.

- Brusatin, M. and J. Clair, eds. *Identity and Alterity: Figures of the Body 1895/1995*. XLVI Venice Biennale. exh. cat. Venice: Marsilio, 1995.
- Eccher, D., ed. *Vettor Pisani: Il Teatro di Cristallo*. exh. cat. Rome: Trento Galleria Civica di Arte Contemporanea, 1993.
- Oliva, A. B., ed. *Vettor Pisani*. exh. cat. Bari, 1970.

Pistoletto, Michelangelo

121 *Mirror Diptych* 1962–71
Plagio. Sonata a cinque dita per Meret Oppenheim 1962–71
silkscreen on mirror, 120.0 x 150.0
Maria Pioppi alla maniera di Meret Oppenheim 1962–71
silkscreen on mirror, 120.0 x 150.0
Courtesy of Collection Giuliana and
Tommaso Setari, Milano.

Born, 1933, Biella, Vercelli
Lives Turin

Pistoletto has been a performance artist, sculptor and painter since 1956. He has arranged substantial 'operas' working with musicians, village mummers and professional actors. He was first recognised internationally for his realist paintings of figures on mirrors. These figures became part of a composition which included the body of the viewer. In this way they continue to remake themselves, forever incorporating the present. These works were often associated with Pop Art although they were far closer to Arte Povera and Conceptual Art. His installations include built environments, sound works and accumulations of found materials.

- Celant, G. and M. Pistoletto. *Pistoletto*. New York: Rizzoli, 1988.
- *Gravity and Grace: The Changing Condition of Sculpture 1965–1975*. exh. cat. London: Hayward Gallery, 1993.
- *Michelangelo Pistoletto*. exh. cat. Rome: Galleria Nazionale d'Arte Moderna, 1990.
- Welish, M. "Pistoletto's American Campaign." *Art in America* (Feb. 1981).

Pollock, Jackson

122 *Naked Man with Knife* c.1938–41
oil on canvas, 127.0 x 91.4
Tate Gallery, London.

Born, 1912, Cody, Wyoming
Died, 1956, East Hampton, New York
Raised in Arizona, Pollock moved to Los Angeles where he met Philip Guston and in 1930 moved to New York where he took courses under Thomas Hart Benton. Together with his wife Lee Krasner, he painted for the government in the W.P.A. – Federal Art Project until 1943. Fuelled by his desire to fill the surface with pictorial incident, he became universally known after 1947 for his 'drip' technique. This loose technique demanded rapid intuitive response and was supposed to allow chance and the subconscious to interact in the realisation of the painting.

- Brusatin, M. and J. Clair, eds. *Identity and Alterity: Figures of the Body 1895/1995*. XLVI Venice Biennale. exh. cat. Venice: Marsilio, 1995.
- Cernuschi, C. *Jackson Pollock: Meaning and Significance*. New York: Icon Editions, 1992.
- *Fémininmasculin: le sexe de l'art*. exh. cat. Paris: Centre Georges Pompidou, 1995.
- *Jackson Pollock*. Paris: Centre Georges Pompidou, 1982.
- Landau, E. G. *Jackson Pollock*. London, 1989.
- O'Connor, F. V. and E. W. Thaw, eds. *Jackson Pollock: A Catalogue Raisonné of Paintings, Drawings and Other Works*. New Haven: 1978.

Quinn, Marc

123 *Self* 1997
(work-in-progress at time of catalogue printing)
Courtesy of Jay Jopling, London

Born, 1964, London
Lives London
After graduating from Cambridge University in 1985, Quinn worked briefly as an assistant to the sculptor Barry Flannagan, before exhibiting his own work in 1988. He has achieved great notoriety for his use of unusual and often controversial materials. Most newsworthy has been his self-portrait in blood, *Self*, made from nine pints of Quinn's blood, collected and frozen into a latex mould of his head, and exhibited in 1991. Many of Quinn's sculptures are self-referential and contain a physical link between artist and work. Frequently a palette of personal viscera, with a preference for fluids, is employed to invoke modern taboos, especially of abject bodily fluids, while exploring the boundary issue. Other materials include coconut milk, bread dough, body casts, personal latex moulds and his own breath, materials which physically infer the works' own lifespan.

- Corris, M. "Marc Quinn (Grob Gallery, London)." *Artforum* 30.5 (Jan. 1992).
- Hall, J. "The Revolution Continues: British Art Now." *ARTnews* 92.7 (Sep. 1993).
- Kent, S. *Shark Infested Waters: The Saatchi Collection of British Art in the 90s*. exh. cat. London: Zwemmer, 1994.

Rainer, Arnulf

124 *Totem-Übermalung (Overpainting Totem)* 1983–84
oil over photograph, 102.0 x 73.0
Kunstmuseum Düsseldorf im Ehrenhof

Born, 1929, Baden
Lives Germany
Almost entirely self-taught, Rainer's early influences included Surrealism, Art Informel and Abstract Expressionism. While he shared with the latter an emphasis on the spontaneous 'act' of painting as a kind of psychical documentation, his work remained anchored to representation, particularly in the form of the self-portrait. In 1953 he began working on a series of *Overpaintings*, a method later applied to photographs. Commenting on this strategy, Rainer has stated that: "Photography alone . . . is not able to communicate adequately a moving or statically concentrated tension. For a closer approximation I draw over the photograph. This isn't retouching, but rather accentuating, the reawakening of the dynamic aspect of the frozen moment. In this way my work became a mixture of performing and visual art" (AR in *Contemporary Artists* 780). The performative aspect of his work, as well as Rainer's emphasis on the expression of repressed or irrational impulses, made him a major source of inspiration for the artists associated with Austrian Aktionismus.

- *L'Art au corps: le corps exposé de Man Ray à nos jours*. exh. cat. Marseille: Musées de Marseille, 1996
- Brusatin, M. and J. Clair, eds. *Identity and Alterity: Figures of the Body 1895/1995*. XLVI Venice Biennale. exh. cat. Venice: Marsilio, 1995.
- Clair, J., ed. *l' âme au corps, arts et sciences, 1793–1993*. exh. cat. Paris: Gallimard, 1993.
- Rainer, A. Artist's Statement. *Contemporary Artists*. Ed. C. Naylor. Chicago: St James P, 1989.
- Ullrich, F., ed. *Arnulf Rainer*. exh. cat. Recklinghausen: Kunsthalle, 1994.

Renoir, Auguste

125 *Jeune Garçon au Chat (Young Boy with Cat)* 1868–69
oil on canvas, 124.0 x 67.0
Musée d'Orsay, Paris
Acquired with assistance from Philippe Meyer, Paris
© photo RMN – R. G. Ojeda

Born, 1841, Limoges
Died, 1919, Cagnes-Sur-Mer
One of the leading exponents of Impressionism, many of Renoir's paintings became the most famous of this movement. Capturing 19th century images of pleasure and the life of the city, in salons, in bedrooms, on boulevards and in cafés, Renoir's paintings were hailed as the essence of realism. Unlike other Impressionist painters, however, Renoir makes no attempt to dissolve the form and have his objects lose their substance. A great admirer of Raphael, Titian, Delacroix and Rubens, Renoir moved away from Impressionism later in life, adopting a more linear style which, by virtue of its formal precision, promised Salon acceptance and portrait commissions. He painted many portraits and increasingly turned to painting nudes, particularly voluptuous women. A distinctive feature of these is Renoir's ability to convey the sensation of touch, as evidenced in *Young Boy with Cat*.

- Monneret, S. *Renoir*. Trans. E. Read. London: Barrie and Jenkins, 1990.
- *Pierre Auguste Renoir*. Intro. by W. Pach. London: Thames and Hudson, 1984.
- *Renoir*. exh. cat. London: Hayward Gallery; Paris: Galeries nationales du Grand Palais; Boston: MFA, 1985–86. New York: Abrams, 1985.
- White, B. E. *Renoir: His Life, Art and Letters*. New York: Abrams, 1984.

Rodin, Auguste

126 *Balzac "Athlete" (study f)* c.1896
cast bronze (recast 1981), 93.0 x 40.0 x 36.0
Newcastle Region Art Gallery
Gift of Mr. William Bowmore, O.B.E. 1991

127 *Assemblage: Torse de la Centauresse et Torse Féminin* 1910
cast bronze, 21.7 x 14.5 x 13.0
Musée Rodin, Paris

128 *Assemblage: Torse de la Centauresse et Adolescent Désespéré* 1910
cast bronze, 31.2 x 24.0 x 13.0
Musée Rodin, Paris

129 *Assemblage: Torse del Centauresse et Étude pour Iris* 1910
cast bronze, 23.0 x 11.5 x 13.0
Musée Rodin, Paris

130 *Main Gauche de Pierre et Jacques de Wissant* 1886
cast bronze, 33.3 x 18.5 x 11.2
Musée Rodin, Paris

131 *Figure Volante (Flying Figure)* c.1890–91
cast bronze, 52.0 x 76.0 x 31.6
Musée Rodin, Paris

132 *Iris, Messenger of the Gods* 1890–91
cast bronze (cast 1970), 50.0 x 60.0 x 25.0
Art Gallery of South Australia, Adelaide
William Bowmore Collection.
Gift of the South Australian Government, assisted by the Art Gallery of South Australia Foundation 1996
Art Gallery of South Australia, Adelaide

Born, 1840, Paris
Died, 1917, Meudon
Rodin's popular appeal and international fame made him, from about 1900, one of the most celebrated sculptors of the modern era. Often reworking and transforming one figure through many commissions, his increasingly rough, unfinished style retained the traces of the creative process itself as a sensory and imaginative response to his models. He regarded the immediacy of the artist-model relationship as indispensable, providing both the literal material and inspiration for his work. "Sometimes," he said, "one believes that there is nothing to be found in a model, and then nature suddenly reveals something of herself, a strip of flesh appears and that scrap of truth reveals the whole truth and allows one to leap with one bound to the absolute principle that lies behind things." (AR in Lampert, 1996, 514).

- Brusatin, M. and J. Clair, eds. *Identity and Alterity: Figures of the Body 1895/1995*. XLVI Venice Biennale. exh. cat. Venice: Marsilio, 1995.
- Butler, R. *Rodin: The Shape of Genius*. New Haven: Yale UP, 1993.
- Clair, J., ed. *l' au corps, arts et sciences, 1793–1993*. exh. cat. Paris: Gallimard, 1993.
- Lampert, C. "Rodin." Entry in *The Dictionary of Art*. Ed. Jane Turner. London: Macmillan, 1996.
- —. ed. *Rodin: Sculptures & Drawings*. exh. cat. London: Hayward Gallery, 1987.
- Levkoff, M. L., ed. *Rodin in His Time*. exh. cat. Los Angeles: Los Angeles County Museum of Art, 1994.

Rouault, Georges

133 *No Title ("Nu de Profil") ("Profile of a Nude")* 1936
illustration intended for unpublished book, "Les Fleurs du Mal"
colour aquatint, etching, 44.4 x 34.0
National Gallery of Australia, Canberra

Born, 1871, Paris
Died, 1958, Paris
Rouault gained admission to the École des Beaux-Arts in Paris in 1890, where he studied under the Symbolist painter Gustave Moreau. His paintings and prints, influenced initially by the brooding tones and Biblical themes favoured by his teacher, evolved through a number of stylistic and thematic phases. At the Salon d'Automne of 1905 he exhibited alongside Matisse and other Fauvist painters. While he shared with them a preference for pure, brilliant colours and boldly delineated forms, his work is distinctive in its deeply religious sentiment and expressive intensity. Drawn to such archetypal motifs as the prostitute, the clown, and nobility in suffering, his works evince a compassionate identification with the physical and psychological ills of contemporary humanity. Equally palpable, however, is a passionate interest in the formal qualities of the human body, articulated primarily through a studied language of colour.

- Hergott, F. and S. Whitfield, eds. *Georges Rouault: The Early Years 1903–1920*. exh. cat. London: Royal Academy, 1993.
- Molineri, D., ed. *Georges Rouault: 1903–1958: Catalogue Raisonne: Collections de la Ville de Paris*. exh. cat. Paris, 1983.
- Soby, J. T., ed. *Georges Rouault: Paintings and Prints*. exh. cat. New York: MOMA, 1945.

Rrap, Julie

134 *Vital Statistics* (from the series, *Prosthetics*) 1997
one of 3 sculptures
rubber, fibreglass and chromed steel
dimensions variable
Represented by Roslyn Oxley9 Gallery, Sydney

Born, 1950, Lismore, NSW
Lives Sydney
Rrap completed a degree in humanities at the University of Queensland before studying fine arts in several Sydney art schools, specialising in photomedia and painting. She then relocated to Europe where she continued to exhibit between 1986 and 1994. Rrap has consistently worked with images of her own body. Her early photographic compositions and installations took the form of feminist critiques of the patriarchal foundations of high art. She became known in particular for her composite reconstructions of famous historical treatments of women in art. Since her stay in Europe she has continued to deal with art history and the body but her analysis has become more personal and less ideological. In *BODY* she presents the negative spaces of her body that nonetheless evoke an intimate presence in the trace of her skin. Rrap has exhibited widely both nationally and internationally, in exhibitions including: 1986 and 1992 Sydney Biennales, *Strangers in Paradise* which toured to Korea and *Photography is Dead! Long Live Photography!*

- Alexander, G. et. al. *Hide and Seek*. Sydney: Piper P, 1997.
- Delvoye, W. "Global Art: Julie Rrap." *Flash Art* 173 (Nov./Dec. 1993).
- Lauf, C. "Permanent New Wave." *Art & Text* 44 (Jan. 1993).
- Maloon, T. "Julie Rrap." *Art & Australia* 33.4 (Winter 1996).
- Moore, C. *Indecent Exposures: Twenty Years of Australian Feminist Photography*. Sydney: Allen and Unwin, 1991.

Salcedo, Doris

135 *Atrabiliarios* 1992
plywood, shoes, cow bladder & surgical thread
27 niches
Courtesy of Alexander and Bonin, New York

Born, 1958, Bogota
Lives Bogota
The work of sculptor Doris Salcedo is inextricably bound to the experience of violence and loss that is the product of Colombia's bloody political conflict. Using touchingly mundane remnants of bodily presence – such as worn shoes or neatly folded shirts – she evokes a palpable sense of absence. Often travelling to isolated Colombian villages to speak with the survivors of guerilla warfare and government purges, Salcedo notes that "The images left behind by the violent act in these places are sometimes evident and sometimes imperceptible although, in any case, indelible. My task is to transform these traces into relics that enable us to acknowledge other people's experiences as our own, as collective experiences" (*Flash Art* 97). As well as recent exhibitions in America, Salcedo's work was included in the 1993 Venice Biennale and the Carnegie International 1996.

- Burke, G. "The Boundary Rider: The 9th Biennale of Sydney." *Art New Zealand* 67 (Winter 1993).
- Cameron, D. "Absence Makes the Art: Doris Salcedo." *Artforum* 33.2 (Oct. 1994).
- Merewether, C. "Naming Violence in the Work of Salcedo." *Third Text* 24 (Autumn 1993).
- Salcedo, D. "Aperto." *Flash Art* 171 (Summer 1993).

Sallé, François

136 *The Anatomy Class at the École des Beaux-Arts* 1888
oil on canvas, 238.9 x 321.2
The Art Gallery of New South Wales, Sydney

Born, 1839, Bourges
Died, 1899, Lyon
Sallé was a student of Luminais and a member of the Société des Artistes Français. His painting in this exhibition, *The Anatomy Class at the École des Beaux-Arts* was included in the 1888 Salon where it received a 3rd class medal. Painted on a grand scale in a traditional, 'academic' style, its subject is a lecture by Mathias-Marie Duval, the author of a number of 'précis d'anatomie' in the 1880s to students and staff at the École des Beaux-Arts where Sallé taught from 1873 to his death in 1899. Although the painting received little comment from critics of the day, it was selected for purchase by the French government for the Luxembourg Gallery but had previously been secured for purchase by the Trustees of the (now) Art Gallery of New South Wales.

- Lynn, E. and L. Rees. "Victorian Favourites: A Conversation." *Art in Australia* 22.1 (Spring 1984).

Schiele, Egon

137 *Eros (Self-portrait Masturbating)* 1911
gouache, watercolour and black crayon, 55.9 x 45.7
Private collection, Melbourne
Courtesy of Richard Nagy, London

138 *Reclining Semi-nude with Black Stockings* 1913
gouache and pencil, 48.3 x 31.4
Private collection, Melbourne
Courtesy of Richard Nagy, London

Born, 1890, Tulln an der Donau, nr. Vienna
Died, 1918, Vienna
Although his artistic career lasted little more than a decade, Schiele was one of the major contributors (with Oskar Kokoschka) to Austrian Expressionism. After a year at the conservative Akademie der Bildenden Künste in Vienna, he was among a group of dissenting students to form the short-lived Neukunstgruppe. By 1910, largely through his contact with Gustav Klimt and his circle, Schiele had participated in a number of major exhibitions and attracted critical acclaim as well as patronage. In his psychological portraits of this period, the human body, obsessively, even anxiously worked and pared down to an almost skeletal essence, articulates the torments of

the soul. Often sexually explicit, his nudes are emphatically de-eroticised, their painful nakedness going far beyond an absence of clothing. Not surprisingly, they provoked public condemnation: in 1912 the artist was imprisoned for 24 days and witnessed the burning of one of his 'immoral' drawings in court.

- Comini, A. *Egon Schiele's Portraits*. Berkeley: U of California P, 1974.
- —. *Schiele in Prison*. London: Thames and Hudson, 1974.
- Kallir, J. *Egon Schiele: The Complete Works*. New York: Abrams, 1990.
- *Klimt, Schiele, Kokoschka: Drawings and Watercolours*. exh. cat. London: Thames and Hudson, 1981.
- Werkner, P., ed. *Egon Schiele: Art, Sexuality and Viennese Modernism*. Palo Alto, CA: Society for the Promotion of Science and Scholarship, 1994.
- Wilson, S. *Egon Schiele*. Ithaca: Cornell UP, 1980.

Schneemann, Carolee

139 From the performance *Up To and Including Her Limits*
1975, photoprint on cardboard
135.0 x 106.0, 130.0 x 103.0
Courtesy of Hubert Klocker, Vienna

Born, 1939, New York
Lives New York
Carolee Schneemann played an active role in the development of performance and body art in the US during the 1960s. Drawing on her early training as a painter, and subsequent involvement with the experimental Judson Dance group in the early '60s, Schneemann's 'Kinetic Theatre' was conceived as a multi-media, interactive ritual. International recognition followed the performance of *Meat Joy* in Paris, London and New York in 1964. Incorporating the participants' semi-naked bodies, as well as the carcasses of chickens, raw fish and sausages, *Meat Joy* was hailed as "a celebration of flesh as material" (Sayre 100). Schneemann's emphasis on the body – specifically the female body – and her commitment to personal and sexual liberation through art were central to the emergence of feminist art practices more generally.

- *L'Art au corps: le corps exposé de Man Ray à nos jours*. exh. cat. Marseille: Musées de Marseille, 1996
- Brusatin, M. and J. Clair, eds. *Identity and Alterity: Figures of the Body 1895/1995*. XLVI Venice Biennale. exh. cat. Venice: Marsilio, 1995.
- *Fémininmasculin: le sexe de l'art*. exh. cat. Paris: Centre Georges Pompidou, 1995.
- Joselit, D. "Projected Identities." *Art in America* 79.11 (Nov. 1991).
- Klinger, L. S. "Where's the Artist? Feminist Practice and Poststructural Theories of Authorship." *Art Journal* 50.2 (Summer 1991).
- McPherson, B., ed. *More than Meat Joy: Carolee Schneemann: Complete Performance and Selected Writings*. New York, 1979.
- Sayre, H. M. *The Object of Performance: The American Avant-Garde since 1970* Chicago: U of Chicago P, 1992.

Schwarzkogler, Rudolf

140 *Aktion Wien* 1965–66
photographs by Ludwig Hoffenreich,
60.0 x 50.0, edition of 40
The Art Gallery of New South Wales, Sydney
Photograph: Jenni Carter

Born, 1940, Vienna
Died, 1969, Vienna
Schwarzkogler was introduced to the Wiener Aktionsgruppe by Hermann Nitsch in 1963. Two years later he held his first *Aktion*, ironically titled *The Wedding*. This and subsequent performances took the form of carefully choreographed and photographically documented surgical 'rituals.' As violent and sexually explicit dramatisations of castration anxiety, these *Aktionen* sought to use art as the 'Purgatory of the Senses'. Schwarzkogler's influences ranged from Eastern Mysticism and the work of Arnulf Rainer and Yves Klein, to Austrian Expressionism and the French Symbolists; but there is also a personal echo to his performances: his father was not only a doctor, but committed suicide in 1943 after losing both his legs in the war. Schwarzkogler's own death was equally unnatural: suffering deteriorating health partly as a result of his experiments with ritual fasting, he died after falling from his apartment window at the age of 29.

- *L'Art au corps: le corps exposé de Man Ray à nos jours*. exh. cat. Marseille: Musées de Marseille, 1996
- Klocher, H. *Rudolf Schwarzkogler: Leben und Werk*. Klagenfurt, 1992.
- Brusatin, M. and J. Clair, eds. *Identity and Alterity: Figures of the Body 1895/1995*. XLVI Venice Biennale. exh. cat. Venice: Marsilio, 1995.

Sherman, Cindy

141 *Untitled* 1992 (MP #264)
colour photograph, 127.0 x 190.5
Courtesy of Barbara Schwartz

142 *Untitled* 1988 (MP #184)
edition 5 (of 6)
colour photograph, 155.6 x 231.8
Courtesy of the artist and Metro Pictures
© Metro Pictures

143 *Untitled* 1992 (MP #259)
edition 6 (of 6)
colour photograph, 100.0 x 150.0
Courtesy of the artist and Metro Pictures
© Metro Pictures

Born, 1954, Glan Ridge (New Jersey)
Lives New York
The exhibition of her untitled 'film stills' in the early '80s established Cindy Sherman as a major figure in the international arena. Since then she has created 'abject' photos evocative of B-grade horror movies (1988–89), parodied the icons of Art History (1990s), and produced a series of *Sex Pictures*. In the latter Sherman manipulates and rearranges the crudely fabricated body parts of mannequins into impossibly perverse poses reminiscent of Hans Bellmer's dolls. Sherman's *Sex Pictures* solicit our curiosity, yet as one critic has remarked,

"The apparent humanity they contain is so closely veiled with inhumanity that it is impossible to apply ethical criteria to any effect" (Brehm 120). Here, as elsewhere, Sherman's work provides a powerful commentary not only on gender and sexuality, but on the uses and abuses of photographic media.

- Brehm, M. "Sex Pictures: The Body and its Surrogates." *Cindy Sherman.* exh. cat. Rotterdam: Museum Boijmans Van Beuningen; Baden-Baden: Staatliche Kunsthalle, 1996–97.
- Brusatin, M. and J. Clair, eds. *Identity and Alterity: Figures of the Body 1895/1995.* XLVI Venice Biennale. exh. cat. Venice: Marsilio, 1995.
- *Cindy Sherman 1975–1993.* New York: Rizzoli, 1993.
- *Fémininmasculin: le sexe de l'art.* exh. cat. Paris: Centre Georges Pompidou, 1995.
- Mulvey, L. "A Phantasmagoria of the Female Body: The Work of Cindy Sherman." *Parkett* 29 (1991).
- Solomon-Godeau, A. "Suitable for Reframing: The Critical Recasting of Cindy Sherman." *Parkett* 29 (1991).

Shiraga, Kazuo

144 *Wild Boar Hunting (part 1)* 1963
fur, paste, oil on plywood, 184.8 x 276.5
Museum of Contemporary Art, Tokyo

Born, 1924, Amagasaki, Japan
Lives Amagasaki
Shiraga was one of the leading figures of the post-war Japanese *Gutai* artists. This was a radical group which experimented with new methods and materials: paint was applied with bare feet, watering cans, even explosives; and objects were made of water, electric bulbs, and tin cans. One of the few *Gutai* artists with art school training in both *Nihonga* and oil painting, Shiraga replaced his brush and palette knife in 1954 with his bare feet, emphasising the notion of painting as action, central to *Gutai*. He balanced on a hanging hope which he grasped with his fists and he dipped and swung his weight through the thick, wet oil paint. "The finished painting stands as a record of his random spins, swirls, and slips" (*Scream against the sky* 92).

- *L'Art au corps: le corps exposé de Man Ray à nos jours.* exh. cat. Marseille: Musées de Marseille, 1996.
- *Kazuo Shiraga.* exh. cat. Paris: Galerie Stadler, 1992.
- Munroe, A. *Scream Against the Sky – Japanese Art After 1945.* New York, 1994.
- Roberts, J. "Painting as performance." *Art in America* (May 1992).
- Sourgnes, M. "Art of the '80s in Japan." *Arts of Asia* (March/Apr. 1990).

Sickert, Walter

145 *Mornington Crescent Nude, Contre-Jour* 1907
oil on canvas, 50.8 x 60.9
Art Gallery of South Australia, Adelaide
AR Ragless Bequest Fund 1963

Born, 1860, Munich
Died, 1942, Bathampton, England
After studying briefly at the Slade School of Art in London in 1881, Sickert gained an apprenticeship with James McNeill Whistler, from whom he learned a fastidious regard for the materials and techniques of his craft. Equally formative was the young artist's meeting with Degas while in Paris in 1883. Moving away from Whistler's method of painting directly from nature, Sickert's carefully composed music-hall paintings of 1887–89 are close both in spirit and in technique to Degas' Parisian theatre scenes of the 1870s. Although he acknowledged an affinity with French Impressionism, Sickert was less interested in capturing the fleeting effects of light than in exploring the stylistic and emotional range of his subjects. In addition to producing a vast – and hugely influential – oeuvre of paintings including figure compositions, portraits and landscapes, Sickert wrote extensively on art.

- Baron, W. *Sickert.* London: Phaidon P, 1973.
- Baron, W. and R. Shone, eds. *Sickert: Paintings.* London: Royal Academy; Amsterdam: Rijksmuseum, 1992/3.
- Lilly, M. *Sickert: The Painter and his Circle.* London: Elek, 1971.

Smith, Kiki

146 *Mary Magdalene* 1994
silicon bronze, forged steel
edition 2 (of 3), 152.0 x 52.0 x 55.0
Private collection

Born, 1954, Nuremberg
Lives New York
Kiki Smith moved to New York in the mid-1970s, and has exhibited widely in the US and Europe. Her work is characterised by an emphatically emotive, often visceral approach to the body and sexuality; as such it is often differentiated from the more conceptual, parodic or ironic approaches to feminism pursued by a number of her contemporaries (such as Barbara Kruger and Cindy Sherman) during the 1980s. Her sculptures and drawings typically deal with the body at its most socially uncomfortable, ambiguous or vulnerable – whether bleeding, defecating, opened up, fragmented or flayed. Equally transgressive is her eclectic use of materials, from hand-made paper and beads to stained-glass, aimed at 'corrupting' (and feminising) the purity of traditional materials like bronze and wax.

- Brusatin, M. and J. Clair, eds. *Identity and Alterity: Figures of the Body 1895/1995.* XLVI Venice Biennale. exh. cat. Venice: Marsilio, 1995.
- *Fémininmasculin: le sexe de l'art.* exh. cat. Paris: Centre Georges Pompidou, 1995.
- *Kiki Smith.* exh. cat. Stockholm: Moderna Museet, 1992.
- Lampert, C., ed. *Kiki Smith.* exh. cat. London: Whitechapel Art Gallery, 1995.
- Lyon, C. "Kiki Smith: Body and Soul." *Artforum* (Jan. 1990).
- Schleifer, K. B. "Inside & Out: An Interview with Kiki Smith." *The Print Collector's Newsletter* 22 (July/Aug. 1991).
- Stoops, S. *Kiki Smith: Unfolding the Body.* Waltham, MA: The Rose Art Museum, Brandeis University, 1992.
- Tallman, S. "Kiki Smith: Anatomy Lessons." *Art in America* 80.4 (Apr. 1992).

Stelarc

147 *Street Suspension* 1984
gelatin silver print, 71.5 x 51.5
The Art Gallery of New South Wales, Sydney
Purchased with funds provided by the Visual Arts and Craft Board
Photograph: Jenni Carter
Represented by Sherman Galleries, Sydney

Born, 1946, Cyprus
Lives Ballarat, Victoria
Stelarc attracted international attention in 1977 when he staged the first of his 'Stretched Skin Suspensions' in Munich. Subsequently suspended and photographed in venues ranging from an elevator shaft to mid-air over the ocean, Stelarc sees these performances in terms of an ongoing evolutionary project based on the 'obsolescence' of the human body. While acknowledging an affinity with religious asceticism, he insists that his corporeal manipulations, penetrations and extensions are motivated by a scientific, not mystical, vision. Since the mid-80s he has used robotics as a means of technologically redefining the limits of the human body. In addition to numerous performances in Japan, Stelarc has staged events in Mexico City (1976 and 1981), Denmark (1985), Holland (1990) and Australia.

- Collins, D. "Digital Somatics: Getting Jack out of the Box." *New Art Examiner* 23 (Summer 1996).
- Stelarc. "Prosthetics, Robotics and Remote Existence: Postevolutionary Strategies." *Leonardo* 24.5 (1991).
- Stelarc. "Towards the Post-Human: From Psycho-Body to Cyber-System." *Architectural Design* 65 (Nov./Dec. 1995).
- Younger, J. *Fuel*. exh. cat. Brisbane: Institute of Modern Art, Oct./Nov. 1991.

Torrado, Laura

148 *Island I and II* 1993
photograph, 90.0 x 60.0
Courtesy of the artist

149 *Red Inside I* 1993
photograph, 90.0 x 60.0
Courtesy of the artist

150 *Untitled (earth sculpture piece)* 1993
photograph, 90.0 x 60.0
Courtesy of the artist

Born, 1967, Madrid
Lives Madrid
Torrado studied at the school of Fine Arts in Madrid and the School of Visual Arts in New York. She exhibits widely both in Spain and the US. Her work explores notions of repetitive actions, actions which are completed without thinking. Of her work, Torrado writes, "the necessity of making these rituals and objects comes from the desire to identify the nonsense of our routine, to question why we let ourselves be animals of habit." Torrado explores this concept through the use of domestic, everyday materials, such as leaves, paper, human hair, flowers and fabric which give her work a perishable and fragile human character.

- Huici, F. *Laura Torrado – El Cuerpo Roto*. exh. cat. Madrid: Centro de Recursos Culturales de la Comunidad de Madrid, 1995.
- Castro Florez, F. "Hueilas Danza de los Sentimientos." *Meridiano*. Madrid: Centro de Recursos Culturales de la Comunidad de madrid, 1995
- Johnson, R. "True Phallacy: The Myth of the Male Power." *New York Post* 2 Dec. 1995
- Munia, A. "El Cuerpa Roto." *Lápiz Revista Internacional de Arte* XXI.103 (1994): 72

Unsworth, Ken

151 *Five Secular Settings for Sculpture as Ritual and Burial Piece* 1975
boxed set of 10 photographs, 30.5 x 25.2 (each)
The Art Gallery of New South Wales, Sydney
Photograph: Jenni Carter
Represented by Roslyn Oxley9 Gallery, Sydney

Born, 1931, Richmond, Victoria
Lives Sydney
Unsworth maintains a number of parallel practices. He regularly creates sculpture, installations, performances, drawing and sometimes relief paintings. The sculptures tend to follow a vigorous abstract line based on balance and equilibrium, and are predicated upon the minimalist art of Richard Serra in the late 1960s. In the mid-70s Unsworth performed a series of body works in which his own body became an element in such sculptures. The installations are often kinetic and sometimes highly theatrical by contrast with the severity and concrete abstraction of the sculpture. Unsworth has a substantial record of exhibitions including Venice and Sydney Biennales.

- Fenner, F. "Chihuahuas and Currawongs: Humour and the Australian Landscape in the Recent Work of Ken Unsworth." *Art and Australia* 33 (Autumn 1996).
- Forsyth, G. "Ken Unsworth." *Art & Text* 48 (May 1994).
- Gamble, S. "Unsworth in Japan." *Art Monthly* 41 (June 1991).
- Wulffen, T. "Ken Unsworth at the DAAD Galerie." *Kunstforum* (Feb. 1988).

Valadon, Suzanne

152 *La Chambre Bleue (The Blue Room)* 1923
oil on canvas, 90.0 x 116.0
Musée National d'Art Moderne, Centre Georges Pompidou, Paris

153 *Nu à la Couverture Rayée (Nude on Striped Blanket)*
1922, oil on canvas
Musée d'art moderne de la Ville de Paris
© Photothèque des Musées de la Ville de Paris

Born, 1865, Bessines-sur-Gartempe, France
Died, 1938, Paris
The illegitimate daughter of a maid, Valadon's birth placed her well outside the boundaries of bourgeois respectability. Her introduction to art was as a model in the Paris district of Montmartre, famous in the 1880s for its prostitutes and artists' studios, and fast gaining a reputation for Bohemianism. Gaining a measure of financial independence with her first marriage, in 1896, Valadon started painting full-time,

encouraged in this pursuit by Renoir (for whom she had modelled), Toulouse-Lautrec, and Degas. Like Degas, Valadon was interested in the unguarded moment: her subjects, many of them female nudes, were very much of the contemporary world, rather than idealised, eroticised and timeless icons of femininity. Valadon's nudes also complicate the usual notion of 'the gaze' as an instrument of male desire and authority directed at a female object, just as they disrupted the traditional artist-model relationship.

- Matthews, P. "Returning the Gaze: Diverse Representations of the Nude in the Art of Suzanne Valadon." *Art Bulletin* 73.3 (Sep. 1991).
- Petrides, P. *Catalogue raisonné de l'oeuvre de Suzanne Valadon*. Paris, 1971.
- Rosinsky, T. D. "Suzanne Valadon." *Woman's Art Journal* (Spring/Summer 1996).
- Weekes, A. O. "Student's Self-Image: Representations of Women in High Art and Popular Culture." *Woman's Art Journal* (Autumn/Winter 1992).

Villon, Jacques
after M. Duchamp

154 *Duchamp's Bride* 1912–34
mezzotint, printed in colour
edition 12 (of 20), 50.2 x 31.5
Courtesy of Galleria Schwarz Collection, Milan

Born, 1875, Damville, Eure
Died, 1963, Puteaux, nr. Paris
Born Gaston Duchamp (brother of Marcel), he changed his name to Jacques Villon when he abandoned the legal studies his father had urged him to pursue. He turned his attention to contributing humorous lithographs to Parisian illustrated newspapers, followed by a move into serious printmaking and painting. Villon's friendship with the Cubist circle and his war experience in a camouflage unit provided him with a new vocabulary of form and colour. In 1922 pressing financial need obliged him to abandon painting once more and begin producing large format aquatints by established modern masters such as Picasso and Matisse. He subsequently included his own selection, including those of family members Marcel and Suzanne Duchamp. Villon received numerous awards during his later years, culminating in 1963 with an election as Grand Officier de La Légion d'honneur.

- *Jacques Villon: Prints from a Particular Collection*. Amsterdam: Rijksmuseum, 1984.
- Robbins, D., ed. *Jacques Villon*. exh. cat. Cambridge, MA: Fogg, 1976.
- Tonneau-Ryckelnyck, D. and P. Cabanne, eds. *Jacques Villon: l'oeuvre grave*. exh. cat. Gravelines, Museum Arsenale Lyon, Museum Imprimerie, Banque, 1989.

Wollheim, Gert Heinrich

155 *Die Siegerin (The Champion)* 1924
oil on canvas, 84.0 x 64.0
Kunstmuseum Dusseldorf

Born, 1894
Died, 1974
Born into a wealthy German Jewish family, Wollheim studied at the Weimar Academy before the outbreak of World War I. Discharged from the German Army with serious wounds in 1917, he began working on a series of anti-war paintings based on sketches done at the front. After moving from Berlin to Düsseldorf in 1919 Wollheim became close friends with Otto Dix, sharing Dix's agenda of social critique as well as his stylistic debt to German Expressionism. The theme of sexual ambiguity present in *Die Siegerin* is most explicitly developed in the artist's *Female Self Portrait – The Golem* (1921), which incorporates military references into an image of a violently divided self. Wollheim's work was included in the Nazi exhibitions of 'Degenerate Art', and he eventually emigrated to the USA.

- *Dix – Pankok – Wollheim: Freunde in Düsseldorf 1920–1925*. exh. cat. Düsseldorf: Galerie Remmert und Barth, May–Aug. 1989.
- Hoffmann-Curtius, D. "Geschlechterspiel im Dadaismus." *Kunstforum International* 128 (Oct.–Dec. 1994).
- Peters, A., ed. *Gert H. Wollheim 1894–1974: Eine Retrospektive*. exh. cat. Düsseldorf: Kunstmuseum; Cologne: Wienand, 1993.
- Wollheim, M. *Gert H. Wollheim: Gedanke und Werke*. Munich: Karl Thiemig, 1977.

Zai Kuning

156 *HYDROGEN: The lightest element*
HYPOCAUST: Hot air was sent as a form of heat
IDIOCY: Extreme mental imbecility: utter foolishness
HYSTERIA: Functional disturbance of psychoneurotic origin
INANE: Enigma of a sexless toad 1996
installation comprising 200 wax objects, metal tools, aluminium tray, water, aluminium sheets
dimensions variable
Courtesy of the artist

Born 1964, Singapore
Lives Singapore
Initially attending La Salle College of the Arts in Singapore, Kuning has most recently completed a Fine Arts Degree in Painting at the Royal Melbourne Institute of Technology. He is both a performance-based artist and an installation artist whose work strongly evokes the body and biological processes. His recent installation at the Asia Pacific Triennial in Brisbane in 1996/97 included what appeared to be joints of meat wrapped in many layers of wax sheeting. The process of producing these forms was in itself a performance enacted with obsessive ritual. Temporality was implied within the work by the dripping water which slowly caused bundles of cloth, themselves suggestive of body organs, to 'bleed' colour from layers within while iron tools slowly rusted away below.

- *The 2nd Asia-Pacific Triennial of Contemporary Art*. exh. cat. Brisbane: Queensland AG, 1996.

Reference Works*

Reference numbers 1 – 28

Cabanel, Alexandre

1 *The Birth of Venus* 1863
130.0 x 225.0
Musée d'Orsay, Paris
© photo RMN

Caillebotte, Gustave

2 *Man at his Bath* 1884
170.1 x 125.0
Josefowitz Collection

Clemente, Francesco

3 *The Five Senses* 1981
66.0 x 49.5
Private Collection
Courtesy of Thomas Ammann Fine Art, Zurich

4 *Heart* 1991–92
77.1 x 64.25
Courtesy of Gagosian Gallery
Collection Diane Von Furstenberg, New York

Courbet, Gustave

5 *An After-Dinner at Ornans* 1848–49
195.0 x 257.0
Musée des Beaux-Arts, Lille

6 *The Bacchante* 1844–45
65.0 x 81.0
The Lefevre Gallery, London

7 *The Bathers* 1853
227.0 x 193.0
Musée Fabre, Montpelier

8 *Country Siesta* early 1840s
13.0 x 18.0
Musée des Beaux-Arts et d'Archeologie, Besançon

9 *Le Fou de Peur (Man Mad with Fear)* 1843
60.5 x 50.5
Nasjonalgalleriat, Oslo
Photograph: J. Lathion
© Nasjonalgalleriat

10 *The Grain Sifters* 1854–55
131.0 x 167.0
Musée des Beaux-Arts, Nantes

11 *Man with the Leather Belt* c.1845–46
100.0 x 82.0
Musée d'Orsay, Paris
© photo RMN

12 *L'Origine du Monde (The Origin of the World)* 1866
46.0 x 55.0
Musée d'Orsay, Paris
© photo RMN – H. Lewandowski

13 *The Painter's Studio* 1855
359.0 x 598.0
Musée d'Orsay, Paris
© photo RMN

14 *The Preparation of the Dead Girl* mid-1850s
188.0 x 251.5
Smith College Museum of Art, Northampton, Massachusetts
Purchased, Drayton Hillyer Fund

15 *The Sleepers* 1866
135.0 x 200.0
Musée du Petit Palais, Paris

16 *The Source* 1868
128.0 x 97.0
Musée d'Orsay, Paris
© photo RMN

17 *Three Nudes* 1868
126.0 x 96.0
Musée du Petit Palais, Paris

18 *The Woman in a Podoscaphe* 1865
170.8 x 208.6
Murauchi Museum, Tokyo

19 *The Woman with a Parrot* 1866
129.5 x 195.6
The Metropolitan Museum of Art, H.O. Havemeyer Collection
Bequest of Mrs. H.O. Havemeyer, 1929
All rights reserved, The Metropolitan Museum of Art

20 *Wounded Man* c.1844–54
81.0 x 97.0
Musée d'Orsay, Paris
© photo RMN

21 *The Young Bather* 1866
130.2 x 97.2
The Metropolitan Museum of Art, H.O. Havemeyer Collection
Bequest of Mrs. H.O. Havemeyer, 1929
All rights reserved, The Metropolitan Museum of Art

22 *The Young Ladies on the Banks of the Seine*
1856–57, 174.0 x 200.0
Musée de Petit Palais, Paris

Ingres, Jean-Auguste-Dominique

23 *The Apotheosis of Homer* 1827
152.0 x 203.0
Musée du Louvre, Paris

24 *The Source* 1856
164.0 x 81.5
Musée d'Orsay, Paris
© photo RMN

25 *The Turkish Bath* 1863
108.0 (diameter)
Musée d'Orsay, Paris
© photo RMN

26 *Venus Anadyomene* 1848
162.8 x 92.0
Musée Condé, Chantilly

Klossowski, Pierre

27 *Milady and D'Artagnan* 1986
154.0 x 139.0
Musée National d'Art Moderne, Centre Georges Pompidou, Paris

Manet, Edouard

28 *Olympia* 1863
130.5 x 190.0
Musée d'Orsay, Paris
© photo RMN–H. Lewandowski

* Works not included in the exhibition

Contributing Writers

Anthony Bond is Head Curator of Western Art at The Art Gallery of New South Wales, Sydney.

Philippe Grand is Registrar at the Musée Contemporain de Lyon, France.

Dr Susan Best is a Lecturer in the Faculty of Design, Architecture and Building at the University of Technology, Sydney.

Dr Sarah Faunce is Curator of European Painting and Sculpture at the Brooklyn Museum, USA.

Dr Jill Beaulieu is a Lecturer in Art History at the University of Western Sydney, Nepean.

Dr Mary Roberts is a Lecturer in Art History at Canberra School of Art, Australian National University.

Dr Jill Bennett is a Lecturer in Art History and Theory at the College of Fine Arts, University of New South Wales, Sydney.

Dr Alan Krell is a Lecturer in Art History and Theory at the College of Fine Arts, University of New South Wales, Sydney.

Dr David Bromfield is a Lecturer in Art History at the University of Western Australia, Perth.

Dr Charles Merewether is Curator of Spanish and Portuguese language cultures at The Getty Research Institute for the History of Art and the Humanities, USA.

Film Programme*

The Performing Body

Victoria Lynn

This programme of films and videos focuses on events, actions and peformances in the late 1960s and 1970s that involved the human body being extended to or beyond a physical limit. The purpose of much of this work was to expand prevailing concepts of what constituted the art object and to manifest new forms of self-expression.

Marina Abramovic and Ulay

A Performance Anthology 1975–80
Volume I: 4 performances by Marina Abramovic
1975–76, video, b&w, 60 min
Volume IIIA and IIIB: Relation Work
17 Performances by Ulay and Marina Abramovic
1976–80, video, b&w and colour, 180 min
Collection: The Art Gallery of New South Wales, Sydney

Vito Acconci

Pryings 1971
with Vito Acconci, Kathy Dillon
video, b&w, 17:10 min
Collection: The Art Gallery of New South Wales, Sydney

Waterways: 4 Saliva Studies 1971
video, b&w, 22:27 min
Collection: The Art Gallery of New South Wales, Sydney

Open Book 1974
video, colour, 10:09 min
Collection: The Art Gallery of New South Wales, Sydney

Adaption Studies 1970
Super 8 colour film transferred to video, 10 min
Collection: The Art Gallery of New South Wales, Sydney

Two Takes 1970
Super 8 b&w film transferred to video, 9:40 min
Collection: The Art Gallery of New South Wales, Sydney

Openings 1970
Super 8 b&w film transferred to video, 15:00 min
Collection: The Art Gallery of New South Wales, Sydney

Joseph Beuys

Coyote: I like America and America likes me 1981
16mm film transferred to video, 37 min
Courtesy of Galerie Rene Block and Helmut Wietz

Gunter Brus

Ana 1964
Directed by Thomas Kren, 16mm film, b&w, 3 min, silent
Collection: Austria Filmmakers Cooperative, Vienna

Selbstersummerlung 1965
Directed by Thomas Kren, 16mm film, b&w, 6 min, silent
Collection: Austria Filmmakers Cooperative, Vienna

Silberaction 1965
Directed by Thomas Kren, 16mm film, b&w, 6 min, silent
Collection: Austria Filmmakers Cooperative, Vienna

Gunter Brus, Otto Muehl, Rudolf Schwarzkogler

Satisfaction 1968
16mm film, b&w, 6 min, silent
Collection: P.A.P Kunstagentur, Galerie Film, Video, Musik

Chris Burden

Documentation of Selected Works 1971–74
Film: Michael Brewster, Barbara Burden, Don Von Valkenburg, Phyllis Lutjeans, Paula Sweet, Charles Hill
Video: Andy Mann
1975, b&w and colour, 34:58 min
Shoot (1971), *Bed Piece* (1972), and *Through The Night Softly* (1973); *220* (1971); *Deadman* (1972); *Fire Roll* (1973); *Icarus* (1973); *B.C. Mexico* (1973); *TV Ad* (1973); *Back To You* (1974); and *Velvet Water* (1974)

Valie Export

Remote Remote 1973
16mm film, colour, 12 min
Collection: Austria Filmmakers Cooperative, Vienna

Gilbert and George with Nigel Greenwood, John Kaldor, Elwyn Lynn, Daniel Thomas

The Singing Sculpture 1969
performed at The Art Gallery of New South Wales, Sydney, 16–21 August 1973
John Kaldor Art Project
Directed by Brian Adams, ABC TV, 16mm film, colour, 32min
Collection: The Art Gallery of New South Wales, Sydney

Joan Jonas

Vertical Roll 1972
Photography: Roberta Neuman
video, b&w, 19:38 min
Collection: The Art Gallery of New South Wales, Sydney

Organic Honey's Visual Telepathy 1972
video, b&w, 17:24 min
Collection: The Art Gallery of New South Wales, Sydney

Ana Mendieta

Ana Mendieta: Selected Works 1973–80 1987
video, colour and b&w, 20 min, silent
Collection: Galerie Lelong, New York

Paul McCarthy and Mike Kelley

Fresh Acconci 1995
video, colour, 45 min
Collection, The Art Gallery of New South Wales, Sydney

Otto Muehl

Leda and the Swan 1964
Directed by Thomas Kren, 16mm film, colour, 3 min, silent
Collection: Austria Filmmakers Cooperative, Vienna

Mama and Papa 1964
Directed by Thomas Kren, 16mm film, colour, 4 min, silent
Collection: Austria Filmmakers Cooperative, Vienna

Dennis Oppenheim

An Electronic Arts Intermix special series

Program Two 1970
video, b&w and colour, 14:56 min, silent
Extended Armour, 1970, b&w, 2:08 min
Gingerbread Man, 1970, b&w, 1:42 min
Nail Sharpening, 1970, b&w, 2:57 min
Toward Becoming a Devil, 1970, b&w, 2:20 min
Rocked Stomach, 1970, colour, 2:48 min
Fusion: Tooth and Nail, 1970, colour, 2:58 min
Collection: The Art Gallery of New South Wales, Sydney

Program Three 1972–74
video, b&w and colour, 24:30 min
Brush, 1973, colour, 4:56 min
I'm Falling, 1972–73, colour, 1:48 min
My Father's Socks, 1972, b&w, 5:50 min
Mittens, 1974, b&w, 4:21 min
Disappear, 1972, b&w, 5:57 min
Collection: The Art Gallery of New South Wales, Sydney

Program Four 1971–72
video, b&w, 44:50 min, silent
Vibration #1, 1971, 13:30 min
Vibration #2, 1972, 11:24 min
2 Stage Transfer Drawing (Advancing to a Future State), 1971, 7:42 min
2 Stage Transfer Drawing (Retreating to a Past State), 1971, 12:04 min

Mike Parr

Mike Parr Performances 1972–75
24 performances, video, colour and b&w, 40 min
Courtesy of the Artist

Jackson Pollock

Jackson Pollock 1951
16mm film, colour, 10 min
Directed by Paul Falkenburg and Hans Namuth
Collection: National Gallery of Australia, Canberra

Carolee Schneeman

Fuses 1964–67
16mm film, colour, 25 min, silent
Collection: London Filmmakers Coop, London

Jill Scott

Stick Around 1975
video, b&w, 10 min, silent
Collection: ZKM, Germany
Queensland Art Gallery, Brisbane
Courtesy of 235 Media Cologne, Germany

Irm and Ed Sommer

Nitsch 1969
16mm film, b&w, 14 min
Collection: London Filmmakers Coop, London

Stelarc

pyscho cyber 1996
video, colour, 57 min
Seaside Suspension (Japan), *City Suspension* (Denmark), *Stretched Skin/ Third Hand* (Japan), *Remote Controlled Suspension* (Australia)

Ken Unsworth

Five Secular Settings for Sculpture as Ritual and Burial Piece 1975
video, colour, 45 min
Courtesy of the artist

Face to Face 1977
video, colour, 30 min
Courtesy of the artist

Hannah Wilke

Gestures 1974
video, b&w, 35:30 min
Collection: The Art Gallery of New South Wales, Sydney

Through the Large Glass 1976
video, colour, 10 min
Collection: The Art Gallery of New South Wales, Sydney

*The list of films was correct at time of printing

Index

Page numbers in bold
refer to illustrations